THE
HISTORY OF
CHILE

Advisory Board

John T. Alexander
Professor of History and Russian and European Studies
University of Kansas

Robert A. Divine
George W. Littlefield Professor in American History, Emeritus
University of Texas at Austin

John V. Lombardi
Professor of History
University of Florida

THE
HISTORY OF
CHILE

John L. Rector

The Greenwood Histories of the Modern Nations
Frank W. Thackeray and John E. Findling, Series Editors

Greenwood Press
Westport, Connecticut • London

Library of Congress Cataloging-in-Publication Data

Rector, John Lawrence, 1943–
    The history of Chile / John L. Rector.
        p. cm. — (The Greenwood histories of the modern nations, ISSN 1096–2905)
    Includes bibliographical references and index.
    ISBN 0–313–31759–3 (alk. paper)
      1. Chile—History. I. Title. II. Series.
  F3081.R43   2003
  983–dc21   2003048521

British Library Cataloguing in Publication Data is available.

Library of Congress Catalog Card Number: 2003048521
ISBN: 0–313–31759–3
ISSN: 1096–2905

First published in 2003

Greenwood Press, 88 Post Road West, Westport, CT 06881
An imprint of Greenwood Publishing Group, Inc.
www.greenwood.com

Printed in the United States of America

The paper used in this book complies with the
Permanent Paper Standard issued by the National
Information Standards Organization (Z39.48–1984).

10 9 8 7 6 5 4 3 2 1

To Irene
Por su amor y comprensión

Contents

Series Foreword ix
 by Frank W. Thackeray and John E. Findling

Preface and Acknowledgments xiii

Abbreviations and Acronyms xvii

Timeline of Historical Events xxi

1 A Crazy Geography 1

2 Origins of the Chilean People, 500–1750 27

3 Independence, 1750–1830 51

4 Miners, Merchants, and Hacendados, 1830–61 73

5 The Triumph of Congress, 1861–91 95

6 New Classes and Conflicts, 1891–1925 113

7 Experiments in Democracy, 1925–58 133

8   Reform Turns to Revolution, 1958–73   155

9   Military Rule and Neoliberalism, 1973–90   185

10   The Democratic Transition after 1990   213

Notable People in the History of Chile   239

Glossary of Selected Terms   249

Suggestions for Further Reading   255

Index   271

Series Foreword

The Greenwood Histories of the Modern Nations series is intended to provide students and interested laypeople with up-to-date, concise, and analytical histories of many of the nations of the contemporary world. Not since the 1960s has there been a systematic attempt to publish a series of national histories, and, as editors, we believe that this series will prove to be a valuable contribution to our understanding of other countries in our increasingly interdependent world.

Over thirty years ago, at the end of the 1960s, the Cold War was an accepted reality of global politics, the process of decolonization was still in progress, the idea of a unified Europe with a single currency was unheard of, the United States was mired in a war in Vietnam, and the economic boom of Asia was still years in the future. Richard Nixon was president of the United States, Mao Tse-tung (not yet Mao Zedong) ruled China, Leonid Brezhnev guided the Soviet Union, and Harold Wilson was prime minister of the United Kingdom. Authoritarian dictators still ruled most of Latin America, the Middle East was reeling in the wake of the Six-Day War, and Shah Reza Pahlavi was at the height of his power in Iran. Clearly, the past thirty years have been witness to a great deal of historical change, and it is to this change that this series is primarily addressed.

With the help of a distinguished advisory board, we have selected nations whose political, economic, and social affairs mark them as among the most important in the waning years of the twentieth century, and for each nation we have found an author who is recognized as a specialist in the history of that nation. These authors have worked most cooperatively with us and with Greenwood Press to produce volumes that reflect current research on their nation and that are interesting and informative to their prospective readers.

The importance of a series such as this cannot be underestimated. As a superpower whose influence is felt all over the world, the United States can claim a "special" relationship with almost every other nation. Yet many Americans know very little about the histories of the nations with which the United States relates. How did they get to be the way they are? What kind of political systems have evolved there? What kind of influence do they have in their own region? What are the dominant political, religious, and cultural forces that move their leaders? These and many other questions are answered in the volumes of this series.

The authors who have contributed to this series have written comprehensive histories of their nations, dating back to prehistoric times in some cases. Each of them, however, has devoted a significant portion of the book to events of the last thirty years, because the modern era has contributed the most to contemporary issues that have an impact on U.S. policy. Authors have made an effort to be as up-to-date as possible so that readers can benefit from the most recent scholarship and a narrative that includes very recent events.

In addition to the historical narrative, each volume in this series contains an introductory overview of the country's geography, political institutions, economic structure, and cultural attributes. This is designed to give readers a picture of the nation as it exists in the contemporary world. Each volume also contains additional chapters that add interesting and useful detail to the historical narrative. One chapter is a thorough chronology of important historical events, making it easy for readers to follow the flow of a particular nation's history. Another chapter features biographical sketches of the nation's most important figures in order to humanize some of the individuals who have contributed to the historical development of their nation. Each volume also contains a comprehensive bibliography, so that those readers whose interest has been sparked may find out more about the nation and its history. Finally, there is a carefully prepared topic and person index.

Readers of these volumes will find them fascinating to read and useful in understanding the contemporary world and the nations that comprise it. As series editors, it is our hope that this series will contribute to a heightened sense of global understanding as we embark on a new century.

Frank W. Thackeray and John E. Findling
Indiana University Southeast

Preface and Acknowledgments

Chile is a country of historians and poets. Although there are no Nobel Prizes for historians, if there were, various Chileans would deserve consideration. Two Chilean poets, Gabriela Mistral and Pablo Neruda, have received the Nobel Prize in Literature. Whether in prose or poetry, Chileans have expressed the uniqueness of their nation with notable success.

The Socialist experiment of Salvador Allende and the military regime of Augusto Pinochet focused the world's attention on Chile. These divisive experiences pitted Chileans against each other and encouraged concerned nations to intervene on behalf of one party or another. With the return of democracy in 1990 some reconciliation between contending parties has occurred, but distrust still remains. The extraordinary material progress of the latter 1980s and 1990s, however, has helped to create some consensus about future policy.

Chile is a cosmopolitan country with its citizens interested in the world around them. Not only do Chileans eagerly follow international news, they read widely and travel extensively. They compensate for their geographical isolation by developing a global perspective. One of the most important sources for relating their own tradition to those of others is through the study of their history.

To write this history, Chileans first needed to identify and preserve its sources. Since the nineteenth century they have collected materials locally, in the Spanish archives, in the British museum, and in the archives of the United States. Prolific bibliographers like José Toribio Medina and Guillermo Feliu Cruz contributed valuable guides to printed sources. Based on these sources, the path-breaking studies of Diego Barros Arana, the Amunátegui brothers, and Benjamín Vicuña Mackenna inspired later generations of Chilean historians. Today many of these sources and histories are available to the public in the Chilean National Library and the National Archives.

Chile's history is one of material, social, and intellectual progress, yet it is also one of crises and controversies. Conservative, liberal, and radical historians have interpreted these events according to their perspective, documenting their views with library and archival resources. Foreign scholars, like myself, owe a great debt to these historians and the nation's research facilities.

When I first began my own work in Chile, I received the counsel of scholars Ricardo Donoso, Julio Heise González, and Eugenio Pereira Salas. Later as a visiting professor at the Catholic University, the University of Chile, and the University of Santiago, professors Horacio Aránguiz, Julius Kakarieka, Armando de Ramón, Juan Ricardo Couyoumdjian, Juan Eduardo Vargas, Rolando Mellafe, Cristián Gazmuri, Luz María Méndez Beltrán, René Millar, Nicolás Cruz, Alvaro Jara, José Manuel Larraín, Sergio Villalobos, Ricardo Krebs, Gonzalo Izquierdo, Sonia Pinto, Cristián Guerrero, Osvaldo Silva, Julio Retamal, and Guillermo Bravo shared their historical views with me. I also benefited from working with Sergio Tuteliers of the Fulbright commission and Emilio Meneses of the Instituto de Ciencia Política of the Catholic University. Eduardo Cavieres, Harold Blakemore, Larry Stickle, Peter DeShazo, Simon Collier, Ann Johnson, Markos Mamalakis, Paul E. Sigmund, Arnold Bauer, and John and Mary Mayo all joined in Santiago's lengthy luncheon seminars over the years.

Charles Boxer first urged me to study colonial Chilean history and shared his awe for the work of José Toribio Medina. James Scobie, Robert Quirk, John Lombardi, John Dyson, Brian and Sharon Loveman, and Roger Burback—all originally associated with Indiana University—provided valuable criticism. Peter Sehlinger not only introduced me to Chilean historians but also encouraged me to write this volume. My history colleagues at Western Oregon University, Narasingha Sil, Kimberly Jensen, Paul Brasil, Max Geier, Bau Hwa Sheieh, and Benedict Lowe, have supported me in this project. Sue Payton's cartographic skills and Mark Van Steeter's geographical advice combined to create the map of Chile.

Western Oregon University also deserves thanks for the release time and resources it provided.

This book would not have been possible without the backing of the series editors, Frank W. Thackeray and John E. Findling. At Greenwood Press, executive editor Barbara A. Rader first supported me in this project, while senior editor Kevin Ohe edited every chapter and provided valuable suggestions.

For their many observations about Chile, I am indebted to Suzanne and Santiago Gordon; Jimmy and María Angélica Dungan; Rigo and Gabiela Toiber; Zoila, Enrique, and Segundo Luengo; Werner and Eliana Bratz; Segundo Nahuel; Afonso Vega; Teodoro and Edith Mättig; and Luis, Manuel, and Inés Montt. I also want to recognize the continued support of my family.

Abbreviations and Acronyms

AFPs   Administradoras de Fondos de Pensiones (Pension Fund Administrators). Private companies which invest pension funds.

CCU   Compañía Cervecerías Unidas (United Breweries Company).

CEMA   Centro de Madres (Mothers' Clubs). Initiated during the Frei M. administration.

CEPAL   Comisión Económica para América Latina (United Nations Latin American Economic Commission). In the 1960s, CEPAL's economic theories encouraged industrialization.

CODE   Confederación Democrática (Democratic Confederation). Organized by the National and Christian Democratic parties to oppose the Unidad Popular.

CODELCO   Corporación del Cobre (Copper Corporation). State-owned company.

CONAMA	Comisión Nacional del Medio Ambiente (National Environmental Commission).
CONICYT	Comisión Nacional de Investigación Científica y Tecnológica (National Commission for Scientific and Technological Research). Primary funding agency for academic research.
CORA	Corporación de la Reforma Agraria (Agrarian Reform Corporation). Expropriated and administered large landholdings.
CORFO	Corporación de Fomento (Development Corporation). Government organization to promote industry and other economic activities.
CRAC	Confederación Republicana de Acción Cívica (Republican Confederation for Civic Action). Organization of Ibañez to control labor politics.
CTC	Compañía de Telefonos de Chile (Chilean Telephone Company).
CTCH	Confederación de Trabajadores de Chile (Chilean Workers Confederation). Created in 1939.
CUT	Central Unica de Trabajadores (United Workers' Federation). Dominant labor confederation from its founding in 1953 to its prohibition in 1973.
DINA	Dirección de Inteligencia Nacional (National Intelligence Service). Involved in assassination and torture during the Pinochet government.
ENAP	Empresa Nacional de Petroleo (National Petroleum Company).
ENDESA	Empresa Nacional de Electricidad (National Electric Company).
ENU	Escuela Nacional Unificada (Unified National School System). Controversial proposal by the Unidad Popular.
FACH	Fuerza Aérea de Chile (Chilean Air Force).

FECH
Federación de Estudiantes Chilenos (Chilean Student Federation). Founded in 1906 by University of Chile students.

FLASCO
Facultad Latinoamericana de Ciencias Sociales (Latin American Social Science Faculty).

FOCH
Federación de Obreros de Chile (Chilean Workers' Federation). Founded in 1909 and later dominated by the Communist Party.

FONASA
Fondo Nacional de Salud (National Health Fund). Individuals can select their own physicians if they contribute to this government healthcare provider.

FTAA
Free Trade Area of the Americas. A proposal to create a common market to include all Western Hemispheric nations.

GDP
Gross Domestic Product. Measurement of the value of annual production.

INDAP
Instituto de Desarrollo Agropecuario (Agricultural Development Institute). A government agricultural extension and credit agency for small farmers.

ISAPRE
Instituto de Salud y Prevención (Health and Prevention Institute). An optional system of private health insurance companies used largely by white collar workers.

JAP
Juntas de Abastecimiento y Precios (Supply and Price Committee). The Unidad Popular distributed food through this committee network.

MAPU
Movimiento de Acción Popular Unitaria (United Popular Action Movement). A splinter group of young Christian Democrats who later joined the Unidad Popular.

MERCOSUR
Mercado Común del Cono Sur (Common Market of Southern Cone). Comprised of Argentina, Brazil, Paraguay, and Uruguay; Chile is an associate member.

MIR — Movimiento de Izquierda Revolucionario (Revolutionary Left Movement). Preferred direct action rather than electoral politics.

PDC — Partido Demócrata Cristiano (Christian Democratic Party).

PPD — Partido por la Democracia (Party for Democracy). A branch of the Socialist Party.

PROCHILE — Instituto de Promoción de Exportaciones (Export Promotion Institute). Created by the Pinochet government.

ODEPLAN — Oficina de Planificación Nacional (National Planning Office).

RN — Renovación Nacional (National Renovation). A moderately conservative party.

SAG — Servicio Agrícola y Ganadera (Agricultural and Livestock Service). Encourages large landholders to implement modern farm technology.

SFF — Sociedad de Fomento Fabril (Industrial Development Society). An industrial employers organization; also known as *SOFOFA*.

TFP — Sociedad Chilena de la Tradición, Familia y Propiedad (Chilean Society for Tradition, Family, and Property). Conservative Catholic lay organization opposed to Frei M. and Allende reforms.

UDI — Unión Democrática Independiente (Independent Democratic Union). Conservative party: originally linked to the Pinochet government.

UECH — Unión de Empleados de Chile (Union of Chilean Employees). Founded in 1925 to bring together white collar unions; replaced in 1949 by the Chilean Employees' Confederation, or *CEPCH*.

UP — Unidad Popular (Popular Unity). A coalition of left-wing parties which governed Chile from 1970–73.

Timeline of Historical Events

13,000–10,000 B.C.	Arrival of first humans in Chile, according to most archeologists.
2000 B.C.	Chinchorro culture in northern coastal area.
500 A.D.	Significant human populations established throughout Chile.
600–1000	Influence of the Tiahuanaco culture on northern Chilean peoples.
1470–1535	Inca conquest of communities north of the Río Maule. Imposition of labor tribute including gold mining.
1520	Ferdinand Magellan explores the strait that now bears his name.
1535–36	Diego de Almagro explores Chile but establishes no settlements.
1541	Pedro de Valdivia leads an expedition to Chile and founds Santiago, February 12, 1541. Mapuche attack in September destroys the community, but Valdivia has it rebuilt.

1543	La Serena, the first town in the Norte Chico, is founded.
1550–53	Valdivia's government establishes the towns of Concepción, Imperial, Valdivia, Villarrica, and Angol as well as the forts of Arauco, Tucapel, and Purén.
1553	Mapuche troops led by Lautaro capture and execute Pedro de Valdivia at Tucapel.
1557	Francisco de Villagra defeats and kills Lautaro at Peteroa.
1557	García Hurtado de Mendoza named governor of Chile. Divests many earlier conquistadors of their privileges.
1558	Hernando de Santillán establishes official limits on Indian exploitation.
1561–62	Emissaries from Chile found towns of Mendoza and San Juan in the territory of Cuyo, eventually part of Argentine territory.
1580	Martín Ruiz de Gamboa tries to eliminate forced Indian labor.
1567	Chile's first royal court, the *audiencia*, inaugurated at Concepción.
1594	English buccaneer Richard Hawkins attacks Valparaíso.
1599–1604	Great Mapuche rebellion destroys the seven towns south of Concepción. Many women and children begin long-term captivity.
1608	Crown authorizes Indian enslavement in Chile.
1612–26	Jesuit priest Luis de Valdivia convinces the crown to build forts north of the Biobío River and turn Mapuche territory over to his order's jurisdiction. Policy called the Defensive War.
1641	Initiation of negotiations, called parliaments, with the Mapuche.
1643	Dutch capture Chiloé and Valdivia with the intention of establishing a colony in southern Chile. For lack of provisions, they abandon this project.

1647	Earthquake destroys Santiago.
1680	English pirate Bartholomew Sharp destroys La Serena.
1700	End of Spanish Hapsburg dynasty with death of Charles II. Beginning of Spanish Bourbon dynasty under Philip V.
1737–45	Eight new towns founded.
1738	King authorizes the creation of the Universidad de San Felipe.
1749	Chilean mint begins operation.
1750	Earthquake destroys Concepción. Rebuilt in new location.
1767	Charles III expels the Jesuit order and confiscates its properties.
1788–96	Progressive administration of Governor Ambrosio O'Higgins.
1791	*Encomiendas* officially abolished.
1808	Francisco Antonio García Carrasco named Chile's interim governor.
1808	Napoleon forces Spanish kings to abdicate and places his brother, Joseph Bonaparte, on the Spanish throne.
1810	Beginning of independence movement. García Carrasco forced to resign. A Chilean, Mateo de Toro y Zambrano, named interim governor. Santiago leaders meet in Junta de Gobierno on September 18 and create first national government.
1811	Government opens Chilean ports to foreign trade with the Decree of Free Commerce. The first national congress meets but is later dismissed by José Miguel Carrera, who assumes dictatorial powers.
1812	Peruvian viceroy sends a military expedition to conquer Chile.
1814	British negotiate a treaty between the Chilean and Spanish forces that is later rejected by the Peruvian viceroy.

1814	Viceroy's troops defeat the Chilean troops at Rancagua. Some patriots escape to Argentina, and others are incarcerated on Juan Fernández Island.
1814–17	Ferdinand VII becomes king of Spain in 1814, and Chile is once again under Spanish rule during a period called The Reconquest.
1817	Chilean-Argentine army led by Bernardo O'Higgins and José de San Martín defeats Spanish forces at Chacabuco, February 12.
1817–23	Bernardo O'Higgins governs Chile.
1818	Chileans formally declare their independence on February 12. Patriot army defeats Spanish again at Battle of Maipú on April 5.
1818–20	Chilean navy formed under the command of Lord Cochrane. It captures Spanish ships, blockades Lima, and expels the Spanish from Valdivia.
1820	Chilean expedition under the command of San Martín sails from Valparaiso in August to attack the Viceroy's troops in Peru.
1821	Execution of José Miguel Carrera.
1822	The United States officially recognizes Chile's independence. British bankers loan Chile £1 million.
1823	O'Higgins renounces leadership; replaced by Ramón Freire.
1827–29	Liberal leader, Francisco Antonio Pinto, becomes president.
1830	Conservatives defeat liberals at the Battle of Lircay, and Diego Portales becomes the political boss of the new government.
1831–41	Joaquín Prieto serves two terms as president. His innovative finance minister, Manuel Rengifo, restores national credit.
1832	Extraordinary silver strike at Chañarcillo in the Norte Chico.

1833	Conservative constitution defines the powers of government.
1837–39	Chile at war with the Peru-Bolivian Confederation.
1837	Diego Portales assassinated near Valparaíso.
1841–51	Two-term presidency of Manuel Bulnes.
1842	University of Chile founded.
1850	Francisco Bilbao and Santiago Arcos found the Sociedad de la Igualdad (Equality Society).
1851	First Chilean railroad inaugurated. Line from Copiapó to Caldera transports minerals.
1851	Unsuccessful revolt to prevent Manuel Montt from becoming president.
1851–61	Two-term presidency of Manuel Montt.
1859	Revolt led by mining baron Pedro León Gallo against the Montt government.
1861–71	Two-term presidency of José Joaquín Pérez. Broad amnesty given to participants of previous political revolts.
1862	Radical Party founded by Pedro León Gallo.
1866	Spanish gunships fire on Valparaíso, severely damaging commercial warehouses.
1878	Chile and Argentina define their common border based on mountain peaks and watersheds.
1879–83	War of the Pacific. Chile defeats Bolivia and Peru, who cede the nitrate-rich areas of Antofagasta and Tarapaca to Chile.
1881–82	Military rebuild forts of Imperial and Villarrica destroyed by the Mapuche three centuries earlier. Part of plan to encircle the Mapuche.
1883–84	Civil cemeteries, marriage, and birth registry enacted over the opposition of the conservatives and the church.
1886–91	José Manuel Balmaceda, president. Nitrate bonanza begins.

1887	Catholic University founded.
1891	Congressional revolt against Balmaceda. Naval commander Jorge Montt and Emil Körner, a Prussian military advisor, help congressional forces win.
1891–96	Jorge Montt's presidency.
1893	Railroad reaches Temuco in the Mapuche heartland.
1904	North American William Braden employs new copper flotation technology in developing the El Teniente copper mine near Rancagua.
1906	Valparaíso earthquake severely damages the port.
1907	Nitrate miners' strike in Iquique brutally suppressed.
1909	Workers' federation, or FOCH, established.
1910	Chilean-Argentine railroad inaugurated. Connects the Atlantic and Pacific Oceans.
1911	Guggenheim company buys Chuquicamata copper mine. Becomes the largest mining company in Chile.
1911	Socialist Workers Party, or POS, founded by Emilio Recabarren.
1914	Panama Canal opens and hurts Valparaíso trade.
1920	Law requires all children attend elementary school.
1920–25	Arturo Alessandri Palma's presidency.
1921	Socialist Workers Party changes its name to the Communist Party.
1922	Gabriela Mistral publishes her first major work, *Desolación*.
1923–24	Pablo Neruda initiates his publishing career with two major poetic works, *Crepusculario* and *Veinte poemas de amor y una canción desesperada*.
1924	Military pressures Alessandri to resign. He goes into exile.
1925	Alessandri returns to the presidency. New constitution strengthens executive powers and replaces the Constitution of 1833.

1927–31	Military government of Carlos Ibáñez.
1928	Worldwide depression has devastating impact on Chile.
1931	Ibáñez issues Labor Code that regulates labor relations for decades.
1931–32	Juan Esteban Montero's presidency.
1932	Brief socialist experiment.
1932–38	Second presidency of Arturo Alessandri; his Minister of Finance, Gustavo Ross, revives the economy.
1933	The Socialist Party is founded.
1937	Ley de Seguridad Interior del Estado (State Interior Security Law) authorizes the president to restrict political attire, meetings, and publications deemed threatening to the state.
1938	Sixty-one Nazi youth executed by Carabineros.
1938–41	Popular Front candidate, Padro Aguirre Cerda, supported by the Radical, Socialist, Democratic, and Communist parties wins the presidency.
1938	Falange Nacional party founded; predecessor of Christian Democratic Party.
1939	Devastating earthquake destroys Chillán. Corporación de Fomento (Development Corporation), or CORFO, created to rebuild the city and promote new economic activities.
1942–46	Juan Antonio Ríos's presidency.
1942	Chile breaks diplomatic relations with Germany, Italy, and Japan.
1945	Gabriela Mistral receives the Nobel Prize in Literature.
1946–52	Gabriel González Videla's presidency.
1947	Construction of Chile's first steel mill begins at Huachipato in the Concepción region.
1947	Communist Party outlawed by Democratic Defense Law.

1948	Congress grants women the right to vote.
1952–58	Second presidency of Carlos Ibáñez.
1952–59	Labor federation, Central Unica de Trabajadores, or CUT, founded.
1956	Formal alliance of Socialists and Communists called FRAP.
1957	Christian Democratic Party created in Chile.
1958	Communist Party legalized.
1958–64	Jorge Alessandri's presidency.
1960	Valdivia earthquake, the most destructive in Chile's history.
1961	Kennedy Administration encourages Alessandri to participate in the Alliance for Progress programs.
1962	Agrarian Reform Law passed.
1962	World Cup held in Chile.
1964–70	Eduardo Frei Montalva's presidency. First Christian Democrat to hold this office.
1966	Government acquires 51 percent of stock in El Teniente mine; begins the Chilenization of the large copper mines.
1967	Militant leftist student group, Movimiento de Iquierda Revolucionario, or MIR, founded.
1967–69	University reform movements at the Universidad Católica and the Universidad de Chile.
1970	Salvador Allende becomes the first Socialist elected president. Supported by coalition of parties called the Unidad Popular.
1970	René Schneider, commander in chief of the armed forces, assassinated in an attempt to block the ratification of Allende's election.
1971	Pablo Neruda awarded the Nobel Prize in Literature.
1971	The March of the Empty Pots; women's protest against food scarcity.

1971	Nationalization of the Gran Minería copper mines; all copper mines now government owned. Rapid acceleration of hacienda expropriations.
1972	The Christian Democrats, the National Party, and smaller parties form the Democratic Confederation, or CODE, to oppose the Unidad Popular.
1972	In August, a national retail merchants strike, and in October, a truckers strike; workers occupy factories. Scarcities encourage proliferation of black market.
1973	In the March congressional election, Democratic Confederation receives 55 percent of the votes and the Unidad Popular, 44 percent.
1973	June 29, tanks roll through Santiago streets in an act labeled the *tancazo*. Prelude to later military uprising in September.
1973	Military overthrows Salvador Allende on September 11.
1973	Military rounds up thousands of Unidad Popular supporters. Begins executions and the routine use of torture.
1973	Military junta suspends constitution, closes congress, and prohibits any political activities.
1975	Friedman delivers economic seminar in Santiago. Initiation of neoliberal economic shock treatment.
1978	Pinochet declares amnesty for political crimes committed since September 11, 1973.
1980	New constitution ratified.
1982	Devaluation of the peso and debt crisis initiate drastic recession.
1983	Strikes on the eleventh day of each month protest the military government.
1987	Pope John Paul II visits Chile. Calls for social justice.

1988	The No campaign wins a majority with 53 percent of the vote; this result denies Pinochet eight more years in the presidency.
1989	First election since 1973. Coalition of Christian Democrats, Socialists, and smaller parties called the Concertación wins presidency and a majority of congressional seats.
1990–94	Patricio Aylwin's presidency (Christian Democrat). Leads transition to democracy. Finance minister Alejandro Foxley, continues neoliberal economic model but with emphasis on eliminating poverty.
1990–91	Rittig Commission investigates human rights abuses during the military regime.
1991	Jaime Guzmán, author of 1980 Constitution, assassinated.
1994–2000	Eduardo Frei Ruiz-Tagle's presidency (Christian Democrat).
1998	Pinochet steps down as commander in chief of the military. Arrested while receiving medical treatment in England. In 2000, released and returns to Chile.
1999	Asian recession hurts Chilean economy. Interrupts over a decade of sustained growth and declining inflation.
2000–06	Ricardo Lagos's presidency (Socialist).
2000–03	United States and European recession raises Chilean unemployment and lowers growth. Argentine financial crisis in 2002 threatens the economies of all MERCOSUR nations.
2002	Conservative resurgence. Unión Democrática Independiente, or UDI, receives 25 percent of the vote in congressional elections. Christian Democrats votes drop to 19 percent.
2002	Supreme Court determines that Pinochet's deteriorating health makes him unfit for trial.

2003   Chile opposes U.S. invasion of Iraq. United States ratifies Free Trade Agreement with Chile. Constitutional amendment eliminates military oversight of government Commemoration of the thirtieth anniversary of the overthrow of the Unidad Popular emphasizing the importance of civic institutions.

1

A Crazy Geography

More than half a century ago, Benjamín Subercaseaux remarked that Chile had a crazy geography. Certainly many of Chile's features defy logic. Why should a country be more than 2,600 miles long and have an average width of only 110 miles? Why should the same country include such extremes as the driest desert in the world, the highest mountain range in the hemisphere, temperate rain forests, and a piece of Antarctica? And why should colliding geological plates make earthquakes and volcanic eruptions an inevitable part of Chilean life? The answers to these questions require a study of Chile's geography and history.

To dwell excessively on Chile's crazy geography fails to highlight the country's picturesque landscapes and abundant resources. Few places, for example, have a more benign climate than the Valle Central where the majority of Chileans live. The north offers not only mineral riches but also a spectacular coastline with year-round sunshine. The south may have heavy rains, but its lush valleys and majestic volcanoes compensate for the humidity. In each of these landscapes, Chileans have fashioned unique communities that together form a vibrant nation.

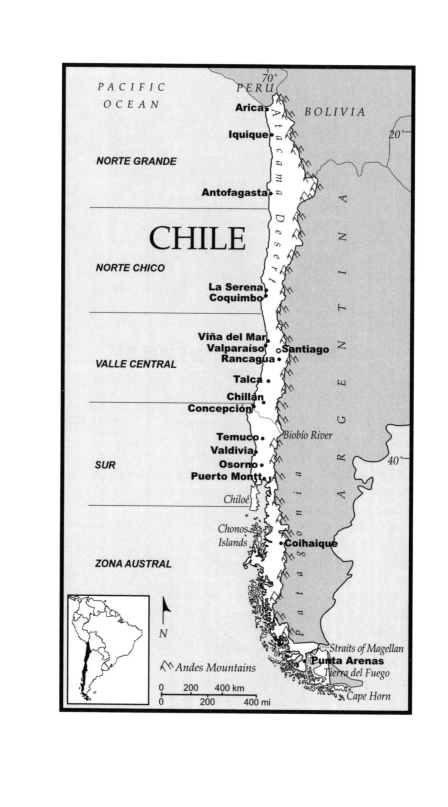

PACIFIC
OCEAN

PERU

BOLIVIA

Arica

Iquique

20°

NORTE GRANDE

Atacama Desert

Antofagasta

CHILE

NORTE CHICO

La Serena
Coquimbo

ARGENTINA

Viña del Mar
Valparaíso   Santiago
Rancagua

VALLE CENTRAL

Talca

Chillán
Concepción

Temuco   *Biobío River*

Valdivia

SUR   **Osorno**
Puerto Montt   40°

Chiloé

Chonos
Islands   **Coihaique**

ZONA AUSTRAL   *Patagonia*

N

Straits of Magellan
Punta Arenas
Tierra del Fuego

⋀ *Andes Mountains*   ⤳ *Cape Horn*

0   200   400 km
0   200   400 mi

THE SHAPE OF A NATION

Defining Borders

Today the Andes Mountains and the Pacific Ocean largely define Chile's borders. This has not always been the case because Chile's borders have been moved frequently. History, as much as geography, has determined Chile's crazy shape. A different history likely would have created a different shape.

Chile could have been part of Argentina had early Spanish attempts to colonize the continent from the Atlantic coast been successful. But twice expeditions failed. Consequently, Chile's explorers and conquistadors came from the north. After subduing the Mapuche, they annexed the colony to the Viceroyalty of Peru. At first this relationship was advantageous, but distance and rival interests eventually led to conflicts.

Chile soon became the base for eastward expansion. In the 1550s Chilean conquistadors crossed the Andes and founded three towns in a region called Cuyo. With the annexation of that region, Chile became more than twice the width it is today. The Andes did not impede close economic and social contacts between the two areas. Chilean governors ruled Cuyo until the crown shuffled administrative boundaries in 1776 and placed the region under the administration of Buenos Aires. Informal ties continued to connect the two regions; commercial and personal ties remained strong.

During the colonial period Chile extended from Copiapó in the north to the Mapuche frontier in the south. In the nineteenth century Chile's economic development allowed the government to push its borders farther north and south. In the 1840s and 1850s it sponsored the colonization of Punta Arenas and the southern Lake District. Nitrate mining and competition for the Atacama Desert pushed the border farther north. When Chile defeated Peru and Bolivia in the War of the Pacific, it annexed territory from both countries. Later international negotiations established the Chilean-Peruvian border just north of Arica, the current boundary. In 1881 a Chilean-Argentine treaty limited the country's eastern border to the Andean peaks and watersheds. After the War of the Pacific, the Chilean military pushed colonization farther south by occupying the Mapuche territory. Then in the early twentieth century, the government helped colonize western Patagonia. Although these efforts fleshed out the current borders of the country, territorial disputes in the Strait of Magellan in the 1980s threatened war between Chile and Argentina. Fortunately these issues were resolved through arbitration, not guns. Chile's territory also includes two Pacific island groups, Juan Fernández and Easter Island, and a section of Antarctica, where the military maintains a permanent base.

Unification

Considerable political will has been required to integrate such a long nation. In both the nineteenth and twentieth centuries Chile subsidized southern settlement, using incentives similar to those used for the North American West. For the extreme north and south, Chile created duty-free ports. It offered salary bonuses to public employees willing to work in hardship areas. It financed communication networks with federal funds. It built a north-south railway in the nineteenth century and the Pan-American Highway in the twentieth century. It subsidized air transportation to isolated areas in the north, the south, and Easter Island. It also underwrote a national television network and an Internet system.

THE LAND

The Pacific Ocean defines Chile's western border, and the Andes Mountains define its eastern border. In many areas a low coastal range separates the ocean from an interior valley. Over the centuries erosion has filled in the depression between the two mountain ranges. In Patagonia, however, there is no coastal range. Furthermore, the shelf that separates the ocean from the Andes in most of the country is either very narrow or nonexistent in this southern region. In contrast, after the coastline of the desert northern region comes a basin, followed by a high plateau, or *altiplano,* that is more than 10,000 feet above sea level. Due to the altitude, extreme day and night temperatures are common. Here are located many of the rich copper deposits. Still farther inland, the Andes rise to heights of up to 22,000 feet. These towering peaks squeeze enough humidity from the dry air to cause snowfall and create snowfields whose runoff feeds the few rivers of the area.

Climatic and Geographical Zones

The regions of Chile can be considered from two separate perspectives. One is based on climate and the other on tradition. Chileans have referred to their nation's five regions as follows: the Norte Grande (Great North), the Norte Chico (Little North), the Valle Central (Central Valley), the Sur (South), and the Zona Austral (Southern Zone). When traveling from north to south, the first 800 miles are desert. Then in the Norte Chico, vegetation and rainfall gradually increase. About 70 miles north of Santiago, the fertile agricultural area of the Valle Central begins and stretches for more than 300 miles until it reaches the humid area called the Sur.

Heavy rainfall predominates in this region as well as farther south in the Zona Austral. Two exceptions in Patagonia are Coihaique and the Atlantic side of Tierra del Fuego where a rain shadow lowers precipitation and produces natural grasslands. At Punta Arenas the average rainfall is only 18 inches. Farther south in the Strait of Magellan, where the shadow disappears, rainfall reaches 200 inches!

In Chile the land is seldom stationary. Anyone who lives for more than a year in the country will likely feel the shaking of a temblor. Large earthquakes are less common; but when they happen, they transform people's lives. Charles Darwin was visiting Valdivia in February 1835 when an earthquake hit that shook the land for two minutes. He recalled that trying to stand up was like being in a boat plummeted by waves. According to him the earth shook "like a thin sheet floating on a liquid." When he visited Concepción a few weeks later, he saw the heaps of ruins and the devastation of neighboring Talcahuano, which was leveled by a tidal wave. An earthquake, he concluded, is sufficient to destroy an entire country's prosperity.

Unfortunately, since the founding of Chile, twelve or more major earthquakes hit the country per century. In 1906, the same year that an earthquake devastated San Francisco, one also destroyed Valparaíso. In 1939 an earthquake leveled the city of Chillán and severely shook the entire Sur. In 1960 the Valdivia earthquake destroyed the city and covered thousands of acres of farmland with shallow lakes. In the mountains people saw trees falling like dominoes and the roads rippling like rivers.

Chile also has more than thirty active volcanoes. In the north, these fiery vents spew rocks and magma into uninhabited areas. In the south, however, people live on the volcanoes' slopes, using the various resources they find there. On Volcán Villarrica, for example, there are lumber operations, cattle ranches, three tourist centers, and a ski resort. An eruption in the 1960s destroyed the town of Coñaripe on the south side of the mountain. Then a decade later another destroyed the roads and bridges on the north side. Today a red glare in the Villarrica crater is visible at night, but local residents pay more attention to its smoke, which they read like a barometer.

An ocean current named after the geographer Alexander Humboldt flows from one end of Chile's coastline to the other. After passing the coast of Antarctica, the current cools Pacific Coast waters as far north as Ecuador. The current brings with it abundant sea life including the diminutive crustaceans at the bottom of the food chain. The crustaceans feed fish and even whales, which are at the top of the chain. In the middle of the chain are the anchovies, which provide a huge catch for national fisheries. Chileans are great lovers of seafood, which ranges from sea urchins, to abalone, to sea bass. The country's fish markets, along the coast and inland, offer the full range of ocean species used in the great variety of local dishes.

Weather

In the far north of Chile, the average annual temperature in Arica is 64 degrees Fahrenheit; 350 miles south in Antofagasta, it is 61 one degrees; in Santiago, 57 degrees, in Puerto Montt 52 degrees, and in Punta Arenas, forty-three degrees. On the northern coast, the day typically begins with a dense fog, the *camanchaca*, which the sun dissipates by early afternoon. Rain is very rare. In the northern interior, daytime temperatures are higher than along the coast, and clouds are rare any time of year. On the altiplano desert the temperature drops quickly after sunset, causing a difference of 40 degrees Fahrenheit between day and night.

During the dry summer months of December to March, the daytime temperatures in the Valle Central are constantly in the eighties, dropping at night to the fifties. Due to sparse rainfall, only irrigated areas remain green during this period. During the winter months of June to September this region receives moderate rainfall, and daytime temperatures drop to the fifties and sixties. Nighttime freezing temperatures are a rarity. In the eastern foothills of Santiago snowflakes occasionally fly but rarely stick. Higher elevations, however, are blanketed with snow, presenting a spectacular view of 15,000 feet of ice. Although residents feel the chill, it rarely damages crops. Oranges, avocados, and palm trees prosper, but this environment is too chilly for mangoes, papayas, and bananas. The one climate that Chile does not have is the humid tropics.

The Andes have permanent snowfields from north to south. In the south both the height of the range as well as the freezing level decreases. As a result, shorter volcanoes such as Llaima and Villarrica, with altitudes of approximately 9,000 feet, have permanent glaciers, quite similar to those found in the Cascade Range of Oregon and Washington. These provide winter recreation and abundant water for lake and river sports during the summer.

On the coast in the Sur and the Zona Austral, early morning coastal clouds that dissipate are common in the summer. In the winter these clouds last for months, bringing heavy rains. Sunny days are rare—only occurring between storms. South of Chiloé, even summer days are cool, and snows are common at lower altitudes during winter months.

Administrative Regions

In addition to the climatic regional concept, there is an administrative one. Using this framework, Chile is divided into twelve regions, plus one—the Santiago Metropolitan area. Each region may contain one or more provinces. In the twentieth century, various governments have changed these divisions. The executive of each region, the *intendente,* is appointed by the president and exercises fiscal control over public works and other services. Regions have no legislative bodies. Administrative divisions determine the distribution of government funds, so when the possibility of redistricting occurs communities try to influence the process.

THE PEOPLE

National Identity

Chileans have a strong sense of nationalism. Chilean historians have traced this sentiment to the country's military, political, intellectual, and cultural traditions. Military tradition underscores Chile's role in liberating South America from Spanish control and the victories over Peru and Bolivia in two nineteenth-century wars. During the military rule of the 1970s and 1980s, critics of the regime had misgivings about tying the nation's identity so closely to military symbols. Nevertheless, many Chileans still fear that Peru and Bolivia may attempt to recover their lost territories and that Argentina may annex parts of Patagonia. In the 1980s there were real threats in both areas, and these threats heightened nationalism.

Whereas the military tradition often has provided symbols for Chilean nationalism, politics provides the everyday process for people to shape their future. Traditionally, Chileans had no fear that political discussions would cause acrimony; but, since the 1970s, people have been more cautious. Nevertheless, many Chileans still feel that politics, not soccer, is their true national sport. They delight in proposing ambitious solutions to major national problems as well as conjecturing over international events.

Chileans have often turned to the political process to undertake major national reforms. In the 1920s a middle-class reform movement tried to address class disparities. In the 1940s the Popular Front movement created innovative programs to promote economic development. In the 1960s and in the early 1970s, Chileans elected parties that attempted sweeping reforms. When the military overthrew the Allende government in 1973, it sought to legitimize its role by eliminating corrupt politics and restructuring the economic system. During all these reform movements, Chileans adhered to a political party and debated the issues from their party's perspective. Regardless of party, the participation in the debate was a national experience that defined being Chilean.

Chile's intellectual tradition has contributed to an informed public. A literacy rate of 95 percent means that most Chileans study national history and literature in school. The people's access to a variety of newspapers, magazines, and books creates a national readership. Historians such as Diego Barros Arana, Banjamín Vicuña Mackenna, Francisco Encina, Ricardo Donoso, and Julio Heise González have created a shared past for Chileans of all political persuasions. Literary figures such as Alonzo de Ercilla, Gabriela Mistral, Pablo Neruda, Jorge Edwards, and Isabel Allende have extolled the beauties of their land and have written of the struggles of their people.

Workers share a variety of legends that bond them together. They repeat the story of Caupolicán, the Mapuche chief, who reputedly could carry a large log on his shoulder for days. They claim that Chilean working class soldiers drank *chupilcas del Diablo,* a mixture of red wine and gunpowder, before charging the Peruvian and Bolivian troops in the War of the Pacific. Workers tell tales of *el roto chileno,* the Chilean worker, which ascribe to him an audacity that allows him to triumph over the greatest odds. Tales of his modern incarnation, *el Condorito,* the scrappy Condor, describe him defeating "Goliaths" with his cunning, not his brawn. When Independence Day, known as *el dieciocho,* comes on September 18, Chileans proclaim their raw patriotism with such earthy expressions as *viva Chile mierda!* (long live Chile, dammit!)

Education

Chile has long supported a public education system with rigorous academic standards. In 1920 the government imposed a universal primary education requirement. However, especially in rural areas, the government did not have the resources to make this rule effective. In the 1960s and early 1970s, presidents Eduardo Frei M. and Salvador Allende invested in school construction, a meal program, and teacher training in a successful campaign to register all children into primary schools. As a result, the literacy rate rose to 95 percent, one of the highest in Latin America. By the 1990s K–12 enrollment exceeded 2,000,000 while higher-education enrollment exceeded 350,000.

Population

Before the arrival of the Spaniards, the Indians lived in either small villages or rural hamlets. The great majority of Chile's population was located between the Valle Central and the Sur. In the sixteenth century, the Spanish quickly founded towns from the north as far south as Valdivia, yet these grew very slowly. Moreover, by 1610 the Mapuche had destroyed half of them. Even the colonial capital developed slowly. By 1700, more than 150 years after the city's founding, it had only 12,000 inhabitants. The growth of trade and government in the eighteenth century boosted its population to approximately 40,000 by the year 1800. The other urban areas were much smaller; Concepción had 10,000 inhabitants, Valparaíso, 4,000, and La Serena 3,500. With the population of 15 other small towns included, the urban population of the colony was only 10 percent of a total of 650,000. More than half of the colony's population was still made up of Mapuche living on their traditional lands, yet a gradual shift of population into the Valle Central and urban areas had begun. The urban population seems small by today's standards, yet for the time it was not unusual. By comparison, the United States had only 4 percent urban population.

The independence placed a new emphasis on international commerce and the commercial centers that handled trade. Santiago and the port of Valparaíso were the greatest beneficiaries with their population growing at a far more rapid pace than the nation in general.

	Valparaíso-Viña del Mar	Santiago
1800	4,000	40,000
1820	10,000	50,000
1865	70,000	115,000
1885	120,000	250,000
1900	150,000	300,000
1930	200,000	700,000
1950	330,000	1,400,000
1960	500,000	1,900,000
2000	625,000	5,000,000

By 1900 Chile was 20 percent urban, in 1960, 50 percent, and in 2000, 84 percent. Interestingly enough, this latter rate of urbanization exceeded that of Mexico and the United States, which were 75 percent and 77 percent respectively. Currently, half of the nation's population lives within the three metropolitan areas of Santiago, Valparaíso-Viña del Mar, and Concepción-Talcahuano. In the twentieth century, the magnetic power exercised by the national capital has overwhelmed that of any other area. Whereas in 1900 only 10 percent of Chileans lived there, by the end of the century, 40 percent did so. The city had grown from 300,000 to 5,000,000 inhabitants in one hundred years! For a brief time in the mid-nineteenth century, the port of Valparaíso competed with the capital. Then the northern nitrate and copper ports emerged as Valparaíso's rivals, while Santiago rapidly created manufacturing and government jobs. Businesses found that closeness to political power was more important than to port facilities. In the 1980s the neoliberal economic model, which theoretically deemphasized the role of government, did not reverse this trend. If the next generation fails to reverse Santiago's congestion and pollution, Chileans may decide to locate elsewhere and contribute to the growth of other urban centers.

Programs to populate more isolated regions have hardly offset the rush of people to the three largest metropolitan areas. Only three other cities exceed 200,000 inhabitants. These latter cities create jobs in commerce and services, but few government or industrial jobs. Therefore, as people flee the rural areas looking for work, they usually bypass regional centers and head straight for the national capital, Concepción, or Valparaíso. With the exception of the Biobío region, the agricultural regions south of Santiago remain more than 50 percent rural. The two northern regions, by contrast, are some of the most urbanized in the country, with 90 percent of the people living in either the port cities or the mining towns.

Although Chile's urbanization is high relative to Latin America, its population growth has been relatively low. In the twentieth century, it has consistently grown at a rate of less than two percent. At its current rate, it will take 50 years for the population to double, as compared to some Central American countries that double every 25 years. Historically, immigration has helped diversify Chile's ethnic make up, but it has never been a major cause of population growth. Except for the rural German immigrants in the Sur, the smaller numbers of British, French, Italian, Swiss, Yugoslav, and Arab immigrants have settled largely in urban areas where they engaged in commerce and industry. Currently, immigrants from neighboring Bolivia and Peru, who largely work in unskilled jobs in the north or in domestic service in Santiago, are more numerous.

ECONOMY

The Norte Grande

In the dry northern region of Norte Grande, except for the ports and a few mining centers, the countryside is practically empty. Water is the main problem, because it almost never rains. River valleys crisscross the northern desert, but they are dry during most of the year. The Andean snowmelt provides insufficient water for the rivers to actually reach the coast. In spite of a lack of water, this is the country's most abundant mineral zone. Chile's nitrate wealth came from this region. With the decline of nitrates in the 1930s, copper soon became the most valuable resource. Huge mines developed such as Chuquicamata, La Escondida, Portrerillos, and El Salvador, and each built company towns. To provide water for these mining oases, companies and governments fought for rights to use one important river, the Loa.

The majority of copper is exported through the port of Antofagasta. A railroad that crosses the Andes into Bolivia also originates in this port. Besides mining, anchovy fishing is an important northern industry, providing Chile with one of the largest fish catches in the world. The ports of Iquique and Antofagasta are centers for the fishing fleet. Due to the year-round mild climate and attractive beaches, coastal cities have tried to develop a tourist industry, but they have achieved only moderate success.

The Norte Chico

In the Norte Chico, rainfall and snowmelt provide a permanent source of irrigation for four river valleys. Historically these areas produced grains for the miners and provided pastures for their draft animals. With mechanization, however, the lands are increasingly devoted to vineyards. Although the Arqueros silver and Tamaya copper mines made important contributions to Chile's nineteenth-century wealth, in the twentieth century, the mining center moved farther north. The Norte Chico produces most of Chile's *pisco,* a clear grape brandy, that when mixed with lemon juice and a few other ingredients becomes the typical *pisco sour.*

The Valle Central

The region known as the Valle Central begins about 70 miles north of Santiago with the Aconcagua Valley and extends to Concepción, about 250 miles south of the capital. Rainfall increases dramatically from the north to the south with Santiago receiving an average of only 13 inches, and Concepción, 52 inches a year. Both the coast and Andes ranges were heavily forested in precolonial times, but the Spanish removed the trees to expand the grazing areas. Reforestation projects on the coast and the protection of native species in the Andes have restored some of the tree cover. Important lumber, pulp, and paper industries have developed as a result.

The valley between the two mountain ranges has been the traditional breadbasket of Chile. The earliest Spanish use of the region was for cattle. Traditionally, the cattle fed in the lowlands during the winter months, and then, as the grasses dried up in the spring, *huasos,* or cowboys, drove them to higher elevations. Colonists also found that grains prospered in this region. Not only were grains raised for national consumption, but also they were exported to a variety of west coast ports. Originally *encomienda* and land grants created huge haciendas. In the eighteenth century the crown encouraged wealthy landowners to entail their estates for a substantial fee. Effectively, this meant that the land would never be sold and would remain in the family. Although this institution ended in the nineteenth century, Chileans replaced it with their own equivalent of the English manor. Wealthy mine owners and entrepreneurs acquired extensive lands, manicured them, and used them to receive distinguished guests. By the mid-twentieth century, however, many Chileans blamed these haciendas, now known as *fundos,* for impoverishing farm workers and lowering farm productivity. A combination of land reform and worker rebellion dismembered most of these *fundos* in the 1960s and 1970s.

This fertile region also is an excellent environment for vineyards, vegetables, and fruit. The great variety and abundance of these products becomes obvious when strolling through Santiago's fresh produce markets, especially el Mapocho. Beginning in the 1970s Chile began shipping large quantities of fresh fruit and wine worldwide. New commercial farms developed, primarily oriented to export. Urban investors, who hired professional agronomists to run their operations, became the dominant landholders. Lands formerly used for grazing or grain now were planted in vineyards and orchards, with adjoining packing facilities.

Not only is this region the most important agricultural zone, but also it contains the majority of industry. Some is natural resource based such as the two large copper mines, el Teniente and Andina, as well as the oil refinery at Concón. Belts of industrial plants extend north and south of Santiago. These include food processing, chemicals, textiles, consumer durables, and construction materials. The port cities of Valparaíso and San Antonio also have some industry.

Tourism, especially on the coast, is very important for the region. Many Chileans head there during the months of January and February. Also, Argentines from the Andean region find the Chilean coast more accessible than Argentina's Atlantic coast. Middle- and upper-class Chileans might have a beach house or apartment in Viña de Mar or another one of the picturesque beach towns sprinkled along the coast. In one of these, Isla Negra, lived the Nobel Prize-winning poet Pablo Neruda. His house, with its collection of artifacts from around the world, is open to the public. In Santiago, historical museums such as the National Archive and the Palace of Fine Arts are popular attractions for tourists and Chileans alike. The same is true of the many theaters and fine restaurants. For those who ski, resorts such as Portillo, Farellones, and Valle Nevado, located east of Santiago, offer abundant snow from June to September. During these months national teams from the northern hemisphere practice skiing and snowboarding when the slopes in their own countries are bare.

Although there are no navigable rivers in this region, during the winter rains and the spring runoff there are great water resources. These rivers include the Aconcagua, Maipo, Rapel, Maule, and Itata. Dams for both irrigation and hydroelectric power are located on the most important rivers. There are no inland river ports, but the seaports of Valparaíso and San Antonio account for 36 percent of Chile's exports and 65 percent of its imports.

The Sur

This region has a climate and topography very similar to that of the Pacific Northwest of North America. Rainfall is heavy on the coast in towns like Valdivia with 90 inches and Puerto Montt with more than 70 inches and increases eastward when the clouds hit the Andes. Although average annual temperatures are in the fifties on the coast and interior valleys, summer daytime temperatures are in the seventies. Winter daytime temperatures are in the forties and fifties with snow only falling in the mountains. Originally, forests covered most of the Sur, but the lowland forests were cleared for grazing and agriculture while slash-and-burn agriculture destroyed many mountain forests. Reforestation and limited burning permits have restored forests and made the area a leading lumber producer.

At the northwest corner of this region is the Concepción-Talcahuano metropolitan area, the second largest in the country with approximately 700,000 inhabitants. Not only does it have the best natural port in Chile, it is also the site of important heavy industry. Chile's only steel mill, Huachipato, is located here as is an oil refinery, chemical factories, and many pulp and paper mills. One hundred and fifty miles farther south is the fast growing city of Temuco, a commercial, agricultural, and forestry center. The region's commercial centers, Valdivia, Osorno, and Puerto Montt, are still farther south. These three cities all have an important German influence dating from the 1850s. Although the descendants of German homesteaders now speak Spanish, they try to conserve their language, work ethic, and land. Their Germanic obsession for cleanliness can be seen in both their impeccable homes and dairies. Their entrepreneurial spirit has created important tourist, milling, brewing, and forest industries.

This region is particularly notable for its many lakes, which ancient Andean glaciers dug and later filled with water. A Chilean folksong, *Los lagos,* or *The Lakes,* names favorites such as Pirihueco, Pangipulli, Llanquihue, Ranco, and Riñihue. When the weather is sunny in January and February, lakeside towns such as Villarrica, Pucón, and Frutillar overflow with tourists. This is rodeo season when riders show off their horsemanship and couples dance the *cueca,* a folk music rendition of the courtship between a rooster and a hen. In the rainy months, by contrast, only the hardy local residents remain, warming themselves in front of wood stoves, telling stories, and drinking tea or mate.

The Sur is the land of the Mapuche who resisted Spanish and Chilean conquest until the 1880s. The Mapuche presence is everywhere in this region. They number nearly 500,000. In downtown Temuco they sell their textiles, woodcarvings, and jewelry. Many live on reservations, or *reducciones,* where they care for sheep, plant potatoes, and weave blankets. Though the elders continue to speak the Mapuche language, the younger generation prefers Spanish. Mapuche youth frequently migrate to Santiago where girls often work as domestic servants and the young men find work in unskilled jobs. Once in the city they quickly assimilate. Except for their last names like Nahuel, Lefiñanco, and Colipe, they are indistinguishable from other Chileans.

South of Puerto Montt is Chile's largest island, Chiloé, which at 4,755 square miles, is approximately the size of Connecticut. The major town on the island is Ancud with 23,000 inhabitants. Native people, the Chilotes, are the dominant ethnic group on the island. Due to a lack of economic opportunities, they often migrate to the Argentine Patagonia in search of work. Evergreen forests once covered much of the island, but many trees were cleared to plant potatoes and raise cattle. Surrounded by a sea with so many abundant marine resources, many people live largely on fish or shellfish. Using only hot rocks to cook their catch, Chilotes prepare their typical *curanto,* or steamed shellfish, which includes crabs, clams, mussels, barnacles, and fish.

The Zona Austral

This region begins just south of Chiloé. From there and farther south, the continental shelf disappears and the Andes plunge right into the Pacific. Some pieces of a shelf or former coastal range stick out as islands and are crisscrossed by channels such as in the Chonos Archipelago. When homesteaders arrived in the early twentieth century, transportation facilities were minimal, so in clearing rangeland, colonists chose to burn the trees rather than harvest them. The fires escaped their control and decimated huge areas, leaving a landscape that still shows the scars. Until the military undertook a major highway construction project in the 1970s, the Patagonian residents had to drive through Argentina to communicate with the rest of Chile by land. Now a partly paved and spectacularly scenic road connects Puerto Montt with the village of Puerto Yungay, 660 miles to the south. Air transportation, which is faster, remains the favorite means of travel. Wind, rain, and low clouds always make takeoffs and landings an adventure.

Most towns are very small, the exceptions being Coihaique with 36,000 inhabitants and Punta Arenas with approximately 125,000 inhabitants. In some ways this region seems sealed in a nineteenth-century time capsule. Not only does the rustic wood architecture seem to reflect another era, but also human relations have a quality atypical of the twenty-first century. People seem to be in no hurry, they both talk and listen, and human relations seem timeless. Perhaps air travel, the Austral highway, and the Internet will bring change and diminish some of the Zona Austral's isolation. Today Web sites beacon outsiders to travel, learn the history, and experience the culture of this region.

Economic Change

Chileans have debated and experimented with economic innovation more than most countries of the world. Salvador Allende implemented a socialist economy in the early 1970s while Augusto Pinochet imposed neoliberal reforms in the mid-1970s. In the 1990s the democratic leaders designed tax and welfare programs aimed at reducing poverty. Throughout the twentieth century, Chile has alternatively emphasized policies to stimulate economic growth and those intended to improve income distribution. Conservative parties have emphasized the former, while center and left-wing parties have emphasized the latter.

The role of the state has been at the center of this economic debate. The government has subsidized agricultural credit and built and operated the national railroad. During the Great Depression, it switched its focus to industrialization. It protected private firms from foreign competition and invested in the steel, petroleum, electrical, and airline industries. In the 1960s and early 1970s the government began to redistribute wealth through agrarian reform. It also acquired foreign-owned copper mines and other industries. It also built public housing, distributed food, expanded education, and provided free health care.

In 1975 the military government turned over economic policy to a group of neoliberal economists who privatized most of the government businesses and many services including health care, the retirement system, and education. Except for the copper companies, it sold most of the businesses acquired by previous regimes. It explicitly encouraged foreign investment and stressed the importance of exports. Although the social costs were high, this model produced exceptional growth, stable prices, and foreign investment.

With the return of democracy in 1990, the Concertación government decided to provide services to the poorest sectors of Chile while at the same time preserving the basic private enterprise model. The government encouraged house construction, paved rural roads, installed running water, and expanded education. The private economy continued to grow, which provided tax revenue for improved services for the poor. So successful was the Chilean economy during the 1980s and 1990s that other Latin American nations tried similar reforms. An economic recession, which began in 1998 and continued until 2003, severely tested the viability of the model.

Growth

In the 1980s and 1990s Chile had the best economic growth rate in Latin America after having one of the worst in the 1960s and 1970s. Between 1990 and 1995 the gross domestic product, or GDP, more than doubled from $30 billion to $65 billion. As of 1997 it reached more than $73 billion. Chile's per capita GDP in 2000 was more than $5,000, second only to Argentina in Latin America. Although in the 1980s Chile's foreign debt equaled its annual GDP, in the 1990s GDP grew much faster than debt, reducing the ratio of debt to GDP to one-half. Much of this growth comes from neoliberalism's emphasis on exports. Whereas in the 1960s and early 1970s, Chile's exports represented 12 percent of GDP, in 1996 they represented 20 percent. Perhaps most interesting was the ability of leaders to diversify exports. As late as the 1970s, copper represented 80 percent of Chilean exports. By the late 1990s, mining exports had dropped to less than 45 percent of the total while other goods including fish meal, fruit, pulp and paper, and chemicals had risen to more than 55 percent of the total. Chile's largest trade partner is the European Union, followed by the United States, Japan, Argentina, and Brazil. The negative side to this emphasis on trade is that the weak Asian and Latin America economies dampened Chile's growth in 1998 and 1999 while the recessions in the United States and the European Union had a similar effect from 2001 to 2003.

Employment and Wages

As with most Latin American countries, Chile has had problems with jobs. Employment and wages have followed parallel trends during the last three decades. When employment fell in the mid-1970s and again in the early 1980s, wages dropped as well. When employment grew in the 1990s, wages rose also. Another important employment trend is the rise in the percentage of female workers. Women represent one-third of all workers, but as is true in most countries, their average salaries lag behind those of males. Disregarding gender and other wage inequality, in the 1990s average personal income surpassed $5,000 while family income exceeded $13,000. Income was not well distributed, however, with the lowest tenth of the population receiving only 1.2 percent of gross household income and the upper tenth, receiving 41.3 percent. One consequence of this unequal distribution is that 20 percent of Chileans live below the poverty line.

Transportation

Chile's communication and electrical networks are advanced by Latin American standards, but within the last decade they even approach those of the developed world. The nation's national railroad network includes rails stretching from Arica to Puerto Montt, with many cross-feeder lines serving the mines in the north and farms in the south. Decreasing public subsidy to the lines, however, has forced many unprofitable passenger trains and feeder lines out of service. For example, the Valparaíso-Mendoza passenger train, which offered scenic views of the Andes as it crossed from Chile with Argentina, no longer runs. A highway network has replaced it and many other trains. An excellent bus system offers regular departures to all points of the nation, and urban bus systems provide daily service to millions of commuters. Santiago's modern subway has terminals adorned with contemporary art. It affords the quickest service to many points of the city. The hub of air transportation are Santiago's national and international airports, with scheduled flights to Chile's twenty-two other airports.

Communication

Chileans want to be connected to important events. Every downtown corner has a kiosk where people pause to read the headlines of recent events or buy a copy of their favorite magazine. Chileans read as they travel on buses, in the subway, and on airplanes. A variety of national daily newspapers are available, although most are published by *El Mercurio*, the oldest daily newspaper in Latin America. Middle-sized cities such as Temuco, where *El Diario Austral* greets people every morning, have their own papers. Other media are important as well. In a country of 15,000,000, there are more than 5,000,000 radios and 3,000,000 television sets. There are three national television networks and major cities also offer cable television with both Spanish and English programming. Not surprisingly, the worldwide boom in cell phones has also hit Chile, with more than 200,000 in use (1996). Computer education and usage is widespread with instruction often included in elementary school curriculum. Many homes and most businesses are linked to the Internet. Friends exchange E-mail addresses as readily as telephone numbers. University programs and library catalogs have their materials available on-line. Major Chilean businesses and government agencies have Web sites adorned with recent video features.

Inflation

Unfortunately Chile has had one of the highest inflation rates in the world. From the late nineteenth century to 1940, the annual rate fluctuated between 5 and 8 percent. In the 1950s it averaged nearly 20 percent, reaching a record 86 percent in 1956. Conservative monetary measures lowered it again in the early 1960s, but by the end of the decade it shot up to more than 35 percent. During the last year of Allende's regime and into the early years of the military government, inflation averaged more than 300 percent, shooting above 600 percent in 1973! Although severe fiscal measures begun in 1975 brought inflation down, it was at a cost of 20 percent unemployment and a sharp contraction of the economy. By 1978 inflation decreased to 30 percent and held between 20 and 30 percent during the next decade. In the 1990s it dropped to less than 4 percent! At long last, Chile had tamed inflation, but not without a high cost. For those interested in studying about Chile's battle with inflation, excellent research publications are available in both Spanish and English.

GOVERNMENT

Constitution of 1980

The military chose to rule by decree until a new constitution went into effect in 1980. This document provided for a gradual transition to civilian rule and defined the military's power in the interim. Augusto Pinochet governed while the Military Junta acted as an advisory legislature. In 1988 Pinochet lost a referendum intended to prolong his tenure until 1997. Congressional elections, as provided by the constitution, were held in 1989. When congress met, instead of in its traditional neoclassical forum in Santiago, it moved to a massive structure in Valparaíso. With the executive and judicial branches still in the capital, the 1980 Constitution literally interpreted the concept of "division of power."

The National Congress consists of the Senate and the Chamber of Deputies. The Senate has 49 members, 38 are elected to eight-year terms, 9 are appointed, and 2 are former presidents. The Chamber of Deputies consists of 120 members elected to four-year terms. The president serves for a six-year term. President Ricardo Lagos's term extends from 2000 to 2006. The president has a cabinet composed of 19 ministers, the Comptroller-General, and the head of the National Energy Commission. The first president elected under the new constitution was Patricio Aylwin, a prominent Christian Democratic leader, who served a four-year term from 1990 to 1994. Originally the president appointed all mayors and city council members, but he could not replace members of the judiciary, military, or bureaucracy. Although Patricio Aylwin tried to reform the constitution, the conservatives blocked his program. His successor, Eduardo Frei R., suffered similar frustrations, but he did succeed in reforming municipal government and the judicial system.

The constitution also created a National Security Council composed of the heads of the armed forces and the police, as well as the president and heads of the Senate and the Supreme Court. This body can advise any branch of government about security matters, creating a power that many consider equivalent to military oversight.

Political Parties

Chile, like most European nations, has a multiparty tradition. The Constitution of 1980 substituted a winner-take-all system of elections for the former system of proportional representation. As a result, most of the parties form coalitions to run a limited number of candidates against the opposition. Those parties that do not join a coalition are at a strong disadvantage. In certain regional races, however, if an individual is particularly well known, he or she occasionally can defeat a coalition candidate.

There are currently six parties and two independent factions that have representatives serving in congress. Two other parties, the Communist and the Humanist, have run candidates but as yet without electoral success. In the congressional elections of 2001, the Unión Democrática Independiente (Independent Democratic Union), or UDI, received 25 percent of the votes, making it the strongest party. This conservative party was originally closely allied with the Pinochet government. Based on the same election, the second strongest party was the Christian Democrats. This centrist/liberal party received almost 19 percent of the vote. This percentage was considerably lower than the 27 and 23 percent it had received in the elections of 1993 and 1997.

The third strongest party is the moderate conservative party, Renovación Nacional (National Renovation), or RN, with 13.8 percent of the vote in 2001. Originally, RN was stronger than the more conservative UDI, but it has declined appreciably since 1997. The fourth strongest party, Partido por la Democracia (Party for Democracy), or PPD, is a subdivision of the Socialist Party. In 2001 it received 12.7 percent of the votes, nearly the same as in the two previous congressional elections. By contrast, the Socialist Party, which received 10 percent of the 2001 total, has declined by almost 2.5 percent since 1993. The Communist Party does not form part of any political coalition. Although it polls from 5 to 7 percent of the vote, it has not succeeded in electing any members to congress since 1989. An even smaller party, based on election results, is the Partido Radical Social Demócrata (Radical Social Democratic Party) or PRSD. It received only 4 percent of the vote in 2001, yet due to its affiliation with the Concertación coalition, it won 6 congressional seats.

The make up of Chile's congress in 2002, based on both coalition and party, was the following:

	Senators	Deputies
Concertación of Parties: Total	20	62
Christian Democratic Party (centrist/liberal)	12	23
Party for Democracy (liberal/left)	3	20
Socialist Party (liberal/left)	5	10
Radical Social Democratic Party (liberal)	0	6
Independent (liberal)	0	3
Alianza por Chile: Total	18	57
National Renewal (conservative)	6	18
Independent Democratic Union (conservative)	9	31
Independent (conservative)	3	8
Designated: Total	10	0
Institutional	9	0
Lifetime members	1	0
Totals	48	120

Elections

In the presidential election held in December 1999, Ricardo Lagos, the Concertación candidate, won the first round by a plurality of 48 percent over the Union for Chile candidate, Joaquín Lavín, who received 47.5 percent. The Communist Party candidate, Gladys Marín garnered a mere 3.2 percent. In the runoff election, Lagos received 51.3 percent to Lavín's 48.7 percent, thus giving him the presidency. Lagos's close victory and the conservative coalition's strong showing contrasted markedly with the presidential election six years earlier. In 1993 the winning Concertación candidate, Eduardo Frei R., received 58 percent of the vote, and the conservative coalition candidate, Arturo Alessandri B., only 24 percent. Based on the strong showing of Lavín in 1999 and the success of UDI in the 2001 congressional elections, the conservatives hope this trend will give them the presidency in 2006. With the economy weak from 1998 to 2003, Concertación must make a dramatic turnaround before 2006 if it hopes to stem the conservative challenge.

Federalism

Soon after its independence, Chile unsuccessfully tried to implement a federal system. Not until the Pinochet regime of the 1980s was federalism seriously considered again. In its desire to privatize and decentralize, the regime decided to create regional advisory councils made up of both public and private representatives. Pinochet retained, however, the power to appoint regional executives, called *intendentes,* as the provincial governors. He also appointed city mayors and council members, called *alcaldes* and *consejales,* but a constitutional reform sponsored by President Aylwin's government made these elected positions. Since 1927, when all police were joined with the Carabineros, there has been no local police system. In 1973, moreover, the Carabineros became a branch of the armed forces.

All education and social services were nationally controlled and funded until the Pinochet government decided to decentralize and later to privatize some of them. Perhaps giving municipal governments more responsibility for education and social services was a good idea, but many municipalities had an insufficient tax base to fund these services and as a result were forced to dismiss teachers and cut back on social services.

CULTURE

Language

Chileans have shaped their language to express their national concerns. A combination of Spanish and Native American words name and describe the land they inhabit. Though the conquistadors affixed Spanish names to the towns they founded in the Valle Central, they accepted the existing Mapuche names for the rivers and mountains. In the Sur, by contrast, Mapuche names are even common for towns, such as Temuco and Loncoche. Pablo Neruda, Chile's most famous poet, grew up in Temuco, where he heard the two languages in constant dialogue. This melding gives Chileans a creative freedom that contributes to their literary tradition.

Music

In some ways Chile can be described as a land of poetry and song. This combination can be seen in the rural *payador,* or minstrel, who invents lyrics as he strums the guitar. The *peña,* or folk music club, is the urban evolution of this tradition. Out of this environment sprang the New Song Movement led by Violeta Parra. Many of her songs, such as *Gracias a la vida* became international favorites. Her children, Angel and Isabel Parra, as well as Victor Jara, protested the conditions of Chilean miners, farmers, and fishermen. Their voices energized supporters of the Allende regime but also brought death and exile under the military government. Folklore groups such as the Parras, Quilapaiyún, and Inti Illimani went into exile where they rallied international opposition to the Pinochet regime, while within Chile the more traditional Huasos Quincheros struggled to create an illusion of harmony.

Although the Chilean folk music tradition is strong, classical music also has important supporters. Two Santiago radio stations with regional affiliates exclusively broadcast classical music. An active vocal music tradition supports classical music through many regional choir performances and festivals. In Santiago, the Municipal Theater is the home of the national symphony orchestra, the opera company, and the ballet company. Foreign conductors and companies complement the excellent national productions. Theatergoers have two dozen companies to choose from. These companies produce both avant-garde and traditional dramas.

Museums

Santiago, as well as important regional centers, has historical museums. The Pre-Columbian Art Museum, the National Historical Museum, and the Museum of Santiago all present panoramas of Chile's past. The San Francisco Church and the National Cathedral have museums that present perspectives on the nation's religious heritage. The National Archive and National Libraries are centers where both local and foreign scholars research Chilean history. The Fine Arts Museum, as well as dozens of private galleries, presents a sampling of Chile's painting and sculpture. Also, many antique shops provide delightful glimpses at colonial and nineteenth-century art and decor.

Religion

Approximately 75 percent of Chileans are Roman Catholic although not all attend mass regularly. Nevertheless, many parishes are overflowing even though they celebrate two or three Sunday masses. Chile is divided into 5 archdioceses and 17 dioceses. Cardinal Francisco Javier Errázuriz currently presides over the Archbishopric of Santiago. During the divisive years of the Allende and Pinochet governments, many fissures developed in the church. Conservative Catholic groups such as Opus Dei and the Chilean Society for Tradition, Family, and Property criticized the church's apparent support of Allende's reforms. Representatives of these groups welcomed military rule and even held important political positions. By contrast, church liberals applauded Allende's programs. When he was overthrown, they supported Cardinal Raúl Silva Henríquez's efforts to defend human rights through the Vicaría de la Solidaridad (Solidarity Vicariate). Since the return of democracy, the church has worked hard to heal these conservative and liberal divisions.

In both the past and the present, the Catholic Church has served as a patron of the arts and architecture. European styles including gothic, Romanesque, baroque, neoclassical, romantic, and modern all are present in Chile's religious art and architecture. In the north, adobe Romanesque structures appear as miniature fortresses in the desert. From the north to the south, some gothic structures were built by immigrant communities, which preferred northern European designs to Mediterranean ones. In the Valle Central, by contrast, renaissance or neoclassical styles predominate, whereas in the suburbs of Santiago and regional capitals, interesting examples of modern religious architecture are common.

Traditional protestant churches arrived in Chile with the merchants who flocked to Valparaíso after independence. First came the Anglican Church, which later developed missionary activities among the Mapuche. With German immigration, especially in the Sur, the Lutheran Church took root. The Methodists and then the Baptists established schools in Santiago and Temuco, respectively, while emphasizing the conversion of Chileans rather than service to an immigrant community. In recent decades Pentecostal and Mormon churches have aggressively spread their message throughout Chile, achieving many conversions among members of the working and middle classes. Small Jewish, Russian Orthodox, and Arabic Orthodox congregations exist in Santiago. The Slavic population of Punta Arenas also supports an Orthodox church. The numerous Middle Eastern immigrants are usually Catholic or Orthodox, rather than Islamic.

Artisan Traditions

During recent decades Chile has rediscovered its artisan traditions. The outdoor fairs in Santiago at the Dominican Monastery, on the Alameda, and in Parque O'Higgins show a wide variety of jewelry, pottery, metalwork, weaving, and woodworking. Just as interesting is a visit to the public markets of Santiago or Temuco where practical artisan products are sold side by side with ones made for tourists. The small town of Pomaire located west of Santiago is a community of potters offering both practical and decorative earthen ware. The copperware available throughout the country attests to the many ways this red metal can be artistically fashioned.

Recreation

Chileans enjoy exploring their country on weekends and on summer excursions. Those with sufficient means own a house near the beach or a bungalow in the southern Lake District. For those of lesser means, camping or renting a cabin enables them to escape the city. In the summer, water sports are popular and in the winter, ski resorts attract Chileans and foreigners alike. Hiking and mountain climbing are especially appropriate in the Andean forests and parks. Many ethnic or occupational groups have sporting clubs, which offer facilities for tennis, swimming, soccer, and track. Chile's world-class tennis players have learned their game at these clubs. Major cities have professional and amateur soccer teams. Aspiring players can be seen working on their dribbling and shooting skills on any street in the country. All Chileans become spectators as the country comes to a standstill when the team plays in the World Cup.

2

Origins of the Chilean People, 500–1750

According to poet Pablo Neruda, Chileans are members of "the Cosmic Race." Just as love and violence formed the cosmos, similar passions fused people from different continents, into Chilean society. For people to find the country, however, was not easy. It was hidden between the Pacific Ocean and the Andes mountains along a narrow corridor of South America's west coast. As the Chileans say, it was *donde el diablo perdió el poncho* or where the devil lost his cape. The earliest humans trekked down the coast and across the Atacama desert, one of the driest places in the world. Wherever they found water, they put down roots and developed communities. As these communities grew into villages, they attracted outsiders. First came the Incas in the fifteenth century and then the Spanish in the sixteenth century. Both conquered them and conscripted their labor. Farther south, however, the inhabitants put up such fierce resistance that the conquerors grudgingly accepted their independence.

During the colonial period, according to British historian Charles Boxer, Chile was the "backwater of the Spanish Empire." Those Spaniards who made the exhausting trip usually came not to conquer but to develop a hacienda or a mine. After Chile gained its independence, new immigrants arrived and made important contributions to commerce and industry. Over the centuries all these outsiders coming together forged Chile's "cosmic race." Although this race cannot forget its conflicts, amid the struggles it developed a tradition of civility. This tradition today serves as the basis of a democratic society.

Early Inhabitants

During much of Chile's past, peoples and their culture moved from north to south. Archeologists are not sure when the first movement of people along the west coast of South America began. They have few Paleolithic sites to document early migrations. Some controversial radiocarbon dates speculate that humans hunted and gathered food in southern Chile 33,000 years ago. More reliable dates come from the Monte Verde site near Valdivia where mastodon bones, weapons, and hearths show inhabitation dating back 13,000 years. Significant populations that archeologists have investigated thoroughly date to approximately 1,500 years ago.

Similar to Ecuadorian and Peruvian settlement patterns, the earliest inhabitants of northern Chile formed communities in river basins fed by snow runoff from the Andes. Some people preferred the coast with its rich ocean fisheries, while others preferred hunting and gathering in the interior. The latter began as nomads, herding llamas and collecting fruit, but when the Peruvian cultures introduced agriculture, they became sedentary. They built stone houses, sometimes with fortifications. From approximately 600 to 1000 A.D. the Tiahuanaco civilization developed in the Peruvian highlands. Either through trade or conquest, it shared ceramic, textile, and construction techniques with people of northern Chile known as the Diaguitas. The Tiahuanacos also introduced potatoes, corn, beans, peppers, and cotton. After this great Peruvian civilization collapsed, it was not until over 400 years later that the Inca Empire expanded deep into Chile.

The Mapuche

The Mapuche inhabited the Central Valley and southern Chile when the Incas first tried to conquer the territory. These people, also referred to as the Araucanos, lived in an environment similar to that of Northern California and the Pacific Northwest. A long, nine-month rainy season with cool temperatures fosters a dense forest and extensive wetlands and bogs in the river valleys. Although living in an area that was similar in topography and climate to Oregon, Washington, and British Columbia, the Mapuche sustained a population of 500,000 to 700,000, or nearly five times that of the Pacific Northwest.[1] Due to a limited number of game animals, agriculture rather than hunting was the primary occupation. The Mapuche routinely planted potatoes, beans, gourds, peppers, and corn. They used these ingredients to prepare gruel, tortillas, and a variety of vegetable dishes. They also made *chicha*, a type of hard cider, with either wild berries or corn. Coastal Mapuche fished while those living in the Andes collected large quantities of Araucanian pine nuts. They raised llamas largely for their wool. The Mapuche living on the west side of the Andes hunted rabbits and a small deer, while those living on the dry, eastern side of the Andes used *boleadoras*[2] to hunt guanacos, wild relatives of the llama, and *ñandú*, a South American ostrich. They built thatched huts, slept on llama pelts, and cooked in a separate hut called a *fogón*. During the long rainy months, family and friends gathered in the *fogón* to chat and chew pine nuts. To celebrate the planting season or a military victory, they played their musical instruments, danced, and drank *chicha* in the *fogón*.

The Mapuche organized themselves into local clans or tribes and formed confederations for military purposes. The northern clans, called Picunches, were located in the region of the Maule River. The Huilliches lived from the Maule south to the Valdivia region, the Pehuenches lived in the western Andes, and the Puelches lived on the eastern side of the Andes.[3] The clans traded with each other, but also raided each other in forays called *malocas*. Given the diverse area the clans inhabited and their decentralized political system, they would seem incapable of confronting a common enemy. Yet, like the Iroquois of North America, they united to fight a common enemy. Twice, the Inca failed to defeat the Mapuche. Although the Spanish momentarily subdued them, they rebelled and successfully defended their autonomy for more than 250 years. Over time, clan alliances shifted. One clan might be allied with the Spanish and fight on their behalf in a particular military campaign. Later, during a general uprising, these "friendly Indians" might join the rebellion. Given the fluidity of alliances, some Spanish governors believed the only solution was complete domination, whereas others believed in negotiations and peace pacts.

Far south in Patagonia lived four other groups: the Chonos, the Alacalufes, Yaganes, and the Onas. The first three groups lived close to the sea and extracted most of their food from it. They built bark canoes capable of carrying five or six people along with their dogs. The Onas, by contrast, hunted a variety of animals especially in the region of Tierra del Fuego. All these groups made their clothing from skins, but according to early European observers, these hardly seemed sufficient to keep them warm. Their small population, distributed over a vast area, made their survival particularly problematic once they were exposed to European diseases and institutions.

Beginning about 1470 the Inca began to annex all of the communities of Chile's northern valleys. The Central Valley clans fell to them as well, but south of the Maule River, the Inca encountered fierce resistance. The dense forests combined with Mapuche unity and mobility prevented the Incas from subjugating them. The Mapuche did develop a trade relationship with the Incas, exchanging gold and raw materials for Inca crafts. They also learned Inca artisan skills, especially weaving.

The conquered people north of the Maule developed very different social institutions than the independent people south of it. The Inca imposed a bureaucratic hierarchy, transplanted natives from Arequipa, Peru, and resettled local people. They forced local inhabitants to do agricultural and mining labor. This domination accustomed them to the work expectations that the Spanish would impose on them a century later.

Early European Exploration

When the Spanish began to explore South America in the sixteenth century, they approached Chile from both the south and the north. Coming from the extreme south was Ferdinand Magellan, who explored the strait that bears his name. He began his exploration of South America by surveying the Brazilian and Argentine coasts, then in November 1520 he headed into the treacherous winds and currents at the southern end of the continent. He was the first European to see Tierra del Fuego and the Andean ice flows plunging into the Pacific. His interest, however, was Asia, not the coast of Chile. Had he known of the existence of the Inca Empire, he certainly would have devoted more attention to the west coast. But, he believed that the American continents blocked access to Asian riches, rather than offering wealth themselves. To his credit, Magellan solved the riddle of the distance between the Americas and Asia. He succeeded where Columbus had failed and found the westward route to Asia. The Spanish, nevertheless, avoided the use of his strait, considering it too dangerous. Instead, they preferred to transport goods from Asia and the Pacific Coast by land across Mexico and Panama.

The second exploration of Chile came from the north and was led by Diego de Almagro. He began his career by helping Francisco Pizarro conquer the Incas. When he heard of the Inca's vast empire, including their Chilean possessions, he decided to explore and conquer them. His expedition included Spaniards who Pizarro had not rewarded with *encomiendas,* Inca servants, and two Inca nobles who served as emissaries to vassal tribes. To encourage the enterprise, King Charles V granted Almagro a charter authorizing him to explore, conquer, and govern a territory called New Toledo, which stretched from Southern Peru to central Chile.

The Incas discouraged Almagro from taking the route through the high northern Chilean desert, claiming that he would find little food for either his people or his animals. He, therefore, decided to traverse the areas that are now Bolivia and northern Argentina before crossing the Andes into Chile at the present site of Copiapó. This harrowing route turned out to be deadly. A combination of hostile Indians, floods, and snow-covered trails decimated his retinue. Many of his Indian porters fled, while others died of cold or starvation. When he and his survivors finally reached Copiapó, their march south became easier due to the frequent river valleys and Indian villages. From the latter he took food and conscripted Indian labor, with no concern about enmity he created for future Spanish explorers. In the Aconcagua and Mapocho river valleys he found environments comparable to the best in Spain. He sent other explorers farther south, but they fared badly, encountering torrential rains and hostile Mapuche. They turned back, therefore, without exploring the fertile regions south of the Itata River.

In Chile, Almagro did not find the gilded temples he had seen in Peru. Some Mapuche worked gold mines to pay the Incas tribute, but historians are uncertain if he visited any of these.[4] The fertile valleys of Chile impressed Almagro, however. He considered establishing a colony, but his men were impatient to find precious metals. They wanted wealth to take back home, rather than to settle down in distant South America. Almagro gave in to their pressure and returned north. This time he avoided the Argentine-Bolivian route, preferring to risk crossing the Atacana desert. On this trek, he and his company again suffered great hardship and arrived in Peru embittered about their lack of treasure. He and his men, therefore, challenged Pizarro for a larger share of Inca riches. Pizarro preferred to fight and a civil war broke out. With the help of Pedro de Valdivia, Pizarro defeated Almagro and executed him.

In retrospect Almagro's Chilean legacy is mixed. He provided first-hand information about the geography on both sides of the Andes. He observed the Indians' valley settlements, what they produced, and the goods and labor they could contribute to Spanish colonization. Unfortunately, his levies of food and labor sent a harsh message to the native inhabitants of Chile. He also discovered that from Copiapó south the vegetation gradually increases, and that the Aconcagua and Mapocho valleys could sustain agriculture and cattle ranching. Although most Spaniards did not wish to sink roots in Chile, others later recognized its potential.

Pedro de Valdivia

Due to Almagro's insubordination, Pizarro claimed that his descendants had lost any claim to New Toledo. Therefore, without King Charles V's authorization, Pizarro rewarded his loyal friend, Pedro de Valdivia, with a charter to conquer and colonize Chile. Given the hardship of Almagro's expedition, Valdivia had difficulty in finding volunteers. Eventually he set off with a modest company along the coastal, rather than the Bolivian, route. Understandably his reception by the Indians was cold, even hostile.

Valdivia chose the Mapocho Valley as the site for establishing his first settlement, which he named Santiago de la Nueva Extremadura. The Mapocho River offered fresh water and a naturally occurring promontory, Cerro Santa Lucía, as a lookout. His founding ceremony underscored both Spain's as well as his rightful claim to the land. He then chose a city council, which elected him governor, following a procedure used by other Spaniards to further legitimate their authority.

Following royal guidelines, he mapped out the city like a chessboard. He located the main plaza a few blocks from the river, allocating the west side for the principle church and the north side for government offices. He divided each city block into four properties, but later subdivisions expanded this number to eight. The colonists then began constructing their first humble structures with adobe walls and thatched roofs. Earlier mistreatment of the Indians came back to haunt them. Not happy to see intruders in their land, the local Indian clan attacked and almost destroyed the fragile settlement a few months later. In fighting for their lives, even Valdivia's consort, Inés Suárez, wielded a sword. Thereafter, the settlers maintained a twenty-four hour alert. The next year when they planted wheat, oats, and corn, they guarded their fields as well.

Valdivia began further explorations. He sought the same wealth that the Inca had derived from Chile: gold and Indian labor. Because the Spanish had conquered the Inca, Valdivia and his colleagues believed that they had a rightful claim to both resources. Near the coast, north of Valparaíso, an Indian showed him the gold mines of Marga Marga, which the Mapuche had worked for the Incas. Valdivia established an *encomienda* of workers who produced gold valued at 7,000 pesos in a few months and, over the next six years, gold valued at 230,000 pesos. Valdivia soon identified other mines and forced more Indians into *encomienda* labor. He obligated men and women to pan gold in the rivers even during the winter months. Their loss of freedom, suffering, and death created enormous resentment among all the clans. Valdivia's fixation on gold also caused him to overlook the commercial potential of farming. Although he introduced grain and cattle, the basic foods in the Spanish diet, he did not to develop their commercial possibilities. To his successors' credit, they discovered the agricultural potential of Chile.

Subduing the Mapuche

Valdivia's passion was to extend gold production into Mapuche territory. In the early 1550s, he led his troops south of the Maule River. He failed to understand why the Incas were defeated during similar campaigns. His belief in Spanish military superiority seemed to be confirmed by the relative ease with which he defeated the Mapuche. In this region of thick forests and wetlands, he established a number of fortified towns, each more than a day's distance from the other.[5] He then rewarded his soldiers with Indians by forcing the latter into *encomiendas*. When his men discovered gold deposits, they used their tribute-paying Indians to work them. Although his practice violated King Charles's requirement that Indian tribute should be in produce, not in labor, they paid no heed to this restriction.

The Mapuche were farmers and warriors unaccustomed to the drudgery of placer mining. The physical abuse and mistreatment of their women, moreover, provoked their rage. They looked for the opportunity to rebel as they observed and learned Spanish military tactics. A few young Mapuche boys served Spaniards as grooms and learned to ride. Some even dared to steal horses and ride to freedom. The Mapuche thus started to build their own cavalry. The Mapuche soon developed exceptional agility as horsemen. Even though their armor was of leather, rather than steel, they became formidable foes. Along with their riding skills, the effective use they made of the thickly forested landscape enabled them to ambush Spanish patrols and settlements.

Mapuche Rebellion

One of Valdivia's former pages, named Lautaro, led his people in a general uprising. In December 1553 he and his troops assaulted fort Tucapel, burned it to the ground, and killed all its soldiers. When Valdivia heard of the massacre, he rashly pursued those responsible, but his small cavalry was no match for Lautaro's army. The Mapuche troops captured and executed Valdivia. No Spaniards survived to narrate the debacle, yet it generated legends that are important in Chilean folklore. These often stress the painful, but seemingly just, methods of Valdivia's execution. According to one version, his captors poured molten gold down his throat to quench his thirst for the precious metal. According to another version, Valdivia paid for the blood of Mapuche people with his own. In this gruesome story, his captors cut off his arms and ate them while he was still alive. Those who narrate these legends rarely show much compassion for the victim. They see the Mapuche, not Valdivia, as the victim and equate social justice with revenge.

Lautaro's uprising brought the Mapuche clans together to fight for the expulsion of the Spanish from their lands. The settlers quickly understood the threat to their lives and abandoned a number of the southern towns and forts. In the meantime the colonial military leaders struggled with each other over who would assume the governorship. Francisco de Villagra temporarily emerged in charge. He saved Santiago, and perhaps the entire colony, when he counterattacked and killed Lautaro. With their leader's death, Mapuche rebellion dissipated and the Spanish settlers returned to their towns. As soon as the Spanish regrouped their *encomienda* Indians, they put them to work again, believing that once again they controlled Mapuche territory.

New Leadership

In gratitude for having saved the colony, Francisco de Villagra thought that the crown would appointment him as governor. He was mistaken. Merit proved a less important criterion for colonial public office than political influence and family ties. The viceroy of Peru named his son, García Hurtado de Mendoza, as governor. Hurtado de Mendoza's social origins were quite different from those of the conquistadors. Whereas the latter were commoners who had triumphed through shear willpower, he belonged to the Spanish nobility. To add weight to his aristocratic status, he brought a retinue of lawyers, priests, and loyal soldiers. Once in Chile, he set a harsh tone for his new regime by arresting Villagra and another conquistador, Francisco de Aguirre. From Valdivia's veterans, he demanded deference in manners and language as befitted the Spanish aristocracy. The veterans believed that by conquering Chile and owning *encomiendas* they had ascended in status, but the new governor reminded them of their humble social origins.

García Hurtado de Mendoza also brought a spirit of new conquests and expansion. First, he encouraged Spanish settlement on the eastern side of the Andes. His lieutenants founded Mendoza and San Juan in the region of Cuyo, which was governed by Chile until the 1770s. Secondly, he marched through the south, founded the town of Osorno, and explored the island of Chiloé. After encountering little opposition, he gave the impression that once again the Spanish dominated the Mapuche clans. Thirdly, he sponsored the exploration of the Chilean coastline, south to the Strait of Magellan. To reward his own followers, he stripped many of the original conquistadors of their *encomiendas* and distributed them to his subordinates. Political influence, not previous service, now determined *encomienda* ownership and rank.

The governor masked his partiality with a set of regulations calling for the humane treatment of the Indians. In an attempt to echo the crown's restriction on *encomienda* abuse, he asked his legal advisor, Hernando de Santillán, to draw up a list of labor prohibitions. Announced in 1559, these restricted the work of women and children and required that all workers be fed and compensated. *Encomenderos,* nevertheless, paid little attention to these regulations. Over twenty years later another governor, Martín Ruíz de Gamboa, took the radical step of eliminating forced labor and replacing it with a tax. This reform, like its predecessor, could not resolve the contradiction between the Spaniards' desire for free labor and the inhumane treatment of the Mapuche. In the seventeenth and eighteenth centuries, other governors faced the same issue in resolving this problem.

As Hurtado de Mendoza increased rather than diminished the Spanish presence in Mapuche territories, a new leader, Caupolicán, incited rebellion near Concepción. Initially he was successful, but in a surprise raid, the Spanish captured him. To revenge Spanish deaths, they impaled him on a stake. Though Caupolicán's struggle was cut short, his name became legendary through the Chilean epic poem, *La Araucana.* Its author, Alonzo de Ercilla, a soldier-poet who fought against the Mapuche, chose to ennoble the Mapuche leader in verse. Ercilla saw the Spanish-Mapuche conflict as a New World version of the Trojan Wars. Through his imagination, Pedro de Valdivia, Hurtado de Mendoza, Lautaro, and Caupolicán emulate the heroic characters of the *Iliad.* The work does not attempt a realistic depiction of either the Spanish or the Mapuche, but the dramatic confrontation it depicts with masterful verse makes it an important source of Chilean identity.

García Hurtado de Mendoza's administration was far from noble as it furthered both his own interests and those of the crown. The veteran conquistadors who lost *encomiendas* and privileges complained bitterly to the king and his council. They sent both letters and personal emissaries pleading their cases. Interestingly enough, the crown learned to use these communications to understand issues and defend its interests in distant territories. After complaints piled up against Hurtado de Mendoza, the crown dismissed him and named a veteran, Francisco de Villagra, as governor. He took over just as a new Mapuche uprising occurred. When he died of natural causes two years later, without having defeated the rebellious clans, a period of political instability ensued. In 1567, in an attempt to resolve the problem, the king created a new administrative body, called the *audiencia,* which served as a judicial board.

The king sought to strengthen his authority by choosing different types of rulers and preventing any group from monopolizing power. One surprising result of the Mapuche rebellions was that they democratized the colony's leadership. Whereas in pacified colonies like Peru and Mexico the crown preferred that its officials come from the Spanish nobility, in Chile the crown usually chose military men. Although these veterans were of lesser social status, the king believed they were more capable of defeating the Mapuche.

Another surprising, but tragic, result of the Mapuche rebellions is that they became the justification for enslaving Indians and an important source of the army's income. Originally the king prohibited Indian enslavement, yet the ferocity and duration of the Mapuche conflict caused him to revise his policy. In 1608 he authorized the enslavement of Chilean Indian rebels. This decree opened the door on two centuries of abuse. Although the decree prohibited the enslavement of women and children, because they were easier to catch they were often the majority enslaved. In many campaigns the soldiers' objective became to take captives rather than to defeat the Mapuche. At 300 pesos a head, each foray into Mapuche territory potentially offered thousands of pesos. This business became so cynical that one governor, Rodrigo de Quiroga, attacked peaceful Indians to harvest captives. He and his successors sold the captives to hacienda and mine owners whose *encomienda* workers had either died or run off. Some governors even sold captives to Peru. Slave hunting became so much a part of military culture that "friendly" Indians captured other Indians and sold them into bondage. Once enslaved, some Mapuche fled and attempted to return to their families. To prevent flight, masters severed the tendon on one leg so they could only hobble and not run. Even crueler punishments were not uncommon.

New Conflicts

By the end of the sixteenth century, the Mapuche desperately wanted to rid their territory of the Spanish. In 1598 they ambushed and killed

Governor Martín García Oñez de Loyola and 50 soldiers when they were patrolling the south. In the next five years they rebelled throughout the south. They either overran the towns, or the Spanish abandoned them out of fear. Upon capturing a town they often executed the men, but they incorporated the women and children into their families. According to one estimate, in just two years the Mapuche killed 700 soldiers, captured 300 women and children, and stole 10,000 horses and 500,000 cattle. Mapuche warriors considered Spanish women as war trophies and taught them their language and customs. If the Spanish ever succeeded in recapturing them, they found them so acculturated to Mapuche life that many refused to return home.

Not only did the Mapuche develop their own cavalry, but they also perfected the ambush. They lured the Spanish onto steep ground, often with only one escape route. Then the Mapuche foot soldiers jerked the Spaniards off their mounts by looping nooses around their necks and attacked them before they could stand up. If the first wave of Mapuche troops was driven back, they sent in reserve waves until the Spanish were overwhelmed. Another tactic was to implant spikes at the bottom of camouflaged pits dug on frequently used trails. When the horses stepped into the trap and plunged to their deaths, the defenseless riders became easy prey to Mapuche warriors. The latter also attached pieces of captured Spanish weapons to their lances and wooden clubs. To further terrorize the Spaniards, they made flutes and drumsticks out of dead Spanish soldiers' bones and used them to create a terrifying racket when they attacked. They frequently executed captives, ate their hearts, and then made their craniums into cider mugs.

This combination of psychological warfare and innovative battle tactics enabled the Mapuche to reverse the Spaniards' military advantage. In the seventeenth century, as the Spanish saw their victories turn to humiliating defeats, they pleaded with the crown for reinforcements. The entire colony panicked and considered abandoning Chile altogether. To reassure residents, Governor Alonso de Ribera fortified the north bank of the Biobío River, but when he tried to reconquer the south, he failed miserably. When news of the Chilean disaster reached the Council of Indies in Spain, it feared for the colony.

In addition to the Mapuche uprising, European enemies attacked Chile. English buccaneers like Richard Hawkins and Bartholomew Sharp plundered coastal towns like Valparaíso and La Serena, while in the south the Dutch tried to establish a permanent colony. The latter was part of the Dutch West Indies Company's global plan to add a base in Chile to the ones they already had in northern Brazil and in the Hudson River valley. Pursuing this objective, in 1643 the Dutch hijacked ships off the Chilean coast, captured the island of Chiloé, and negotiated an alliance with the Mapuche. Health problems and a lack of provisions, however, forced them to abandon the Chilean project.

To deal with these many threats, the crown decided to create a standing army. As in most colonies, it had preferred the more economical, local militia. With a paid army, hacienda and mine owners were relieved that they would no longer have to supply men and provisions. Chilean revenues, however, were insufficient to cover this new expense, so from Peru the crown allocated an annual subsidy, or *situado*, of 120,000 ducats to maintain a force of 1,500 men. This army may seem small, but by colonial standards, it was large. Even wealthier colonies, like Peru and New Spain, relied exclusively on militias for their defense. Over the years even this army failed to subdue the Mapuche, which kept the crown searching for other solutions to this conflict.

Missionary Efforts

The Catholic Church proposed its own solution. It was concerned about the Mapuche rebellion, but for different reasons. Beginning with the colonization of the Caribbean, the church had defined its mission in the Americas as the conversion of the native peoples to Christianity. Priests followed the conquistadors to Mexico and Peru, baptizing millions of recently conquered subjects. As the clergy witnessed the cruel exploitation of these new Christians, they threatened the conquistadors and *encomenderos* with excommunication. Passionate defenders of the Indians such as Father Bartolomé de las Casas took this cause to the king himself and persuaded him to place severe restrictions on the use of native labor.

The first priests in Chile did not share las Casas's passion for justice and therefore did not object to Pedro de Valdivia's conquest and mistreatment of the Indians. After Valdivia's death, however, friar Gil González, a Dominican, preached that Valdivia had waged an unjust war against the Indians. He warned that soldiers, who pursued such tactics, risked eternal damnation. Reinforcing this message was Franciscan friar Antonio de San Miguel, the first bishop of southern Chile. He refused to hear confessions and give absolution to soldiers who fought the Indians. Not surprisingly, this message disconcerted both the military leaders and the *encomenderos*, whose wealth depended on the exploitation of Indian labor. They successfully opposed the clergy's campaign for social justice.

The "Defensive War"

A dramatic change occurred when the Jesuit order arrived in Chile in 1593. Its most important leader was a friar, Luis de Valdivia, unrelated to

Pedro de Valdivia, who believed that the Mapuche rebellion was exclusively a result of their exploitation. As a solution, he proposed a radical policy called the "defensive war," which called for the exclusion of the Spanish from Mapuche territory. According to him, only the Jesuits charged with converting the Mapuche to Christianity would be permitted to enter the region. The military and the *encomenderos* adamantly opposed this policy, but Luis de Valdivia and his religious order successfully lobbied the crown to adopt it.

The Jesuits persuaded the crown to implement a similar program in Paraguay, where initially it succeeded. The Chilean case proved different. Not only did the Jesuits confront a half-century of hostilities and distrust in Chile, but they confronted entrenched interests which benefited from war. Military leaders supplemented their income by selling captured Indian slaves, and hacienda and mine owners gained additional workers. Some of the Mapuche also benefited from what they robbed from Spanish haciendas. How could the Jesuits change this situation? Hardly had the defensive war gone into effect, when a major tragedy occurred. According to one version, the wife of Anganamon, a Mapuche chief, converted to Christianity. Afterwards, she took refuge in a mission and refused to return to him. To exact revenge, the infuriated chief and some warriors attacked three Jesuit missionaries who were preaching nearby at Elicura. After assassinating the priests, they rode north across Valdivia's defensive line and raided Spanish settlements.

Since most Spaniards opposed the defensive war, to them the Elicura tragedy confirmed that the Jesuit's policy would never work. They implored the crown to let the military solve the Indian problem. For a different reason, other religious orders and the secular clergy came out against the defensive policy. They objected to the virtual Jesuit monopoly of Mapuche missionary work. As the defensive war policy came under criticism from all quarters, Luis de Valdivia decided he must return to Spain to defend it. He failed, however. Two years later, the new governor, Pedro Osores de Ulloa, opened a full-scale war with the Mapuche. In justification of his action, he blamed them for the deaths of 400 Spaniards, the loss of 2,500 horses, and the flight of 1,500 workers. He also claimed that 46 Spanish soldiers had deserted the army, fled to live with the Mapuche, and were supplying them aid. To raise troop morale and provide the hacienda and mine owners with additional labor, he decided that soldiers could enslave and sell any Mapuche captured in battle.

Although in the 1620s the Jesuit peace plan seemed dead, certain aspects of it resurfaced periodically. In the 1640s, for example, the Marquis de Baides began his governorship by recognizing Mapuche sovereignty in the Sur. He invited their leaders to conference at Quillín and, as a goodwill gesture, distributed gifts to them. Both sides agreed on peace and then they toasted with wine and hard cider. The peace agreement was followed by a barbecue with music and dancing. This peace, like others, unfortunately did not last, but it initiated a tradition of parliaments, gifts, and festivities in which leaders tried to resolve hostilities through negotiations.

Life in Captivity

The Mapuche wars created many histories including that of the captive officer Francisco Núnez de Pineda y Bascuñan. He was taken prisoner in 1629 and converted into a Mapuche chief's servant. Later he narrated his experiences in *Happy Captivity and the Cause of the Prolonged Wars in Chile*. There are interesting parallels and distinctions between his narrative and that of Captain John Smith's of the early Virginia colony from 1607–09. As with Smith's relationship to Pocahontas, an Indian princess also cares for Pineda y Bascuñan. She does not, however, negotiate his release. Other differences between the histories of the two men are also interesting. Pineda y Bascuñan offered a sympathetic view of Mapuche culture. For example, he credits a shared code of military honor by the Mapuche and the Spanish for his humane treatment and his eventual release. Instead of being barbarians, Pineda y Bascuñan views the Mapuche as civilized. His history also has a political agenda, for in it he pleads for the restoration of friar Valdivia's defensive war policy. The author, educated by the Jesuits, wanted to give the policy another chance.

Gradually hostilities with the Mapuche diminished as trading opportunities between the two peoples gained more importance. The Mapuche bartered cattle, hand-woven ponchos, feathers, and baskets for Spanish textiles, ironware, grain, and wine. In contrast to the military's distrust of Mapuche promises, the merchants had considerable faith in them. After they distributed goods to the Mapuche, the latter paid them in a timely fashion. As the value of this trade increased, however, the military leaders sought to monopolize it. They prohibited anyone but themselves from bartering with the Mapuche. They tried to jack up prices and force the Indians to buy unwanted goods. When rebellions occurred, increasingly they resulted from this heavy-handed conduct.

Building the Church

While the military and the merchants were inventing new relations with the Mapuche, the church concentrated on ministering to the growing population in Spanish-controlled Chile. The church needed parishes, but building proceeded slowly due to the colony's relative poverty. Pedro de Valdivia allocated the entire west side of Santiago's main plaza to the church, but nothing was built until the colonists themselves provided the resources. In the meantime the clergy celebrated mass in the entryway of Valdivia's house. The first chapel of rustic adobe walls and a thatched roof was so poorly built that it collapsed after a few years. Later, priests with architectural skills and more resources supervised the construction of the cathedral, the Franciscan monastery, and the Dominican church, which are still prominent Santiago landmarks. The Augustinians, Mercedarians, and Jesuits also added their parishes to the heart of the city. A reflection of the importance of these churches is that streets bear their names. Although never as lavish as the churches of New Spain and Peru, as Chile prospered the clergy adorned their churches with ceramic tiles, gilded altars, and carved tableaux. Paintings and woodcarvings of Christ, the Virgin, and the saints inspired devotion.

Prominent parishioners donated land and mortgaged their lands to support the church. They also encouraged their sons and daughters to join the clergy. During religious festivities, they participated in processions. Fasting, vigils, retreats, and pilgrimages were common. When elite family members died, after a wake and funeral mass, they were buried beneath the church floor and their names inscribed upon the flagstones. By contrast, the common people were buried in humble cemeteries. In addition to its parishes, the church built hospitals, orphanages, and educational institutions. It usually charged no fee for these services; rather, they were paid for by income from other activities including the taxes collected by the state but turned over to the church.

In an era without clocks, the church bells served to tell time. They rang for mass, to signal someone's death, and to announce the coronation of a new king. Chileans believed that the sacraments such as baptism, marriage, confession, and communion were needed to sustain them in this life and the next. Although the church was revered as an institution, people sometimes joked about the foibles of the clergy. The union of church and state left no room for non-Catholics in the colony. The church guarded against heretical beliefs and imposed conformity through its power of excommunication and inquisition. The church did accept considerable latitude in personal behavior. Sin was acceptable: opposition to the church was not.

As its wealth increased, the church invested in land. It also loaned money to hacienda and mine owners at the standard 6 percent interest. The church thus became the equivalent of a colonial bank. The clergy's management of both finance and land was the most advanced in the colony. To develop their haciendas, they improved farming and ranching methods. The Jesuits' skill in building irrigation systems, seeding alfalfa, and fattening cattle made their haciendas some of the most valuable in Chile. The income from them supported their schools and parishes. Since their schools educated civilians as well as the clergy, not surprisingly, a Jesuit education was common among colonial leaders.

In rural Chile affluent hacienda owners built small chapels on their estates, which priests only visited a few times a year. In the clergy's absence, rural folk learned to provide for their own spiritual needs. Not surprisingly, many poor couples were not married nor were their children baptized; yet when someone died, members of the community conducted the wake. Given the limitations of folk medicine and the tragedies of everyday life, when they had health problems or a family crisis, they petitioned a saint or the Virgin Mary to intercede for them. In return, they promised to undertake an act of faith such as a pilgrimage. During the festival of the Tirana in the far north, the Indians offered their traditional dances as acts of faith. The clergy generally encouraged folk religious practices, but they defined what was acceptable and what was not.

Rural Traditions

In addition to traditional religious practices, the Spanish strove to recreate the rural life they left back home. In much of Spain this revolved around cattle ranching. Although mining soon became the backbone of Chile's commercial economy, even mine owners wanted to own a ranch. In addition to giving them status, they used the hacienda to breed the mules for transporting and grinding their minerals. Although the colony's first horses, cows, and sheep were exorbitantly expensive, they reproduced with little effort, so that within a few decades, they became abundant and cheap.

The summer hacienda rite was the rodeo in which the *huaso*, or cowboy, rounded up, slaughtered, and skinned mature cattle. He then stripped the fat from the carcasses, melted it, and poured it into jugs. Later, families used it to prepare a variety of dishes including *sopaipillas*, a traditional fried bread. On rainy winter days, the entire family would stand around the fire pit gobbling up hot *sopaipillas* as they came out of the pot. Chileans also converted the fat into tallow for manufacturing candles. As tallow became abundant, they shipped it north to Pacific Coast ports. They also made jerked beef, some of which they exported. It formed a key ingredient in the local diet especially in the winter when they served it with chopped vegetables as *charquicán*, or jerked beef hash. In a largely rural economy, there was little market for meat, so after stripping the fat off the carcasses, many them were left for condors to feast on.

Out of necessity the Spanish incorporated a number of Mapuche foods into their diet. Most important was corn. They ate it fresh on the cob, as cornmeal gruel, and as *humitas,* or the Chilean equivalent of a tamale. In spite of the abundance of corn, the tortilla never became part of their diet. Other Native American foods that soon became staples were potatoes, tomatoes, peppers, and beans. Native hazelnuts and pine nuts also were widely consumed.

The Spanish found that wheat and other grains flourished in Chile. As a result bread became the most important staple of the Chilean diet. They baked it fresh daily in brick ovens. Poor farm workers, who did not have ovens, buried the dough in the ashes and baked it in an open hearth.[6] European nuts, fruits, and vegetables, especially almonds, walnuts, apples, pears, oranges, garbanzos, and lentils, adapted well to Chile. Another European plant that flourished was the grapevine. The monks produced wine on their haciendas and then the secular estates followed suit. Quality was a problem, however, because Chileans used unfired ceramic jugs to ferment and store the wine. These were porous, allowing the wine to turn to vinegar after a few months. To solve the problem, some people waxed the inside of the jars, but as the wax dissolved, it fouled the wine. Of course, when drunk early, this was not a problem. Chileans also developed a taste for recently fermented wine, called *chicha.* Being both sweet and alcoholic, it encouraged consumption. The Mapuche who made their own chicha quickly developed a taste for Spanish liquors, which became standards for trade and peace negotiations.

The Spanish transplanted livestock such as horses, cows, donkeys, goats, sheep, pigs, and chickens. The Mapuche quickly adopted all of these animals and developed their own herds and flocks with animals they either traded or pilfered. Although the llama was universally used by the Mapuche, they later rejected it in favor of European animals. Even the women switched from llama to sheep wool for weaving ponchos and blankets. Meat became a central part of the Mapuche diet and cattle became important as a war prize and trade item. The Pehuenches, for example, rode as far as Buenos Aires to capture animals, which they traded with Chilean merchants.

Population Trends

Unknowingly the Spanish also introduced a variety of Old World diseases to Chile. Measles, smallpox, and influenza pathogens encountered a population with no immunity to European diseases. The *encomenderos* complained that their working population died off and therefore they needed additional laborers. Demographic studies suggest Chile's pre-Columbian population dropped by more than 40 percent within 50 years of the Spanish conquest. It then stabilized until in the eighteenth century when it began to grow moderately. Mexican, Peruvian, and North American native populations, by contrast, suffered far more dramatic population losses. As yet scholars do not understand why the Mapuche, in spite of constant war casualties, did not suffer similar catastrophic declines.

A gradual increase occurred in the non-Mapuche population. In 1600 the Spanish population was 10,000 and grew slowly the next century to 25,000. Also growing substantially were mestizo, mulatto, and black populations. Totaling almost 40,000 in 1600, they reached 100,000 in 1700. By this date the African slave trade with Buenos Aires and Lima had already affected Santiago's population distribution. About 14 percent of the city were mulatto and 6 percent were black, whereas 19 percent were Indians, only 4 percent were mestizos, and 56 percent were Spanish. In the colony as a whole, in 1700 slightly less than half, or 215,000, Native Americans were under Spanish domination, whereas the remainder, or 235,000, lived free in Mapuche territories.

Trade

The growing population increased agricultural and mining exports, which in turn paid for imports. The latter came from many distant points. Silks came from China while a wide variety of textiles, ironware, and mercury came from different European nations. Peru and Ecuador sent fine woolens. Tropical goods from South America such as cane sugar, chocolate, and yerba mate—known as Paraguayan tea—were also favorite items.

The official trade route from Spain to Chile began in Seville, and later Cádiz. Merchants shipped goods in annual escorted convoys to Panama. There they loaded them on mule trains that crossed the isthmus and reloaded them again on ships when they reached the Pacific. These vessels usually headed directly to Peru, but they might stop in Guayaquil. Once the goods reached Lima, Peruvian merchants selected certain goods for the Chilean market, which they sent to Valparaíso. During most of the colonial period, the crown prohibited direct commerce between Chile and Spain via the Strait of Magellan. In part the crown was concerned about the dangerous passage, but more importantly, it wanted to guarantee a control over the flow of goods. The fixed Panama route facilitated tax collection and guaranteed the merchant guild a commercial monopoly. Guild members paid the crown import, export, and sales taxes in return for excluding everyone else from colonial commerce. This reciprocal arrangement may have benefited guild members and the crown, but it hurt Chilean consumers and producers. By driving up import prices and driving down export prices, Chileans profited less from international trade. For those willing to circumvent the monopoly system, however, the incentives were considerable.

A more direct, but illegal, system developed in the seventeenth century via Rio de la Plata. Dutch and British ships engaged in contraband in Buenos Aires and across the river at Colonia do Sacramento. After foreign merchants smuggled the goods in, local traders loaded them on wagon trains that headed across the pampas. Some wagons turned north toward the silver mines of Charcas (today Bolivia), while others went west to the town of Mendoza. The Jesuits in Paraguay also sent hundreds of sacks of yerba mate, valued at more than 300,000 pesos annually, across the pampas to Mendoza, located at the base of the Andes. Here mule drivers strapped all these goods on pack animals and followed a treacherous trail over a 12,500-foot pass to Chile. When the goods finally reached Santiago, customs agents inspected them and assessed duties. Resourceful merchants used both collusion and evasion to keep the duties below official levels. In the eighteenth century direct trade with Europe began to flourish thanks to audacious efforts of French, British, and North American traders. After sailing through the Strait of Magellan and up the Chilean coast, they conspired with Chilean agents to import goods duty-free, while risking the embargo of their entire cargo.[7]

International trade was vital to Chile in spite of its inefficiency. The colony had small urban markets, so hacienda owners needed external markets for their tallow, hides, grain, and wine. Also, credit was limited, so by selling imports on installment merchants helped fill this void. Trade was a necessity for mining because imported iron and mercury were needed to excavate and refine the minerals. Ironically, it was the expansion of contraband that improved the terms of trade and provided new incentive for hacienda and mine owners to increase their production. Only in the late eighteenth century did the expansion of internal markets rival the importance of external markets.

Bureaucracy

The political system by which Spanish officials allocated resources and privilege was also challenged in the eighteenth century. Originally hacendados, miners, and merchants depended on state support for land, labor, and privilege. But as the private economy developed, the state increasingly impeded rather than encouraged expansion. The crown highly regulated commerce and mining in order to tax them. Although officially the tax burden was onerous, the collection rate was low. Approximately half of the agricultural and mining production avoided any tax. The state's most lucrative source of revenue was the monopoly it had on the sale of tobacco, liquor, and playing cards. The great majority of Chileans paid no direct taxes because they did not participate in the commercial economy.

As part of the Spanish Empire, in theory, Chilean officials were subordinate to the viceroy of Peru. When a governor of Chile died in office, the viceroy named his temporary replacement. Permanent appointments, however, came directly from the crown. Often acting on behalf of the king was the Council of Indies to which he allocated broad executive, legislative, and judicial powers. In the viceregal capitals and later in Chile, the king created a judicial body called the *audiencia*. This body tried to resolve disputes over *encomiendas,* mining claims, land, and official decisions. People who could afford to hire an advocate could appeal the *audiencia*'s or governor's decisions to the Council of Indies. Chilean authorities often disagreed with their superiors in Peru, so they used this appeal option.

The distance of Chile from both Peru and Spain gave Chilean officials considerable autonomy. This isolation had another interesting consequence. Officials learned that they needed the local elite's support to govern. Without the cooperation of a *criollo,* a Chilean-born Spaniard, officials could not collect taxes and they could not enforce the law. Miners and landowners learned to influence government and church leaders to their advantage. No *criollo* ever occupied the position of governor, but members of this group did serve as bishops, on municipal councils, in bureaucratic positions, and as advisors. From these positions they helped execute policies that were favorable to their relatives who were hacendados, mine owners, and merchants.

Social Status

The majority of Chileans were rural dwellers who rarely, if ever, came in contact with government officials. The people who controlled their lives were their *patrones,* or bosses, who were *encomenderos,* hacendados, or mine owners. For the Indians in the north and the Central Valley, they had little choice but to accept their *patrones'* authority with resignation. By contrast, in the south, the Indians rebelled against it. The mestizos had some freedom of employment but usually settled to work on a mine or hacienda. In the first case, their salary consisted of a small portion of the minerals they produced each day. In the second case, these workers, called *inquilinos,* were allotted some land to use in return for their labor. Another landless, rural population occasionally hired by hacendados during harvests or roundups was called *afuerinos,* or outsiders. Both *inquilinos* and *afuerinos* learned to accept their employers' authority, because the government offered them no protection.

For some people, however, Chile represented a new beginning. The first Spaniards who entered Chile often were so poor that they borrowed money to buy weapons and a horse to participate in the conquest. After the conquest, their situation radically improved when the crown compensated them with *encomiendas,* land, or mineral rights. Their wealth and status improved immensely, far more than they could ever have achieved in Spain. But this wealth could be fleeting. Pedro de Valdivia distributed *encomiendas,* but then retracted some due to an insufficient number of Indians. Bitter ex-*encomenderos* either sued Valdivia or rebelled against him, but they were defeated and executed. Later governors also confiscated *encomiendas* and used them to reward their own men. The injured parties reacted with litigation and petitions. In addition to losing *encomiendas* for political reasons, the Mapuche rebellions terminated them as well. Impoverished former *encomenderos* and their descendants formed the lower echelon of colonial society, above the Indians, slaves, and mestizos, but far below *encomenderos* and merchants.

There were ways to improve one's status besides controlling Indian laborers. Men with capital formed partnerships with the conquistadors, and if they were successful, shared in their rewards. After the sixteenth century, trade became a favorite avenue for advancement. Often they invested their commercial profits in mines and haciendas. As a result, by the eighteenth century many prominent families came from merchant, not conquistador, backgrounds.

Less profitable professions, but still in demand, were blacksmiths, cobblers, tailors, candle makers, and carpenters. As towns grew, butchers, bakers, and shopkeepers added diversity to colonial society. Most Chileans, however, spent their entire lives laboring on a hacienda or in mines. Their social and racial origins forced them to seek pleasure through family, friends, and the rituals of daily life, not through advancement.

Women, like most men, rarely rose above their social caste. Indian women rarely married Spanish men, but might cohabit with them. Women gained few benefits from these relationships, but their mestizo daughter might marry a *criollo* if her father contributed a dowry. Although Spanish men usually preferred a Spanish wife, some were attracted to mestizo women. For those Chilean families having relatives in Spain, encouraging them to emigrate presented new opportunities. These female immigrants were especially attractive as prospective wives for single *criollos* and Span-iards. For a married woman, her spouse controlled the entire estate, but when he died the widow inherited half and the children divided up the other half. Some tried to manage their estates on their own, but most preferred the security of a new marriage.

Racial and cultural assimilation in colonial Chile sometimes occurred by force and other times by choice. The Mapuche who were obligated to form part of Chilean society created a basis of a mestizo culture. Their language, foods, and customs fused with those of Spain. Elite society was more Spanish and working-class society was more Mapuche, but the two interacted continually. A Chilean identity that was separate from Spain gradually evolved. After more than 250 years as a colony, a European crisis forced Chileans to decide whether this identity was sufficient for creating a nation.

NOTES

1. Most calculations of the Native American population in Chile are based on Spanish observations. For a variety of reasons, Spanish observers were prone to exaggeration. Pedro de Valdivia, for example, wrote that his companions who had been in Mexico thought the Chilean Indian population was larger. The widespread use of agriculture by the Mapuche, however, did sustain larger populations than those of the Pacific Northwest.

2. This weapon, used by Native Americans from Peru to the southern end of Patagonia, consists of two or three polished stones that are each attached to a separate leather thong that are joined to a single thicker thong. The hunter twirls these stones around his head then throws them at the legs of a fleeing animal. When the animal is hit, the thongs wrap around its legs and stop it in its tracks. The hunter can then either herd it home or butcher it. After the Spanish introduced the cattle industry to Argentina, the gaucho appropriated this device and often used it instead of a lasso. The Chilean *huaso*, however, did not appropriate it, perhaps because when badly thrown it can seriously injure the animal.

3. In Mapuche, *che* means people. The following are meanings of the diverse prefixes of *che*: *mapu* = land, *picun* = north, *huilli* = south, *pehuen* = pine tree, and *puel* = east. Sometimes words can take on a secondary meaning such as the word Puelche, which literally means people of the east but also means east wind and is comparable to double meaning of Chinook (people/wind) of the Pacific Northwest.

4. Many historians have emphasized the disappointment of Almagro and his men at not finding gold in Chile, but there must have been some

positive information for Pedro de Valdivia to believe that there was enough wealth there to merit another expedition. By contrast, the failure of the de Soto and Coronado expeditions to find gold did not lead to renewed visits of conquistadors to the regions that they explored.

5. He founded the following towns: Concepción in 1550, Imperial in 1551, Valdivia in 1552, Villarrica in 1552, and Angol in 1553. In the same period he built forts at Arauco, Tucapel, and Purén.

6. This tradition is alive and well today in rural Chile. On Sunday evenings, for example, when Santiago residents return from a weekend at the beach or in the mountains, they stop at roadside stands to treat themselves to this *pan de rescoldo*, or ashes bread, that is sold by rural folk.

7. The last governor of Chile, Francisco García Carrasco, conspired to kill the captain of the British merchant vessel, *Scorpion*, and take the ship and its goods as a prize. Although he gained considerable wealth, Chileans considered his action foul play. The colony had an informal code of conduct that included respect for life and property even of those engaged in contraband.

3

Independence, 1750–1830

Few Chileans would have thought that the changes taking place around them in the eighteenth century were leading to independence. Increased immigration, education, and wealth transformed society. Immigrants injected new energy and ideas into commerce, mining, and agriculture. They developed a market economy that was less dependent upon government subsidies and more on trade with other regions. In mining and agriculture they expanded both production and markets. When they encountered official opposition, they resorted to contraband and later to rebellion.

Changes also occurred in education. The establishment of schools and a university enabled trained professionals and clergy to assume leadership roles in colonial government and in the church. Chileans also gained military experience through the Mapuche wars. Gradually during the latter eighteenth century, leaders developed who were capable of running a nation and managing an economy. Therefore, when Napoleon invaded Spain in 1808 and turned the Empire upside down, Chileans were ready to shape their own future.

THE LATE COLONIAL PERIOD

Bourbon Reforms

The Spanish Empire underwent a fundamental change when a new dynasty, the Bourbons, inherited the throne in 1700. The new monarchs initiated a series of reforms meant to modernize the Empire and, in turn, produce more revenue. They restructured government, liberalized the trade network, and encouraged some social changes. For the first time, they allowed the Basques from northern Spain and the Catalans from northeastern Spain to trade directly with the American colonies. Taking advantage of this reform, merchants from these two regions established commercial houses throughout the colonies. In Chile they soon dominated trade and then moved into mining and agriculture. When the crown offered them the opportunity to purchase noble titles and entail their estates, those who could afford these status symbols eagerly acquired them. In contrast to the Basques and Catalans, many descendants of the conquistadors suffered economic difficulties. The rise in immigrant families and the fall of traditional ones contributed to social tensions.

Although colonial Chile was officially closed to non-Spaniards, some foreigners did settle in Chile during the eighteenth century. They or their children often played important roles in Chile's independence. Ambrosio O'Higgins and Juan Mackenna both emigrated from Ireland. O'Higgins rose to the positions of governor of Chile and viceroy of Peru, but, more importantly, his son Bernardo led Chile's independence struggle. Later he became the first ruler of independent Chile. Mackenna briefly fought for independence, but a quarrel with another leader led to a fatal duel. Some French immigrated to Concepción; whereas, some Portuguese immigrated to Santiago. Even a few Englishmen such as Jorge Edwards settled in Chile. He and his descendants played important roles in mining, banking, and politics.

The Spanish monarchs, like their European peers, feared that if they named colonists to leadership positions they would promote local, not royal, interests. As a result, they never selected a Chilean as governor and prevented Spanish officials from marrying Chileans without royal permission. Nevertheless, in the eighteenth century, the Bourbon monarchs increasingly gave leadership opportunities to Chileans. The crown appointed two Chileans to the *audiencia,* the highest colonial judicial body, another as director of the customs house, and still another to oversee the mint. Various Chileans also held important offices in the army and militia. Local clergy attained a surprising number of leadership positions in the church. Of 17 bishops in the eighteenth century, 13 were Chilean.

Education and Government

The greatest influence that Chileans had, however, was as the advisors to the governors and *intendentes.* The Spanish military officers who occupied these posts had little civilian administrative experience and no legal training. By the 1760s they could find talented advisors among the law graduates of the Universidad de San Felipe, which had opened its doors in 1758. These attorneys had ties to prominent families and influenced the governor to support these families' interests. One prominent lawyer, Juan Martínez de Rozas, served as counsel to Governor Ambrosio O'Higgins until the latter was promoted to viceroy. He then influenced the selection of his successor.

Whereas Chileans learned firsthand about how bureaucracy works, they lacked a similar opportunity with a legislature. Spain created no institution equivalent to a colonial congress in which Chileans could debate tax, budget, and security legislation. The monarchs issued all civil and criminal laws. There was one type of organization, however, that collectively resolved local problems, and this was the *cabildo,* or city council. The city councils granted franchises, regulated prices, and handled local security. Although council members were usually not elected and were both Spanish and Chilean, through the cabildo local leaders gained experience in regulating their urban affairs.

Church Reforms

While the Bourbon monarchs allowed greater participation of the Chilean clergy in the hierarchy of the church, they attacked what they viewed as the excessive autonomy of the institution. Throughout Europe in the eighteenth century, Catholic European monarchies strove to subordinate the church to royal control. In Spain the Bourbons observed that the clergy outnumbered civil officials, the religious orders owned vast, tax-exempt estates, and church revenues rivaled those of the state. Officials in Chile, as in the rest of the empire, recognized that through the tithe the church taxed all farm production while receiving annual *censo* or mortage payments from many private estates. In addition to these sources of financial strength, the church exerted power through its control of almost all of the schools.

Of the various religious institutions that concerned the Bourbons, the Society of Jesus, or Jesuits, appeared especially threatening. This order, founded by the former Spanish soldier Ignatius de Loyola, included submission to the pope as one of its religious vows. For the Bourbons this vow meant that Jesuit loyalty to the papacy took precedence over that to the king. Deciding to apply a radical remedy to this papal allegiance, in 1767 King Charles III decreed the expulsion of all Jesuits from the empire. It befell on Chilean governor Antonio de Guill y Gonzaga to execute this order. Although he was a personal friend of the Jesuits, regretfully he put all members of the order under house arrest, closed their schools and convents, and confiscated their properties. He then expelled the priests to Italy and sold or rented the sixty haciendas that they owned.

Due to the competition between the religious orders, some clergy approved of King Charles's action. Neither they nor the king had anticipated the extent that this measure would weaken the church and the state. A half-century later, when the independence movement began, the Jesuits were not there to support the old regime. The Jesuits would have defended the Spanish Empire against the secular ideas of John Locke, Jean Jacques Rousseau, and Thomas Jefferson just as they had earlier defended southern Europe against the ideas of Martin Luther. After their expulsion, some embittered Jesuits managed to encourage independence even from their distant exile.

Few of the Bourbon monarchs' reforms were as dramatic as the expulsion of the Jesuits. In their commercial reforms, for example, they did not try to eliminate the mercantile system, but to modernize it. Through subsidies, protection, and public works they reformed the system in the hope of stimulating private enterprise. This approach was evident in Chile where the Bourbon governors developed roads, mercury mines, a gunpowder factory, and new methods of tax collection. Some of these projects contributed to increased production and government revenue, but much of the colony's growth occurred because merchants and mine owners increasingly operated outside of the Spanish economic system. Quietly these entrepreneurs sought more freedom; the opportunity for an open declaration of independence would come later.

Mining

This very traditional gold panning activity slowly changed. By the seventeenth century, the depletion of gold-bearing sands and gravels forced miners to develop pit mines. Gradually Chileans opened up copper and silver mines as well. In these mines it was common for a dozen or fewer workers to follow a vein of gold or silver ore, hollowing out irregular tunnels as they went. In their minimalist approach they dug only the rich minerals and left all other rock, even if the cramped tunnels and shafts created hazardous work conditions. One group of workers chiseled out the ore with a long iron rod, while others scooped it into leather sacks and scampered up rickety ladders to the surface. Mule drivers loaded it on their animals that packed it to *trapiches,* or grinding mills. Located along rivers, the hydraulic power moved the mill. Once ground they mixed the gold or silver ores with mercury and salt to leach out the precious metals in a process called amalgamation. After a few months of periodic stirring, the workers washed the ores, separated out the mercury, and smelted the ores. Then they poured the liquid gold and silver into bar-shaped molds. Because mercury was a scarce, expensive ingredient, during smelting they tried to capture as much of it as possible for reuse. They were unaware of its toxicity, however, and many workers suffered serious health problems as a result. In contrast to the precious metals, copper was smelted without the lengthy amalgamation process. Regardless of the mineral, after smelting, miners transported them to port on pack trains. There, merchants shipped them to Peru where the precious metals were minted into coins and the copper forged into bronze. Merchants also illegally trafficked the metals to non-Spanish traders.

From their first arrival in Chile, the Spanish sought cheap mine laborers. First they coerced the Mapuche through the *encomienda* system. By the seventeenth century, however, the combination of high mortality levels and Mapuche uprisings made Indian labor no longer viable. So mine owners created a labor system to attract mestizos. Lacking cash to pay their workers, they compensated them with a proportion of the minerals that they dug from the mine daily. Frequently the last sack of ores hauled from the mine at the end of the day belonged to the worker. The latter then traded his ores to a smelter or merchant for supplies.

With the rise in gold production in the eighteenth century, the Santiago *cabildo* petitioned King Charles III to establish a mint. If Chilean miners could mint their gold locally rather than send it to Peru, they would cut costs and benefit the colony with its own currency. An ambitious entrepreneur, Francisco García Huidobro, pursued this issue further and offered to create a private mint at no cost to the crown. The king considered this petition favorably because royal coinage taxes collected at the mint would compensate for those lost to the Peruvian mint. Furthermore, he hoped that a local mint would reduce smuggling. Therefore, he granted García Huidobro the franchise he requested. In 1749 the mint began operation, averaging a production of between $400,000 and $600,000 of gold coins a year.

Unfortunately for García Huidobro, the mint's success led the crown to want full control of the business, so it canceled his franchise. Also, due to increased local silver production, in 1772 when the government took over the mint's management, it began to coin silver as well. As a result, smuggling decreased temporarily, but with coinage and other mint expenses comprising about 30 percent of the ore's value, miners and merchants had strong incentives to engage in contraband. Increasing opportunities to trade with Buenos Aires and ships bound for Spain, England, or the United States facilitated the clandestine shipping of precious metals. The merchants who controlled the precious metal trade continued to profit through contraband.

Mining was definitely the backbone of Chile's colonial trade. In the 1770s, Chile exported $650,000 of gold annually and three decades later this figure reached at least $850,000. Gold represented more than twice the value of all minerals exported. Silver exports grew as greater mercury supplies enabled miners to refine lower grade ores. Peru increased mercury shipments to Chile and some local mercury mines began production. From $130,000 per year in the 1770s, silver exports more than tripled to $400,000 in the 1800s. In the case of copper, favorable copper prices and a drop in transportation costs combined to make this ore increasingly profitable in the latter eighteenth century. As a result copper exports grew from $120,000 a year in the 1770s to $200,000 in the 1800s.

Although mining was Chile's most dynamic activity, most mines were small. Large-scale mining, which occurred in Mexico and Peru, simply did not exist. In an effort to modernize Chilean mining, both the state and the miners' guild proposed solutions. To improve the amalgamation process, governor Ambrosio O'Higgins contracted a German metallurgist over a five-year period. Other governors joined with private investors to develop three mercury mines. To increase the supply of blasting powder, O'Higgins underwrote a state gunpowder factory. Although the factory had its ups and downs, it produced for both local consumption and exports. In spite of this progress, other northern Europe innovations for draining flooded mines, designing tunnels, and smelting sulfide ores unfortunately remained unfamiliar to Chile.

The lack of credit was a constant complaint of mine owners who were forced to sell their ores to merchants at below market prices. These merchants, called *habilitadores de minas*, advanced goods in return for future production. To compete with these *habilitadores* the government created a state purchasing agency and a state lending institution. Unfortunately the state lacked the resources to fully fund either institution. Those funds that it did have went to a select group of influential miners. Miners who received loans did not always use the funds for mining. Also, the slow repayment of old loans reduced the funding for new ones.

To limit access and regulate mining, Spain created a mining guild and court, the Tribunal de Minería, in its wealthiest mining colonies. Not until Chile's mining boom in the eighteenth century did the Bourbons do likewise in Chile. The guild enabled mine owners to settle the numerous disputes over miners' claims and contracts, but in return the crown expected the miners' support. Guild members, however, found taxes too high and often defied the crown by funneling their ores though the unofficial trade network. Although the king originally appointed the guild's leadership after 1802, elections of prominent *criollo* leaders gave them experience dealing with mining issues.

Agriculture

Mining was far more risky than agriculture, so successful mine owners usually invested in land. They typically bought haciendas in the northern river valleys where they grazed the mules and donkeys that they used for transportation. If their estate was large, they also might raise wheat and cattle for export. Many of the successful merchants who traded with the mine owners also bought land. They purchased property in the Valle Central where they raised cattle and wheat and planted orchards and vineyards. They sold some of their produce locally and exported the rest.

The value of land depended on its water resources and its proximity to markets. Irrigated land that was close to towns or ports brought the best price. This was used to fatten cattle or grow grain. Conversely, the lowest-priced land was dry, marginal grazing land in the coastal range or the Andean foothills. Property did change hands as people with wealth invested in haciendas. Beginning in the seventeenth century, but particularly under the Bourbons, for a fee the crown offered the elite the right to establish *mayorazgos,* or entailed estates, and the opportunity to purchase titles of nobility. Since a *mayorazgo* could not be sold or divided and was inherited by the oldest son, hacendados purchased this privilege to assure the long-term wealth of the family. Due to the high cost, only eighteen families purchased the *mayorazgos,* and of these, only ten, the noble titles. Even if *mayorazgos* were uncommon, large estates dominated colonial Chile. Although over 10,000 people owned land, the 2,000 largest haciendas controlled most of the country.

Outside visitors remarked about how depopulated the countryside was. The widely scattered rural people, or *campesinos,* represented various categories. About 15 percent were landowners, most who worked their own fields. Thirty percent were *inquilinos,* or the dependent workers who lived and worked on the large haciendas. Typically they worked for the hacienda owner in return for permission to build a hut, plant a garden, and graze some cattle. Day workers or *afuerinos* represented another 30 percent of the rural population and were contracted for planting, harvesting, and the cattle roundups. Servants and slaves, respectively, represented 10 and 5 percent of the labor force. They worked in the house and the field of the hacienda. Rural women, though not officially considered farm laborers, cultivated their own gardens and helped the hacienda owner during harvest time.

Those who farmed near urban markets grew potatoes, corn, and vegetables to sell in town; whereas others grew crops largely for family consumption. The main crop was wheat. To grow it, the *campesinos* plowed their fields and seeded them in the fall. They worked with oxen much like the European peasants did in the Middle Ages. In early summer they used scythes to cut the wheat, then bundled it and loaded it on an oxcart. Later they spread it on a patio, threshed it with horses, and finally cleaned it by hand. These traditional methods became so ritualized that even late eighteenth-century immigrants failed to change them.

Trade

Although the majority of farm products were consumed in Chile, internal markets were limited. Exports, therefore, were important to hacienda owners. Farm goods represented between 35 and 40 percent of all exports. Chilean consignees of Lima and Guayaquil merchants purchased the largest amounts of these goods for West Coast markets. Peru was Chile's largest customer, yearly buying over 200,000 fanegas, or 15,600 tons, of wheat, as well as tallow, hides, wine, cordage, and lumber. With the exception being yerba mate, from Paraguay, few farm goods were traded with the colonies on the eastern side of the Andes. The limited size of West Coast markets and the high transportation costs crossing the Andes restricted agricultural exports. Hacienda owners needed new markets, but under the colonial trade system these were unavailable.

The Spaniards liked the existing trade system because it protected them from outside competition. Commerce was one of most attractive careers for Spanish immigrants. Of the important firms in the late colonial period, Spaniards controlled 70 percent of them. By contrast, *criollos* controlled less than 18 percent of these firms. Among smaller firms, the percentage of *criollos* increased, but they still were less than half of the total. *Criollos* lacked overseas connections and commercial skills. Few owned ships, and the one who did, José de Mendiburu, invariably is cited as an exception. Being a merchant, even in the protected Spanish commercial system, involved considerable risk. Court records attest to numerous bankruptcies.

But the successful Spanish merchants married into elite Chilean families, bought large estates, and assimilated into society.

In 1700 the official Spanish trade network began to crack when the Bourbons ascended the throne. When Phillip V became king, he allowed the French South Sea Company to operate on South America's West Coast. The company's ships were prohibited from trade, but for over a decade neither he nor his officials took steps to prevent it. Between 1701 and 1724, the company sent 153 ships around Cape Horn to trade in Chile, Peru, and points north. Striking a deal with the local governor was often the only prerequisite to trade. The governor benefited, the French merchants benefited, and Chilean producers benefited. Of course the losers were the Spanish merchants and the Spanish treasury. When the losses began to hurt his treasury, Phillip ordered a squadron and licensed corsairs to drive the South Sea Company's vessels out of the Pacific.

Contraband came from many other sources and eventually undermined the Spanish fleet system. In an attempt to recapture South American trade, in 1720 the crown created a system of *navíos de registro,* or registered ships. Instead of sailing together in the traditional fleet system, these vessels sailed individually. The monarchy implemented this reform first with Buenos Aires and then with Peru. From 1743 to 1761 a total of 56 ships arrived in Callao, the port of Lima, and often stopped in Valparaíso on their return voyage. According to regulations, the *navíos de registro* could only trade in Chile after first trading in Peru. In any case, from the 1740s until the end of the century, these ships sold millions of pesos of manufactured goods on the west coast in return for copper, precious metals, and hides.

International conflicts, however, often blocked Spanish shipping to America. During the American Revolution and the Napoleonic War, *navíos de registro* rarely appeared in Chile. As a result Spanish imports dropped precipitously, forcing Chile to look for other sources. The colony found that the La Plata region, which encompasses the present counties of Argentina, Paraguay, and Uruguay, offered the best new markets. Whereas only 15 percent of imports came from that region in the 1770s, by the 1800s almost 60 percent came from there. These included 300,000 pesos of yerba mate from Paraguay, 100,000 pesos of Argentine produce, and 1,000,000 pesos of European cloth, hardware, and assorted goods. By comparison, imports from Peru and Ecuador, Chile's traditional markets, declined to 400,000 pesos of local cloth, 500,000 pesos of tropical farm goods, and 100,000 pesos of European goods.

The arrival of United States ships in Chile in the 1770s complicated Spain's attempt to enforce its monopoly. In a series of treaties, Spain granted American vessels the right to fish, but not to trade, in Pacific Coast waters. Many whaling and sealing vessels, however, violated this restriction. Under the pretext of seeking repairs or fresh supplies, ship captains requested permission to enter Chilean ports. If granted, they proceeded to trade. Some were arrested, but most found accommodating local merchants and officials. Over 250 American vessels fished and traded in Chilean waters from 1788 to 1809, enabling American ship captains to profit and familiarize themselves with the local ports, merchants, and customs.

One group that was little affected by colonial trade were the artisans who worked in apparel, construction, and transportation. Shoemakers, hat makers, and tailors made the variety of clothes worn in the colony. Carpenters, masons, and building material manufacturers worked in the construction trades, whereas saddlers, cart makers, and shipwrights worked in transportation. For most jobs, there was no system for introducing new methods. Especially in rural areas where people engaged in part-time artisan activities such as construction, wine making, spinning, weaving, and leatherwork, the traditional methods rarely changed.

Public Works and Taxes

The Bourbons believed that change had to occur from the top down. They preferred to name competent, progressive men rather than the nobility as governors. Most of them emphasized public works. To aid commerce, for example, they built a new road from Santiago to Valparaíso and improved the mountain trail to Mendoza. To enhance the capital, they built dikes to prevent flooding and hired architects to design and build the Casa de la Moneda, or the mint; the Consulado, or the merchant guild; the Cabildo, the Aduana, or the customhouse; the Audiencia, or the royal court; and the San Borja Hospital. These neoclassical but austere structures fittingly represented the renovated character of colonial authority. The public administrators who worked in these buildings developed new fiscal controls and reformed the *cabildo,* the police, and the militia. In Concepción a new regional minister, the *intendente,* tried to modernize that region as well.

Although colonial Spanish America taxes seem excessive compared to those of colonial English America, compared to other European empires they were not. In colonies like Chile, the Bourbons kept their bureaucracy small. Services such as charity, the hospitals, the mail, and some law enforcement were the responsibility of the church or other institutions. The state granted franchises to private parties to collect taxes as well as to run the mint and the tobacco and playing card monopolies. To raise additional revenue, it also sold public offices. Due to the threat of Mapuche rebellions, the crown maintained a standing army paid for by public revenue, yet it also encouraged a volunteer militia of about 16,000 men. When uprisings occurred, private citizens supplied soldiers, arms, and money to supplement the state's resources.

In examining the tax burden on the different groups within Chilean society, those who were most heavily taxed were the mine owners. In the decade from 1801 to 1810, their collective burden was approximately 150,000 pesos yearly. This represents about 10 percent of the value of mineral exports. The next highest tax burden fell on farmers. Agriculture's major tax was the *diezmo,* or tithe. This tax revenue went to the church, not the state, although the state farmed the tax out through public auction. In the 1790s, this produced about 125,000 pesos in revenue. With agricultural production about 2,000,000 pesos yearly, the tax amounted to 6 percent, rather than the 10 percent the name suggests. In calculating the tax burden on miners and farmers, one must also consider the export duties on their products. Although it was the merchants who paid these duties, the effect was to lower farm and mineral export prices, which in turn reduced profits for all concerned.

Because the Spanish colonies never had any participation in tax issues, when they disagreed with a tax, they had no legislative forum in which to protest it. Their only recourse was to try to evade it. For this reason the issue of taxation without representation was not a principle motive for independence as it was in the English colonies. Nevertheless, economic issues such as trade with other nations did play an important role in Chile once the independence movement was underway.

THE INDEPENDENCE MOVEMENT

The Chilean elite was familiar with both the United States independence and the French Revolution. Although some *criollos* sympathized with the first, all but a few feared the second due to its attack on privilege. Some *criollos* resented Spain's preference for *peninsulares,* or people born in Spain. Nevertheless, they recognized that their own socioeconomic status was based on Spanish institutions. They had virtually no interest in transplanting the revolutionary changes they saw in France. The colonial elite was comfortable with classes based on separate estates that granted privileges to the large landholders, militia members, and the clergy.

At the beginning of the nineteenth century, Napoleon Bonaparte hijacked the French Revolution and began transforming Europe. He dethroned kings, demolished old empires, and created new ones. In 1807 he invaded Portugal and forced its monarchy to flee to Brazil. Then, in 1808, he marched into Spain and coerced King Carlos IV and his son, Ferdinand VII, to abdicate. He placed his own brother, Joseph, on the Spanish throne and sent out emissaries to the colonies to persuade them to accept the new dynasty. The Spanish colonies rejected French domination and asserted loyalty to Ferdinand VII, living under house arrest in France. The Chilean colonists then confronted the practical and legal issue: Who had the right to rule? Spanish officials argued that their authority remained valid in spite of the king's abdication. They intended to continue in their posts at least until Ferdinand recovered his crown. The colonists, however, split on this issue. Some supported the presiding officials while others used religious and legal theory to assert that when the legitimate government ceases, the power reverts to the people. Based on this latter argument, in many colonies the local elite gathered in a *cabildo abierto,* or town meeting, to decide who should govern.

A Leadership Crisis

In the case of Chile, Governor Luis Muñoz de Guzmán died just as Napoleon invaded Spain. Unaware of this momentous event, the Audiencia proceeded according to its administrative rules and selected an interim replacement. Concepción attorney, Juan Martínez de Rozas, disagreed with the Audiencia's choice and lobbied on behalf of the Spanish military commander, Francisco Antonio García Carrasco. After some negotiation, the Audiencia reversed its decision and named García Carrasco as interim governor. Conveniently, Martínez de Rozas, a *criollo,* acted as his advisor.

Unfortunately for García Carrasco, he soon became embroiled in an academic dispute over the selection of the rector of the Universidad de San Felipe. No sooner had he extricated himself from this issue, than he soiled his reputation in the *Scorpion* affair. The latter began when Martínez de Rozas and some of his friends learned that a British merchant vessel, *Scorpion,* was trading illegally on the Chilean coast. Rather than arrest the captain and confiscate the ship, García Carrasco schemed to assassinate the captain, Tristan Bunker, and appropriate the ship's cargo. The accomplices carried out their plan, each gaining about $250,000.

This sordid affair destroyed García Carrasco's reputation. Not only was assassinating a British captain repulsive to most Chileans, but clandestine trade with the British was accepted among the Chilean elite. In the *Scorpion* case, García Carrasco trampled on the business interests of José Toribio Larraín, an extremely powerful member of the Santiago aristocracy. Captain Tristan Bunker's contact was Larraín, the owner of a *mayorazgo* and the noble title "Marqués de Casa Larraín." Martínez de Rosas should have known better than to trump the business of a prominent Santiago family, but being from an affluent Concepción family, he disregarded the capital's aristocracy. His mistake, nevertheless, cost him his position as García Carrasco's advisor and tarnished both of their reputations.

García Carrasco's reaction to events outside of Chile further discredited his authority. When on two separate occasions the British invaded Buenos Aires, the local population drove them out. The viceroy, Viscount Rafael Sobremonte, acted cowardly and fled rather than lead the resistance. When the crises passed and he tried to return, Buenos Aires citizens refused to let him. Instead, they created their own government. García Carrasco learned of communications between Buenos Aires and Chile and feared that Chileans might follow the Argentine example. Acting on his suspicions, he arrested three prominent Chileans and accused them of plotting to overthrow the government. When he ordered their deportation to Lima, he set off a political revolution. The Santiago Cabildo met in an emergency session and forced García Carrasco to rescind the deportation. Then it forced him to resign and replaced him with a high-ranking Chilean officer, Mateo Toro de Zambrano, also known by his title, "Conde de la Conquista." García Carrasco learned too late that without the monarchy's backing, a Spanish military officer was no match for the Chilean aristocracy.

Steps toward Independence

At first the patriots were uncertain about the extent they wished to change the government. On September 18, 1810, they called a *cabildo abierto* of Santiago's most influential community members. After listening to passionate pleas for a new order, the *cabildo* voted to create the first national government. Those who initiated this process foresaw a new era, but proceeded with caution. After installing a Junta, they proclaimed their loyalty to Ferdinand VII. They avoided any declaration of independence. To avoid antagonizing the many people who were frankly against independence, those who supported this change feigned loyalty to the king. Even ardent patriots feared that hostility might erupt between the nationalists and royalists. They also feared a military response from the Peruvian viceroy. They believed that if they could postpone conflict, an independent government stood a greater chance of success.

Free Trade

To promote the Chilean economy, the new government believed that it had to dismantle some aspects of Spain's closed trade system. The native

Spaniards, referred to as *peninsulares,* feared that such changes threatened their livelihood and presence in Chile. In November 1810, when the National Junta sent a proposal to the Tribunal del Consulado to open up international trade, the Spanish merchants of the Consulado attacked the proposal. In an attempt to hide their motives, they claimed that the measure would encourage foreign immigration and religious heresy, not that it would hurt their business. On December 4 the guild voted, not surprisingly, to reject the proposal. The Junta, nevertheless, observed that Buenos Aires and other former colonies already opened up trade, so it published the "Decree of Free Commerce" on February 21, 1811. This reform struck at the heart of Spanish mercantilism by declaring that four of Chile's ports were henceforth open to international trade.

The Decree of Free Commerce began by stating that the Junta acted in the name of Ferdinand VII. Then in a quick shift of language, it paraphrased the United States Declaration of Independence saying, ". . . all men have certain inalienable rights granted by their Creator in order to achieve happiness, prosperity, and welfare. . . ." The decree then enumerated four ports, Valdivia, Talcahuano, Valparaíso, and Coquimbo as open to "foreign powers, friends and allies of Spain, and also neutrals." Other ports in the country were closed to foreign commerce in an effort to reserve the coastal trade for the national merchant marine. To foster Chilean retail commerce, foreign merchants were not allowed to sell goods on their own account outside the cities of Valdivia, Concepción, Santiago, and Coquimbo. Although the government promised foreign merchants "consideration, protection and assistance," the decree did not mention merchant property rights. The rest of the decree, however, reiterated Spanish trade legislation, thereby leaving many aspects of mercantilism in place.

Chilean leaders had many reasons to believe that international commerce would bring prosperity. The United States, France, and Great Britain, all had traded with Chile long before the *cabildo abierto* met in 1810. Now with legal impediments removed, not only would the flow of goods increase, but immigration, new technology, and foreign capital should grow. Some leaders feared that cheap imports might disrupt local industry and that foreign shipping might undermine a national merchant marine, so they raised tariffs to protect these activities. The Junta opened trade, not to destroy Spanish merchants, but to promote Chilean agricultural and mining interests.

After the trade reform, the pace of change accelerated and the consensus supporting the new government began to break down. The Junta hoped to reform the political institutions by calling a national congress. An early controversy over regional representation threatened to disrupt this process, but a compromise enabled the congress to inaugurate its first session on July 4, 1811. Disputes between radicals and conservatives, unfortunately, soon paralyzed this assembly's work. The impetuous and charismatic military officer, José Miguel Carrera, decided to resolve the impasse by dismissing congress and putting himself in charge. His opposition coalesced around the former viceroy's son, Bernardo O'Higgins. Each man put together his own army and in 1812 they confronted each other on the battlefield. This paralyzed the country and made it vulnerable to attack.

Reconquest of Chile

The Spanish merchants in Chile accommodated themselves to these changes better than did the merchants in Peru. The latter saw that the prices of European goods imported directly to Chile undercut their markets. In an effort to block the Chilean trade reforms, they lobbied the Peruvian viceroy, José Fernando Abascal, to act. In response, in December 1812, he sent an expedition to reconquer Chile. In addition, he authorized corsairs to capture any foreign ships entering the colony's ports.

Chile was under attack and tried to fight back. On the economic front, the government prohibited grain exports to Peru. When the royalists soon captured Concepción, the heart of Chile's grain region, this measure proved ineffectual. Grain producers and merchants from other regions suffered from the loss of Peru's market, but they failed to persuade the government to reopen trade.

On the political front, José Miguel Carrera and Bernardo O'Higgins set aside their differences and united against the common enemy. They acted too late, unfortunately, and were soon defeated. The British then stepped in and offered to mediate between the two sides. Understandably the British sought to preserve some of the reforms such as open trade. The English naval captain James Hillyar persuaded both sides to sign a peace treaty that included a clause guaranteeing the right of neutral ships to trade in Chile. Not surprisingly, Viceroy Abascal and the Lima merchants found the treaty unacceptable. He wanted to renew the war, yet the viceregal treasury lacked the resources to do so. Abascal, therefore, turned to the wealthy Lima merchants, who loaned him $100,000. He then named Mariano Osorio as commander of the new expedition.

In Chile, radical independence advocates like José Miguel Carrera also rejected the treaty. Moderates such as Bernardo O'Higgins originally supported it, believing that it gave Chileans time to reorganize their internal affairs. Carrera, however, took the initiative again and seized control of the government. O'Higgins tried to dislodge him with his army, so once again Chileans fought each other. By the time they recognized the danger posed by Osorio's expedition, they reacted too late. Osorio defeated their combined forces but failed to prevent them from escaping over the Andes. Those who did not escape were arrested and incarcerated on Juan Fernández Island.

Mariano Osorio succeeded on the battlefield, but his trade and financial policies severely hurt the reconquered colony. To prevent Chile's military leaders from infiltrating into the colony, he terminated all communication with Argentina. The impact on Andean trade and customs revenue was startling. The latter dropped from $130,495 in 1813, to practically nothing during his two years in power. According to Osorio's trade policy, any goods that crossed the Andes were considered contraband. His maritime policy, however, was more liberal. He reopened trade with Peru and allowed some neutral trading. Customs revenue responded favorably, rising from 74,287 pesos in 1814 to 139,000 pesos in 1816. Other treasury income fell sharply, especially that from the tobacco monopoly. Looking for other sources of revenue, Osorio expropriated at least 24,000 pesos of the patriots' properties and raised about 64,000 pesos through loans and levies. Nevertheless, treasury income fell to less than half its prerevolutionary level, while military expenditures nearly doubled. The viceroy decided to relieve Osorio from command, replacing him with Francisco Marcó del Pont in December 1815. In a desperate effort to deal with the financial crisis, the new governor imposed more levies and impounded neutral vessels.

Patriot Strategy

While the Spanish governors were wrestling with finances on one side of the Andes, on the other side of the Andes, the exiled Chilean leaders developed strategies to overthrow the regime. O'Higgins formed an alliance with the Argentine leader, José de San Martín, whereas José Miguel Carrera traveled to the United States to purchase arms. When he returned to Argentina, he put together a separate army, which clashed with that of the O'Higgins-San Martín coalition. He escaped but his two brothers were arrested and shot. The enmity caused by that tragic event poisoned relations between the Carrera family and O'Higgins's supporters and left a long legacy of divisiveness.

Early in 1817 O'Higgins and San Martín's armies made a spectacular crossing of the Andes to defeat the royalists at the Battle of Chacabuco. A year later they triumphed again at the Battle of Maipú. The royalists, including at least 70 prominent Spanish merchants, fled to Peru. There they addressed a letter to Ferdinand VII asking him to intervene and protect their property in Chile. Chilean patriots now returned from their exile in Argentina or their imprisonment on Juan Fernández Island. Chilean leaders offered the supreme director's position to San Martín, who declined, and then to O'Higgins, who eagerly accepted.

O'Higgins was reticent to create a legislative branch after witnessing earlier dissention. When urged by Theodoric Bland, the chargé d'affaires from the United States, to establish a legislature, O'Higgins responded that the bickering of the first congress had undermined the patriotic government and contributed to the royalists' victory. Nevertheless, he did establish a small senate, which acted in an advisory role. Neither of two constitutions written during O'Higgins's tenure significantly limited his power.

Liberating Peru

O'Higgins's main concern was to help San Martín organize an invasion of Peru to overthrow the viceroy, Joaquín de la Pezuela. He believed that until all Spanish government officials were expelled from the continent, Chile's independence would be vulnerable to another royalist attack. San Martín and O'Higgins encouraged the soldiers who fought with them in the Chilean campaign to join the expedition to Peru. O'Higgins then faced the problem of financing the expedition. Since his own national treasury was empty, to raise funds he expropriated royalists' properties and imposed levies on them and patriots alike. From 1817 to 1824, the treasury collected more than 900,000 pesos in money seized from the enemy and expropriated property. It also collected more than 400,000 pesos more in forced levies. O'Higgins also collected 150,000 pesos in ransom from two royalist merchants who were captured in 1818 trying to finance another viceregal invasion.

To control the seas, O'Higgins authorized the creation of a navy. He encouraged newly established foreign merchants to acquire ships and outfit corsairs while he named a former British naval officer, Lord Cochrane, to command of the Chilean fleet. To support him some experienced North American officers were commissioned. Beginning in March 1819, Cochrane declared a blockade of Peruvian ports and began to interdict Spanish shipping. The Chilean fleet also transported San Martín's forces to southern Peru, and from there they marched to Lima. San Martín took the city and declared himself the ruler of Peru, but he hesitated to attack the retreating viceroy's forces. Lord Cochrane eliminated all Spanish shipping on the Pacific Coast then quarreled with San Martín over his conduct of the campaign. He abruptly submitted his resignation and offered to help Brazil achieve independence. The Venezuelan liberator, Simón Bolívar, also preparing a campaign in Peru, persuaded San Martín to turn his command over to him. While San Martín sailed to exile in Europe, Bolívar's forces defeated the viceroy at the Battle of Ayacucho in 1824. After fourteen years of struggle, South America was liberated. Although a Chilean commander was not present at the final battle, Chile made an extraordinary contribution of soldiers, seamen, and financial resources to the ultimate victory.

O'Higgins's Administration

While supporting the liberation of Peru, O'Higgins also began transforming Chile into a viable nation. He had a clear vision of Chile's commercial potential as he planned economic policy. In support of this vision, he encouraged trade by moving the main customs house from Santiago to Valparaíso and converting the port into a West Coast distribution center. As Chilean merchants observed the rapid growth of commerce, the majority controlled by foreign firms, they protested this apparent favoritism. While they were right that some early programs favored foreigners, later programs alienated many of them. In his search for revenue, for example, he imposed a levy on them, he enacted harsh, anticontraband measures, and abolished government warehouses. When he rewrote the basic commercial law in 1822, it was equally unpopular among foreign and domestic merchants who pressured him to suspend its implementation for six months.

O'Higgins wanted to create a more homogeneous society, but not one without social classes. He tried to eliminate some exclusive, aristocratic institutions while raising the cultural level of the common people. In a decree that struck at the pride of a few elite families, he abolished noble titles and forbid the display of their coat of arms. He tried to abolish the *mayorazgos*, but failed. He chipped away at the Catholic Church's power by creating a public cemetery and allowing some concessions to Protestants. To educate the general public, he founded a national library, reopened the Instituto Nacional, and encouraged printing. He also lent support to an educational system based on an English model.

O'Higgins was scrupulously honest and well intentioned, but he forced many changes on people without popular support. To his admirers, he was an enlightened despot; to his enemies, he was a dictator. He used the army to impose order, obligating even the Chilean aristocrats to obey him. He falsely assumed that he could transform Chile without their cooperation. By the end of 1822, however, he lost control of the army in Concepción, commanded by his former junior officer, Ramón Freire. The Santiago aristocracy took their cue from Freire, gathered in a *cabildo abierto,* and demanded O'Higgins's resignation. At first in disbelief, O'Higgins rejected their demand. When the persistent *cabildo* convinced him that he had no choice, he made a dignified and patriotic abdication statement and went into lifelong exile in Peru.

New Leadership

An interim junta briefly governed Chile. It quickly ingratiated itself with merchants through a new commercial law, which lowered and simplified tariffs. Then military commander Ramón Freire took over as supreme director. Freire acquiesced to elections of an assembly and the ratification of a new constitution. Controversies among assembly members unfortunately prompted Freire to dismiss them and assume dictatorial powers. Nevertheless, Freire did implement some liberal measures. He abolished slavery, which liberated approximately 10,000 Africans and Mapuches engaged in agricultural and domestic service. He also undertook a controversial expropriation of church property. This action, as well as a conflict with the bishop of Santiago, alienated the visiting Vatican envoy and postponed the normalization of relations with Rome.

Financial Issues

Soon after Freire assumed power, a British loan contracted by O'Higgins arrived in the country. Of approximately 3,000,000 pesos, half of this the Chilean government loaned to Peru to cover military expenses. Instead of investing the remainder in public works, Freire used over 500,000 pesos to fund the 1823 budget and some to pay for his campaign against the Spanish on the island of Chiloé. The rest of the money was unaccounted for. In less than a year the money was gone, but the country was left with annual payment of over 350,000 pesos to an English bank. This amount represented 20 percent of annual government revenue. Freire's fiscal solution was to contract a private firm to make the payments in return for granting the firm a tobacco and liquor monopoly, or *estanco.* The firm awarded the *estanco*—Portales, Cea and Company—failed to make the payments, went bankrupt, and had to be liquidated. The government, also in grave financial difficulties, suspended payments and did not resume them until twenty years later.

Part of Freire's financial problems stemmed from a sharp contraction of commerce, which after independence had become the country's main source of tax revenue. Freire's attempt to sell the expropriated church properties produced little income. Adding to the difficult economic situation was the disorganization of the treasury. Faced with empty coffers, the Freire administration refused to pay its own notes. When it later attempted to borrow, its poor credit closed all the doors of financial institutions. By 1826 chronic financial problems combined with political disputes prompted Freire to resign. He dreamed of returning to power and several times conspired unsuccessfully with friends in the military to take over the government.

During the unstable period from 1826 to 1831, a number of leaders served as president. Francisco Antonio Pinto was the most notable. As a lawyer, mine owner, merchant, general, and diplomat, Pinto had exceptional leadership skills. Rather than being from Santiago, he had mining operations in La Serena. He favored federalism for the autonomy it would give his prosperous region, which accounted for over half of all Chilean exports. He therefore supported the federal system embodied in the liberal Constitution of 1828, which also eliminated *mayorazgos*. The conservative Santiago elite opposed both measures and worked to undermine Pinto's government.

Authoritarian Rule

In September 1829 new elections reaffirmed Pinto as president, but the position of vice president remained undecided. When the struggle over this issue made the country ungovernable, Pinto resigned. In support of Pinto's federal system, both Concepción and La Serena withdrew their recognition of the new national government. The Santiago conservatives managed to persuade a group of Concepción's military leaders to ally with them. Liberal and conservative military factions clashed on the battlefield of Lircay. When the conservatives won, they dominated government for the next three decades.

In the 1820s congresses and constitutions failed to create a governing consensus. Now conservatives achieved this through force. According to historian Julio Heise, the conservatives resurrected the colonial system by abolishing civil liberties and eliminating religious freedom. In their economic policies, however, they were far more liberal. It is sad the force was the only way to unite the nation because the divisiveness of the period was not between social classes, but between factions of the elite. The government's critical financial situation further exggerated disputes.

To gain power, a leader had to put together a coalition of interests, which usually included a faction of the military. Once in power, he was tempted to dismiss a quarrelsome congress and impose authoritarian rule. Although some historians consider that O'Higgins acted like a dictator, nevertheless, when challenged by the Santiago aristocracy, he chose to resign rather than fight. Far more authoritarian were the conservatives who ruled in the 1830s. Only in the 1840s and 1850s did this group include more participants and viewpoints, but not without some serious rebellions. During this regime's tenure, the liberal ideas of the 1820s were not forgotten; rather, they served as a landmark for the parliamentary rule that emerged in the 1860s.

4

Miners, Merchants, and Hacendados, 1830–61

ORDER VERSUS FREEDOM

During the period from 1830 to 1860, only three presidents served, each for a decade. Senators served for nine-year terms and deputies for three-year terms. Presidents handpicked the candidates for congress, who invariably won elections. Presidents also appointed the municipal and regional officials. To squelch any opposition they declared a state of siege, often subordinated the judicial branch to their control, or favored one group over another. The government was nominally a representative democracy, but due to property requirements few people voted. In 1834, for example, less than 7,000 people went to the polls out of a population of more than a million. In 1849, the number of voters rose slightly to over 18,000 but then declined again in the following decade.

This lack of participation in government partly explains why two serious rebellions against authoritarian rule occurred in the 1850s. Liberal leaders such as Benjamín Vicuña Mackenna and the Matta brothers demanded greater political freedom, and the liberal mine owner Pedro León Gallo financed his own army in an attempt to overthrow authoritarian rule. Although rebel leaders of 1851 and 1859 fought on behalf of liberal ideals, their regional motivations were also important. They were largely from the north and south not the Valle Central. In the south the military was dissatisfied with its compensation, and the landowners were unhappy with the lack of government support. In the north the mine owners were upset that their taxes financed government but gave them few benefits in return.

Latin America's Troubles

Chile's restrictions on political liberty as well as its regional tensions need to be seen in the context of the rest of Latin America. Throughout the hemisphere dictators or revolutions trampled people's rights and often threatened their lives. Instead of independence and self-government opening a new era of progress, they produced stagnation and even depression. Mexico, formerly the prosperous colony of New Spain, suffered such political instability that only one president completed his term of office before 1860. Fifty years after independence, Mexico's per capita income was less than in colonial times. Although Brazil and Argentina made important economic progress, both suffered from strong regional secession movements.

Given Latin America's dangerous political climate, opposition leaders and writers often fled to other countries for safe haven. Andrés Bello, a brilliant Venezuelan scholar, avoided the dictatorial regime in his own country and chose to live in Chile instead. There he became head of the University of Chile and the author of the country's civil law code. Domingo F. Sarmiento, the noted Argentine author and future president, immigrated to Chile to escape Juan Manuel de Rosas's despotic regime. In Valparaíso he dedicated himself to journalism and later became Chile's minister of education. To foreign visitors Chile seemed so orderly that they referred to it as the England of South America. Numerous scientific expeditions such as those of Charles Darwin and Claudio Gay were escorted around Chile so they could study its natural and political history. Gay even received government support to research and publish his multivolume work.

All the new republics of the Western Hemisphere struggled to invent viable political and economic institutions once they achieved independence. Earlier the United States had experienced a decade of political and economic troubles until the country scrapped the Articles of Confederation in favor of the Constitution. Similarly, Chile experimented with constitutions, seeking a balance between order and freedom. During the period from 1830 to 1860, as the country consolidated its institutions, economic freedom preceded political freedom. Government defined the economic rules, while the market set prices, exchanged goods, and distributed wealth. This freedom encouraged the growth of foreign and domestic markets. Not surprisingly, as businessmen accumulated wealth, they demanded participation in political decisions. Those who felt their voices were unheard resorted to armed uprisings in 1851 and 1859. Their goal was not to overthrow the economic system but to open up the political one.

Economic Changes

Limited political participation did not prevent Chileans from creating an era of great material progress. Nowhere in the country was this more pronounced than in Valparaíso. Merchants transformed the port from a sleepy town to the "emporium of the Pacific." Ships from all over the world stopped there on their way to Asia, California, or Europe. The dozens of firms with their home offices in diverse locations such as Philadelphia, Liverpool, Bremen, Marcella, and Cádiz operated in the port. Further south in Concepción, whalers from all over the world purchased supplies, while in the north, copper made Coquimbo an international port.

The merchants helped transform economic policy from one that explicitly favored particular groups to one in which private enterprise defined the rules of the marketplace. Originally the government attempted to protect national artisans, manufacturers, merchants, and the merchant marine. When conflicts of interest and problems of enforcement failed to make these mechanisms effective, the government gradually dismantled many of them. Tax reduction was another matter; all groups lobbied congress for tax cuts. Nevertheless, they also wanted the government to build roads, docks, warehouses, and irrigation canals, but scarce resources postponed most of these projects. Increasingly, private capital undertook some of these projects. Investors created the first steamship line, built railroads, and dug irrigation canals.

Unfortunately, at the beginning of the 1830s the Chilean treasury was empty, and both local and foreign creditors wondered if they would ever be repaid. Regardless of the state's desperate situation, leading economic groups wanted taxes reduced or eliminated. So the minister of treasury, Manuel Rengifo, made cuts. It is doubtful whether these reductions contributed to the economic growth, but the regime garnered additional political support. The silver discoveries of the 1830s were the main stimulus to the economy and government revenues, which grew from just over 1,600,000 pesos in 1830 to over 8,500,000 pesos in 1860. This wealth finally gave congress the opportunity to fund public works and services. In addition to roads and railways, the legislature supported education and the military.

MINING

More than any other activity, mining served as the motor to the Chilean economy. During independence this area was spared the destruction that devastated the haciendas in the agricultural regions. Although traditional mining methods frustrated foreigners who tried to change them, silver discoveries in the 1820s increased output. The price of ores also shot up, in part due to advancements in shipping and commerce. This growth enabled foreigners in the 1830s to introduce industrial mining using steam engines, reinforced tunnels, railroads, and reverberatory furnaces. These innovations required capital and skilled personnel, as well as political support.

Charles Lambert

After independence British investors founded three mining companies with the objective of buying mines and introducing Wales mining technology. One firm, the Chilean Mining Association, sent Charles Lambert along with two commissioners to set up operations in Chile. Lambert was a trained geologist who already had explored the Chilean mining region. Instead of sailing directly to Chile, the three disembarked in Buenos Aires, crossed the Pampas on horseback and then hiked over the Andes during the winter. Lambert arrived in the Norte Chico in September 1825 and immediately began essaying ores, meeting with mining owners, and acquiring properties. He was cautious, yet optimistic about the prospects for the business. In February 1826 Lambert wrote Commissioner Charles Dobson "... that with something like two hundred thousand pesos ... within a few years, I am certain, if things are well run, millions could be made." Yet when the London stock market collapsed, the company declared bankruptcy. These dreams never materialized because the collapse of the London stock market forced the company into bankruptcy. Dobson committed suicide while another commissioner became an alcoholic. Lambert lost all the investments he had made on the company's behalf, but he had enough capital to initiate mining ventures on his own.

Lambert's most important assets were his knowledge of mineralogy and his ability to adapt to the local culture. He first employed these talents in purchasing a slag heap of copper sulfide ores from Bernardo del Solar, who considered them worthless because the Chilean technology was unable to smelt them. Lambert, however, knew how to build a reverberatory furnace that achieved the higher temperatures needed to smelt these ores. At great savings he processed del Solar's ores with no expense in mining them. Lambert also astutely recognized that offering credit to other mine owners guaranteed him a constant supply of ores, while he reaped a commission on the sale of copper overseas.

Lambert understood how much government policy could affect his enterprise. Wishing to cut his copper export expenses, he audaciously loaned 100,000 pesos to the Coquimbo provincial government to encourage it to lower tariffs. Although this caused a conflict between the regional and national government, Lambert achieved his goal. But Chilean politics were sometimes too unpredictable even for such an astute entrepreneur as Lambert. In 1851 rebellion broke out in La Serena, and the revolutionaries seized Lambert's steamship, the *Firefly*. Lambert sided with the government, who defeated the revolutionaries and returned his ship. In the process he alienated many prominent local mine owners who backed the revolution. Lambert decided to migrate to Swansea, South Wales, where he already had strong business connections with the copper smelters there. He left his son, Carlos Segundo, to handle his many business affairs in Chile. More than two decades later in 1876 Lambert died in Wales leaving a fortune estimated at 5,000,000 pesos.

Silver

While Lambert improved copper technology and production, others expanded silver production. In the 1820s prospectors discovered silver lodes at Arqueros and Tres Puntas in the Coquimbo region. These rich mines raised silver exports from 500,000 pesos in 1820 to 1,100,000 pesos in 1830 while boosting a slumping economy. Then in 1832 at Chañarcillo, near the northern city of Copiapó, occurred the largest silver strike in Chilean history. A poor Indian woman, Flora Normilla, originally revealed to her son, Juan Godoy, the abundance of silver ores at Chañarcillo. Together with the property owner, Miguel Gallo, they registered the claim. This deposit, followed by others in the region, pushed up silver exports from 1,600,000 pesos in 1840 to 4,100,000 pesos in 1850 and nearly 8,000,000 pesos in 1855. Unfortunately, after this date the high-grade ores were depleted and production declined.

Candelaria Goyenechea and Pedro León Gallo

Miguel Gallo's wife, Candelaria Goyenechea, assumed administration of the mine when her husband died in 1842. Realizing the importance of modern transportation in developing her mine, she invested in Chile's first railroad, which ran between Copiapó and the port of Caldera. She recognized the value of education so she sent her son, Pedro León Gallo, to the exclusive Instituto Nacional in Santiago. While there he wrote for a newspaper and enrolled in the national guard. When a revolution broke out in 1851 in opposition to the presidential candidacy of Manuel Montt, Gallo's guard unit was ordered to defend the government. Pedro fought on behalf of Montt even though many mine owners from Copiapó opposed him.

Two years later Gallo returned home and with Montt's support was elected to the municipal council. Later, Montt dismissed him for refusing to enforce an executive order. He soon began collaborating with Montt's opponents who called for a revision of the 1833 Constitution. When the government rounded up some of his political sympathizers and shipped them to Liverpool, Gallo decided to form his own army to overthrow Montt. Using both his abundant silver and copper wealth, he hired his own army, coined his own money, and forged his own cannons. On March 14, 1859, with an infantry of 1,200, a cavalry of 200, and an artillery of 60 he defeated the government troops at Los Loros, outside the city of La Serena. A month later, however, fresh government troops defeated him at Cerro Grande and he was condemned death. But Gallo escaped to Argentina where Candelaria supported her son during his exile. In his absence she assumed control of the family business, and with her own resources she offered relief to the soldiers' families. Two years later a new president, José Joaquín Pérez, approved an amnesty law for all the revolutionaries of 1859, allowing Gallo and many others to return home as heroes. He built a successful political career, being elected to the Chamber of Deputies five times and to the Senate once. When he died in 1877, Candelaria survived him. Among her many activities, after the War of the Pacific, she helped out the soldiers.

José Tomás de Urmeneta and Matias Cousiño

Although silver reigned supreme in the middle of the nineteenth century, increasingly investments flowed into copper. By the 1870s Chile was producing over one-third of the world's supply. José Tomás de Urmeneta was Chile's most successful nineteenth-century copper baron, as historian Ricardo Nazer Ahumada explains in his biography. Urmeneta, like Lambert before him, realized the need for mining technology. In developing the Tamaya mine, he abandoned the traditional irregular mine shafts and built reinforced tunnels with rails for pushcarts. He used steam engines to operate the mine's pumps and its grinding mills. Although he employed skilled foreigners in his smelters as mechanics and carpenters, the great majority of workers were Chilean. The total number of workers in his mines and foundries exceeded 10,000. By 1871 his foundry produced more than half the smelted copper in Chile, although this percentage declined thereafter. He developed smelters and export facilities at Guayacán, Tongoy, and Totoralillo, in the Coquimbo region. Whereas ores from his own mines were used at Guayacán, other producers, often those who had received credit from Urmenata, supplied the ores used at Tongoy and Totoralillo. He connected the Tamaya mine to the Guayacán smelter with a railroad, and later he formed a coal company to produce fuel for his smelter.

Urmeneta also branched out into other businesses. One of his earliest was a Santiago flourmill. When gas lighting became popular, he developed this utility with his son-in-law, Máximiano Errázuriz. Among his other investments were the Banco Nacional de Chile, an insurance company, a credit company, a construction company, railroads, and steamships. Somehow he found time to serve in congress, twice as a deputy and once as a senator. In 1870 he ran for president as the opposition candidate, but the election was fixed, so he withdrew in disgust.

Another innovative mine owner was Matías Cousiño who originally devoted his energy to copper mining. Like other mine owners, he used local wood to run his smelters, but excessive logging exhausted the wood supply, so he imported English coal. He believed, however, that Chile could produce its own coal, so he bought some struggling mines in the Concepción region and began to develop them. Rather than haul the coal north to his copper smelters, he shipped the copper ore to his coal mines. To reduce transportation costs, he also invested in two railways. Soon he became one of the largest coal producers in Chile as well as a prominent grain merchant. His economic success led to a political career and he served in the House of Deputies from 1849 to 1855 and in the Senate from 1855 to 1864. His son enhanced the family's fortune after he died. Since the wealthy were building luxurious residences in Santiago, his son followed suit with an ornate mansion and magnificent gardens located near the capital's horse track. Later he donated it to the city, which converted it into a public park called Parque Cousiño. In the 1970s the benefactor's name was lost, when in a patriotic gesture the government renamed it Parque O'Higgins.

TRADE

After the 1820s declining tariffs encouraged trade. A wide variety of European products flowed into the country with textiles dominating, followed by mining materials, and household furnishings. Textiles included inexpensive cloth for workers as well as high-priced fabrics for Santiago's elite. Chilean and foreign merchants of many nationalities imported a wide variety of wares. The British dominated the market with woolens, cottons, paper, musical instruments, liquors, crockery, knives, machinery, mercury, hats, glass, and arms. The Americans were second, importing tobacco, rice, naval stores, candles, whale oil, furniture, rum, and manufactured goods from France, China, and India. Other firms included merchants from France, the German and Italian states, Spain, and South America. Chileans received consignments from foreign firms as well as traded on their own account. Merchants paid for imports preferably with copper and silver, but they also shipped wheat, hides, wool, jerky, and fresh produce.

The coastal trade between national ports, as well as the retail trade, was reserved for Chileans. Liberal citizenship laws and lax enforcement, however, enabled immigrant merchants to participate actively in both areas. Merchants helped create a national economy by shipping grain and other foodstuffs from the south to the mining districts of the north. For example, grain merchants like Juan Antonio Pando and Matías Cousiño built flour-mills on the Maule River and then shipped their products north. During the California Gold Rush, they competed in the San Francisco market as well. They guaranteed their grain supply through a credit with hacendados. The latter developed their own system to supply miners with both fresh meat and jerked beef. Their *huasos* herded sheep and cattle from the Valle Central to the north and sold jerky to the merchants, who shipped large quantities of it north.

José Tomás Ramos Font

Some merchants like José Tomás Ramos Font specialized largely in Chilean and South American produce. He competed with the larger European commercial houses mainly by dealing in agricultural goods from Peru, Ecuador, Paraguay, Uruguay, and Brazil. According to his biographer Juan Eduardo Vargas, after starting with little capital, eventually he became one of Chile's ten wealthiest men. His father was a Portuguese immigrant who began with a modest retail store in Santiago, but with the rise of Valparaíso's trade he moved to the port. When the independence wars began, his father sent José Tomás to Lima to live with an uncle and continue his studies. After San Martín invaded Peru, José Tomás went back and forth between Lima and Valparaíso, learning about politics and trade. In one of his first ventures he set up a brewery in Valparaíso to compete with imported beer. He also won a government tax collection contract. Later he developed interests further south where he bought wool for the North American merchant August Hemenway and invested in a modern flourmill near Concepción.

His ethnic background helped Ramos develop a partnership with the affluent Portuguese merchant, Francisco Alvarez. The latter owned four ships and Ramos owned one. Together they traded grain, flour, jerky, wine, cheese, and wood along the Chilean coast and north to Peru, Ecuador, and Colombia. On the return voyage from these northern nations, they imported sugar, rice, and Panama hats. In an exchange with Brazil they exported hats, wheat, copper, anise, and nuts and imported sugar, yerba mate, and coffee.

When the California gold rush began, it seemed to offer instant wealth. To take advantage of skyrocketing San Francisco prices, Ramos formed a new partnership to ship food, liquor, wood, and clothing. At first eggs sold for as high $4 a dozen, but after a year prices crashed and the partners lost money. They also offered credit to Chilean miners heading to the gold fields, but the miners did not repay them. Falling prices and bad loans cost the partners over $17,000 for their California adventure.

Fortunately Ramos did considerably better in other markets. Based on his experience in sugar trade with Peru, Ramos calculated that he would make more producing sugar than he did owning ships. In 1861 he sold his vessels and bought two plantations in Chiclayo, Peru. He paid 136,000 pesos for 4,858 hectares of prime sugar land and 7,702 hectares of uncultivated land. The sugar refinery needed modernizing so he invested more than 200,000 pesos importing machinery from England and making other improvements. Finding workers was another problem. His imported Chilean workers returned home, and the Peruvian government barred some Polynesian workers he tried to import. He finally turned to free and indentured Chinese workers. By 1874 he employed over 1,600 workers on the plantation and at the refinery. Output over a thirty-year period climbed from less than 200,000 to more than 2,000,000 kilos of sugar per year, which quadrupled the plantation's value to 1,700,000 pesos.

Following the pattern of other successful merchants, Ramos bought a 19,000 hectare hacienda north of Santiago for 300,000 pesos in 1881. He also made urban investments in gas, insurance, and banks. By the time he died in 1891, the value of his fortune had reached more than 4,000,000 pesos. His children unfortunately did not have their father's business talents and eventually sold his enterprises to pay off debts. Unlike other wealthy families of his generation, his children neither established notable political, economic, or cultural lineages, nor did they marry into older, established families.

Diego Portales

Even in a generally prosperous economy, many merchants were unsuccessful. Diego Portales, for example, failed in various commercial adventures before he eventually made his name in politics, not business. Portales' father, Santiago, was superintendent of the colonial mint and a strong supporter of independence. Diego, however, played no role in Chile's independence, but preferred to speculate in the Peruvian trade. In the 1820s, he and his partner, José Manuel Cea, saw an opportunity to operate a government tobacco monopoly, or *estanco,* in return for paying the interest on a British loan. The *estanco* failed, however, and Portales's company defaulted on its loan payments. When the government liquidated the *estanco,* critics believed that Portales and Cea faired better than they should have. This affair plunged Portales into the political arena and he became the author of satirical commentary in the newspaper, *El hambiento,* or "The Hungry Man." Opponents referred to him and his followers as the *estanqueros,* or "the monopoly men."

Portales liked power but was impatient with the mundane duties of public office. He played a major role in installing General Joaquín Prieto to the presidency in 1831, but after holding several ministerial positions he resigned and returned to his business affairs in Valparaíso. He was not hesitant to use his political influence with the Prieto government. For example, he assisted William Wheelwright to win a franchise to operate steamships between Chile and Peru. His own businesses, however, were rarely profitable. With a partner he invested $5,400 to fatten beef for the port's market. As his debts mounted, he tried to develop a copper smelter. Desperately he tried to collect money owed him by Manuel Cea, while being unable to honor a letter of credit to his friend Juan Diego Barnard.

His businesses were still floundering when he was shot in 1837. Were it not for his exceptional political career, historians would never distinguish him from dozens of other struggling merchants.

William Wheelwright

Portales's friend, William Wheelwright, did have an illustrious business career. Although he was originally from Massachusetts, he devoted his life to South American trade and transportation. During the 1820s he headed a commercial firm in Guayaquil, but in the 1830s he moved to Valparaíso due to its growth as a trade center. He soon recognized how new transportation systems could revolutionize trade. The success of these enterprises often depended on his forging ties between the private and government sectors. He successfully lobbied for an exclusive government franchise for the Pacific Steam Navigation Company. Unable to find investment capital in Chile or the United States, he turned to Great Britain for start-up money and a government contract. After considerable effort he attracted British investors, purchased a ship, and began operations in 1840. The company lost money its first few years and would have failed were it not that British Parliament gave it a mail subsidy of annual cash payments. Even in the age of private enterprise, political support often was the difference between success and failure.

With the steamship line operating, Wheelwright moved on to railroads and telegraph projects. Among others he persuaded prominent mine owners such as Candelaria Goyenechea and Matías Cousiño to invest in his railroad company. The firm gained the distinction of inaugurating Chile's first railroad in 1851, which ran from the Copiapó mines to the port of Caldera. Originally the firm imported coal from Great Britain, but after finding sufficient coal near Concepción, Wheelwright, Cousiño, and other investors opened their own mine. They sold coal to the railroad and the copper refineries.

Merchants needed timely market information to reduce their business risks. To solve this Wheelwright introduced the telegraph in 1852 with a line he built between Valparaíso and Santiago. Other Chilean business ventures went sour, so he decided to shift his efforts to Argentina, where he built the first railroad across the Pampas from Rosario to Cordoba. Again both political and business support were important as he successfully lobbied the Argentine government for a franchise and raised the needed capital in Great Britain. Wheelwright's ability to lobby the governments of Chile, Argentina, and Great Britain and to raise capital in both South American and Europe where the keys to his success. Other entrepreneurs, who were unable to bring government and investment interests together often failed.

CHANGES IN LAND OWNERSHIP

Many successful businessmen invested at least part of their earnings in land. With land values rising while other prices were volatile, land was a secure investment. Land also acquired a new status as the Chilean elite visited Europe. Their ideas evolved from the rural ideal of the colonial hacienda to that of the manicured French or English manor. Following the latter example, Chilean entrepreneurs built luxurious country mansions with tree-lined entrances and landscaped gardens. These entrepreneurs also brought an investment mentality to the lands they purchased. They built irrigation canals, bought machinery, and experimented with new crops.

The new landed elite sought to marry their children into traditional affluent families. They identified with new educational and business values. If their offspring were sons, they usually encouraged them to study law and engage in real estate, banking, investment, and political activities. By contrast they encouraged their daughters to learn to run a large household, entertain peers, and resolve family issues.

Numerous elite members involved themselves in politics. They might write passionately about national issues but did not confine themselves to journalism. They served in congress and occupied ministerial positions. If they ran their hacienda, they did so from a distance, making decisions about crops, purchases, and sales, but relying on an overseer to handle daily operations. Others preferred to lease the land to someone else. Although in the summer it was fashionable for the family to vacation on the estate, the rest of the year they engaged in urban activities.

The Larraín Family

To understand the evolution of powerful landed families, one of the most interesting families to study is the Larraín. Works by the historians Arnold Bauer and Mary Lowenthal Felstiner offer valuable insights into the family. According to them, the first Larraín settlers in Chile arrived in the seventeenth century. They dedicated themselves to education and government, holding such positions as head of the Universidad de San Felipe, mayor of Santiago, and commander of the militia. At the same time the family accumulated large tracks of land. In 1787 José Toribio Larraín had sufficient capital to entail his estate and acquire the title "Marqués de Larraín." He was actively engaged in commerce including the contraband trade with the English vessel, *Scorpion*, which led to a crisis in Governor García Carrasco's administration.

Larraín's wife, Dolores Moxó, likewise descended from a wealthy family. Although she and her husband were Chilean-born, they refused to endorse the independence movement that endangered their status. By contrast another branch of the same family, which did not have a noble title, avidly supported independence. In spite of favoring the royalist side, José Toribio and Dolores managed to retain their wealth and avert persecution.

In 1822 a British observer, Maria Graham, visited *Viluco*, the Larraín hacienda, located just south of the Maipo River and a day's journey from Santiago. She marveled at its beauty, especially the variety of orchards, vineyards, and fields. She estimated that the crops and the 9,000 cattle produced an income of about 25,000 pesos a year. The oldest son, Rafael Larraín Moxó, born in 1813, later inherited this hacienda, the family fortune, and its conservative politics. When he took over the hacienda, he chose to sell a cattle ranch that was farther south in Cauquenes to raise capital to improve Viluco's productivity. He actively worked with other landowners in the National Agricultural Society to introduce modern agricultural practices in Chile.

Like so many wealthy hacendados of his era, Rafael had a special attraction to politics. His marriage to Victoria Prieto, the daughter of President Joaquín Prieto Vial, certainly did not hinder his career. In 1849 he was elected to the House of Deputies where he served for nine years and then moved on to the Senate where he served from 1855 to 1882 and once acted as its president. His political career enabled him to associate with a group of investors who founded the Banco de Chile and who elected him as the bank's president. He also invested in the railroad from Santiago to Talca. When this project stalled, he supported government participation in it. Later his son, Luis, saw new opportunities in manufacturing, but to raise capital he had to sell part of the family's estate. Although he diversified the family's economic interests, nevertheless, he remained faithful to its conservative political roots.

Fernando Lazcano Mujica

Another landowning family strongly committed to politics was that of Fernando Lazcano Mujica. Fernando, like his father before him, studied law. In 1832 he was named secretary of the Court of Appeals. In 1851 President Manuel Montt named him Minister of Justice, Religion and Education. Acting on his conservative religious principles, he provoked a scandal at the Instituto Nacional when he attempted to replace secular professors with priests. Montt judiciously decided not to antagonize the students and moved him to interim Minister of Treasury. That same year Lazcano was elected for a nine-year term to the Senate and later served as Senate president.

In addition to practicing law and developing an important political career, he also managed the hacienda El Guaico that was 100 miles south of Santiago, which he and his wife, Dolores Echaurren Larraín, had purchased. To improve the land's productivity, they built canals and irrigated over 4,000 hectares. By the 1880s these improvements had raised the value of El Guaico to over 600,000 pesos. Surprisingly, Lazcano failed to spread his investments as widely as did colleagues like Rafael Larraín. When Lazcano died his estate was valued at over 1,500,000 pesos, but only 5 percent was invested in stocks and bonds. His three sons inherited his passion for politics, serving as legislators, ministers, and ambassadors. One son, Fernando Lazcano Echaurren, even ran for the presidency in 1906 but was defeated by Pedro Montt. Unfortunately as politics increasingly dominated the family's interests its economic fortunes declined.

Josué Waddington

Immigrants who purchased haciendas came from very different backgrounds than the Larraín and Lazcano families. Josué Waddington, for example, began his career as a merchant. After spending five years working in Buenos Aires for an English firm, he immigrated to Chile in 1817. He opened his consignment business in Valparaíso as a distributor of British goods along the South American west coast and an exporter of agricultural goods and metals. In order to produce his own farm exports, he bought the hacienda San Isidro for 30,000 pesos. It was located about twenty-five miles northwest of Valparaíso near the town of Limache.

Limited rainfall in this region restricted his activities to cattle ranching and raising winter wheat. He could not grow the variety of fruits and vegetables demanded by the shipping community. To solve this problem Waddington audaciously constructed a seventy-two mile irrigation canal from the Aconcagua River to his farm. Other hacienda owners were astounded that someone would undertake such a large project at his own expense. Nevertheless, when they saw the increased value of the hacienda, they committed themselves to similar, though smaller projects. Years later when Waddington's heirs sold San Isidro to Agustín Edwards, it was one of the most valuable haciendas in the nation.

For Waddington, agriculture was one of many businesses. Others included urban real estate, mining, and railroads. In 1833, for example, he bought land from the St. Augustine Convent at Valparaíso, built his own luxurious residence, and subdivided the rest. In mining, he advanced goods to mine owners in return for exclusive purchasing contracts. Although he owned copper mines in the vicinity of La Serena, in 1860 he sold them to Urmeneta for 15,000 pesos. To improve the transportation of goods from his hacienda to the port, he invested in the Valparaíso-Santiago railway. During the war with the Peru-Bolivian Confederation, he arranged financing for the Chilean government. Unfortunately, three decades later in 1866 during a brief conflict, Spain bombarded Valparaíso, destroyed Waddington's warehouses, and forced him into bankruptcy. He struggled back and soon won a contract to build a waterworks for the port. Although one of Valparaíso's most influential entrepreneurs, he never ran for public office. All three of his sons, however, were elected to the Chamber of Deputies.

For the three hacienda owners discussed, agriculture represented one of numerous activities. They did not live at their haciendas but in the city. They were investment minded, as they employed many resources to improve the land's productivity. But they did not limit their interest to land; they invested in railroads, banking, and urban property. Of the mine owners, merchants, and hacendados discussed above, six served in important government positions. Gallo, Urmeneta, and Cousiño were liberals, whereas Larraín, Lazcano, and Portales were conservatives. Ramos was the anomaly. As a wealthy Chilean he could have aspired to political office but chose instead to dedicate himself to his business. The three immigrants, Lambert, Wheelwright, and Waddington, lobbied government intensely for special concessions but did not hold public office. All of these men benefited from the combination of Chile's market economy and social stability. The liberals demanded more political freedom, while the conservatives worried that increased freedom might mean less stability.

PROFESSIONS AND POLITICS

As Chilean leaders defined the nation's political culture, disagreements led factions. At first, true political parties did not emerge; rather, alliances formed based on families, clans, or political principles. To galvanize loyalties, rival factions labeled their opponents with colorful names. Conservatives derided as *pipiolos,* or beginners, all those who favored federalism, freedom of expression, and secularism. Liberals ridiculed as *pelucones,* or bigwigs, those who favored strong central government, limited civil rights, and the union of church and state. Only the affluent, the well educated, or the military participated in government, nevertheless, the political culture they developed during this period conditioned the dynamics of government when other groups later gained access to the system.

Mining and commercial families were more likely *pipiolos,* whereas hacendado families were more likely *pelucones.* The *pipiolos* drew more on people of new money and talent, yet some people like Manuel Montt and Manuel Rengifo who shared this background became *pelucones.* Neither party made any attempt to appeal to the farm or mine workers. Chilean constitutions, liberal and conservative alike, only granted the vote to property owners.

Though most politicians came from the same social class, economic, regional, and family interests sharply divided them. In the period from 1830 to 1860, when disputes reached an impasse, the military stepped in. Political leaders lobbied commanders hoping to bring them in on their side of the controversy. When this happened, the military often split with different units opposing each other on the battlefield. For example, liberals encouraged general Freire to rebel against his former commander, Bernardo O'Higgins, in 1822. Conservatives likewise encouraged Joaquín Prieto to opposed his former commander Ramón Freire in 1830. Even more surprising, two cousins, Manuel Bulnes and José María de la Cruz, conservative and liberal generals respectively, fought each other in the in the civil war of 1851.

Originally the military contributed to the divisiveness of the republic, not to its stability. The presidents from 1831 to 1851 were career officers, but after them, four decades passed before another officer reached the presidency. Manuel Montt, the first civilian president, subordinated the military to civil government and thereafter it strengthened rather than undermined the state. Also, while the governments from 1830 to 1861 frequently suspended civil liberties, allegedly to protect the state, thereafter leaders permitted diversity of opinion and relied upon rhetoric and politics, not guns, to resolve disagreements.

The Era of Portales

One of the most dominating yet elusive figures in Chilean politics was Diego Portales. His strength was in controlling others, not in public administration. A government crisis in 1829 gave him his first opportunity to promote his conservative allies to power. When another crisis occurred in 1830 he took control of the government, not as president, but as minister. In a unique power grab, he held all the cabinet positions simultaneously. As the country divided into warring camps, the military split as well. With conservative support, general Joaquín Prieto routed former liberal president Ramón Freire at the battle of Lircay on April 17, 1830.

This victory enabled Portales to consolidate his control. First he eliminated federalism by canceling local elections and exiling prominent liberal leaders. Then he sacked 136 military officers who had supported Freire and denied them any retirement benefits. Knowing from experience how military leaders often used their troops to overthrow the government, he shrank the army and strengthened the national guard. He counted on the guard to impose order whenever civil unrest occurred during conservative rule.

Once Portales had confidence that conservatives firmly controlled the government, he returned to his business ventures in Valparaíso. To their credit, the conservatives who remained at the helm did not seek personal gain, rather they sought to create durable, conservative institutions. First they began with a new constitution. The authors, Mariano Egaña and Manuel José Gandarillas, decided to increase presidential power and diminish legislative power. Ratified in 1833, this constitution permitted the president to serve two consecutive five-year terms. Not only did it allow him to control the elections of congressmen and to appoint all local officials, he could also suspend the constitution and declare a state of siege at his discretion. The presidents who ruled from 1830 to 1861 found this article a useful device for muzzling dissent.

While the conservatives' political system discouraged new ideas, their economic system encouraged innovation. Manual Rengifo, the treasury minister, crafted new trade, tax, and public finance reforms. He found government records in total disarray: not only was the treasury empty, records of income, expenses, or debts were in complete confusion. Miners, merchants, and hacendados had expected tax cuts as a dividend of independence, yet a combination of war expenses and poor management had often increased them. To gain these men's support, he offered them benefits. For mine owners, Rengifo raised the price the mint paid them for gold. Then for the first time he permitted them to export unminted bars of silver. For merchants he designed the 1833 tariff with a sliding scale of duties that reduced rates for most imports. He also expanded bonded warehouse regulations with the objective of encouraging merchants to import goods to Valparaíso for distribution to other Pacific ports. He also offered tariff discounts for imports consigned to national merchants as a way to encourage the growth of Chilean firms. Finally, to please landowners, he lowered the sales tax on farm goods and temporarily eliminated the agricultural tithe.

Like treasurer Alexander Hamilton of the United States, Rengifo sought to bolster government credit. In 1830 Chile had a foreign debt of 5,000,000 pesos and an internal debt of over 2,000,000 pesos. With annual expenditures exceeding income, the country's credit continually deteriorated. To solve the problem, Rengifo used a dual approach. He cut government expenses while earmarking a fund to pay off creditors. Striving for the support of national creditors, he concentrated on paying them first. Later, when the country was fiscally healthy, he began to pay Chile's foreign creditors.

The conservatives, as well as many of the liberals, were in favor of Rengifo's reforms. As the presidential election of 1836 approached, a group of liberals referred to as *filopolitas* began to support Rengifo rather than a second term for Prieto. When Diego Portales observed this movement, he quickly abandoned political retirement, forced Rengifo out of office, and took over two ministerial positions. Together he and Prieto engineered the latter's reelection.

During Prieto's second term, domestic and foreign politics intertwined and led Chile to war with its northern neighbors. Bolivia and Peru suffered from greater instability than Chile. The Bolivian general, Andrés Santa Cruz, first took over the government in his own country and then that of Peru, creating a new state, which he called the Peruvian-Bolivian Confederation. Tensions between Chile and the Confederation began with a tariff war over sugar and wheat duties. They increased in 1836 when Santa Cruz supported an invasion of Chilean liberal exiles headed by Ramón Freire. Portales broke relations with the Confederation, and a few months later a Chilean emissary declared war.

Most Chileans felt no need to go to war with Peru. The foreign merchants community opposed it as well. Portales, however, saw this conflict as a rivalry for trade supremacy in the Pacific and refused to listen to the opposition. Prieto declared a state of siege to silence all dissenters. Unexpectedly, a faction of the army rebelled. In June 1837, when Portales was reviewing some troops, Colonel José Antonio Vidaurre suddenly arrested him. The following day one of Vidaurre's men executed Portales on a hill above Valparaíso.

The government quickly squelched the Vidaurre uprising. The martyred Portales inspired greater domestic support for the war with Peru, although foreign merchants cringed at the harm they feared it would inflict on west coast commerce. When the war started, the first Chilean expedition north proved a humiliating failure. A second expedition, led by General Manuel Bulnes, was much more successful, destroying Santa Cruz's forces January 20, 1839, at the Battle of Yungay. As a result of the Chilean victory, the Peruvian-Bolivian Confederation split up, Valparaíso increased its domination of Pacific commerce, and Bulnes became a national hero. Upon his return to Santiago, the people celebrated as if they had just won their independence.

Bulnes became the perfect candidate to provide continuity to the conservative regime while at the same time ushering in a new era of tolerance. Not only was he a victorious general, he had family ties to two presidents. Outgoing President Joaquín Prieto was his uncle and former President Francisco Antonio Pinto was his father-in-law. Since Pinto was a liberal, these family ties encouraged Bulnes to soften the regime's hostility toward the opposition. Before Prieto left office he restored the rank to some of the officers dismissed in 1830 and normalized civil rights. As soon as Bulnes assumed office in 1841, his minister, Manuel Rengifo, pushed a general amnesty through congress. This measure went so far as to offer pensions to widows of cashiered officers.

A honeymoon of cordial relations between Chile's political factions created a fertile environment for the nation's intellectual and cultural life. Not only did prominent families insist on their male children studying at the Instituto Nacional, they sent a number of them to Europe. The statesman Vicente Pérez Rosales remembered sailing to France with the cream of upper-class youth. He and his friends enjoyed the delights of Paris but showed scarce interest in their academic work. In spite of the meager accomplishments, nonetheless, French acculturation became a rite of passage for upper-class youth.

While Chileans were discovering Europe, the reverse was true as well. A number of European professors and literary figures made pioneering contributions to the country's intellectual life. Ignacio Domeyko, from Lithuania, first taught mineralogy in La Serena and then in Santiago. His interests extended to educational reform as well. He helped implement the six-year secondary school curriculum and later became head of the University of Chile. Somewhat more controversial was the French economist, Jean Gustave Courcelle-Seneuil, who taught at the University of Chile Law School. In his lectures and publications he emphasized free trade, a doctrine that some later critics blamed for Chile's slow industrialization.

Reprinted European articles, along with local essays on European trends, increasingly contrasted Chile's modernizing economy and its backward political and social system. Liberal intellectuals tried to transplant ideas such as the separation of church and state, freedom of the press, fair elections, and greater social equality to an authoritarian environment. One of the most influential liberal leaders was José Victorino Lastarria. In a public address at the University of Chile in 1844, he blamed the colonial church, state, and property relations for the country's backwardness. These were precisely the institutions revered by the *pelucones*.

Without fanfare, the Bulnes administration initiated a move toward liberalism. It began secularizing the state and subordinating the church to government. To support the Protestant commercial community, Bulnes recognized non-Catholic marriages. To eliminate church privilege, he subjected the clergy to civil law and regulated religious vocations. These measures, not surprisingly, angered Archbishop Rafael Valentín Valdivieso, who mobilized conservatives to fight any further limitations of church power. This set the stage for greater confrontations in the future.

In spite of Bulnes's apparent nod to liberalism, when he ran for reelection in 1846 he muffled any opposition by censuring the press and limiting civil liberties. In 1848 when revolutionary movements spread throughout Europe, he felt no contradiction in applauding such liberal reforms abroad while blocking similar ones at home. However, he sought to portray himself as favoring liberal reforms when he publicly applauded Europe's revolutionary movements. Two young idealists, Santiago Arcos and Francisco Bilbao, organized Santiago craftsmen in a reform movement called the Society for Equality. In 1850 they published a paper, *The Friend of the People*, with articles demanding greater freedom including the right of Chileans to choose their next president. Unimpressed by such arguments, Bulnes followed his predecessors' example and imposed his candidate, Manuel Montt, on the country. When the Society for Equality protested, Bulnes shut it down. He then closed other liberal publications and exiled his most vociferous opponents. Even so, voters in the northern mining center of La Serena and the southern port of Concepción supported his opponent, José María de la Cruz. Montt won easily, but de la Cruz and protesters took up arms. Bulnes himself took to the battlefield and defeated him while other army commanders stamped out insurrections in other areas.

Even though Manuel Montt was chosen by the old guard, he represented a major change in Chilean politics. He was from a civilian rather than a military background. His exceptional intellect distinguished him early in his career. After receiving his law degree from the Instituto Nacional in 1831, his alma mater hired him to teach Roman law, and, four years later, named him as director. In 1837 President Prieto named him to his first ministerial position, followed by other positions including Foreign Relations, Justice and Education, and War and the Navy. Later he presided as president of the Supreme Court and president of the Chamber of Deputies.

Montt began an intellectual tradition in which most Chilean presidents were graduates of the state-run Instituto Nacional. This academy included both secondary and college programs such as law. The University of Chile was founded in 1843, but the law school remained at the Instituto Nacional until years later. The Instituto offered rigorous education available to all who could meet the admission requirements. Although children from the elite predominated, many less affluent attended as well. Talented men like Montt and his close friend, Antonio Varas, achieved prominence largely due to their education at the Instituto, in spite of their family's limited resources.

Based on Montt's own background, he believed that men of ability, not just landed aristocrats, could govern Chile. But he failed to build a political base for a new class of leaders. He did not extend democracy; rather, he allied himself with the *pelucones*. He thought efficient administration and modernization would establish a tradition of merit, not money, as the qualification for leadership. He failed to realize, however, that class was becoming more important, not less, in nineteenth-century Chilean politics. Not until the social movements of the twentieth century opened the door did the middle class challenge the upper class for political office.

Montt's policies actively cultivated the support of the landed aristocrats. He eliminated the sales tax on farmland and the agricultural tithe. He abolished the entailed estates so henceforth all heirs would inherit land. More importantly, these same estates became part of the commercial land market. To make farm credit more available to hacendados he created a Mortgage Loan Bank. To improve rural transportation, he made government the most important investor in the Santiago-Valparaíso and the Santiago-Talca railroads. Finally, he promoted settlement of southern Patagonia and Chile's control of the Strait of Magellan.

In spite of benefiting the elite, many *pelucones* abandoned him when Montt asserted the government's authority over the church. In a church employment issue the Supreme Court accepted jurisdiction in the case and Montt backed the court. In response, fiery Archbishop Valdivieso stirred up pro-church *pelucones* against Montt and eroded support in his own party. This issue caused a strange political realignment with the ultra conservatives and liberals forming a coalition opposing Montt while moderates of both camps backed him. Believing that they might overthrow a weakened regime a group of liberals revolted in 1859. They were wrong because the military backed the government and defeated the revolutionaries. Though they failed to oust Montt, his opponents convinced him not to impose his protégé, Antonio Varas, as president. Instead Montt selected a more moderate figure, José Joaquín Pérez, whose liberal policies changed the direction of Chilean history.

Pérez's selection not only initiated a shift toward liberalism, but also a shift of power. Gradually congress checked presidential authority, which initiated the parliamentary era. This period was characterized by intense rivalry and political infighting. In this era, government respected freedom of expression and a diversity of political parties. Successful parliamentary leaders demonstrated rhetorical elegance and bargaining finesse. While middle- and working-class Chileans began to form parties which would challenge the elite, some conservative critics wrote with admiration of the more austere and forceful presidents of an earlier era. As national wealth increased, so did the fortunes of the members of congress. To many Chileans, congress appeared to be an affluent club. They extolled the military backgrounds of generals José Joaquín Prieto and Manuel Bulnes, who rose to the presidency out of merit. Perhaps less appreciative of Montt, nevertheless, particularly critics recognized his intelligence and devotion to public service. They praised all three presidents for their honesty and fiscal conservatism. They overlooked, however, that the authoritarian presidents limited the diversity of opinion and often incarcerated or exiled vocal opponents. These presidents imposed incumbents and handpicked congressional candidates from the elite. Even though the presidents themselves were not from the elite, their programs certainly favored this group. From 1830 to 1861, Chile was truly an authoritarian republic, with all its virtues and defects.

5

The Triumph of Congress, 1861–91

Contrary to popular belief, modernization is often not a peaceful process. Chilean history from 1861 to 1891 witnessed not only great economic progress but also considerable violence. Mining and agricultural expansion accelerated the pace of economic change. New land and ocean transportation expanded domestic and international markets. Booming mining and farm exports fueled consumer and capital imports. The first national industries emerged. Yet this economic expansion lead to a controversy over Chile's exploitation of Bolivian mines and a war against both Bolivia and Peru.

Chile won the war and acquired new mineral resources, especially nitrates. Taxes on nitrates filled the treasury, but congress and the president quarreled over the right to spend them. Additionally presidential power eroded as the executive lost his ability to manipulate congressional elections. A fight over the budget appropriation process led congress to declare the president in violation of the constitution. A civil war broke out, pitting the congress against the president. Congress triumphed and restored order, but at a high cost to the nation.

THE NATIONAL IDENTITY

In this era of growth and conflict, Chile also developed a clear sense of its national identity. Early historians played an important role in this process. The first important historical work was that of the French naturalist Claudio Gay. During the 1830s he researched the country's natural and political history, collecting specimens and documents that became the basis of a 24-volume work. His example inspired a generation of Chilean historians who were born in the 1830s and studied together in the Instituto Nacional law school. The most prolific historian was Diego Barros Arana who served as professor, legislator, minister, and diplomat. His contribution was a 15-volume work that spanned over 300 years of the nation's history and was based on a painstaking collection of documents from both Spanish and Chilean sources. Another educator, legislator, and minister was Miguel Luis Amunátegui. He concentrated on the independence period, especially on such leaders as Bernardo O'Higgins, who he criticized as a dictator.

The most flamboyant historian was Benjamín Vicuña Mackenna. In the 1850s he was twice exiled as a revolutionary but was later pardoned. After his rehabilitation, he was elected to congress, served as *intendente* of Santiago, and then unsuccessfully ran for president. He sought to engage the public with his entertaining biographies, although he was less concerned with documenting his work. His histories of Valparaíso and of Chilean mining today are considered his most important works. Born twenty years after the first generation of historians, José Toribio Medina was Chile's foremost bibliographer, who also developed special interest in colonial history, literature, the Mapuche, and the Inquisition. His organization of the colonial archives and dozens of bibliographies on diverse historical subjects continue to serve researchers today. All these authors shared a critical vision of the Catholic Church and the colonial era while fully endorsing the nineteenth-century liberal trends of free trade, secularism, and public education. They fully endorsed modernization and progress. Their academic and political careers lent valuable support to the ascendancy of liberalism over conservatism.

ECONOMIC AND SOCIAL CHANGES

Silver

Mining continued to dominate Chile's development. It drew thousands of laborers from the Valle Central to the Norte Chico and the Norte

Grande. It provided markets for agricultural products and revenue for public works. The silver boom of the 1870s and 1880s was in large part due to Bolivian mines. Chilean silver production oscillated between 75,000 and 125,000 kilos per year from 1857 to 1878, but a silver export boom occurred in the 1870s largely due to exports from Bolivia's Caracoles mine, which produced approximately 900,000 kilos of silver in a decade.

The Caracoles mine was largely owned and worked by Chileans. Since most of the silver was also traded through Chilean ports, during two years of the 1870s, this boosted exports to 300,000 kilos. This figure represented about 15 percent of the world's silver production. In the 1880s, when the Caracoles lode began to run out, Chileans began exploiting two other Bolivian silver mines in Oruro and Huanchaca. Over a six-year period these mines produced approximately 200,000 kilos of silver exports per year.

Copper production demonstrated some of the same volatility as silver. It climbed from 33,000 metric tons in 1861 to a high of 52,000 metric tons in 1875. This figure represented over one-third of world production. A gradual decline began, however, so that by 1890 production had dropped to 26,000 tons, or approximately 15 percent of world production. As high-grade ores ran out and the price declined, entrepreneurs searched for other mining investments.

Nitrates

The great attraction became nitrates. These mineral salts, which occur naturally in the Atacama Desert, have a high nitrogen content useful for making fertilizer or gunpowder. Although the majority of the nitrates were located in Peru and Bolivia, Chilean firms gained franchises to operate in the two countries. In the 1870s the firms employed fewer than 3,000 workers to produce approximately 200,000 metric tons of nitrates. Then in 1879, the War of the Pacific enabled Chile to annex both the Bolivian and Peruvian nitrate fields. By the end of the 1880s approximately 12,000 workers produced nearly 1,000,000 metric tons. This represented a value of $23,000,000 and more than half of the nation's exports.

Modern technology, driven by international demand, enabled Chileans to radically transform their traditional mining system. A law in 1857 encouraged the creation of joint stock companies to mine, build smelters, and construct railroads.

Entrepreneur José Tomás de Urmeneta used a combination of the new corporate model and technology to develop the Tamaya mine. To do so he needed to transport minerals, coal, lumber, and supplies on a scale never faced previously by a Chilean mine owner. He began in 1856 with traditional methods, for example, when he built a toll road for oxcarts. When this proved insufficient to handle his production volume, he convinced investors to invest 700,000 pesos in the stock of a railroad planned between the mine and the port of Tongoy. By 1867 the railroad was operating and carrying over 50,000 metric tons of cargo yearly.

The investments, like those of Urmeneta, transformed the lives of all those involved in mining. Rather than live near the mines, owners of large-scale operations hired professional administrators to supervise the daily operations. The owners operated out of offices in Valparaíso or Santiago where they handled the commercial and financial aspects of the business. Urmeneta employed a general administrator who oversaw the Tamaya business office, an engineer who designed the tunnels and supervised the mining, and another engineer who assayed the ores. His administrative staff was cosmopolitan, consisting of Chilean, British, North American, and German supervisors.

Mine workers were now specialized with one group handling explosives, another breaking up the ore, and another loading it. Steam engines propelled cars that hauled the ores from the mine to men who sorted them by hand. Urmeneta later eliminated this labor-intensive work and installed a cable car to carry the ore straight from the mine to the railroad cars.

Mine Workers

Urmeneta employed as many as 1,500 men at the Tamaya mine. Although his workforce was largely Chilean, he also brought in some Welshmen. Miners and their families formed a company town, which was larger than many farm towns. Later during the nitrate boom of the 1870s, mining camps grew even larger. Typically employers paid their workers in script, a substitute for money, which workers used to purchase supplies at the *pulpería* or company store. Their homes were made of adobe with metal roofs. They had no running water or sewers, a common deficiency suffered by the working class in major urban areas also. Tuberculosis was rampant and periodic small pox and cholera epidemics took heavy tolls.

The attraction of mining jobs, with the illusion of steady employment, encouraged floating rural workers to migrate north. Urban workers believed that mining jobs offered higher pay. Mine owners frequently paid the boat fare to transport workers from the Valle Central. When economic crises periodically left many miners out of work with no alternative employment, workers became destitute. To combat unemployment, poor working conditions, and low salaries, some foreign workers, especially Spaniards, campaigned to form labor organizations. By 1890 their efforts achieved success. As a sharp recession hit, mine workers helped stage the first national strike.

The worst working conditions were those in the coal industry. Most of these mines were located on the south coast, with some tunnels actually extending under the ocean. Often standing in water as they worked, miners risked their lives to floods, explosions, and cave-ins. Instead of receiving their salary in money, they were paid with script that they spent at *pulperías*. Much of their diet consisted of fish and shellfish. Nearby vineyards and orchards supplied them with cheap wine and hard cider.

They lived with their families in precarious shacks perched on hills and linked by dirt footpaths. After observing these miners' tragic lives, Baldomero Lillo wrote a testimony to them in his stories, later published as *Under the Earth*. His narratives initiated a literature of social protest that awakened Chileans to the harsh reality of miners' lives.

Border Issues

Chilean and foreign firms operating in Chile aggressively sought to invest in the mines in neighboring countries. With borders somewhat undefined, sovereignty emerged. In the case of its northern border, in 1866 Chile made an agreement with Bolivia that 24° south latitude would be the official division between their nations. Although Chilean prospectors shortly thereafter found silver north of this border, without major conflict Boliva granted them franchises to develop the mines. But when other miners discovered nitrates in Bolivian territory and negotiated similar franchises, new issues emerged.

To exploit these nitrates, Chilean and British investors, along with some members of Chile's congress, created the Antofagasta Nitrate and Railroad Company. This firm then obtained a Bolivian franchise. The company seemed unconcerned with the sovereignty of this area; rather, their objective was to keep down taxes. Chilean diplomats seemingly resolved this concern in 1874 through a treaty. According to this agreement Chile ceded all rights to the region in return for no future nitrate tax increases.

Chileans not only invested in Bolivian nitrate mines but in Peruvian ones as well. The two countries, fearful of the spread of Chilean influence, signed a secret mutual-defense treaty in 1873. Two years later, in hopes of controlling nitrate prices in the volatile international market, the Peruvian government nationalized all the mines in its territory. As compensation to the companies, the government gave them interest-bearing certificates.

Although the government's intention was to pay the certificate holders in two years, it lacked the money to do so. As a result the certificates' value dropped sharply and speculators traded them at sharp discounts. Some certificate owners, believing that a change in sovereignty would restore their lost mines, pressured the Chilean government to intervene, but it did not.

While Chile negotiated with Bolivia to the north, issues with Argentina threatened to the east. Both Chile and Argentina claimed large sections of Patagonia. In 1878 the Chilean representative, Diego Barros Arana, agreed with his counterpart to define the border with Argentina using the Andean peaks and the Atlantic and Pacific watersheds. The Chilean public, who wanted all of Patagonia, decried this agreement as a sellout, but northern tensions with Bolivia and Peru obliged the country to accept it.

War of the Pacific

Bolivia's instability soon precipitated a conflict with Chile. In 1878 Bolivian general Hilarión Daza overthrew his government. He rejected his country's previous agreement with Chile and raised the tax on the Antofagasta Company's nitrate exports. The company refused to pay, confident that the Chilean government would force Daza to rescind his decision. This confrontation, however, quickly escalated as Bolivia embargoed the company's machinery. Chile retaliated by invading the Bolivian port of Antofagasta. Out of desperation, Bolivia declared war and attempted to expel all Chileans from its territory. Peru initially offered to mediate the conflict, but when Chile discovered that Peru and Bolivia had a mutual defense treaty, it declared war on Peru.

Soon named the War of the Pacific, this conflict took place in one of the driest places on earth. The landscape is not rolling desert sands, but bluffs, escarpments, dry valleys, pampas, and salt flats. Since the strategic points were mostly ports, a strong navy represented a decisive advantage. Ships transported soldiers between distant coastal battlefields and they blockaded and bombarded the enemy's ports. In this conflict, Bolivia had a tremendous disadvantage because it had no navy. Both Chile and Peru had small navies, with the latter having a slight advantage. The Chilean merchant marine, however, was considerably larger, which proved valuable in transporting men and supplies.

The combined Peruvian and Bolivian armies quadrupled that of Chile, yet the two countries had trouble mobilizing and supplying their troops. Neither country had a truly national economy. The mostly indigenous population of both nations was poorly integrated into national life and could not offer much help in an international conflict. Chile, by comparison, had a mobile workforce, which could be converted to soldiers in wartime. Its railroad and shipping network had integrated the society and the economy. The civilian-led political system was stable and could generate the resources to supply its armed forces.

With almost no resistance, Chilean soldiers quickly occupied the entire territory of Antofagasta. Bolivia was unable to counterattack because of the barrier that the Andes represented between the interior and the coast. As Chile took effective control of the land, in 1879 two naval battles determined the control of the Pacific. On May 21, off the coast of Iquique, the Peruvian ironclad, *Huáascar,* rammed Chile's wooden vessel, the *Esmeralda.* Before the Chilean ship sunk, Captain Arturo Prat stormed the *Húascar's* deck and was shot and killed. His martyrdom soon became a patriotic symbol, not only during the War of the Pacific, but for generations of Chilean school children. In this battle the Peruvians suffered a grave loss of the ironclad vessel, the *Independencia.* In October, in a second battle, the Chileans succeeded in boarding both the *Húascar* and the *Pilcomayo* after heavy shelling. When these two ships surrendered, the Peruvians were left without a navy, enabling Chile to move troops up and down the coast and blockade Peruvian ports with virtually no opposition.

The next month the war shifted inland as Chile landed 9,500 troops at the Peruvian port of Pisagua. Peru had an army south of the port and Bolivia had one to the north, so the two armies had an opportunity to box the Chileans in, but they failed to do so. By the end of July 1880, the Chileans defeated or forced all Peruvian and Bolivian troops to withdraw north to Tacna. In the crucial Battle of Arica, Chilean troops stormed the highly fortified *Morro,* and in less than an hour dislodged 2,000 Peruvian soldiers. The victory completed Chile's conquest of the nitrate region and added another page of patriotism to Chilean school textbooks. It also prompted the United States and England to offer mediation, but when Peru learned of Chile's territorial demands, it rejected the gesture.

Chilean politicians and the public played an important part in the war even though they were distant from the battle lines. Political factions wanted commander appointments for their leaders in order to increase their popularity for the next election. Incompetent leadership resulted from this political intrigue, yet Chile was victorious. For rank-and-file Chileans, the *roto chileno,* or Chilean worker, won the battles, not the generals. Although the army impressed the *rotos* into service and then mistreated them, out of patriotism the workers fought anyway. A legend developed that they raised their bravado before battle by drinking *la chupilca del Diablo,* a devilish mixture of gunpowder and wine.

Public pressure as well as expansionist ambitions pushed the war farther north. The Chilean president, Aníbal Pinto, ordered his commander,
Manuel Baquedano, to take Lima. Troop reinforcements brought the number of Chilean soldiers up to 25,000. Peru had an even larger number of
troops defending their capital, but to no avail. In January 1881 the Chileans overran the Peruvian lines at the battles of Chorrillos and Miraflores
and the city surrendered. No Peruvian was ready to cede national territory,
so for two years the country resorted to guerrilla actions as a desperate
defense. In the meantime, Chile signed an agreement with Argentina in
1881 to eliminate any risk of war with this neighbor. Two years later Peru
made the bitter decision to concede territory to Chile in order to rid itself
of the occupying army. In October 1883 it signed the Treaty of Ancón in
which it relinquished the territory of Tarapacá and consented that Chile
govern Tacna and Arica for ten years until a plebiscite determined the
sovereignty of the provinces. In the case of Bolivia, Chile exercised de
facto control over Antofagasta until years later when it officially ceded
the province to Chile. Tragically Bolivia became landlocked.

The War of the Pacific not only expanded Chile's territory by one-third,
but it also added a region that supplied enormous wealth. The question
now was who would exploit this wealth? The Chilean government could
have taken over the nationalized Peruvian mines, paid off the certificate
holders, and run the mines as a state monopoly. For a variety of reasons,
however, it chose not to do so. Some Chilean politicians had investments
in the Antofagasta Nitrate and Railroad Company, and they did not want
it to compete with a state company. The government also had war debts
and was hesitant to assume the financial obligation of nitrate certificates.
Also, Chile wanted to deflate European opposition to its annexation of
Bolivian and Peruvian territory. Its offer to return the nitrate properties
to the certificate holders created strong support, especially among British
and French investors. Though in the 1880s the decision seemed reasonable,
later politicians and historians strongly criticized their leaders' decision
to turn the nitrate mines over to private owners rather than nationalize
them. It retrospect, as mostly foreign firms developed the nitrate mines,
to many Chileans it seemed that they had fought the War of the Pacific
on behalf of these companies.

John Thomas North

One British citizen, John Thomas North, soon became the Nitrate King.
He began his career in Chile as an engineer, but later established himself

in Iquique as an importer, proprietor of a water works, and a ship owner. When the War of the Pacific began, he lost a ship and his waterworks was damaged, but he made valuable friends. One was a Chilean admiral, Patricio Lynch, who later supported some of North's business ventures. Two British citizens helped him as well. Robert Harvey, who had worked in nitrates for the Peruvian government, enabled him to identify the best nitrate fields in Tarapacá, and John Dawson, a banker, opened up access to capital. During the war, when the price dropped on Peruvian nitrate certificates, North used Harvey's knowledge and Dawson's banking connection to buy the certificates on credit. For this speculation to succeed depended on Chile's decision to turn nitrate properties over to certificate holders after the war. Perhaps he lobbied influential Chilean friends to that effect; the record is not clear. In any case, in anticipation of a favorable policy, he bought very cheaply the certificates of the most valuable nitrate fields in Tarapacá.

North also needed to buy machinery, employ workers, and transport the nitrates to market. For this purpose, he returned to England to raise capital. In February 1883 he convinced a former business acquaintance to help him create the Liverpool Nitrate Company. He took this risky step eight months before Peru officially ceded Tarapacá to Chile. With money raised from stock sales, he bought boilers, steam engines, and pumps. Robert Harvey, along with other contracted English engineers, then sailed to Chile to set up this nitrate processing machinery, while North chose to remain in England and handle the company's financial affairs. By 1884 they had everything installed and were producing 3,000 tons of nitrates a month.

The company proved a success. It paid annual dividends of 20 percent or more until 1886 when North and his partners liquidated it to found other companies. As the stock prices of the new firms soared, he sold some of his holding to invest in other ventures. One was the Nitrate Railway Company, which for a decade had a monopoly on the rail transport of nitrates in Tarapacá. He developed a similar monopoly over Iquique's water supply. When other entrepreneurs tried to develop competing companies, he hired lawyers to block them in both the courts and congress. So flagrant were North's manipulations that even the Chilean president, Manuel Balmaceda, came out against him. Under pressure to enact reform, the congress adopted measures to undercut North's monopoly and restore competition. Eventually North's speculative ventures unraveled in Chile and Great Britain, but not before he thoroughly enjoyed his tenure as "Nitrate King."

Nitrate Production and Tax Revenue

The demand for nitrates continued to grow, as did production, but the two were not always in sync. Between 1886 and 1889, for example, nitrate production doubled from 1,000,000 to 2,000,000 metric tons. Then a recession hit and the price dropped by half. During such recessions nitrate prices dropped below profitability. Producers tried to solve the problem by forming a cartel to restrict production and drive up prices. Then when the market recovered and prices rose, the cartel dissolved.

After the War of the Pacific, the Chilean government's fortunes closely followed those of nitrates. Between 1878 and 1882 it increased the export tax from 4.00 to 22.00 pesos a metric ton. This boosted customs revenue during the period from 6,000,000 to 29,000,000 pesos. The government became so affluent that it cut both land and income taxes. In effect this eliminated most taxes on farming. The periodic downturns in nitrate production, however, reminded leaders how dependent the country's finances were on one product. Sharp tensions then occurred between the nitrate producers, who tried to curtail output, and the government, which tried to increase it. With the tax on the volume of exports, not the price, whenever the cartel curtailed output the government lost money. Unable to solve this problem, the government cut expenses or printed money. As the latter became increasingly common, the Chilean peso lost value relative to stronger currencies and inflation became rampant.

Changes in the Sur

The War of the Pacific affected many other aspects of national life quite distant from the nitrate fields. The Mapuche in the south, who had resisted conquest for over three centuries, lost their autonomy in the 1870s. Even before this decade, their isolation had already eroded as they increasingly engaged trade. They sold cattle and hand-woven textiles to Chilean merchants and bought ironware, cloth, and trinkets. Although they became familiar with money and markets, they held land communally, with no sense of land ownership or property transactions.

For some time Chilean leaders had designed strategies to occupy Mapuche territory. In the 1850s Colonel Cornelio Saavedra drew up a plan to build forts and advance the government's control southward, eventually encircling Mapuche territory. In 1862 while establishing three forts, Saavedra ran into one of the most bizarre figures in Chilean history. He encountered a Frenchman, Orélie-Antoine de Toumens, who alleged himself to be "King of Araucanía and Patagonia." Although de Toumens had convinced some local Mapuche tribes to recognize him as their leader, Saavedra was unimpressed. He arrested the intruder and turned him over to Chilean officials, who declared him mad. Seeking to avoid an international incident, they consigned him to the French diplomatic representatives, who with much embarrassment and apology shipped him home. De Toumens's delusions of grandeur persisted, and he tried repeatedly to slip back into Chile. When he died, he conferred his royal title to his descendents, who, with better judgment, did not pursue the issue.

With the French pretender gone, Saavedra completed the encirclement of Arauco with forts. The Mapuche struck back briefly in 1868, but later agreed to a truce. They made a grave miscalculation and rebelled again during the War of the Pacific. After the conquest of Lima, Chilean officials decided to dispatch some of the army south to complete Saavedra's plan. In 1881 and 1882 the military built forts on the sites of Imperial and Villarrica, which the Mapuche had destroyed almost three centuries earlier. These forts were supported by others and controlled strategic points of the region.

In contrast to an earlier era, modern transportation now tied these forts to the towns and cities of the Valle Central. In the 1870s the railroad reached the edge of Mapuche territory. A deep canyon in Malleco temporarily halted its southern advance, but after the construction of an impressive steel bridge, in 1893 the line reached Temuco in the Mapuche heartland. Telegraph lines, surveyors, land speculators, and squatters followed. The Chilean government declared that all Mapuche lands belonged to the state, setting off a frenzied land grab. Officials distributed the majority of lands to men who formed large haciendas, but in the least fertile areas they did allocate some homesteads to landless peasants from the Valle Central. Also, the government sponsored European immigration, which brought approximately 10,000 Germans, Swiss, Italians, and Frenchmen to the region. The overwhelmed Mapuche, unprepared to negotiate with surveyors and notary publics, lost most of their lands. They continued some trade, but with their cattle lands sharply curtailed, their herds dwindled.

Agricultural Expansion

An important motivation behind the rush for Mapuche lands was that Chilean agriculture was rapidly expanding into overseas markets. From a value of approximately 4,000,000 pesos a year in exports in the early 1860s, this amount more than doubled by the end of the decade. This trend continued in the 1870s, reaching an all time high of almost 16,000,000 pesos in 1874. In that year, for the first and last time in Chilean history, the value of agricultural exports nearly equaled that of mining. The following decade agricultural exports declined, but recuperated somewhat in the 1890s. The world price of cereals declined in the 1880s, and only countries that cut their costs through new technology could compete. Unfortunately, in this period few Chileans acquired threshing machines or modern flour mills. They were, therefore, increasingly limited to the national market.

A growing number of urban consumers demanded more fresh meat. In response Chilean hacendados improved their herds and imported cattle from Argentina. Another lucrative farm activity was making wine and *aguardiente,* a grape brandy. Consumption of wine from 1875 to the end of the century more than tripled, to 90 liters per capita. Originally hacendados paid no tax on liquor production, but during a recession in nitrate revenue, congress begrudgingly imposed a tax on spirits. Just as North American farmers had once indignantly opposed a whisky tax, the Chilean hacendados reacted with similar emotions. They did not organize an armed uprising, but some were tempted. In a climactic episode in Eduardo Barrios's novel, *Gran señor y rajadiablos,* a hacienda owner, José Pedro, staged a one-man rebellion. When revenue agents entered his land, rather than pay a liquor tax he took an axe to his still, uprooted his vineyard, and shot the agents.

Urban versus Rural Living

The hacendados increasingly gave up the pastoral life of their estates to enjoy the cosmopolitan life of Santiago. Not only did the city offer hacendados more interaction with people of their own class, but it offered economic opportunities as well. In Santiago they could invest in urban property, banks, insurance companies, and mining firms. As hacendados diversified, their estates became only one of various business ventures, which they managed from the capital. Often through the land mortgage bank, they obtained credit to speculate in other ventures. As the commercial side of farming became more important, they followed grain and beef prices more closely than was possible on their estates. New transportation links facilitated this commercialization as railroad lines extended south and lowered shipping costs.

Living in the city enabled hacendados to oversee their sons' and daughters' education. They usually enrolled them in a religious order's elementary and secondary school. Only the boys continued on to college, frequently studying law at the Instituto Nacional. Santiago also offered receptions, dances, and theater performances where the elite developed a circle of friends and met their future spouses. In the summer families returned to the hacienda where they competed in rodeos, danced the *cueca*, or folkdance, and entertained relatives and friends. Hacendado families tried to maintain these rural ties while becoming increasingly cosmopolitan. Inheritance problems and financial necessity, however, caused many descendents to sell their land and become exclusively urban professionals.

While hacienda families loosened their ties to the land, hacienda workers remained firmly tied to it. They saw only the shadows of Chile's modernization. As the railroad approached, they drove cattle or hauled grain a short distance to the railhead. They devoted more time to grain, alfalfa, and fattening the cattle than to riding the range. Rarely did they have a chance to operate machinery because few farms owned any. Due to low worker salaries, most hacendados had little incentive to buy machinery and save on labor costs. Although marketing changed in rural Chile, everyday life on the hacienda did not. One generation after another depended totally on the will of the patron or his administrator. With primary schooling being unavailable on the hacienda, the workers' children remained illiterate. Less than 20 percent of Chilean children attended school, and those who did usually lived in urban areas.

The Origins of Industry

While change occurred slowly in agricultural areas, cities witnessed the beginning of manufacturing. From the beginning industry competed with imports and with local artisan ware. The value that industries added to raw materials such as hides, grain, and fruit contributed to the growth of national income. Sometimes local industry brought foreign raw products to be processed locally. For example, Julio Bernstein imported raw sugar from Peru and Brazil and refined it in his Viña del Mar factory for the national market.

Railroad construction stimulated local industry. Between 1860 and the War of the Pacific Chileans built over 1000 km of railroads. Half of these were private mining railroads in the north, while the other half were government owned, dual-purpose passenger and commercial lines. Originally the rails and rolling stock were imported, but later Valparaíso and Santiago industries supplied some of these materials. Unfortunately Chile had to import the iron and steel for this purpose because it did not yet have its own iron smelters or steel mills. The national lumber industry sawed thousands of railroad ties, although many were imported from Oregon and Washington.

Most of the machinery for Chilean industry was imported. Bernstein, Urmeneta, and North imported steam engines, boilers, and grinders from England and the United States. Railroad contractors like Henry Meiggs, even when they worked for the Chilean government, imported most of their rails and rolling stock. Chile did have various foundries and machine shops, but they did not produce machinery on a scale capable of transforming the country into an industrial nation. The industries remained small islands of modern production within an economy devoted to mining, agriculture, and commerce.

There was no official policy to promote industry; however, public policy played an important role in shaping the economy. Though free trade was the official policy and had the support of the visiting French economist Jean Gustave Courcelle-Seneuil, nevertheless there were important exceptions to this policy. Railroad, steamship, and industrial entrepreneurs constantly petitioned the government for exclusive franchises that prohibited competition with their firm for a specified period. John North, for example, enjoyed two state-sanctioned monopolies in Iquique. And Julio Bernstein enjoyed a similar one for his Viña del Mar sugar refinery. In addition to this direct state support, there was an indirect one as well. According to Chilean economic historian Gabriel Palma, when the government printed money to solve its budget woes, the national currency lost value and imports became more expensive. Chileans therefore found national goods cheaper than imported ones. Consciously or unconsciously, by devaluing the peso, policy makers encouraged the initial stage of industrialization.

POLITICAL ISSUES

Liberals versus Conservatives

Interestingly enough there was greater controversy over religious issues than economic ones. The Liberal Party policy was to separate the church and state, especially regarding marriages and birth records. Influential Masonic leaders wanted to liberate people from church control by granting the state authority to perform marriages and record births. A third measure on the Liberal agenda was the secularization of cemeteries. Not surprisingly, the staunch church supporters in the Conservative Party viewed the Liberal's proposals as atheistic and a corruption of the nation's Catholic identity.

For the Liberals to pass their program, they had to build coalitions in a three-party system that emerged in the 1860s. The Radical Party, with strong ties to the Masonic movement, was a natural ally. It attracted professionals, some hacienda owners, and men of new wealth who enthusiastically supported a secular state. In a complex three-party system the president increasingly had trouble disciplining the members of his own party. The electoral reforms of 1874, which allowed all literate males to vote and gave more local control over voting, weakened presidential control over congress. Within four years after this bill passed, the number of voters had tripled as well as encouraged more candidates to run for office. An unforeseen result was that candidates spent large personal resources purchasing votes for their election. As a result, even when candidates belonged to the president's party, they did not owe him their election.

Political alliances were highly volatile. The Liberal Party divided, with some members allying with the Conservatives and others with the Radicals. In this struggle for political advantage, surprisingly enough, Radical Party legislators often made tactical alliances with the Conservatives. In spite of shifting coalitions, when Liberal Domingo Santa María became president in 1881, he believed that he could muster enough votes to secularize marriage, birth registry, and cemeteries. To accomplish this daunting task, he called on his interior minister, José Manuel Balmaceda. The latter fulfilled Santa María's expectations, but he had to manipulate elections and distribute political patronage to a degree that offended Conservatives, Radicals, and even some Liberals. Santa María rewarded Balmaceda for his efforts with the Liberal nomination for president. Yet when Balmaceda was elected, he had to deal with the animosity he created during the past administration.

Balmaceda's Troubles

Before becoming president, Balmaceda served in congress for more than twenty years and represented his country in international relations. He also had experience using the press and public forums to push for reforms. After his election, in a gesture to diffuse some of the Conservative Party's hostility, he accepted the church's candidate for archbishop, Mariano Casanova, and selected a cabinet that brought together Liberal and Radical factions. Within two months, however, congress censored his cabinet and forced him to put together a second one. This was the beginning of his difficulties.

The economy was booming at the beginning of Balmaceda's administration. Due to a bonanza in nitrate exports, government income increased from 37,000,000 pesos in 1886 to 53,000,000 pesos in 1890. With the government's credit strong, he decided to borrow 30,000,000 pesos from foreign banks and 23,000,000 pesos from local investors to begin a record building spree. Public works included bridges, viaducts, 1,000 kilometers of railroad, telegraph lines, hospitals, schools, wharves, and even jails. He gave Santiago a facelift, constructing ministry buildings, a medical school, a military school, an art school, and a canal for the Mapocho River. To coordinate all the projects, he created a new ministry of public works in 1887. He also doled out political patronage, which fueled tenacious opposition rather than strengthening his leadership. The competition for patronage encouraged coalitions with the opposition rather than a submission to party discipline. As spending soared, so did the public debt, which prompted some legislators to question Balmaceda's fiscal control.

When an economic recession hit in 1890, congress prevented Balmaceda from acting. When it censured his cabinet, he became so incensed that he refused to negotiate new cabinet appointments. Congress then refused to pass his appropriations bill. In January 1891, he decreed that if congress refused to act, he would use the previous year's budget. Congress fought back and declared him in violation of the constitution. It then persuaded naval officer Jorge Montt to take over the northern customs house, which supplied the majority of the nation's revenue. Not to be outdone, Balmaceda won the army over to his side. Tragically, the two branches of the armed forces then fought each other. The navy's control of northern nitrate revenue and the intervention of German military advisor General Emil Körner on behalf of congress proved decisive in defeating the army. When Balmaceda realized that he had lost, he took refuge in the Argentine embassy. On the day his term expired, September 18, 1891, he committed suicide. while his supporters lamented his death, they considered his act heroic.

Balmaceda's death closed an era. Between 1861 and 1891 the Chilean government had gone from a small, frugal institution to a wealthy corporation. It was the engine of national progress. To be a member of congress, a minister, or president no longer meant just service, rather, it meant an opportunity to participate in wealth. Although government salaries were unimpressive, contracts, commissions, and legal fees were attractive. More importantly, the investment information available to those within government offered many avenues for enrichment. Chilean government was less corrupt than in many nations experiencing such affluence, but leaders understandably participated in the business opportunities surrounding them.

The growing Chilean state faced many challenges. The balance of power among parties and branches of government shifted toward congress and away from the president. This diversification of power presented the opportunity for middle- and working-class leaders to win congressional seats and address their problems. While the number of those participating in power broadened, the source of national wealth narrowed. Excessive dependence on nitrates made the entire nation vulnerable to the demand of one product. A difficult question ahead was whether Chile could broaden both political participation and national wealth.

6

New Classes and Conflicts, 1891–1925

When congress won the Civil War of 1891, the domination it established over the president consolidated parliamentary power. The elite used congress to further their own goals, but they formed coalitions with new groups that broadened their participation in public life. The developing economy fortified the middle and working classes who then demanded a voice in national politics. Leaders from these classes formed professional and labor organizations, created new political parties, and elected representatives to congress. Through education and expanded voter rights they shaped policies undaunted by recurring crises that undercut prosperity and slashed government budgets.

Rather than develop a comprehensive solution to the national problems, political parties more often quarreled and concerned themselves with the spoils of office. When strong Liberal leadership emerged in the 1920s, the opposition blocked its reforms. Frustrated that the politicians failed to act, the military stepped in and shut down congress. Later, when a civilian government returned to power, the president imposed a new constitution that shifted power from congress to the executive, officially ending the parliamentary era. Middle- and working-class Chileans hoped the new political system would respond more to their needs. Difficult times during the next decade tested the system's ability to fulfill the needs of these groups.

SOCIAL CHANGES

Demographic Trends

Between 1891 and 1925 Chile's population grew by approximately 61 percent, from 2,600,000 to 4,200,000. This growth, however, was uneven. Santiago's population more than doubled in size from 275,000 in 1891 to 650,000 in 1925. The urban mining region of the Norte Grande experienced a similar growth, from 180,000 to 350,000 inhabitants. The percentage of people living in cities grew from 20 to 30 percent. By contrast, in the rural area of large haciendas in the Valle Central, there was little growth. The only rural area with impressive growth was the newly settled Sur. Yet most of the towns in this region were stagnant as well. With few new jobs, many of the youth migrated to the cities.

The cities did create employment opportunities. Here middle and working classes developed that began to rival the elite. While the middle class tried to take over elite institutions, labor organized and bargained for increased benefits. The great contribution of the parliamentary system, according to Chilean historian Ricardo Krebs, was that the middle class rose to power without a revolution. Initially the Chilean elite class allied itself with the middle class in order to reinforce its own power. In contrast to labor, however, the middle class was not a cohesive group with a single ideology. They represented a diversity of wealth, professions, and political inclinations. Partly due to this diversity, the elite viewed at least some of the middle class as allies with the expectation that they would support rather than challenge their power.

With the rise of labor unions, the middle class could ally with the workers if they tired of compromising with the elite. Populist middle-class politicians such as Arturo Alessandri made such an alliance. Later, in the 1930s and 1940s, the middle class formed a coalition with labor called the Popular Front. As long as middle-class leaders ran the coalition and established its priorities, this alliance prospered, but when labor took over the leadership and threatened middle-class interests, the alliance disintegrated.

THE RISE OF THE MIDDLE CLASS

The development of the middle class in Chile differs somewhat from that in Europe and the United States. Modest shopkeepers and government employees initiated this class in the decades following independence. Successful merchants and mine owners were absorbed by the elite, while those of modest means added additional support to the middle class. After 1850 the rise of industrial entrepreneurs and professionals reinforced this class. By contrast, very few farmers belonged to the middle class. Only in the Sur did immigrants and Chilean homesteaders successfully create a modest middle-class farming group. The growth of government after the War of the Pacific added an important group of state employees to the middle class. Whereas in 1875 the government employed 2,500, in 1900 this rose to 5,500, and by 1925, to 26,500. Many, if not all of these employees, identified with the middle class even if their income was significantly less than that of merchants or professionals. Although these heterogeneous origins of the middle class inhibited unity, an identity gradually evolved that sometimes coalesced in times of crisis.

The advance of the middle class depended on the growth of educational institutions. By 1891 total school enrollment was only 80,000 students and national literacy was less than 30 percent. By 1900 enrollment had more than doubled to 170,000, and by 1920 it reached nearly 400,000. By this latter date, approximately 50 percent of the population was literate. In 1920, congress made the first four years of primary school obligatory. Slower enrollment growth occurred in secondary education. In 1900 less than 10 percent of total school enrollment was at the secondary level, and in 1920 this figure had not appreciably improved. Not surprisingly, university enrollment was also low. In 1920 only 4,000 attended college, a figure representing a mere 1 percent of those enrolled in elementary and secondary schools.

A potential for larger university enrollments developed during this period. In 1888 the Catholic Church decided to offer an alternative to secular higher education when it founded Universidad Católica de Chile. In 1919 the government founded the Universidad de Concepción, the first institution of higher education established outside of the national capital. Now students in the Sur had a greater opportunity to pursue professional careers. From this college's inception, the Radical Party and the Masons controlled its administration. These two interlocking groups created an institution that was far more critical of the status quo than the two existing universities in Santiago.

The middle class supported the growth of secondary and university enrollments. In 1906 the students formed an association called the Federación de Estudiantes Chilenos (Chilean Student Federation), or FECH, which focused on middle-class issues. As labor activism underscored national social problems, the FECH increasingly joined with workers in their strikes and protests. But the FECH, like government employees' unions, had a problem of class alliance. Should it ally itself with unions, increasingly dominated by the communists, or should it ally itself with the middle class, with its ambiguous relationship with the elite? In recognition of the importance of student politics, parties of all persuasions cultivated student leaders and intervened in their elections to gain control of the FECH.

The rising educational level of the middle class enabled it to play a dominant roll in the nation's intellectual and political life. By 1920 many engineers, lawyers, writers, historians, and artists came from this middle-class background. The values that they expressed in their works represent their status. Sometimes these values were openly hostile to the elite, but more often they reflected accommodation. Although often critical of upper class mismanagement, the middle class believed in a gradual, rather than a revolutionary, change.

There are numerous examples of the middle-class gradualist approach. One of the most interesting examples is found within the changing leadership of the Radical Party. Originally, wealthy mine owners and merchants dominated the party, but gradually middle-class professionals and government employees transformed it. The elite welcomed the new members because they contributed to the party's rising fortunes. In 1891 the party had the smallest number of representatives in the House of Deputies with only 23 deputies. By 1924, they had the largest with 42. How could upper-class members of the party complain about such success although the party leadership became increasingly middle class.

The Radicals believed in an academically rigorous educational system with little or no church participation. They did not push for universal education as did working-class parties. Their strong educational commitment attracted many teachers. When they formed the Primary Schoolteachers' Society in 1915 and the General Teachers' Association in 1922, these organizations affiliated with the party. Following the teachers' example other public employees recognized the importance of organizing a union. In 1925 the chaotic public employment situation created by party politics and the military led public employees to establish the Unión de Empleados de Chile (Union of Chilean Employees), or UECH, which loosely allied itself with the Radical Party. They fought for contracts and social-security benefits. They also lobbied for an eight-hour day and a minimum wage. Although some of these issues were similar to those of blue-collar workers, public employees cherished their middle-class identity and rejected overtures to join the Communist-dominated federation of unions.

In Chile belonging to a party was as much a social as a political experience. The Radical Party fully understood this social function and developed clubs in most urban areas. In these clubs members could drink and dine with friends in addition to participating in political activities. By 1920 the rank-and-file members of the middle class dominated the clubs' social life. That year the Party endorsed the Liberal Party presidential candidate, Arturo Alessandri, who himself was a highly successful professional with a middle-class political agenda. While many of the Radical Party's congressional candidates came from a similar background, Conservative and Liberal party candidates were more often drawn from the elite.

In the economic sphere, the Radical Party supported laissez faire and private enterprise in theory, but in practice it aggressively sought to expand government services. Public employees appreciated this political position and often lent the party their support. With the influx of both educators and government employees into the party, leadership shifted toward the middle class.

This group also inserted itself into professional organizations dominated by the elite. In the case of the Institute of Chilean Engineers, founded in 1888, the organization included both middle- and upper-class professionals. Although its journal addressed both technical and policy issues, an early twentieth century article on scientific management fused the two criteria. To run government agencies efficiently, it urged that administrative principles, rather than political criteria, be used. To accomplish this objective, numerous engineers ran for congress, served as ministers, or ran public agencies. In 1915 five engineers were elected to senate seats and eight to deputy seats. Miguel Letelier and Francisco Mardones, two leading engineers, headed up ministries from 1921 to 1924. Not surprisingly, once in power they espoused a more technocratic approach to public administration.

Chilean engineers were drawn into politics more so than in many other nations because so many worked for the state. The largest employer of engineers was the government-owned National Railway Company. The engineers campaigned to de-politicize the National Railway Company and convert it into a public corporation. They believed that they could eliminate waste and make the system run profitably. Engineers were also prominent in the Ministry of Public Works and the military where they emphasized that education, not political criteria, should be used for placement and promotion.

Engineers became increasingly eager to apply their knowledge to social and political reform. In 1916 the council of the Institute voiced impatience with political bickering and urged reform. Eight years later the military overthrew the civil government and offered engineers new leadership roles. Francisco Mardones was named Minister of the Interior, the most important cabinet position. Two years later Colonel Carlos Ibáñez's government gave engineers an even stronger ministerial role.

In addition to the growing influence of middle-class engineers in national life, other middle-class professionals found ways to extend their influence. Lawyers, doctors, dentists, pharmacists, accountants, and architects also formed professional organizations.

Due to the diverse party affiliation of their members, these organizations originally avoided political commitments. When the crises of the 1920s and 1930s hit, however, the organizations took positions on issues as well as candidates. Although they were not as visible as labor unions, they had greater access to power and influence.

Another organization in which the middle class exercised power was the Masons. Aware of its role in national politics, aspiring leaders joined the Masons. The great majority of Liberal and Radical party members were Masons. A less political organization, but very influential one on the local level, was the volunteer fire department or Club de Bomberos. Every town of any significance had a Bombero organization that brought people together, often of middle-class status, to discuss common issues and politics.

The Sociedad Nacional de Agricultura (National Agricultural Society) was one organization in which the middle class never gained much influence. This organization served as a forum for elite hacienda or *fundo* owners as well as a lobby for their interests. In the cities the Sociedad de Fomento Fabril (Industrial Development Society), or SFF, served a similar purpose. This was composed of both elite and middle-class manufacturers. Over half of the members were foreign born. Other employer associations were founded in the 1920s including the Cámara de Comercio (Chamber of Commerce). These groups lobbied the government for special recognition, but they also coordinated their opposition to labor demands. Few of the members of these organizations could be considered part of the elite. Many were affluent members of the middle class, but they lacked the pedigree and the land to be included among the upper class.

Upper-class women founded a number of organizations in this period, which soon had a majority of middle-class members. Some like the Club de Señoras (Women's Club) emphasized developing women's educational and cultural interests, while others like Acción Nacional de Mujeres de Chile (Women's National Action) emphasized women's rights and suffrage. Still others like the Asociación de Damas Protectoras del Obrero (Ladies Worker Protection Association) provided services and education to the poor. Whereas most of these organizations were secular, there were also women's religious organizations such as the Sociedad del Apostolado Popular (Popular Apostolic Society) and the women's auxiliary of the Salvation Army. Their social and missionary activities were directed toward working women and their families.

THE RISE OF THE WORKING CLASS

While the middle class exercised its growing influence through professional and social organizations, the working class likewise sought to expand its influence. Urban artisans formed mutual societies to protect themselves and their families in case of sickness, accident, or death. The societies also served as cooperatives and social organizations. By 1900 there were more than 200 organizations, and by 1925, over 700. Mining, construction, and industry created new jobs, and in 1925 approximately 25 percent of workers belonged to one of these three categories. The number of female workers grew very quickly especially in Santiago and Valparaíso. By 1920 they totaled more than 60,000 and made up over one-third of the labor force in the two cities. They engaged largely in domestic service but worked in manufacturing as well.

Chile's first unions began in the mining, railroad, urban transit, and typesetting industries. Their outlook was heavily influenced by anarcho-syndicalist ideas, which were brought into Chile by immigrants and foreign publications. The strong Spanish anarcho-syndicalist movement spread to Argentina, Cuba, Chile, and other Latin American republics. Members of this movement believed that government, institutions, and laws reflected elite values. Convinced that they could never reform government, the anarcho-syndicalists preferred to abolish it. Due to this conviction, anarcho-syndicalist labor groups originally refused to join political parties, nominate candidates, and vote in elections.

In 1887 the leaders who founded the Democratic Party took quite a different perspective. For the first time, labor and middle-class groups founded a party with no elite connections. Although it did not have the money that was available to other parties, its first member was elected to the House of Deputies in 1894. In 1924, after three decades of slow growth, the party reached 10 deputies and 4 senators. Although nationally it only received 8 percent of the votes, its showing in some areas was more impressive. In Santiago it received 21 percent of the votes; Concepción, 37 percent; and in Cautín, 100 percent. It also joined the Alliance, which supported Arturo Alessandri, the winning presidential candidate in 1920. After achieving success, however, the party gradually moved to the political right, forcing labor to look for a more representative party.

In 1909 mutualist labor groups founded the Federación de Obreros de Chile (Chilean Workers' Federation), or FOCH, with relatively conservative goals. Three years later Luis Emilio Recabarren organized the radical labor party Partido Obrero Socialista (Socialist Workers' Party). After the Russian Revolution, Recabarren sought to move both Chilean organizations in the same direction. He captured the leadership of the FOCH, steered it leftward, and mobilized support for his congressional election in 1921. The following year, under his leadership of the Partido Obrero Socialista, the party renamed itself the Communist Party. This party's domination of the FOCH drove out noncommunists such as the anarcho-syndicalists who rejected labor's participation in politics.

Labor relied on direct action rather than politics to force employers to increase their benefits. In 1890 northern workers struck at the nitrate and copper mines, and soon the southern coal miners joined in. Although there had been previous strikes, this was the first truly national one. The government mobilized troops while employers pretended to give in to the strikers' demands. Then, when workers returned to the job, employers cynically backed out of their agreements. The Valparaíso stevedores struck in 1903 and again 1907. Also in 1907 the Santiago workers staged an unsuccessful general strike, and tragically government troops killed striking workers and their families in the northern port of Iquique.

For a decade this repression intimidated labor, but after World War I when inflation cut the buying power of workers' salaries, they again took to the streets. Fearful of potential violence, the government declared a state of siege. A few years later, in 1921, a recession hit the nitrate industry an raised unemployment. In addition to using violence against protesting miners, the government shipped 20,000 of them to the south.

The recurring strikes emphasized the rising power of labor. Still, the great majority of workers remained unorganized. While nitrate, copper, and coal miners were unionized, farm laborers were not. Agricultural workers outnumbered industrial workers more than three to one. Even in Santiago and Valparaíso where there were over 175,000 workers in 1920, most did not belong to unions. Furthermore, conflicting political beliefs and rival federations divided the unionized industrial and mining workers. To bring labor together under one tent required a populist politician who could energize labor while de-emphasizing the differences between the groups. In 1918 such a charismatic politician, Arturo Alessandri, began a political career and attracted many labor votes. With their support he won a landslide victory in the northern province that gained him the nickname El León (the Lion) of Tarapacá.

AGRICULTURE

As new groups entered the political arena, the hacienda or *fundo* owners found it increasingly difficult to dominate the system that they had controlled for nearly a century. Within their own congressional districts they still controlled workers' votes, but their relative strength in congress diminished with the growth of the cities and the mining region. From a political perspective, modernization represented a threat, though, ironically, their mining and industrial investments accelerated the process.

Although mining and industrial workers represented a political threat to landowners, nevertheless they comprised an important, but volatile, market for farm goods. To supply urban markets hacendados specialized in dairy products, vegetables, or tobacco. As world farm prices dropped and Chileans failed to compete with countries with cheaper production costs, landowners depended increasingly on domestic markets. One exception, however, was the wool exports from the huge sheep ranches in Patagonia, largely developed by English immigrants.

From 1900 to 1930 landowners doubled their cultivated land, increased irrigation by one-third, and expanded their cattle herds by over one million head. Urban workers complained about the high price of food, which due to inflation seemed outrageous, yet real cereal prices dropped rapidly during the latter nineteenth century, although they raised somewhat between 1900 and 1930. Still some farm goods were more available to Chileans than to people in other countries. Chileans, for example, consumed twice the meat of New Yorkers and considerably more wine.

Some hacienda or *fundo* owners increased farm productivity by using machinery to plow, seed, and harvest their crops. Most, however, preferred to raise output by cultivating more land, expanding irrigation, or getting more labor from their workers. In the 1920s these traditional methods were sufficiently effective to raise the production of potatoes, corn, wheat, and barley by more than 50 percent. As long as labor was cheap and machinery relatively expensive, landowners postponed modernization. Unfortunately, their rate of mechanization dropped far behind other agricultural exporting nations.

Increasingly haciendas, now called *fundos*, took on another function.

They provided their owners with capital for investment in other enterprises. Congressional landowners passed legislation creating the Mortgage Land Bank, which provided the best credit system in the country. Between 1900 and 1930 its loans to farmers swelled from 94,000,000 to 1,471,000,000 pesos. The Mortgage Land Bank did not stipulate that loans be used for farm improvement, so farmers often used the money to invest in urban property, mines, banks, and insurance, which paid a higher return than their farms. As a result, rural Chile helped finance the modernization of urban Chile. Additionally, landowners used this credit to build lavish Santiago residences, take trips to Europe, and finance their political campaigns. Inflation, moreover, gave them the best of all possible worlds. When they paid off their loans, they owed less than they borrowed.

Land continued to be heavily concentrated in the hands of an elite; 10 percent of fundo owners possessed 80 percent of the land. The composition of the rural elite did change, however, as inheritances and declining fortunes caused some families to cash out their farms. Wealthy miners and merchants purchased these lands as they came to market. The copper baron Agustín Edwards Ossandón, for example, acquired seven haciendas valued at over 600,000 pesos; two he foreclosed on and the others he bought at public auction from their indebted owners. Edwards exemplified how new wealth mixed with old. These lands provided him a constant source of income, access to credit, and a hedge against inflation. They also symbolized that Edwards had become an authentic member of the elite. To solidify this position, his widow, Juana Ross, and their son, Agustín Edwards Ross, bought six more rural estates valued at 1,500,000 pesos.

The great majority of landowning Chileans owned parcels of less than five hectares. Sixty thousand yeoman farmers owned less than one-tenth of Chilean farmland; whereas, fewer than 3,000 hacendados owned more than half of it. There were some mid-sized farms, but credit and marketing arrangements often subordinated these farms to the large *fundos*. Chile's total rural population in 1900 was approximately one million people. Over 90 percent of these owned no land at all. Less than half were permanent residents, or *inquilinos*, on large estates. The others moved from one *fundo* to another seeking work. Due to inflation their wages increased, but the pesos' purchasing power declined. Not surprisingly, railroads, mining, and industrial jobs, which paid higher wages, encouraged workers to flee the farm. Urban domestic servant positions, as nursemaids and washerwomen, provided a similar incentive to many young women. A few young families headed south with the goal of acquiring former Mapuche lands. Those who succeeded did so with great hardship.

INDUSTRIAL DEVELOPMENT

With growing urban markets, some entrepreneurs saw the opportunity to transform agricultural goods into more valuable consumer products. They built industries that turned barley into beer, wheat into flour, wool into textiles, and logs into lumber. From 1891 to 1925 these industries revolutionized production in Chile. Although the majority of firms emerged in Valparaíso and Santiago, some developed in Concepción and as far south as Valdivia. Immigrants played a key role in this process.

Industry stressed consumer rather than capital goods. By 1925 nearly 50 percent of national industry was devoted to producing food and beverages. Next in importance were textiles, clothing, and shoes, representing almost 25 percent of the total. The production of metal goods was disappointingly low or less than 8 percent of the total. Although some important foundries grew up to service the railroad and mining industries, they did not develop export markets. It was hard, therefore, for them to attain a scale on which to compete with the large multinational corporations. Similarly small was the wood industry, producing less than 6 percent of the total. It neglected the immense forests of southern Chile, so peasant farmers resorted to burning the trees to clear the land.

Many firms produced national goods for local markets previously supplied by imports. This was the case with beer, virtually unknown during the colonial period, but imported to Valparaíso immediately after independence. Within two decades a number of the port's merchants experimented with small-scale breweries. Further south in Valdivia the German immigrant Carlos Anwandter opened a brewery in the 1850s. Not only did he produce beer for the local market, but he shipped it to the mining regions of the far north.

In 1902 a consolidation of the beer industry began with the fusion of important breweries in Santiago and Limache. The Cousiño and Edwards families, with capital acquired in coal and copper mining, created the Compañía Cervecerías Unidas (United Breweries Company), or CCU. In 1916 the CCU bought out three other breweries, including the firms owned by Carlos Anwandter and Andrés Edner. The latter acquisition by the CCU was a real prize because the brewery also produced soft drinks, some under exclusive foreign licenses. Between 1923 and 1932, CCU went on another buying spree, acquiring the local breweries in five other regions. It also used its dominant market position to control Cristalerías de Chile, the only bottle-making company in the country.

Other industries such as sugar refining, tobacco, chemicals, paper, and cement repeated this pattern of expansion and market control. Immigrants initiated many new industries, but the elite families with larger capital resources often bought out these firms. Industrialization added some new entrepreneurs to the economic elite, but the agricultural and mining elite, with residences and offices in either Santiago or Valparaíso, soon recognized the opportunities presented by industry. Rather than rejecting this new activity, many became its leading entrepreneurs.

Industrial leaders quickly recognized the value of favorable government policies. They formed an employer organization, the Sociedad de Fomento Fabril, which enabled them to lobby the government effectively. For example, when two sugar refineries were threatened by competition from imported sugar, they and the SFF successfully lobbied congress for an increase in tariffs, which cut imports by 75 percent. To protect the cement, textile, and match industries, the SFF also encouraged higher tariffs. Although in 1928 the congressional Tariff Committee complained that higher import taxes were contributing to local monopolies, this did not deter the SFF from pushing for even higher tariffs.

The role of foreign participation in Chilean industrialization is a controversial one, not because of the role of immigrants, but because of the role of foreign corporations based in Europe or the United States. British, German, Spanish, Italian, French, and North American companies were all early participants in Chilean industrialization. In the nineteenth century, merchants in Valparaíso and Concepción began to process agricultural products for export or local consumption more cheaply than they could import them. These included woolens, paper, metal products, canned goods, shoes, liquor, and furniture. As they persuaded congress to give their products tariff protection, overseas corporations sought to participate in this lucrative market. Sometimes they formed joint ventures with established Chilean manufacturers. Other times they established independent manufacturing facilities as a wholly owned subsidiary. Examples of the latter are Siemens-Schuckert, electrical equipment; E.I. Du Pont de Nemours, explosives; and Abbott Laboratories, pharmaceuticals. So strong was the presence of such companies that by 1925 they owned 50 percent of Chilean industry, which was largely administered by foreign managers.

Monopolies became an early feature of Chilean industry. Their disadvantage was that they limited innovation and raised consumer prices. When owned by Chileans, however, they had the advantage of greater bargaining power when multinational corporations wanted to enter the Chilean market. In those fields in which Chilean companies already had a strong presence, foreign companies preferred to form joint ventures rather than compete with them. For example, in glass manufacturing the

Corning Glass Company of the United States decided to establish a partnership with the Chilean firm, Cristalerías, rather than compete with it. Swiss Match, United States Steel, and the British American Tobacco Company are similar examples of foreign firms partnering with Chilean ones.

MINING

From 1890 to 1925 nitrates dominated mining, but after 1910 the modernization of copper production established the basis for a dramatic recuperation of this industry. During this period nitrate output grew from 1,000,000 to 2,500,000 tons, with the price fluctuating from as low as 24 dollars to as high as 49 dollars a ton. World War I caused a huge swing in demand based on shipping availability. The need for laborers encouraged migration from central and southern Chile. Whereas in 1890 the nitrate region of the Norte Grande had less than 180,000 inhabitants, by 1925 it exceeded 345,000 inhabitants. Iquique became the nation's fourth largest city and Antofagasta, the seventh. In the north, almost everyone lived in towns or mining camps in order to have access to water. For this reason, in spite of the north's vast spaces, urban, rather than rural, residence predominated.

The leading nitrate companies hired European chemical engineers to oversee their processing plants. Although these industries were quick to employ the most recent processing technology, they were slower to introduce new mining techniques. As a result the mining itself remained primitive until the early twentieth century. Digging and transporting of the nitrates was a labor intensive, dirty, and unhealthy activity. William H. Russell, a *London Times* correspondent, observed the miners' daily routine when visiting John North's Primitiva nitrate field in the 1880s. He watched an explosive team dig a hole through the hard crust and into the nitrate strata, perhaps to a depth of 10 to 12 feet. Then a young powder monkey climbed down the hole and stuffed a sack of explosives under the strata, and another worker lit the fuse. The explosion broke the strata into blocks, while covering the workers with a fine dust. Then the workers hand loaded the blocks into carts that were pulled by mules to a processing factory where workers dumped the blocks into crushers that ground the nitrate into a salt. Other railcars transported the salt and emptied it into boiling tanks. The liquefied mineral was then purified, dried, and sacked for export.

A new era of nitrate mining began in World War I when the Guggenheim brothers decided to invest in Chile. Their company already owned many copper mines in Colorado and Mexico. It also had large capital resources that enabled it to introduce many capital-intensive methods previously lacking in Chile. Mechanical shovels, railroads, and conveyer belts eliminated much of the manual labor. The cost of these innovations, however, was a staggering $130,000,000.

Nitrate mining provided an illusion of wealth that was periodically shattered by international crises. The problem was not foreign ownership but the dependence on foreign markets. In fact Chilean ownership, which was as low as 10 and 15 percent in 1890s, rose to 60 percent in 1918. Even before the rise of Chilean ownership, the combination of export taxes and workers' salaries assured that more than 50 percent of the value of production remained in Chile. The problem was that Europe and the United States purchased almost all the nitrates, so market conditions in those countries determined price and production. During World War I when the Allies blocked German access to nitrates, unfortunately, German scientists succeeded in synthesizing them in the laboratory. After the war, Germany protected this domestic industry by prohibiting Chilean imports. Eventually other nations succeeded in producing artificial nitrates, further undermining the Chilean industry.

From the 1890 until 1910 the fortunes of Chilean nitrates and copper were nearly the opposite. While nitrate production increased, copper decreased. From a high of 52,000 tons, it dropped to a low of 26,000 tons. Until the 1880s Chilean copper miners had worked high-grade ores using world-class technology. As these ores ran out, the only way to remain competitive was to develop a technology for processing low-grade ores. But nitrates appeared as a more attractive investment. Families like the Edwards and Urmeneta, who had made fortunes in copper, now abandoned this industry and moved into nitrates and other investments.

The rehabilitation of copper mining, therefore, fell on foreign investors. A flotation system for processing low-grade ores had been invented in the United States in the late nineteenth century. In 1904 William Braden introduced it to Chile when he purchased El Teniente mine located at an altitude of 10,000 feet in the Andes, southeast of Santiago. Snow caused transportation problems but did not effect the extraction of the ore from deep, underground tunnels. Braden found the mine's investment needs beyond his resources, so four years later he sold out to the Guggenheims. In 1911 the latter firm expanded its investment in Chile by purchasing the Chuquicamata mine in the province of Antofagasta. In contrast to El Teniente, the new mine was open-pit. Viewed from the air, it appears as a huge spiral circling ever deeper into the earth. Under the corporate name Kennecott Copper Company, the Guggenheims invested 100 million dollars in these two mines.

Another major North American firm, the Anaconda Copper Company, acquired the Chuquicamata mine and then developed a new one called Potrerillos. With these mines, plus the one it owned in Butte, Montana, Anaconda attempted to control an important part of the world's copper production. Increasingly Chileans became hostile to foreign control of copper production and marketing. They referred to the three large-scale mines as *la Gran Minería* in contrast to small-scale mines, or *la Pequeña Minería*. The large-scale mines are capital intensive and produce the majority of the nation's exports, while the small-scale mines are labor intensive and produce very few exports.

The investments of North American companies began to turn Chile's copper industry around. Chile's share of world production, which had been as low as 4 percent at the beginning of the century, rose to 7.5 percent during World War I. Initially Chileans saw few benefits from this growth because the companies imported most of the machinery and other supplies. Although the workers were Chilean, the engineers and administrative personnel were North American. Furthermore, the government was slow to tax copper exports, so it provided little fiscal revenue.

TRADE

During this period two terrible blows hit Valparaíso and tarnished the port's image as the emporium of the Pacific. On August 16, 1906, an earthquake devastated the city just four months after a similar quake hit San Francisco, California. More than 2,000 people died and property damage reached millions of pesos. Although the government rebuilt its offices, private investors increasingly moved their businesses from the port to Santiago. The other blow was less violent but longer lasting. The opening of the Panama Canal enabled shipping companies to save time and money by taking this short cut rather than the traditional Cape Horn route. Valparaíso lost all the business of supplying in-transit ships. After a century of being the preferred port of call in the Pacific, the only ships stopping at Valparaíso after 1914 were those intending to trade there.

Valparaíso's problems did not affect nitrate and copper exports, which moved mostly through northern ports. Especially due to nitrates, exports grew from 1890 to 1920 at an annual rate of between seven and nine percent. The post-World War I recession temporarily reversed this trend, but after 1925 the growth temporarily rebounded. Export income allowed Chileans to import a wide variety of goods ranging from railroad equipment to apparel. Until 1914, Great Britain was Chile's most important trade partner, but during World War I and thereafter the United States usurped that role. The following figures, in U.S. dollars, illustrate this tend.

	Great Britain	United States
1910	$139,400,000	$64,400,000
1920	$113,100,000	$299,600,000

Chile was not diversifying its exports or the countries with which it traded. Nitrates represented between 70 and 80 percent of all exports from 1890 to 1914. Only when copper began to flourish during World War I, reaching nearly 20 percent of total exports, did another product gain importance. After 1890 wheat exports dropped as productivity lagged behind population growth. This drop contributed to a further concentration of mining exports. Indeed, this was the "nitrate era."

The taxes on nitrate exports contributed 50 percent of all the government's revenues. Leaders employed this money in building a modern railroad system, improving roads, educating youth, and beautifying the cities. Although some money was ill spent, most was not. Improved transportation reduced shipping costs. Educated citizens were more creative and productive. Yet the very structure of government limited incentives. The government subsidized the landowners' transportation and credit system, thus giving them "a free ride." No similar credit was available for Chileans to develop new mines. Huge amounts of capital were required to produce nitrates or copper competitively, but few Chileans had the resources. Some opportunities beaconed in industry, but large firms were already consolidating and pushing small firms out of the market. The tax revenue from nitrates, therefore, did not encourage new enterprises. Instead, it supported impressive public works projects, which created the illusion, but not the substance, of development.

Perhaps the most obvious sign that important aspects of the Chilean economy were faltering was the battle with inflation. Chile's first experience with inflation occurred during the War of the Pacific when the government printed money to pay for expenses. (During the Civil War in the United States, however, both sides also used this method of financing.) By the end of the war, the peso had lost more than 30 percent of its value. The following two administrations struggled to reverse the fall of the peso, but when the Civil War began in 1891, president Balmaceda resorted to the printing press again. As a result, within a year the peso lost half its value.

From 1891 to 1925 world economic instability and World War I directly affected Chile's economy. When demand was up, so were Chilean exports

and government revenues. During these good times, leaders tried to re-
deem the paper money and return to the gold standard. But when demand
fell, exports and government revenues did likewise. To pay the bills and to
save the banks and creditors, the government printed enormous amounts
of money. In 1898 it more than doubled the number of pesos. In 1907 it
increased the number by over 80 percent, in 1914, by 50 percent, and from
1924 to 1925, by over 75 percent. Belatedly the government raised taxes
on some consumer goods, income, and property. These taxes, however,
still left the government too heavily reliant on nitrate exports. Until other
sectors of the economy paid their share in taxes, the government could
not resolve irregular revenues and chronic inflation.

Because some people benefited from inflation, it was hard to develop a
consensus to fight it. Industrialists benefited from it. When the peso lost
value, the prices of imports rose faster than those of local goods; therefore,
more local goods were purchased. Debtors also benefited from inflation.
The money they used to pay off their loans was almost always worth less
than the money they had borrowed. This amounted to a negative interest
rate. Landowners, with some of the largest debts, found this a windfall,
but the policy did not encourage them to make productive investments.
Speculating on inventories or property seemed to offer better returns than
productive investment. Both the government and the private sector failed
to design policies that would promote national development.

POLITICS

Electoral reforms in 1874 and 1891 opened the door for middle-class
and worker participation and shifted power toward congress. Parties became more competitive, and this competition produced broader representation in congress. Local electoral control strengthened political bosses and
further weakened the president's influence on elections. Initially these
reforms were intended to benefit the elite, but the middle- and working-
class voters found that the reforms enabled them to elect members of their
own classes to office.

While these reforms diminished the president's manipulation of elections, they encouraged party manipulation. Election fraud unfortunately
became commonplace. Candidates tried to defeat their opponents by buying votes. This was not cheap. In the congressional elections of 1909, for
example, Eduardo Charme spent 400,000 pesos on votes while his opponent spent 300,000 pesos. Charme won by slightly more than 1,000 votes,
but he mortgaged his personal estate in the process. Occasionally a candidate ran unopposed. Perhaps the opposition candidate received a gov-

ernment job in return for his withdrawal from the race. So accustomed did voters become to selling their votes, according to historian Julio Heise, that when an election was not contested, voters became incensed because there was no one to buy their votes.

Candidates were willing to invest their own money in an election, not so much for future economic benefits, but because of the prestige of serving in congress. Membership in the exclusive Club de la Union confirmed a person's elite status, but serving in congress was a step higher. The highest example of civic spirit was to be a congressman or a minister. These men were the celebrities of their age.

Congressmen who spent more than one term in office generally served as minister at least once during their career. The intense party rivalry forced repeated cabinet turnovers. Parties used the power of censure to demand ministerial change. Rarely did a minister serve a year in office; a few months was more common. Sometimes congress would censure a minister to block his political career such as when it removed president Balmaceda's protégé, Enrique Salvador Sanfuentes, to end his presidential aspirations.

Ministerial turnovers became so commonplace during the parliamentary period that congress forced an average of twenty ministerial changes per president. Government might have come to a standstill had there not been continuity at the subministerial level, which allowed public works and services continue with little disruption.

The selection of the presidential candidate was a complicated process that forced parties to form pacts. One pact was called the "Coalition" and generally included the Conservatives. The other pact was the "Alliance" and generally included the Radicals. The other parties or factions within parties would join a pact based on their election strategies or promises of future jobs. Not uncommonly, the Liberal party would split. On two occasions, however, all parties agreed on the same candidate. In 1891 Vice admiral Jorge Montt was elected unopposed and in 1910 Ramón Barros Luco was similarly elected. The elections of 1896, 1915, and 1920, however, were exceedingly close, with the electoral college deciding the victors by narrow margins.

Although jockeying for the next election occupied a large amount of a congressman's energy, considerable efforts were also devoted to encouraging public works. Congress appropriated funds to spend on railroads, bridges, and ports, which exceeded that of private capital. In railroad construction, the state built and operated 56 percent of the nation's lines. It financed the entire southern railroad between Santiago and Puerto Montt. It also built two international lines, one to La Paz, Bolivia, and the other to Mendoza, Argentina. In addition, the state built roads and offered public services, which in many other nations were private. By the early twentieth century, Chile had already supplemented inadequate private investment with public funds. As the century progressed, domestic investment increasingly came from the state while private investment was increasingly foreign.

What congress did not do was pass significant social legislation. Until the 1920s most members of congress agreed on the doctrine of laissez faire. According to this belief, the free market, not the government, should resolve people's needs. Had world events not plunged Chile into serious crises, the political landscape might have retained this conservative homogeneity. World War I and the European revolutions, however, shook Chile to its foundations. Even though Chile did not participate directly in World War I, the war came close to home. The British and the Germans fought a naval battle off the coast of Concepción and later the *Dresden* was sunk near Juan Fernández Island. The economic crises of the 1920s also demonstrated to Chileans how vulnerable they were to world events. The middle and working classes began to demand change. Seeking their support, some politicians responded to their social concerns. The elite vetoed these initiatives until the balance of power quickly shifted toward the middle and working classes in the 1920s.

In the presidential election of 1920, the middle class and the working class found an attractive reform candidate named Arturo Alessandri who ran his campaign with a populist style entirely new to Chile. He and his supporters in the Alliance won a sharply contested election by a narrow margin. He frightened the elite with his rhetoric, but conservative senators vetoed his proposals when he submitted his reform legislation to congress. After a stalemate of four frustrating years, the congressional election of 1924 offered Alessandri the chance to gain a majority in both houses. He campaigned passionately for his Alliance supporters and they won a majority. But before he could enact his agenda, the military foiled his plans.

In early September a group of junior officers entered the legislative galleries and interrupted debate. Senior commanders, led by General Luis Altamirano, were more fearful that junior officers threatened their control of the armed forces than that they were of undermining the government. So Altamirano pressured Alessandri to include him and other commanders in the presidential cabinet. They also used their ministerial positions to dictate a legislative agenda to congress. At first Alessandri believed he could gain the upper hand, but when he realized that he was wrong, he resigned. The military granted him a six month leave of office, so he chose exile in Europe. The senior officers formed a governing junta and teamed up with conservative politicians to draw up an agenda. The progressive junior officers, however, felt betrayed. So on January 23, 1925, under the leadership of Colonel Carlos Ibáñez, they overthrew their senior colleagues, reinstated civilian government, and restored Alessandri to the presidency.

Alessandri gave his new regime an authoritarian twist by retaining Colonel Carlos Ibáñez as Minister of War and refusing to call congress back into session. Instead, he ruled by decree. To increase the power of the presidency permanently, he appointed a commission to revise the 1833 Constitution. The commission produced a document that strengthened the president's power to initiate and veto legislation, but congress retained the power to censure ministers and remove them from office. The structure of elections left political parties and coalitions unchanged. Alessandri was pleased with this 1925 Constitution, so he submitted it to a referendum by the voters, who approved it overwhelmingly.

Alessandri soon found that it was not the congress, but his power-hungry Minister of War, who challenged his authority. Carlos Ibáñez began his own campaign for the presidency while demanding that Alessandri consult with him on important issues. Frustrated and unable to oust his Minister of War, Alessandri resigned for the second time. This suited Ibáñez, who presided over the selection of his replacement. Ibáñez chose not to run himself, however, but to manipulate the victor.

The military had now become the most important player in Chilean politics. Although the military had determined the outcome of 1891 Civil War, it had not imposed its rule on the nation. Vice admiral Jorge Montt, who served as president from 1891 to 1896, was elected by congress. The last time the military had taken over the government by force was in 1830. By contrast, the officers who initiated governmental changes in 1924 ushered in a new era of military power that the 1925 constitution failed to correct. In the next decade when the depression hit, the military further weakened the political system so that it nearly collapsed.

7

Experiments in Democracy, 1925–58

By the 1920s the nation's cities offered an environment that allowed the middle class to flourish and rise to positions of leadership. Driven by ambition and education they challenged the elite, not only in politics, but also in the professions and the arts. The most notable example of middle-class impatience with elite institutions was in the support that it gave the military when it intervened in civic life in the 1920s. Nevertheless, when the depression struck in 1930 and the military proved incapable of combating it, the middle class turned its back on the military and remembered the virtues of democracy and civic institutions.

The five presidents who ruled Chile from 1932 to 1958 emerged from the middle class. Some administrations from 1938 to 1952 actually included working-class parties in their coalition. Though the policies of these regimes strengthened the middle class and increased benefits to the working class, they did not undermine the elite's economic power. They did achieve a compromise among Chile's social factions, which solidified the political system. To their credit, they kept their country functioning as an open, democratic society during a period in which authoritarian regimes ruled much of Latin America.

The middle class created a political culture in which it decided that the state should provide for the general welfare of all groups. To benefit workers, it passed social legislation, expanded education, and regulated consumer prices. To benefit itself, it created government jobs, modernized public services, and negotiated stability. To benefit the elite, it protected agriculture and industry while preventing the expropriation of wealth.

There was a price, however, of government being so accommodating. These programs should have been paid for with increased taxes, but new tax legislation and collection fell short, so the government resorted to foreign borrowing and to printing money. Consequently, the value of the peso declined, which eroded people's standard of living and discouraged long-term investment. As a result, Chileans were deprived of the affluence enjoyed by North American and European consumers. When they placed blame, they usually held the party in power responsible. This concern produced a dynamic political dialog in which people usually preferred greater state controls not less.

THE POWER OF IDEAS

Chile's tradition of freedom of expression led to a vibrant press, an active publishing industry, and a stimulating university environment. More than most people in Latin American countries, Chileans kept their eyes on European intellectual and social trends. This interest began in the nineteenth century, but with improvements in travel and communication, this became even more the case in the twentieth century. Bookstores carried important European and North American works in both original and translated versions. The educated public eagerly read about world events and ideas, so newspapers expanded their international coverage to include cultural and literary supplements that reviewed major works.

The distributors of North American and European films found eager audiences in Chile. Entrepreneurs built luxurious theaters in the large urban areas and more modest ones elsewhere. For the middle class, the typical weekend often included at least one movie. The stars of the silver screen became as much a part of national culture in Chile as they were in their own countries. The newsreels preceding feature films graphically portrayed the mass movements of Europe and the United States in the 1930s and the contrasting styles that Mussolini, Hitler, Roosevelt, and Churchill used to control labor and to combat the depression.

When radio became prominent in the 1930s, it likewise gained quick acceptance in most urban homes. The typical programming included popular music, soap operas, sports, political commentary, and news. Often stations clearly identified with a particular political party, emphasizing that viewpoint in both news and commentary. Some stations appealed to the working class by playing Mexican ballads and Argentine tangos, while others appealed to the middle and upper class by playing jazz or classical music. As much as half of program content originated outside Chile.

The same social issues debated in popular media were explored in more depth by Chilean historians and writers. Somewhat surprisingly, historians were actively involved in politics. Their views on contemporary issues considerably influenced their perspectives on the past. Writers and artists less often held political office but had strong political commitments, which were often evident in their works. Their own middle- or working-class origins powerfully influenced their views on social issues.

Whereas in the nineteenth century Chile was distinguished for its historians, in the twentieth it was distinguished for its poets. A culture of poetry developed in which every community had a poetry society. These groups published poetry magazines and sponsored regular readings. Train conductors, retail clerks, schoolteachers, and even bureaucrats wrote poetry. Although most poets came from the middle or working classes, a few came from the aristocracy. Regardless of their class origins, Chilean poets read widely, including such authors as Lord Byron, Walt Whitman, and Gustavo Bécquer. Chile's three most celebrated poets of the twentieth century, Vicente Huidobro, Gabriela Mistral, and Pablo Neruda, all lived abroad for extensive periods. Although foreign authors' styles and themes influenced them, Chilean themes were a central element of their works. While Huidobro avoided social issues, both Mistral and Neruda placed them as the center of their work. Both emphasized a common indigenous heritage, one that unifies the Americas. They recognized their own Indian ancestry and contributed to *indigenismo,* or renaissance of Native American culture.

An exception to the social origins of most of his contemporary poets was that of Vicente Huidobro, who could trace his aristocratic ancestry to colonial times. Perhaps this explains why, contrary to his peers, he had little interest in business or politics. From his early school years he showed such a love for literature that he began publishing poetry in his teens. By the time he was 23 he had developed his own style, which he called creationism. He rejected the modernist style of imitating nature; rather, he strove to create his own worlds outside of nature. In 1916, he traveled to Paris where he soon joined the local vanguard poets and began writing and publishing in French. He later moved to Spain where his style influenced many writers. In addition to poetry, he experimented with novels and dramatic works.

Gabriela Mistral came from a family of educators who lived in the small northern community of Elqui. Like her parents, she began her career as a teacher, moving constantly from one school to another. In her first six years she taught in a different town every year, ranging from the far north to the far south. In 1922, she published her first volume of collected poems, *Desolación* (Desolation), in New York. These poems are a lament, but one in which nature's beauty offers consolation. Love in her poetry is spiritual, not erotic, in contrast to most other Latin American writers of her generation. In recognition of her talent and to encourage her writing, the Chilean government granted her an early pension. Later the government named her to diplomatic posts in Italy, Spain, and Brazil. In 1945, she became the first Spanish-speaking poet to be awarded the Nobel Prize in Literature.

Coming from a more humble background than Mistral, but having an even greater impact on Spanish poetry, was Pablo Neruda. Although his father worked on the railroad, early on Pablo developed a precocious love for literature. He published his first verses at thirteen while still attending the *liceo*. He studied to be a teacher but never taught due the fame he gained though *Crepusculario* (Twilight Verses) and *Veinte poemas de amor y una canción desesperada* (Twenty Love Poems and a Song of Despair), published respectively when he was 20 and 24. Like Gabriela Mistral, the Chilean government rewarded his genius with a series of diplomatic appointments.

Neruda showed an early sympathy for laborers, and his work with refugees during the Spanish Civil War radicalized him and made him more sympathetic to proletarian causes. His *Canto general* (General Song) offers a panoramic view of the Americas from a socialist perspective. In addition to his prolific writing, he helped to run political campaigns. In 1969, the Communist Party nominated him as its candidate for president, but he withdrew in favor of Salvador Allende. His views highly politicized some of his poetry, but it also endeared him to the working class. Far less political were his *Odas elementales* (Elemental Odes) in which, like Walt Whitman, he sang about the fruits of the earth and the people who till the land. When Salvador Allende was elected president in 1970, he appointed Neruda as Chile's ambassador to France. A year later, the Nobel Prize committee awarded him its distinguished prize for literature.

Chilean novelists had less success in attracting foreign audiences. Their focus on local customs and social problems had less universal attraction than Chilean poetry. Joaquín Edwards Bello's novels, set in Valparaíso, depict the class antagonisms of the port while evoking its rugged hills, winds, and seascapes. He was highly critical of both the elite and the middle class, although his cousin was one of the wealthiest men in Chile. Another innovative writer, Augusto D'Halmar, developed his own imaginative school of literature as his work *Pasion y muerte del Cura Deusto* (Passion and Death of the Priest from Deusto) exemplifies. His spirit of innovation led him to found an art commune near Santiago, but he later took up residence in Spain and India.

More concerned with the problems of rural workers was the novelist Pedro Prado. In *Alcino,* he sympathetically portrays children born to impoverished *campesinos.* The author avoids endorsing ideological or even practical solutions for poverty, but envisions a transformation of both man and nature. A contemporary novelist, Eduardo Barrios, committed himself to public service and literature after having traveled abroad extensively. During the governments of Carlos Ibáñez, he served as the director of the National Library and the Minister of Education. Although his novels like *Gran Señor y Rajadiablos* (Gentleman and Rogue) offer earthy portraits of Chilean rural society, he is rather uncritical of traditional class relationships.

In the area of history a more diverse ideological panorama developed. On the right, conservatives challenged nineteenth-century liberal interpretations. In 1929 Alberto Edwards Vives, a close collaborator of Colonel Carlos Ibáñez's military government, published *La fronda aristocrática* (Aristocratic Opposition), one of the most thoughtful syntheses of Chilean history ever written. He attributed much of Chile's success to the leadership of a Basque-Castilian aristocracy. A more prolific yet less analytical of conservative was Francisco Antonio Encina, whose *Historia de Chile* encompassed twenty volumes. He attacked liberals by employing a controversial psychological method and a folksy narrative style that endeared him to the general public. His lack of academic rigor, however, made him an easy target for professional historians. His most acclaimed work, *Nuestra inferioridad económica* (Our Economic Inferiority), offers valuable criticism of Chile's economic problems. Jaime Eyzaguirre was a more scholarly, conservative historian who taught legal history at the Catholic University Law School. In his many historical publications, he emphasized Hispanic and Catholic values. He authored a critical biography of Bernardo O'Higgins and began a general *Historia de Chile.* He was also active outside the classroom, encouraging a conservative trade union movement as a counterbalance to radical labor unions.

The liberal historical tradition still had excellent practitioners in twentieth-century Chile. The long-time director of the *Sociedad Chilena de Historia y Geografía* (Chilean History and Geographic Society), Ricardo Donoso, vehemently defended the reforms that opened up opportunity for the middle and working classes. He contributed incisive analyses of Chile's political evolution in works such as *Las ideas políticas en Chile*

(Political Ideas in Chile). Another liberal historian, Julio Heise González, taught history at the University of Chile Law School for many years. His two-volume work, *Historia de Chile, 1861–1925,* mapped the evolution of Chilean democratic institutions and defended these institutions from conservatives with authoritarian inclinations. A less controversial cultural historian was Eugenio Pereira Salas, who explored such themes as theater, sports, and commerce. Mario Góngora was a historian who began interpreting history from a labor point of view but later brilliantly defended traditional Hispanic values. His works on the colonial labor institutions and the nature of the Chilean state have been widely read and translated.

On the left, Marxist historians criticized capitalism and the exploitation of the working class. Hernán Ramírez Necochea, in addition to his writing, became heavily involved in the university reform movement as dean of the School of Education of the University of Chile in the 1960s. His most important work, *Historia del imperialismo en Chile* (The History of Imperialism in Chile), emphasized how British and North American commerce and investment had dominated the country. Another Marxist interpretation of Chile was that of Julio César Jobet, *Ensayo critico del desarrollo economico-social de Chile* (Critical Essay on the Socioeconomic Development of Chile). His assessment of elite domination encouraged students to question the social order.

Although the majority of Chilean authors and historians in this period belonged to the middle class, they did not necessarily identify with it. Most criticized the upper class, had ambiguous feelings about their own class, and usually empathized with the working class. The middle class enjoyed works criticizing the upper class and laughed at the antics of *siúticos,* or social climbers, from their own class. In contrast to German angst or French existentialism, they found humor to be a better defense against modernity. National Chilean culture did not exist in a vacuum; rather, international themes were interpreted through unique Chilean experiences.

SOCIAL AND ECONOMIC CHANGE

Demographic Trends

From 1940 to 1952 Chile grew, but unevenly. Urban population increased by 42 percent, whereas rural population grew by barely 3 percent. The rural birthrate was as high or higher than the urban one, but young people migrated to the towns and cities looking for work. Santiago was the great job creation center, with 37 percent of national industry in 1930 and 65 percent in 1952. Not surprisingly, its growth rate outstripped the nation. In 1930 the population in Santiago accounted for 16 percent of the total population in Chile, and by 1952 this had risen to 30 percent. The rise of the nation's urban population from 50 percent in the 1930s to 60 percent by 1952 showed that Chileans increasingly preferred living in cities.

The fastest growing social groups were the middle and urban working classes. By the late 1950s, based on income, the middle class represented between 15 and 20 percent of the population. Based on education and self-identification, however, close to 33 percent of Chileans considered themselves middle class. This discrepancy between income and expectations represents the failure of the economy to provide an income commensurate with a person's education. Even though middle-class earnings were low, they were approximately seven times those of farm workers. The farm workers represented 29 percent of the economically active population, but were the least paid. Urban workers represented 45 percent of the economically active population and earned wages approximately three times those of farm workers. With their rent and food expenses higher, however, they were not much more affluent. The smallest social group was the elite who represented less than 10 percent of the population and owned the large businesses and haciendas.

In the later 1920s, Chileans experienced an improvement in their standard of living. Then in 1930, Chileans were devastated by the depression. Already under stress, the political situation became chaotic but then surprisingly stabilized. To combat the depression, the state promoted industry, engaged in labor arbitration, and regulated prices. The state also influenced the relative share of national income each group received. Given these extensive roles of the state, understandably, professional organizations, business associations, and organized labor sought to influence government policy.

As the state's responsibilities expanded, so did its need for revenue. Taxes on nitrates and copper accounted for 15 to 25 percent of the total, and the rest was borne largely by consumers, commerce, and industry. *Fundo* owners managed to keep agricultural taxes very low. Although the government raised taxes to meet expenses, it frequently circulated more currency. This contributed to 7 percent yearly inflation in the 1930s, rising to 15 percent by 1946, to 21 percent by 1951, and to a demoralizing 84 percent by 1955.

To combat inflation, some leaders relied on the unpopular policy of holding down wages. Such measures provoked labor protests and failed to effectively halt rising prices, because the government did not increase revenue or curtail its own expenses. In 1932 the military-led socialist republic tried a different approach by freezing prices on basic foods and services, rather than freezing wages. This action did not stop inflation, but it gave consumers the temporary illusion that it did. Due to the popularity of this approach, later governments increasingly used it. Nevertheless, by keeping farm prices low, the policy discouraged local production and made the country more dependent on food imports. The government's failure to tame inflation did not lead people to demand less government control over the economy, rather just the opposite. People believed that private enterprise was incapable of providing cheap, abundant goods, so they looked to the state to resolve the problem.

Industry

Due to a belief that promoting industry was the road to prosperity, the state made this the most innovate area of the Chilean economy. After the devastating earthquake of Chillán in 1939, President Pedro Aguirre Cerda proposed a new agency called the *Corporación de Fomento* (Development Corporation), or CORFO. This institution brought government and private capital together to create innovative companies. CORFO borrowed a large portion of the capital for these firms from the United States Export-Import Bank. It built the nation's first steel mill near Concepción, explored for oil in the Zona Austral, and built hydroelectric dams in the Valle Central. It also encouraged import substitution industries to produce appliances, cement, and sugar. These industries made Chile less dependent on imports while increasing industrial employment by nearly 20 percent.

Still Chile's industrialization had many weaknesses. There was a lack of large firms; only three percent of the factories employed more than 200 workers. Small firms employing fewer than five workers, which employed more than 40 percent of the industrial work force, were more common. Although there were over 6,000 industrial firms, the concentration was such that only 20 companies produced nearly 40 percent of industrial goods and represented more than 50 percent of the fixed capital. Moreover, most firms were not efficient. Had the government not raised tariffs to protect them, they would have succumbed to foreign competition.

Copper Mining

Important changes occurred in mining from 1925 to 1958. While nitrate production declined, copper production rose. In the 1920s this trend was not apparent as nitrate exports nearly doubled those of copper. The depression, however, devastated nitrate demand and by the mid-1930s copper exports tripled those of nitrates and continued to rise. Employment in the nitrate industry dropped by almost half. The capital-intensive copper industry used relatively few workers, so it offered few jobs to the 60,000 unemployed nitrate-industry workers. These jobless men and their families migrated south, causing a population loss in the Norte Grande. World War II began a new employment cycle as copper and iron production expanded rapidly to meet worldwide demand.

Foreign ownership of the nitrate mines was an issue, but with copper mines the issue was compounded. As early as 1920, Chilean-owned mines produced only 3 percent of national copper while foreign-owned ones produced 97 percent. Of the latter, United States companies accounted for over 80 percent of the total. Two of these companies, Anaconda and Kennecott, owned the largest mines in the country. By the 1930s the value of the latter mines exceeded $400,000,000 and represented the majority of United States investment in Chile. The example of the Bolivian and Mexican nationalization of oil in the 1930s was not followed by the Chilean government. Instead, it preferred to increase taxes on the copper companies' profits, reaching a rate of 80 percent in the 1950s. With little incentive to expand, the companies allowed production to stagnate. In an effort to encourage new investment and production, in 1955 the government lowered the tax rate to 50 percent. This policy, however, failed to produce the expected results and leftist parties began to demand nationalization of the companies.

The Agricultural Crisis

To encourage farm output, the government subsidized farm credit and machinery imports, yet the outcome of this policy was poor. Agricultural output declined from the 1920s to the 1940s as a result of low food prices and large, inefficient *fundos*. Presidents prevented the unionization of farm workers, which helped landowners keep down salaries and avoid strikes. The poor salaries, however, accelerated the migration of farm laborers to the cities. Agricultural production fell behind population growth, requiring Chile to import ever-larger amounts of food. By the late 1950s, agricultural imports surpassed 45 million dollars annually. Due to state price controls, large landowners often bought goods from their less-affluent neighbors and held them off the market until the government raised prices. Many found that food speculation returned a higher profit than food production.

Bucking the trend of declining production was the Sur, especially the

Mapuche heartland. By the 1930s this region produced approximately 30 percent of the nation's cereals. The area's cattle production grew from less than 10 percent of the nation's total in 1920, to more than 40 percent in the 1950s. Likewise, the Sur produced the majority of the country's dairy products. A major reason for these increases was the influx of settlers into the region. The government opened these lands for homesteading, but was far from impartial in allocating them. Attracted by the promise of free land, thousands of *inquilinos* and farm workers flocked south from the Valle Central. The influx of homesteaders into the Cautín province helped raise the population from 280,000 inhabitants to over 400,000 in this period, making it the fourth most populous province in the country. North American geographer George McBride, who witnessed Chileans converting the wilderness into small farms, said they reminded him of a similar epic in the American West a century earlier.

Near the coast and in the valleys, wetlands covered large areas, whereas dense evergreen rainforests covered the uplands. In the uplands, massive trees with names such as *coihue, roble, raulí, tepa, ulmo,* and *laurel* had hidden generations of Mapuche from marauding Spanish cavalries. Ancient footpaths ran through valleys and along mountain ridges. As homesteaders arrived, they planked the trails in the swampy lowlands and widened mountain paths so that their oxcarts could pass. To clear the land, homesteaders girdled the trees, and when the foliage dried up, they lit fire to the trees. They used the leftover charred trunks for fence posts and firewood. They used this slash-and-burn, *roce del fuego,* method to clear a thousand miles of Andean forests. For shelter, they built log houses, and beside them, the *fogónes* where they cooked, sipped mate, and ate meals like the Mapuche before them.

According to homestead legislation, a surveyor needed to measure a land claim before a settler received a permanent title from the government. Because settlers moved faster than the government agencies and surveyors, the claimed land was without clear title. In 1927 approximately 47,000 settlers lacked property deeds. The next year the government created La Caja de Colonización Agrícola (Agricultural Colonization Bank) to resolve this property problem. As the government acted, influential people used the legal quagmire to their advantage. They persuaded officials to grant them large tracks of occupied land and then forcefully evicted the residents. In 1934 the settlers in the locality of Ranquil resisted when the Carbineros, the national police, tried to drive them out. A gun battle ensued and left over 100 homesteaders dead.

As similar tactics and force were used elsewhere, *campesinos* fled to higher elevations and to poorer soils where they began again. Desperate to feed their families, they cleared forests on steep mountainsides never meant for cultivation. To survive, they raised a few cattle, planted gardens, hewed railroad ties, and gathered pine nuts. Occasionally they engaged in contraband with neighboring Argentina. Many of their children, to escape poverty, also crossed the mountains seeking work in the orchards of the Río Negro valley or in the Patagonian coal mines. Others joined the stream of migrants heading for the industrial cities of Santiago and Concepción.

In the Sur where the mountain passes separating Chile and Argentina are low, people frequently move back and forth in search of opportunity. Segundo Luengo, for example, was born in southern Chile in the 1890s and migrated with his father to Argentina when he was still a boy. There he grew up living as a gaucho, herding cattle throughout Patagonia. When large Argentine estates began fencing the pampas, he returned to Chile hoping to find land. He married Zoila in 1917 and together they homesteaded near Cunco. A wealthy landowner chased them off their claim, so they headed farther into the mountains to a beautiful but scarred terrain near Lake Caburgua. There, along with his brother's family, they successfully homesteaded 80 hectares each.

They raised cattle, sheep, and goats and cultivated potatoes and a garden. During the spring, Señora Zoila milked cows and made cheese. While still young, Segundo was occasionally hired to drive large cattle herds from Argentina to Chile. He raised a few dozen cattle of his own and sold them to roving buyers, usually in the fall before the government raised official meat prices. He also planted apple, cherry, and quince trees. In the fall he collected the apples, took them to a local press, and filled half a dozen barrels with cider. Life was hard, especially when living three hours by horseback from the nearest town, but he and Zoila managed to rear three children. The oldest remained on the farm, the second taught school in a northern copper town, and the third immigrated to Chicago.

In contrast to the Luengos, the nearby Compton family, which obtained thousands of hectares in a large land grant, contracted sharecroppers to till the *fundo*'s flat, rich fields. Among the sharecroppers were German families who had originally immigrated to Brazil but later moved to the temperate climate of southern Chile. Though poor, their farming and mechanical skills soon enabled them to buy land and eventually become middle-class farmers. The same region was inhabited by Mapuche, who raised cattle, cultivated gardens, and planted orchards. One Mapuche patriarch, Hilario Nahuel, lost part of his land to a government employee. He complained for years about the loss to the Indigenous Affairs office, but to no avail. His son, Segundo Nahuel, preferred to invest his energies in the education of his children, assuming that the family would never regain the land. With education, he believed that his children might get ahead when they migrated to Santiago or Argentina. Without it, his girls would work as maids or in fruit-packing plants, while his boys would work in low-paying service jobs.

In the 1950s various social and political groups in the Valle Central began to organize and defend *campesinos* from the abuses of *fundo* owners. Catholic priests, Catholic Action groups, the National Falange, and the Federación Nacional de Trabajadores Agrícolas (National Federation of Farm Workers), actively recruited *campesino* support. In 1953 the workers in the community of Molina, supported by the clergy and the National Falange, staged a successful strike. The latter, a progressive Catholic youth group, founded in 1935, continued to build support in rural areas. When the National Falange became part of the Christian Democratic Party in 1957, its experience organizing *campesinos* helped rural Chileans seek redress of their problems.

Labor Unions

Although the economically active population increased from 1,300,000 to 2,300,000, in the period from 1925 to 1958, the proportion of industrial workers remained constant, at approximately 20 percent. In 1925, out of 280,000 industrial laborers, 198,000, or over 70 percent, worked for small firms. By 1958, although industrialization had advanced, small firms continued to employ almost half of the industrial labor force. Not surprisingly, under these circumstances, most factory unions were small. In 1932, the average size was 130 members, diminishing to less than 90 members in 1940. Because unions were so fragile, their size depended heavily on government policy. With hostility or repression, they shrank, but with patronage they flourished.

By 1925, total union membership reached 204,000, but when Carlos Ibáñez became president in 1927, he attacked the unions and membership dropped. He repressed the Federación de Obreros Chilenos (Chilean Workers Federation) as well as the Communist-dominated unions. He succeeded in destroying the latter and seriously weakened the Communist Party. In place of leftist unions, he sought to create government-dominated ones. In 1931 his administration published a labor code that established union organizing criteria, collective bargaining, and government procedures for intervention. His labor department created 300 labor organizations with a total of 50,000 members who were all organized into a national confederation of unions called the Confederación Republicana de Acción

Cívica (Republican Confederation for Civic Action), or CRAC. To give CRAC leaders active political roles, he allocated them nineteen congressional seats. Through these actions, Ibáñez reduced the FOCH to a shadow of its former size and established the precedence for political control of labor.

By the time Ibáñez fell from power in July 1931, official union membership was only 56,000. His successor and second-term president, Arturo Alessandri, decided to reverse this trend. He used the 1931 Labor Code to both promote and control unions. With his encouragement, membership increased to 125,000 by 1938. Simultaneously the Communists attempted to resurrect the FOCH, but the Socialists, who had cooperated with Ibáñez, initially refused. After a failed railway strike, the Socialists recognized the need to collaborate with the Communists, so in 1936 they formed the Confederación de Trabajadores de Chile (Chilean Workers Confederation), or CTCH.

In the 1930s fascism gained prominence in Europe. In an attempt to block it, the Soviet Union urged world Communist parties to form broad coalitions. In Chile this policy led the Communist Party to join other leftist parties to form the Popular Front. This coalition won the presidency in 1938, and though it later fragmented, it helped the left control the presidency until 1952. Under the Popular Front, unionization expanded rapidly, rising to 193,000 members in 1942 and to 284,000 in 1952. In spite of the CTCH's growth, it fell short in two areas. It achieved few wage gains and it failed to recruit agricultural workers. In 1952 it was put on the defensive again as Ibáñez returned to the presidency for a second term. He pushed union membership down again, but not as sharply as during his first administration.

Unions were strongest in the mining regions of the north and in the meatpacking and mining region of the extreme south. Although both areas had sparse populations, people worked for large firms that were relatively easy to organize. Union membership fluctuated widely according to the business cycle, especially with the decline of the nitrate industry. Although the copper mines employed relatively fewer workers, they successfully organized and became the backbone of the labor movement

Two opposing ideas about union political activities clashed in this period. An apolitical perspective supported by the anarcho-syndicalist unions rejected party affiliation and preferred to bargain directly with employers. Another perspective supported by most other unions sought strong political ties. With the establishment of a Chilean branch of the Industrial Workers of the World, or IWW, the apolitical stance gained strength. The various IWW-affiliated unions held their first congress in 1919, but a year later in reaction to labor protests, the government arrested many IWW leaders. Ibáñez's repression also hurt the IWW, so that by the 1930s anarcho-syndicalist unions had withered away or joined the Socialist or Communist Parties.

The political perspective of the labor movement, therefore, gained strength. It developed its own party or affiliated with an existing one. Labor leader, Luis Emilio Recabarren, led many unions to the Democratic Party. Then, when he founded the Socialist Worker's Party, which became the Communist Party in 1922, he strove to incorporate all unions into the Party.

The Socialist Party, founded in 1933, organized unions and tried to get members to adhere to the party line but was less successful than its competitors, the Communists. It was a far more heterodox organization serving as an umbrella for disaffected Communists, Marxist idealists, alienated Radical progressives, revolutionary Trotskyists, and Social Democrats. The diversity of the party was both its weakness and its strength. When Gabriel Gonzalez Videla outlawed the Communist Party in 1947, the Socialists escaped similar repression due to their heterogeneity. Although both Socialists and the Communists often helped strengthen the unions, they also made them more vulnerable to political repression than if they had been more apolitical.

The rivalry among the parties prevented the unions from taking a united stand. The Cold War exaggerated these divisions as the American Federation of Labor urged Latin America's non-communist unions to break with the Communist Party. Furthermore, due to divisiveness on the left, the Soviet Union urged Communist unions to take an aggressive stance against the Socialists. These tensions were highlighted in 1947 during a major coal strike. President Gabriel González Videla, in reaction to Communist efforts to prolong the conflict, persuaded congress to pass the Law for the Permanent Defense of Democracy that outlawed the party. The government did not repeal the act until ten years later. With the Communist Party illegal, the government could intervene more easily in the unions. In 1953 the noncommunist unions formed the Central Unica de Trabajadores (United Workers Federation), or CUT. This organization became especially powerful when the Communists again became legal and contributed their leadership.

Unions had surprisingly little ability to affect the general wage level in Chile. Industrial workers' wages declined during the 1930s, rose somewhat during both World War II and the Korean War, and declined sharply in the latter 1950s. The best paid workers were the copper miners, followed by urban manufacturing workers. The poorest paid were the maids and the farm workers. Due to inflation, especially toward the end of the

1950s, the workers' salaries played catch up. In contrast to North American and European laborers, Chilean workers were marginal participants in consumer society. Their salaries provided only for their basic needs.

Thanks to government efforts, workers did benefit from health and education improvements. Servicio Nacional de Salud (National Health Service) reduced infant mortality by half, from one-in-four to one-in-eight deaths per live births. It helped add 20 years to a Chileans' life span, raising the average to 54 years for men and 60 for women. State-supported schools decreased illiteracy from approximately 30 percent in 1925 to about 17 percent in 1958. Thus, services for workers and their families improved, although their disposable income did not.

The Middle Class

Even in working class parties and institutions, the majority of leaders were middle class. Similarly, administrators of elite-owned estates and businesses were often middle class. The upper middle class owned medium-sized industries, businesses, and construction firms, while a less affluent middle class owned small stores and farms, worked for the government, or served as teachers. Often the latter's incomes did not much exceed the working class, but due to their education they identified with the middle class

The less affluent, middle class was particularly dependent upon government. In contrast to Europe and the United States, in which private industry provided many jobs for the middle class, in Chile this was not the case. So the state became a major avenue for middle-class employment. Given this demand, promises of employment weighed heavily in electoral politics. All parties managed to fulfill the promise of more jobs, boosting public employment during the period by nearly 250 percent. Not surprisingly, to pay salaries, taxes rose as well, reaching 20 percent of GDP. Sales taxes grew from less than 15 percent of government revenue to nearly 25 percent. But the worst tax of all was inflation. Until inflation corroded salaries in the 1950s, middle-class workers fared well. Their incomes grew by nearly 50 percent in the 1940s, in contrast to blue-collar workers whose salaries remained stagnant.

The middle class was largely urban and committed to modernization. Middle-class voters did not coalesce in one party, but spread across the political spectrum, as they sought a party or coalition that best represented their interests. In the 1920s, the Radical Party, which stressed education and secularization, appealed to many of these voters. While some of the upper middle class identified closely with the upper-class agenda of the

Liberal or Conservative parties, other middle-class public employees sympathized with the more working-class agenda of the Socialist or Communist parties. During Colonel Ibáñez's two administrations, many middle-class voters supported him, believing that by eliminating traditional politics he could rapidly transform the country. When he failed to deliver, however, they quickly turned their backs on him.

GOVERNMENT

Colonel Carlos Ibáñez

Some powerful personalities dominated Chilean politics from 1925 to 1952. The period began with Colonel Carlos Ibáñez assuming the role as "kingmaker." He forced Arturo Alessandri's resignation and prepared the terrain for a compliant Emilio Figueroa to be elected in the same year. During Figueroa's brief presidency, Princeton economics professor and financial advisor Edwin Kemmerer visited Chile to advise the government on more effective management of the economy. His proposals included the creation of a Central Bank, a more efficient tax structure, and a return to the gold standard. When Chile's congress approved these measures, Kemmerer notified United States banks that Chile was a prime candidate for new loans.

In early 1927 when Ibáñez took over the powerful position of minister of the interior, Figueroa resigned and Ibáñez arranged his own election. He received an unprecedented 97 percent of the vote. To intimidate congress, he expelled many political leaders. He also abolished the Communist Party and squashed independent labor unions. In his desire to emphasize efficiency rather than political debate, he named engineers rather than lawyers to ministerial positions. He began to borrow heavily from United States bankers and with the money undertook ambitious public works. Among the projects were feeder railways to the main trunk lines, bridges, and port facilities. To better control finances, he created the Contraloría General (Comptroller General), with enough independent authority to demand accountability from all branches of government, particularly the executive.

He also reorganized the armed forces, creating Fuerza Aérea de Chile (Chilean Air Force), or FACH, as a separate institution. He brought all police departments together into a national police called the Carabineros. The working-class origins of rank-and-file Carabineros ingratiated them with the people. In foreign relations, United States arbitration helped

Chile and Peru resolve their common boundary issue, with Chile taking permanent possession of Arica and Peru of Tacna.

Ibáñez dismissed public employees he believed hostile to his regime and created 9,000 new positions. These changes generally benefited the middle class. In spite of persecutions and censorship, a temporary aura of prosperity made many people optimistic. In fact, many middle- and upper-class people agreed with his cult of efficiency and his criticism of traditional politicians. When the Depression hit, however, Chile found that the Ibáñez formula for prosperity failed.

Like Herbert Hoover and other world leaders, Ibáñez did not anticipate the severity and duration of the Depression. With the country heavily dependent on nitrate and copper exports, when the commodity markets crashed and prices plummeted Chile lacked the means to pay for its imports and its debts. As mines cut back, unemployed mine workers became destitute and fled south in search of jobs. Yet there were no jobs, because as the economy faltered Ibáñez followed the conservative policy of cutting government expenses and employment. He clung tenaciously to the gold standard while American credit dried up and loan payments came due. As unemployment skyrocketed, people reacted with massive protests against Ibáñez's regime. Seeing no solution to this desperate situation, Ibáñez resigned on July 26, 1931, and fled to Argentina.

The Socialist Republic

An interim government organized new elections in which the Radical Party leader Juan Esteban Montero defeated Arturo Alessandri's attempt to win a second term. Montero attempted to provide food and shelter for the unemployed as well as reduce rents and taxes. Unfortunately, after only eight months in office a military conspiracy overthrew him. The leaders included Marmaduke Grove, an Air Force officer; Carlos Dávila, a journalist; and Eugenio Matte, a socialist. The conspirators declared Chile to be a "Socialist Republic," although they did not really define what they meant by socialism. It certainly was not Troskyist or Marxist socialism. Due to infighting within the junta, it spent much of its energy selecting who was in charge. The military found Grove and Matte too radical and expelled them to Easter Island. Carlos Dávila then appointed himself president but could not deal with the overwhelming problems of the Depression. The Socialist Republic only lasted 100 days, but that was long enough to frighten many upper- and middle-class Chileans and to further tarnish the military's reputation.

Arturo Alessandri Restores Democracy

The military again decided to act and overthrew Dávila. Then they presided over a new election that brought Arturo Alessandri to power again. He not only returned Chile to civilian rule, but reinforced the country's democratic tradition. For forty years thereafter, Chile enjoyed an open, civilian-led government, in contrast to the dictators that plagued many Latin American nations. A consensus developed among parties from left to right, and even among the military, that Chile's welfare was better served with a democratic rather than an authoritarian government.

Alessandri, who had frightened conservatives in the 1920s, now provided them with security. To reassure conservatives that the traditional economic system would remain intact, he chose the affluent business man Gustavo Ross as his finance minister. Although no friend of labor, Ross was surprisingly adroit at restarting the economy. Recognizing the construction industry's ability to create jobs quickly, he offered a it ten-year tax break on new projects. With agriculture, he continued the policy of fixing low farm prices, but as a stimulus he encouraged farm machinery imports and farm export subsidies. For industry, he raised tariffs and increased access to credit. In addition to generous government loans, he pumped money into the economy through public works. As both industrial and agricultural production grew, the nation became increasingly self-sufficient. With restrictions on purchases from abroad, the rise in spending generally provided jobs at home. The downside of pumping money into the economy was rampant inflation and a decline in workers' purchasing power. Ross also had a radical solution for Chile's lack of foreign exchange; he shocked world banks by defaulting on foreign loans. Then he used copper and nitrate revenue to buy back the same loans at discounted prices. International bondholders cried "foul play," but for Chile the decision proved advantageous.

To keep the military in its barracks, Alessandri retired some officers and undertook an institutional reorganization. He had his own authoritarian side, however, as he showed in his treatment of labor. He ordered the Carabineros to evict homesteaders from Ranquil in 1934 and then under the Labor Code of 1931 used the army to squash a 1936 railroad strike. He then declared a state of siege to prevent worker protests. Taking advantage of congressional fear of social unrest, in 1937 he persuaded the legislature to pass the Ley de Seguridad Interior del Estado (State Internal Security Law). This law granted him the power to incarcerate anyone the government deemed a threat to domestic order. When a group of Nazi youth planned a coup and occupied the Social Security building, he ordered them shot. He believed that if the democratic state did not maintain a monopoly on violence, the state would not survive.

The Popular Front

In spite of his heavy hand, Alessandri's political decisions gained him widespread popularity. But when Gustavo Ross tried to succeed him in 1938, he failed because he lacked Alessandri's charisma with the working class. International events also radically changed party alliances. The Chilean Communist Party joined with the Socialists and the Radicals to form the Popular Front. The Radicals had the largest congressional representation of the three, so their candidate, Pedro Aguirre Cerda, became the Popular Front's nominee for president in 1938.

The Popular Front's campaign successfully attracted voters by emphasizing land reform, housing, health care, and education. Aguirre Cerda won a narrow victory, but the Popular Front lacked a majority in the legislature. To intimidate the congressional opposition, the Front encouraged unions, protests, and strikes, but to no avail. In 1939, two conspiracies emerged in the military, which Aguirre Cerda defused. Then the right wing threatened to boycott the congressional elections of 1941, but this tactic proved self defeating. A month before the elections they suddenly decided to run candidates who failed to attract voters. Their percentage of votes for deputies dropped 34 percent from that of the previous contest. The left wing parties, by contrast, doubled their percentage of votes and the Radicals increased theirs by almost 15 percent. Unfortunately for the Popular Front, the Socialist-Communist rivalry led the Socialists to withdraw from the alliance. The Popular Front received enough support from the right to pass legislation that improved housing and education and created CORFO, the economic development agency.

In 1942 Carlos Ibáñez made another run for the presidency, giving the fragmented left no alternative but to support the Radical Party's candidate, Juan Antonio Ríos. In general, Chileans were pleased with the country's improving fortunes, so they supported Ríos. Unstable political alliances, however, made governing very difficult. He did initiate hydroelectric projects and Empresa Nacional de Electricidad (National Electric Company), or ENDESA. He encouraged oil exploration in the Zona Austral, leading to important discoveries in 1945. He also created the nation's first steel mill, the Compañia de Acero del Pacífico (Pacific Steel Company).

His administration also had to deal with both internal divisions and the diplomatic issue of World War II. Many German-Chileans sympathized with the Axis, but Ríos's leftist supporters tenaciously opposed it. At first the president tried to remain neutral and avoid internal and external conflict. After consistent pressure and negotiation with the United States, in 1943 he broke relations with the Axis, in spite of fears of a German naval attack. Chile received both credits and some military supplies from the United States, but his administration's decision to sell copper to the allies below world market prices stirred up local controversy. The allies, however, were grateful for this support, which they had not received from Argentina. The latter remained neutral and sold its agricultural products at inflated prices.

Clouding Ríos's administration were party conflicts and increased labor unrest. His own health failed and he died in 1946 before completing his term in office. Chileans then elected a third Radical Party president, Gabriel González Videla, in 1946. While his two predecessors were from the right wing of the party, González Videla was from the left wing. Taking office at the beginning of the Cold War, pressures from both the left and the right led him to adopt contradictory positions. He first supported, and then opposed, peasant unions. He included Communists in his cabinet, then after a prolonged coal strike outlawed the party. In 1949 he signed a law enfranchising women but failed to attract many of them to his party. He created new government industries like the Empresa Nacional de Petroleo (National Petroleum Company), or ENAP, and a national sugar company but could not rejuvenate the faltering economy.

The Return of Carlos Ibáñez

Such contradictions left Chileans perplexed as to what the Radical Party stood for. To its credit, during a time of increased political polarization, it brokered a moderate position. In the process, unfortunately, it often appeared self-serving and even unscrupulous. Carlos Ibáñez took advantage of the Radical Party's tarnished image and made another run for the presidency. In his campaign he contended that he would liberate the country from party politics, stabilize the economy, regulate the copper industry, and fight inflation. Although victorious, once inaugurated, he found that governing Chile in the 1950s was no easier than in the 1930s.

Inflation had risen gradually during Gonzalez Videla's administration until it reached 21 percent in 1952. Although periodically the government raised salaries to compensate for the lost purchasing power, Chileans felt their salaries shrinking. Ibáñez promised to solve the problem by tax reforms, but congress would not support his proposals. He rejected the other alternative of cutting expenses, because that would have raised unemployment. As he ran deficits of 25 to 30 percent, suddenly in 1954 inflation exceeded 50 percent. The copper miners struck, so he declared a state of siege to force them back to work. He contemplated a military takeover, but when he met with junior army officers, he found the conditions for their support unacceptable. Frantic for a solution to the deteriorating situation, he invited the North American financial consulting firm Klein-Saks to examine the problem. They recommended a reduction in government spending and credit. He followed these guidelines and lowered the deficit to below 20 percent by cutting workers' salary adjustments and by making other reductions. As a reward, United States financial institutions offered Chile a $75,000,000 loan. Inflation eased up somewhat, but it never dropped below 20 percent.

In preparation for the 1957 congressional elections, the Socialists, Communists, and Democrats formed the Frente de Acción Popular (Popular Action Front). The move proved a success, especially for the Socialists, who doubled their representation from 12 to 24. Most other parties, except those supporting Ibáñez, made important gains. The next year, as presidential elections approached, congress passed a reform bill that implemented the secret ballot for the first time in Chile. Henceforth landowners could not observe how their *campesinos* voted, but this did not deter political bosses from offering them free transportation to the polls. In Chile's highly competitive political culture, politicians bent over backwards to please the people.

FOREIGN POLICY

Foreign events gave the country less flexibility than it had previously enjoyed and had a major impact on domestic policy. Chile lacked the resources to finance its state development model, so it turned to outside credit. Most of this credit came from the United States in the form of Export-Import Bank loans. The terms were that Chile had to use credits to buy capital goods from the United States for its steel mills, its oil industry, and its electrical industry. Since North American companies produced and marketed most of Chile's copper, which generated a large part of its foreign exchange, the United States had a dual influence on Chilean policy.

From the middle 1930s until the Cold War, Chilean political parties from all parts of the political spectrum generally sympathized with the United States. During World War II Chile broke relations with the Axis, and, during the Cold War, for a decade it outlawed the Communist Party. This cordiality with the United States avoided outright conflicts, but it diminished Chile's flexibility to develop an independent credit and copper policy. Chile, like much of Latin America, found its foreign policy options severely narrowed during important periods of the twentieth century.

CONCLUSION

In spite of the fighting over issues such as rural unionization, private participation in public corporations, and monetary policy, Chilean politicians forged a consensus in favor of a state-led model of industrialization. Middle-class politicians created a steel mill, a state petroleum company, a state electric company, and state sugar mills. These firms offered investment opportunities and jobs to all classes. These same politicians used tariffs to protect local goods from imports, although middle-class consumers might have preferred foreign imports. The middle class supported unionizationm, for they saw it as a way to control labor. What the middle class did not find, however, was a formula to reproduce the European and North American consumer societies that had become familiar to them in the media. This remained a politician's greatest challenge.

8

Reform Turns to Revolution, 1958–73

During the period from 1958 to 1973, pressures for reform came from both within and without Chile. Even the conservative Alessandri government could not avoid the pressure to initiate land reform when the Kennedy administration offered economic support in return for reform. By contrast, both the Christian Democratic government, 1964–70, and the Unidad Popular, 1970–73, had strong ideological commitments to reform and needed no outside prodding. All three administrations shared the principle that the state should promote economic development, but they disputed the role that private property should have in this process.

A coalition of right-wing parties elected Jorge Alessandri, son of Arturo, to the presidency in 1958. He narrowly defeated the left-wing candidate, Salvador Allende, by 33,000 votes. Eduardo Frei, the Christian Democrat, polled more than 20 percent of the votes, and the Radical candidate, Luis Bossay, polled less than 16 percent. These two parties represented the middle ground of the political spectrum, and had they agreed on a common candidate, the center could have won the election. During the following two presidential elections, the parties had to decide their alliances carefully because the proportion of votes on the right, center, and left was nearly equal. This balance between the various ideological positions represented the health of the Chilean political system but also a potential vulnerability. As long as the various players in the political forum reached a relative consensus, then the democracy remained stable, but, should one group gain a domineering position, which threatened the other two, then confrontation could result.

THE ELITE

The wiggle room that the upper class had for protecting their privileged position constantly contracted during this period. *Fundos,* urban real estate, and industrial investments all came under greater government control. The first change affecting *fundo* owners was that labor legislation increased workers' benefits. A more radical change followed in which a majority of *fundo* owners in the Valle Central lost their land. Urban landlords frustrated by rising inflation confronted laws that prevented rent increases and the eviction of tenants. As the government and workers expropriated industries, owners withheld new investments. Landowners feared losing their assets and so neglected to repair them, fatalistically believing they would lose them soon.

As opportunities for profitable ventures shrank, wealthy Chileans moved their money out of the country. Their demand for dollars rose, causing the informal exchange rate to soar far above the dollar's real value. In hotels, restaurants, and even professional offices Chileans offered foreigners to exchange money. Carriers then took the funds out of Chile where they were and invested in stocks and bonds. It became increasingly common for affluent Chileans to have overseas portfolios.

The social justice movement deprived the wealthy of some of their land and businesses, but the inability of the government to prevent the flight of capital meant that a substantial amount of it left the country. With little incentive to invest in Chile, this capital contributed to the growth of other nations' economies. As private investment declined, government investment tried to make up the difference, but as the private sector stagnated so did the local tax base. Government investment increasingly had to come from abroad, which meant borrowing from the country's future export earnings.

THE MIDDLE CLASS

The growth of educational institutions, social service agencies, and state industries created a boom in government employment, largely benefiting the middle class. From approximately 85,000 employees in 1958, it grew to 128,000 in 1968, and 360,000 in 1972. Whereas the growth before 1970 was largely though the creation of new jobs, between 1970 and 1973 the growth was due to both new jobs as well as the nationalization of private firms. This growth in public employment paralleled the growth in the number of high school and college graduates. For example, 27,000 students enrolled in the universities in 1960, over 70,000, in 1970, and 145,000 in 1973. Due to the stagnation of the private sector, graduates increasingly saw the state as their only employer. Since the executive branch largely controlled government employment, the stakes of winning the presidency increased enormously.

The middle class split along diverse party lines. Those tied to the private sector supported either the National, Radical, or Christian Democrat parties. Those in the public sector supported the Radical or Christian Democrat parties, with the exception of public teachers, who usually supported the Socialist or Communist parties. These political divisions within the middle class prevented it from acting as a unified group even though it shared many consumer, educational, and civic values. For a majority of the middle class, property values were important, but for some lower paid public employees, such as public school teachers, rent control took precedence over property rights.

Although government legislation improved health care, housing, and the job market, the state controlled these services and allocated them through a political process. As public housing flourished during the Frei and Allende eras, party connections were especially important for obtaining a dwelling, because the demand far exceeded the supply. Relationships with public employees played an important role in establishing priority for services. Terms such as *palita, cuña,* and *padrino* signified bureaucratic connections or influence. Elections, therefore, became much more than a contest between ideologies. They affected party members' access to services, housing, and jobs.

Due to the erosion of middle-class income during periods of high inflation, this group looked for a party that would restructure the economy. They wanted the value of money to stabilize, the purchasing power of salaries to increase, and the creation of more jobs. In the 1950s and 1960s, parties promised most of these goals in their electoral platform, but once in power they proved unable to deliver. As a result, no party succeeded in winning the presidency for two successive terms. The middle class and to a lesser extent the nonunion working class, looked for a party that could provide both security and prosperity. Except when the right wing decided to vote for Eduardo Frei in 1964 to block Salvador Allende, presidential elections were close. In 1958, for example, 33,000 votes separated the first and second candidates and in 1970, only 39,000 votes separated them.

A shift of 20,000 votes, therefore, could have changed the outcome in either election.

LABOR

The working class likewise saw its salaries stagnate, then erode, during periods of rampant inflation. They saw the beginning of a consumer society but barely participated in it. Their salaries hardly provided for food and shelter. Families had to pool their scarce resources to buy and build on a piece of property. Working single sons and daughters helped their parents acquire furniture or basic appliances. Rural relatives might send food and charcoal in winter. During the Allende administration when a black market for potatoes, meat, and wheat flourished, urban relatives consumed and sold some of these farm products.

With many young people coming of age during this period, entry-level jobs were difficult to find. While the population grew by 1,800,000 from 1960–70, the economically active grew by approximately 523,000. Schooling slowed the influx of new workers, but to meet the demand for jobs the government had to spread around scarce resources. Although job creation was impressive, with over 500,000 jobs created during the decade, real wages were low. From 1970 to 1973, the pace of job creation accelerated, so that in those three years the economy created 245,000 new positions. Of those employed, approximately 250,000 were unionized in 1960, and this figure multiplied to 533,000 a decade later. By 1973 union membership reached 600,000; approximately 20 percent of those who were farm workers. The overall percent of workers belonging to unions from 1965 to 1973 doubled, from 11 to 22 percent.

The 1931 Labor Code established the criteria for forming a union and for collective bargaining. The government often fixed maximum salary increases in an effort to control inflation, and this limited unions' latitude for negotiation. As a way to circumvent this compensation limit, unions also included in their contract proposals employee housing, health care, and family benefits. To initiate collective bargaining, the union presented the employer with a formal list of petitions to include in the contract. When a bargaining impasse occurred, a government representative tried to mediate. Unions used strikes to increase pressure for an agreement or to uphold a contract. Although strikes were common, they rarely paralyzed the economy. For example, in 1960 unions struck 257 times involving 88,000 workers, whereas a decade later unions struck 1,000 times involving 300,000 workers. Administrations that were sympathetic to workers succeeded in reducing the duration of strikes. Under Frei the average length was 7 days; whereas under Allende it was only 3.7 days.

During the Frei administration, rural unionization added a new dynamic to the labor movement. When Frei took office in 1964, there were only 24 rural unions with 1,658 members. Six years later, at the end of his administration, there were 421 unions with 104,000 members. Until 1968 over half of the organized rural workers were affiliated with Triumfo Campesino, a union controlled by the Christian Democratic Party. After 1968 the majority joined Libertad and Ranquil, two unions controlled by the Communist, Socialist, and MAPU parties, which supported Allende. All three unions helped secure improved working conditions and economic benefits for *campesinos.*

Labor made important progress in the 1960s and early 1970s as unions expanded into new areas and governments supported their economic and social goals. Still, nearly 80 percent of labor remained unorganized, with low levels of unionization in construction, retail, and services. Most unions were affiliated with the CUT, which was largely dominated by the Communist and Socialist parties. Although these unions supported collective bargaining, the goal of the parties controlling the CUT was state ownership of farmland, industry, and other economic activities. When these parties finally won the presidency in 1970, workers had the opportunity to see the benefits or disadvantages of state ownership.

JORGE ALESSANDRI'S PRESIDENCY, 1958–64

Jorge Alessandri had no taste for stirring up crowds with inflammatory oratory like his father, Arturo. He emphasized that he was not a politician. His charisma was his name, not his demeanor. With him, conservatives felt secure that he would not adopt radical measures. Yet, the dynamics of Chilean politics led him to approve policies which in a more conservative age he would have likely rejected.

Economic Program

One of his main objectives was to lower the inflation that had plagued the preceding administration. To do so, he changed the monetary unit from the peso to the escudo and pegged the latter at par with the dollar. He also encouraged Chileans to bring their money back home, allowing them to open dollar accounts in local banks. He tried to reduce the government deficit and keep down wages. These steps were similar to those recommended by the Klein-Saks economic mission to the previous government. They reflected a belief that a stable currency and open markets would encourage the private sector to raise economic growth.

Valdivia Earthquake

During the first year, the economic program seemed to work because industrial production grew while unemployment dropped 2 percent. Although imports were up 30 percent, enough capital was coming into the country to maintain a favorable balance of payments. There were two unforeseen events, however, that seriously undermined this program. The first was that Chilean exports did not keep up with imports, thus pointing toward a trade deficit. The second more drastic event occurred in May 1960 when one of the largest earthquakes ever recorded struck the south of Chile. It killed hundreds of people and destroyed the equivalent of 10 percent of the nation's annual production. Houses and businesses sank as the terrain liquefied, while miles and miles of farmland became lakes as the land level dropped below the water table. In the Andes, rockslides and falling timber terrorized local residents. A tsunami accompanied the quake, washing away entire communities from Concepción to Chiloé.

For Alessandri to aid the Sur, he had to increase government spending. More damaging to his economic program, however, was his trade imbalance. The combination of foreign aid for the earthquake zone and United States Alliance for Progress funds did not provide sufficient dollars to meet Chile's trade deficit. In October 1962 Alessandri gave in to the inevitable and devalued the national currency by 33 percent, thus destroying the parity of the dollar and the escudo. As businesses saw import prices rise, they jacked up the price of locally produced goods. Inflation jumped to 29 percent in 1962 and over 40 percent for the following two years. To increase government revenue, Alessandri raised taxes, pegging the sales tax at an all-time high of 20 percent. By 1964, the total of all taxes equaled 24 percent of GDP, a large burden for both producers and consumers. Alessandri's stabilization program failed and dissipated the hope that the private sector could produce economic growth.

Achievements

Alessandri's presidency was not without accomplishments. The Kennedy administration offered Alessandri $100,000,000 or more per year if Chile agreed to participate in Alliance for Progress programs. The Alliance sought to create a Marshall Plan for Latin America with rapid growth similar to that of post–World War II Europe. Kennedy's advisors believed that a combination of growth and reform would prevent Cuban revolutions from occurring elsewhere in Latin America. Alessandri willingly cooperated with the Alliance's educational, housing, and land reform objectives. He expanded public schools and doubled university enrollments. He persuaded congress to offer tax exemptions for new housing construction, resulting in an annual increase of 40,000 new units. The state financed some buildings, whereas private capital financed others.

Alessandri's most radical initiative was land reform. His conservative colleagues in congress approved a bill authorizing the government to expropriate idle farmlands, paying the owners 20 percent of their value in cash and the remaining 80 percent over a ten-year period. To administer the process, congress created the Corporación de la Reforma Agraria (Agrarian Reform Corporation), or CORA, and another organization to provide extension services to *campesinos* called the Instituto de Desarrollo Agropecuario (Agricultural and Livestock Development Institute), or IN-DAP. Under Alessandri, CORA expropriated and distributed only 60,000 hectares to only 1,000 *campesinos.* He established the precedent, however, that the state could expropriate private farmland, which later administrations considerably amplified. Also, under later administrations CORA and INDAP supported the radical farm politics that ended Chile's traditional hacienda system.

CHRISTIAN DEMOCRATS IN POWER

Party Origins

The party leadership was made up of young men from the middle class, many who met when studying at the Catholic University. Although the young men originally joined either the Falange or the Social Conservative Party, they realized that they had much in common, so in 1957 they fused the two parties to form the Christian Democratic Party, or PDC. These leaders emphasized their belief that Catholicism could be progressive, in contrast to the conservative Catholicism of an earlier era. They admired the ideas of the French philosopher Jacques Maritain, the intellectual father of the of the Christian Democracy movement. Maritain developed his version of Catholic humanism from two papal encyclicals, *Rerum novarum* of 1891 and *Quadragesimo Anno* of 1931. The Chilean Falange complimented the French scholar's vision with a communitarian ideal, while rejecting the fascism of the Spanish Falange and the Marxist concept of class warfare. Once formed, the Partido Demócrata Cristiano (Christian

Democratic Party), or PDC, promoted a community responsibility for social justice. The PDC hoped to initiate social legislation, which would provide for everyone's basic needs, while reinforcing democratic institutions and human rights. The party also wanted to accelerate economic development by implementing the research recommendations of the Comisión Económica para América Latina (Economic Commission for Latin America), or CEPAL.

In the 1958 presidential election, the Christian Democratic candidate, Eduardo Frei, did amazingly well, coming in third with 20 percent of the vote. The party's percentage dropped in two bi-elections, but in the city council elections of 1963, it rose to 22 percent, or only 1.5 percent less than the two leading coalitions. The Christian Democrats suddenly realized that with only a small increase in votes, they could win the presidency the following year. The PDC leadership, therefore, invested an energy in the campaign such as Chile had rarely seen.

Presidential Campaign

In his presidential campaign Frei proposed a "revolution in liberty" to show that there is a middle way between capitalism and socialism. To achieve this he and his party proposed the following goals. In housing, it planned to build 60,000 units yearly for six years. In agrarian reform, it would distribute land to 100,000 families. With inflation, it promised to lower it but did not specify an exact rate. Regarding copper, its goal was to "Chilenize" it, which meant that the state would buy a majority interest in each of the large mines. To help the poor, in rural areas it called for peasant unions and in urban areas neighborhood action groups. In education, it wanted to end illiteracy, restructure public education, and increase enrollment. In addition, it included an ambitious program of public works such as a subway for Santiago. The party set a goal for economic growth at 6 percent yearly, which over six years would increase the average income of Chileans by one-third.

In spite of the attractiveness of this platform and the growing popularity of its charismatic leader, Eduardo Frei, the right-wing parties determined the results of the election. In a special parliamentary election that was held in March 1964, a victory by a coalition of left-wing parties prompted the right-wing and the Radical parties to drop their presidential candidate, Julio Durán, and support Eduardo Frei. They feared that if they voted for Durán, the next president would be the Socialist candidate, Salvador Allende. With right wing and Radical support, Frei polled 56 percent of the vote, Allende 39 percent, and Durán 5 percent.

How many of Frei's votes were Christian Democratic and how many from other parties? The previous year the right wing and the Radicals together had polled more than 44 percent of the vote; whereas in the congressional elections of 1965 they polled just less than 26 percent. Although the latter number represents approximately the number of votes the right cast for Frei, without these votes Allende, not Frei, would have been elected in 1964. The Christian Democrats, however, did not fully appreciate this reality, in part because they refused to allow either the right or the Radical Party to modify their platform. They discovered even before the next presidential election that in Chilean politics, allies are a necessity.

Although the Christian Democrats wanted to interpret the presidential victory as a mandate, they did not have enough congressional votes to pass their legislation. Nevertheless, they refused to ally with the Radicals or the right to avoid compromising their legislative program. Like most twentieth-century Chilean presidents, Frei faced a very uncooperative congress. In 1965, however, parliamentary elections renewed the entire lower house and one-third of the senators. The PDC campaigned to convince voters to give the party a majority in order to accomplish its ambitious program. Chileans accepted this argument and gave the PDC 85 out of 147 deputies and increased the number of senators from 3 to 13. Still lacking a majority in the Senate, the PDC adopted the strategy of seeking Senate votes from the opposition to pass important bills.

Within the PDC, one faction believed that economic growth was the prerequisite for development. The state would promote economic growth, but while doing so it had to lower inflation and maintain a positive balance of payments. Another faction, however, gave social development priority. According to this faction, house construction, land distribution, and workers' salaries should not depend upon balanced budgets. If achieving these goals caused inflation, according to this group, then that was unavoidable.

Economic Plan

To fine-tune the economy, the Frei administration established a comprehensive Oficina de Planificación Nacional (National Planning Office), or ODEPLAN. By carefully balancing both state and private interests, ODEPLAN sought to reduce inflation, increase production, achieve a five to six percent growth, and promote savings. In foreign trade and finance, it sought to raise copper prices, encourage exports, and renegotiate the foreign debt. There was little margin for error in this program. The failure to achieve any one of these goals could affect the entire program.

Copper Policy

In 1966 the PDC pushed new copper legislation through congress. According to this law, the Chilean government could buy the stock of the major copper corporations. Using this new power the state agency, the Corporación del Cobre (Copper Corporation), or CODELCO, bought 51 percent of the El Teniente mine owned by the Kennecott Corporation and, in 1969, bought 25 percent of Chuquicamata and El Salvador mines owned by the Anaconda Corporation. The PDC touted this achievement as the "Chilenization" of copper. Chile was moving toward the control of copper just as other developing nations were doing with oil. The future challenge would be to manage these mines in a way that would be both competitive and profitable.

The rise in copper demand due to the Vietnam War and a decision to market the ore through the London market increased revenue and investment. Mine workers, however, wanted more benefits, so when negotiations between their union and the government broke down they called a strike. Concerned that a drop in production would affect other programs, in March 1966 Frei mobilized the Carabineros to quell the strike at the El Salvador mine. The miners resisted, and the Carabineros fired, killing seven. Left-wing parties blamed the deaths of the miners on the government, but Frei responded, with some truth, that the left had exploited the conflict for political purposes.

The government also acquired other branches of multinational corporations operating in Chile. It bought the Chilean Electric Company from the South American Power Company and the Chilean Telephone Company from International Telephone and Telegraph. In the latter case, the telephone service was notoriously deficient, so Chileans were hopeful that the state would upgrade the system. The Frei government believed that profits from these enterprises would cover new investments and that state ownership would facilitate economic planning.

Education

Education was high on Frei's list of reforms. His advisors recommended that he restructure the education system into three parts: early childhood; elementary school, consisting of grades 1 through 8; and secondary school, consisting of grades 9 through 12. To improve registration and nutrition the government provided scholarships and meals for needy students. At the university level, the government opened enrollment to all social classes by implementing a national entrance exam, which replaced the *liceo* diploma as the criteria for admission. These reforms also encouraged technical and adult education.

To handle the rise in student enrollment, the state went on a building campaign, more than doubling the total number of classrooms by adding 3,000 new schools. Total registration climbed from 1,840,000 students in 1964 to 2,690,000 students in 1970. The greatest percentage of growth was in secondary and university registration; both exceeded 100 percent. At the university level, the government recognized the need to give more support to research, creating the Comisión Nacional de Investigación Científica y Tecnológica (National Commission for Technological and Scientific Research), or CONICYT, to both fund and supervise viable projects.

Rural Development

The energy that the Christian Democrats brought to their tasks enabled them to achieve many of their goals even in remote areas. In the Sur they engaged in road and school construction, organized farmer cooperatives, and formed mothers' clubs. INDAP provided credit to small farmers while Servicio Agrícola y Ganadera (Agricultural and Livestock Service), or SAG, offered technical support. New Zealand dairy specialists sponsored by SAG encouraged Chilean farmers to adopt their highly productive system. Dairy farmers like Rigo and Gabriela Toiber from Pucón, who enrolled in the SAG program, subdivided their *fundo* into separate paddies, seeded high yielding pastures, and built a modern milking barn. Increased milk production enabled them and other southern farmers to meet the nation's growing demand for dairy products.

Over 450 Peace Corps Volunteers served in Chile during the Frei administration. Although the Communists and Socialists often accused them of being CIA agents, they collaborated with the government in a wide variety of rural development programs. In the province of Cautín, for example, Bruce Weber and Robert Spich worked with *campesino* cooperatives to improve pastures and build an innovative, portable sheep bath. Patricia Soloman worked with promoters from the Pucón Centro de Madres to organize mothers' clubs. To assist residents in the rural village of Trovolhué, which flooded every spring, Volunteers Brian and Sharon Loveman helped them relocate their town to higher ground. In 1965 the government developed a Reforestation and Forestry Management program to combat erosion and encourage the forestry industry. Peace Corps representative Jimmy Dungan collaborated with government agencies and *campesino* co-ops to reforest large areas of the Sur. In this program,

SAG and the Instituto Forestal provided technical support and distributed seedlings, and volunteers enlisted farmers in this program.

Frei's government also responded to many people's social needs. For Lake Caburgua residents, who had only oxcart roads to travel on, it lent support to community leader Berni Bratz and his neighbors to gravel the road and open a bus line. In the same region, where local children walked miles to a distant school, the education department helped community leaders Alfonso Vega and Segundo Nahuel build a neighborhood school. While local residents had fundraisers and organized work crews, the government supplied prefabricated materials. Many rural children had never received school health care, so Servicio Nacional de Salud (National Health Service) nurses in Villarrica initiated a school vaccination campaign.

Parallel to implementing these social programs, the Frei administration achieved many economic goals. In two years, industrial production rose by 20 percent. Improved copper output and prices contributed to a favorable balance of payments. A more progressive tax system funded increases in public employees' salaries. Farm workers' wages and farm prices increased, and moderate price increases in other consumer goods reduced inflation to half its rate during Alessandri's last two years in office. Considering that construction was booming and employment was up, Frei's economic team could congratulate itself on its achievements.

There were two areas, however, in which Frei's economic team failed. One was wages and the other was savings. Collective bargaining and strikes enabled workers to gain wage increases above the rate of inflation. Moreover, private savings and investment dropped, putting a greater obligation on government, which now represented 75 percent of the total. Eduardo Frei criticized the private sector for its low contribution to savings. Later, in November when finance minister Sergio Molina proposed a forced savings plan for workers, the opposition of Socialist and Communist parties derailed the plan through a national strike.

Frei's public projects were certainly oriented to the modernization of Chile. He built new airports, a tunnel linking Santiago and Valparaíso, and modernized the railroad. Along with new dams, port facilities, and Santiago subway construction, public works contributed to a rise in employment and an annual growth of four percent. Yet while public investment grew, private investment contracted. Foreign corporations realized that as long as Chile was nationalizing companies, major new investments were risky. Chilean investors likewise were nervous that after the expropriation of *fundos* and foreign corporations, nationally owned companies might be next.

In a national municipal election in April 1967, the percentage of votes that the Christian Democrats received dropped below the elections of 1964 and 1965. When the party met to discuss the results, its left wing claimed that voters desired more rapid changes. At another party assembly a few months later, the left-wing leader Jacques Chonchol pushed for rapid nationalization of major mining companies and banks. He also pushed for state control, rather than private control, of the economy. To push this program, he put together a coalition, which wrested party control from president Frei's supporters. Instead of the party strengthening its position through alliances with other parties, it weakened itself through infighting.

Agrarian Reform

The expropriation of land, begun under Alessandri, moved at a pace that satisfied very few people. In 1964 Frei had promised to create 100,000 new property owners if he was elected president. To keep this promise, his administration expropriated an average of 450,000 hectares yearly from 1965 to 1967 and 718,000 yearly from 1968 to 1970. But, he created few property owners. The Corporación de la Reforma Agraria decided that *campesinos* had to work the expropriated *fundos* as a group before they could opt to have the land subdivided into private plots. The government feared that many small holdings would be inefficient and diminish farm production.

When Frei's Land Reform bill passed in 1967, it changed the criteria for determining the expropriation of haciendas. Rather than identify only idle lands for expropriation, now the maximum acreage the government allowed was 80 hectares of irrigated land or its equivalent. In an effort to undermine the law, landowners sometimes subdivided the land among children or relatives.

Also high on Frei's agenda for agricultural reform was the unionization of *campesinos.* Although government officials were explicitly prohibited from promoting unions, the head of INDAP encouraged employees to do so anyway. The Christian Democrats competed with Socialist and Communist parties in organizing *campesinos* as all three parties sought political dividends. In 1968 when salary negotiations broke down on the Fundo San Miguel, the Socialist Party encouraged the *campesino* union to strike. Even this action failed to achieve an agreement, so the union took over the *fundo* with arms. When the government sent Carabineros to retake the *fundo*, the *campesinos* resisted them with guns. Students from the FOCH showed solidarity with the *campesinos* through numerous demonstrations. The Carabineros, however, arrested the *campesinos* without loss of life, thus deflating a very dangerous confrontation.

The San Miguel takeover signaled a new strategy by the Socialist Party and another left-wing group, the Movimiento de Izquierda Revolucionario (Revolutionary Left Movement), or MIR. Both groups rejected the legal process for redistributing wealth and instead encouraged direct action. Unfortunately for Frei, the left wing of his own party espoused similar actions. In the last two years of his government, *campesino* unions took over 400 *fundos*. This equaled 30 percent of all the *fundos* expropriated by the CORA. The speed of this extralegal process signaled that a rural revolution was beginning.

University Politics

Another sign that direct action, rather than traditional institutional procedures, was increasingly the norm occurred with various student movements. In 1967 students at the Universidad Católica de Valparaíso boycotted classes for fifty days, demanding more participation in the curriculum and in the choice of administrators. When their movement achieved its goals, student leaders of the Universidad Católica campus in Santiago followed their example. In close alliance with political parties, they sought a role in selecting the academic hierarchy. Students associated with the Christian Democratic Party had an even more defined agenda. They wanted to remove the conservative Catholic heads of the institution and replace them with progressive leaders aligned with the PDC.

In August 1967 students occupied the central administration building and blockaded themselves there until the Vatican and Chilean Cardinal Raúl Silva Henríquez intervened and named a Christian Democratic leader, Fernando Castillo Velasco, as the new head of the Universidad Católica. His appointment ended the student protest, because it also forced the resignation of Santiago's bishop and all existing deans of the university. Some PDC student leaders became more radicalized from this experience and formed the Moviemiento de Acción Popular Unitaria (United Popular Action Movement), or MAPU, which later split from the Christian Democrats. Catholic conservatives, by contrast, decided to organize their own *gremialista,* or employers association movement, led by law student Jaime Guzmán. This group successfully wrestled power from the left in 1968 when it won control of the student federation of the Universidad Católica.

In May 1968 the student movement spread to the University of Chile. The left-wing students of the Instituto Pedagógico (Education School) of the university took over the administrative building. To preempt a leftist group from also occupying the main campus buildings, more moderate students did so. Protracted negotiations between students and administrators kept classes closed for months, obligating students to return in the summer to make up some of the lost time. In 1969 according to new law governing the universities, elections were held to choose the head of the University of Chile. In a three-way contest, Edgardo Boeninger, the Christian Democratic candidate, won. This important victory, coupled with that at the Universidad Católica, meant that the Christian Democrats now controlled the two most important universities in the country. This student movement, however, disconcerted most adults. Even though they were accustomed to student activism, the disturbances in Chile, Europe, and the United States of 1968 were incomprehensible. They could not understand why privileged university students devoted so much time to politics rather than attending classes and studying.

Military Demands

Chilean political culture had an amazing tolerance for diversity of opinion. The Christian Democrats' dramatic reforms generated national debates at both ends of the political spectrum. The military, a somewhat forgotten player in this debate, suddenly startled the nation with its own demands. General Roberto Viaux took over the Tacna Regiment in downtown Santiago on October 21, 1969, and refused to obey either the Minister of Defense or the president. According to Viaux, his rebellion was strictly a protest over low military salaries and poor equipment. Frei, however, interpreted the Tacnazo as a threat to civil government. He declared a state of siege and sent loyal troops to surround the rebellious regiment. Before violence occurred, leaders of Frei's administration resolved the impasse by promising a raise for the military in the next budget, so the Tacna soldiers put down their arms. To celebrate this solution, Frei's supporters filled up the plaza in front of Chile's presidential palace, la Moneda, and during a vibrant political rally listened to him speak in defense of democracy.

In 1969, military governments ruled in Argentina, Paraguay, Bolivia, Brazil, and Peru. Frei had reason, therefore, to be fearful of a military takeover. Conservatives in Chile whose *fundos* were in jeopardy, whose *campesinos* were organizing, and who were paying higher taxes, openly talked about how a military coup in Chile would protect their interests. According to a book titled *El Kerensky chileno*, Frei's reforms were preparing the way for a Marxist takeover in Chile. A Catholic conservative group called Sociedad Chilena de la Tradición, Familia, y Propiedad (Chilean Society for Tradition, Family, and Property), or TFP, accused Frei of undermining traditional Chilean values in their magazine, *Fiducia*. But, in

1969 the military was not plotting to unravel the Christian Democratic reforms. Such action would be too divisive within the military itself where there were numerous PDC sympathizers. Fortunately, negotiations prevailed over force.

In March 1969, parliamentary elections were held. All the parties considered them an indication of who might win the presidential elections in 1970. The results were as follows: National Party, 20.1 percent; Communist/Socialists, 28.2 percent; Christian Democrats, 29.7 percent; and the Radicals 12.9 percent. The right wing, represented by the Nationalist Party, had increased in votes by almost 6 percent since the elections in 1967, the Christian Democrats had lost almost the same percentage of votes, and the left changed by less than 1 percent. This election showed that some of the middle class, which had voted for the Christian Democrats hoping for improved well-being, now were moving to the right. In order to win the presidency in 1970, the Christian Democrats would have to persuade either the Radical or the National Party to support a coalition candidate. Alone they could not hope to win.

1970 Election

To achieve a victory in the 1970 presidential elections, the PDC needed an ally. A center party and a natural choice would have been the Radical Party. But, in a special election in the Sur, the Radicals developed a provisional alliance with the Communists to elect their candidate, Alberto Baltra. Communists urged both the Radicals and the Socialists to resurrect the Popular Front of the 1930s and 1940s. When the Socialists nominated Salvador Allende and the Communists and Radicals dropped their own nominees in favor of Allende, the alliance was reborn, this time under the name Unidad Popular (Popular Unity), or UP. As a sign of change, the platform of the UP was far more radical than the Popular Front. State control over the Chilean economy had advanced considerably since the 1940s, and the Cuban Revolution presented a credible model of a state-owned economy. The UP proposed, therefore, to nationalize large mining firms, banks, most large industries, foreign trade, and wholesale distribution firms. In its social agenda, it wanted to expand public housing, the agrarian reform, health care, and education.

Former President Jorge Alessandri ran ostensibly as an independent, but the National Party backed him as its candidate. He promised to eliminate the popular movements of the Christian Democrats and restore order. Supporters believed that he would curtail agrarian reform, impose discipline on the universities, and deal harshly with strikes. Understandably, this agenda appealed to the upper class, but it also appealed to a growing sector of the middle class, which believed that the price of PDC reforms was inflation and economic uncertainty.

The Christian Democrats chose Radomiro Tomic. Their candidate was a former ambassador to Washington and a long-time party leader. Tomic represented the left wing of the party, which wanted greater state control of the economy. More conservative members of the party like Frei feared that Tomic's enthusiasm for socialism blurred the distinction between Christian Democrats and Marxists, but they did not attempt to block his nomination. Although Tomic applauded Frei's accomplishments, he asserted a need for more radical change. His charismatic delivery of this message appealed to the party's youth, but other middle-class voters found him almost as threatening as Allende.

Alessandri and his supporters were sure he would win; perhaps some were even overconfident. When the votes were counted showing Allende won, they and most other Chileans were shocked by the results. After voters rejected Allende in three previous elections, they now chose him as president. The victory margin was narrow; of a total cast of more than 3,000,000, he won by only 39,000 votes. Allende received 36.2 percent of the vote; Alessandri, 34.9 percent; and Tomic, 27.8 percent. Although Tomic quickly congratulated Allende on his victory, Alessandri called upon democratic forces to unite and block an Allende presidency.

Since no candidate had received a majority of the votes, the constitution required that congress decide the victor. In three-way or four-way presidential contests, it was rare that one candidate would receive a majority. A tradition existed, however, that congressmen cast their votes for the front runner. As political pundits conjectured whether this would also be the case with Allende, he threatened to use workers to shut down the country if congress did not elect him. The Christian Democratic party had enough congressional votes to determine who would be the next president, but they rejected any tactic to block Allende's election. They did insist, however, that Allende support changes to the constitution that they called the "democratic guarantees," which sought to de-politicize the armed forces and protect the media from government expropriation.

While the Christian Democrats and the Unidad Popular worked out an agreement so congress could elect Allende, some right-wing groups sought just the opposite. In the United States, the International Telephone and Telegraph Company sent representatives to discuss with Richard Helms of the CIA and Henry Kissinger of the State Department ways of blocking an Allende presidency. Agustín Edwards, the influential Chilean business leader, conferred with them as well. As rumors circulated that perhaps the United States would support a military coup in Chile, various American civic and business leaders counseled against it. Nevertheless, the CIA proceeded with a plan called "Track II" that explored kidnapping the head of the Chilean armed forces, René Schneider. The latter opposed military intervention, so according to this plan, with him removed, officers below him could act. But the CIA's contacts assassinated rather than kidnapped Schneider, and provoked consternation among most Chileans and especially the Christian Democrats. Two days after the shooting, PDC congressmen, along with those of the Unidad Popular, elected Allende as the first Marxist president in the western world.

THE GOVERNMENT OF THE UNIDAD POPULAR

Salvador Allende explicitly stated that he intended to socialize Chile, not by force nor with the sacrifices of other socialist nations, but with *"vino tinto y empanadas,"* red wine and turnovers. In his speeches, he pledged a commitment to pluralist, democratic institutions. Although Allende had served twenty-five years in the Chilean Senate and had a strong commitment to Chile's political system, he did propose a major constitutional change to replace the bicameral legislature with a unicameral one.

Some of his Unidad Popular colleagues were less committed to a democratic system, which they derisively referred to as bourgeoisie democracy. As the latter discussed their strategy for socializing the economy, they questioned the relevance of bourgeoisie political institutions in a socialist state. Two groups in Allende's coalition, the Socialists and the MIR, had used arms to take over property during the Frei administration. Although they halted these activities after Allende's election, they did so only temporarily. The Communist Party leaders, by contrast, consistently rejected the use of violence. They agreed with Allende about the need to adhere to democratic procedures. To do otherwise, they reasoned, might provoke a military coup.

Economic Changes

One of Allende's first initiatives was to send to congress a bill expropriating all existing foreign mining companies in Chile. The bill, which passed unanimously, stipulated that Chile should compensate the companies. When the comptroller calculated the fair compensation, he found that most mines should receive none; rather, they owed the Chilean government money for the illegal repatriation of profits. Unidad Popular supporters found this decision just, but they failed to anticipate how the copper companies would use it in their legal strategy to tie up copper sales in international markets.

Allende picked Pedro Vuskovic as economic minister to deal with both domestic and international issues. Vuskovic developed plans to raise production, increase employment, distribute wealth, and nationalize industry. Since Chilean industry had unused capacity, he reasoned, if he raised workers' salaries, the increased demand would encourage industry to employ more people and raise production. His first step, therefore, was to grant all workers a 35 to 40 percent raise, in part to compensate for inflation. To prevent an equal or greater rise in prices, he froze them. Chileans did not hesitate to take advantage of their new affluence and went on a buying spree. One result was that inventories decreased and stores placed new orders. Industries then hired more workers to fill the increased number of orders. Unemployment dropped to a historic low of 3.8 percent, inflation dropped to less than 20 percent, and the economy grew by over 8 percent. Vuskovic basked in success; he had accomplished his first three goals.

In the March 1971 municipal elections, in ratification of their increased affluence, many Chileans supported UP candidates. Fifty percent of the electorate voted for the Unidad Popular, which caused a surge in the confidence of government leaders. They interpreted this vote that Chileans wanted to accelerate the pace of socialism. It did not occur to them that the vote really meant that people were pleased with their new level of consumption and hoped the trend would continue.

Signs soon appeared, however, that too much demand was making some goods scarce. Chile's supplies of all products were limited, especially in the case of imports. When the supply of sugar dwindled, people began to hoard it and it disappeared from the stores. As soon as a new shipment arrived, lines formed, sometimes a block long. By 1972, to limit hoarding, stores began rationing the amount they sold to each customer. Some goods such as fresh vegetables and fish were always plentiful. With foods like beef, as a conservation measure, the UP imposed meatless days or weeks. It feared that ranchers might butcher their entire herds and send the money out of the country.

With money plentiful, but some goods scarce, a black market developed that offered goods above the official price. Stores without coffee or toilet tissue on their shelves might sell these prized items from a back room to well-known customers at inflated prices. In other cases, peddlers would go through neighborhoods offering sacks of potatoes or sugar at prices that were considerably higher than the official price. Ironically, as store shelves became bare, restaurants still managed to find most ingredients, which encouraged people to eat out. Every night crowds packed the restaurants. Over dinner and wine, some celebrated the progress of socialism while others debated how to slow it down or how to stop it.

As the traditional means of distributing goods broke down, Allende's opposition decided to publicly emphasize scarcity. On December 1, 1971, a group of women organized "the march of the empty pots." As they paraded through middle-class neighborhoods beating on their pans, supporters rained confetti on them. When they approached working-class neighborhoods, however, angry MIR supporters physically attacked them. Rather than be intimidated, the women developed a long-range strategy of beating their pots nightly and holding more marches. This unique female-led protest caught the Allende administration off guard. Though Allende debunked the women's affluence and referred to them as pawns of international capitalism, he never found convincing arguments to allay the fears of increasing scarcity. He had told Chileans that his revolution would not require sacrifices and now women challenged this point.

Allende was organizing a new method of getting food to the poor through a distribution system that parallelled normal commerce. He established the Juntas de Abastecimiento y Precios (Supply and Price Committees), or JAP, which put together a bag of groceries, called a *canasta popular,* or people's basket, to supply a family for two weeks. The committees distributed these sacks to poor neighborhoods at below cost. Those who did not receive these sacks and opposed this new distribution network questioned whether this was the beginning of a rationing system similar to those in many socialist nations.

One reason that food became scarce was that the UP accelerated the agrarian reform to a pace that disrupted many agricultural activities. In 1971 the CORA, led by Jacques Chonchol, expropriated more land than during the entire six years of Christian Democratic government. As the process accelerated, *campesinos* often decided to expropriate the land themselves. To do this they waited until the owner or administrator was away on business. When he returned, they stood with guns at the gate, preventing him from entering his property. In the south, Mapuche groups occupied ancestral lands that had been lost a century earlier. Reticent to offend any *campesino* group that occupied lands, the Allende government generally accepted this spontaneous land reform. Landholders, however, decided to fight back and formed vigilante groups to defend their *fundos.* In the Sur, for example, a group named Rolando Matos engaged *campesinos* in shoot-outs if they tried to occupy a *fundo.* Clashes between farm workers and owners, not the government, increasingly determined who possessed the land.

Neruda and Castro

Few events in the early 1970s could have united most Chileans, but there was one exception. In October 1971, the Nobel Literature Prize committee distinguished Pablo Neruda for his outstanding contribution to poetry. Since publishing his *Twenty Love Poems* and *General Song* many considered Neruda the most creative poet of the Spanish language of the twentieth century. The Noble Prize gave him additional international stature. His prize along with the earlier one bestowed on Gabriela Mistral convinced Chileans that they were a nation of poets.

A somewhat more divisive event was the arrival of Fidel Castro for a three-week visit. Fidel traveled to the mines in the north and the rural areas of the south making speeches, greeting people, and thoroughly enjoying himself. Although he was obviously enthusiastic with Chile's journey toward socialism, when asked if he believed socialism could be achieved through the democratic process, he responded that every country must act out its own history. On this topic as well as others, he avoided controversy. Although the opposition press claimed it was scandalous that an official visit should last so long, supporters of the Unidad Popular enjoyed the unique opportunity to meet the hero of the Cuban Revolution.

Polarization

In the Valle Central a fascist-style group called Patria y Libertad (Land and Freedom) developed a very aggressive attack against the Unidad Popular. The organization's leader, Pablo Rodríguez Grez, preached confrontation with the Unidad Popular, attracting those who felt that the democratic means were too ineffectual. Although another Patria y Libertad leader, Roberto Thieme, reputedly died in an airplane crash, he was, in fact, very much alive and carrying out acts of sabotage against the government. He caused numerous blackouts by blowing up electrical transmission towers. The conservative press, nevertheless, blamed these acts on leftist terrorists. Later he severed an oil pipeline and conspired with military officers in the June 1973 coup attempt.

Violence from the left further polarized the democratic opposition. A radical leftist group decided to avenge the 1969 death of Puerto Montt squatters by assassinating Edmundo Pérez Zujovic, formerly Frei's Interior Minister. This brutal attack on a leader antagonized the PDC and further separated the nation into opposing blocks. Likewise, the impressive UP election victory in 1971 seriously worried the Christian Democrats. With 50 percent of the electorate favoring the UP and the implementation of its programs gaining speed, the PDC leadership found that they could no longer remain isolated. For decades it had refused any formal alliance with the right wing; now it decided that it had no choice. After forcefully attacking privilege during its six years in power, the PDC now decided to block a revolution. It formed the Confederación Democrática (Democratic Confederation), or CODE, with the National Party, and together they controlled enough congressional votes to block the Unidad Popular's legislation.

As the Unidad Popular sought greater control of the media through acquisitions in the publishing industry, the PDC realized how difficult its role as the opposition might become. First, the publishing house Zig-Zag, which edited the widely circulating weekly, *Ercilla,* succumbed to rising labor costs. The government took it over and soon began publishing a variety of titles reflecting its ideology. The largest paper mill, La Papelera, as well as the newspaper chain, *El Mercurio,* experienced similar economic problems. If the government also bought out these industries, this would likely muzzle the opposition. So, a national campaign, which even involved the CIA, struggled to save both companies from government acquisition.

While CODE developed a strategy to oppose the Unidad Popular, radical workers and *campesinos* accelerated illegal property seizures. In the case of factories, when the owners demanded their return, the Allende government refused. It based its denial on a 1930s decree, which permitted the state to temporarily take over a firm that had labor problems. Newspaper headlines reported that workers seized factory after factory. CODE feared that this haphazard process could soon end private industry, so it confronted Allende and demanded a bill to establish a procedure for socializing property. Allende agreed to negotiate a solution.

Representatives from both CODE and UP met and drew up a constitutional amendment call the "tres areas." The first area was a socialized sector made up of large mining and industrial firms. The second area was a mixed sector with joint government and private ownership. And the third area was the private sector. Although Allende accepted this proposal, radical Socialists like Carlos Altamirano rejected it, fearing it would prevent additional worker takeovers and put breaks on "accelerating the revolution." Congress passed the measure, but divisiveness within the UP prompted Allende to veto it. CODE tried to override his veto, but a constitutional controversy stalled its efforts. The measure died, and with it, the opportunity for Allende to resolve with CODE this explosive issue. In this case, a minority faction within Unidad Popular showed its power to paralyze the president's efforts to compromise.

The Nixon administration closely followed the rising tensions between

CODE and UP. After failing to prevent Allende from taking office, its strategy shifted to supporting CODE to keep the opposition to the Unidad Popular alive. Nixon and Kissinger were fighting communism in Asia. To them, Allende's regime represented a communist beachhead in South America, and they were determined to destroy it. They encouraged the opposition press and labor by pouring money into CODE-affiliated publications, *la Papelera,* and trade-union strike funds. To hurt Allende's foreign credit, they cut off new loans and opposed grants to Chile from international organizations. The Nixon administration, however, continued to disburse existing loans and private banks continued to grant Chile some credit. Both government and private financial institutions avoided an outright boycott of Chile, in part because they were renegotiating the repayment of past loans.

The Unidad Popular needed increasing amounts of foreign credit to finance its consumer revolution for the poor. To compensate for declining loans from the United States, officials turned to Canada, Western Europe, the USSR, and China. Though these countries provided Chile some new loans, the USSR offered little short-term credit, preferring instead to grant over $400 million in long term credits. Chilean officials also obtained $80,000,000 in loans from the International Monetary Fund and agreed to a new debt repayment schedule with private banks and the governments belonging to the "Club of Paris." The decline of new loans from the United States, therefore, was more than compensated by those from other sources. Nevertheless, with trade revenue dropping and local consumption rising, the country developed a chronic need for credit to finance rising imports.

National Strike

By August 1972, CODE confronted the Unidad Popular with the same "scorched earth tactics" that the UP had used to take over private property. On August 21 the retail merchants locked their doors for twenty-four hours. In an attempt to reopen these businesses, the government began to break the locks, which provoked riots and arrests. On October 11 a truckers strike in the Zona Austral quickly spread nationwide. Two days later the retail merchants and industries joined in, followed by professional organizations of doctors, lawyers, and architects. Even peasant cooperatives went on strike. All complained of scarcities, inflation, and insecurity. As in any strike, the participants were willing to hurt their short-term interests for a long-term goal. The strikers believed the very survival of private property and the middle class was at stake.

The Military Cabinet

The only way that Allende found to resolve the strike was to invite the military to join his cabinet. Although many of his own colleagues opposed this move, on November 2, 1972, he named General Carlos Prats, commander and chief of the armed forces, to the position of Minister of the Interior. Other officers filled additional key ministerial positions. Three days later, Prats negotiated an end to the strike. With this confrontation seemingly behind them, Chileans now shifted their focus to more traditional party rivalry: the March 1973 parliamentary election. While CODE campaigned to win enough seats to remove Allende from office, the Unidad Popular asked people to show their support for the government.

The military served as a buffer between the two coalitions and allowed the country to return to a semblance of normal life, which enabled the hotly contested election campaign to proceed with a minimum of confrontation. Parties covered every post, wall, and fence with their candidates' posters. Frequently, one party would paste their posters on top of the others'. The radios were filled with jingles and songs supporting the candidates. Periodically, Pablo Rodriguez Grez of Patria and Libertad, who was not running for office, predicted impending doom. Apart from him, people lived the illusion that the country had returned to normality.

Except for an occasional rumor of fraud, the election occurred without problems. CODE fell short of its unrealistic goal of 66 percent, ending with 55 percent versus 44 percent for the Unidad Popular. Both sides claimed victory, but little had changed. The military indicated its willingness to remain in the cabinet after the elections, but the left wing of the UP wanted them out. Therefore, they resigned and Allende named a civilian cabinet.

The minister of education set off the next controversy when he announced plans for a new education system called the Escuela Nacional Unificada (Unified National School System), or ENU. It proposed that a national curriculum based on a new socialist society be taught in both public and private schools. CODE immediately reacted against what it believed to be the imposition of Marxist ideas in the curriculum. The Catholic Church, generally friendly to the Unidad Popular, feared this measure would undercut its control of the curriculum and asked for time to discuss the program.

The next month the copper miners at the El Teniente mine struck for higher wages. Allende reminded workers that the mine was nationalized, which meant that they owned it and should not push for higher wages. CODE, however, encouraged the strike because it not only cut government revenue, but also it seemed to belie the claim that the Unidad Popular benefited workers. Supportive of the miners strike, the middle-class professionals welcomed the workers when they marched from the mine to Santiago. Before Allende finally settled the strike 77 days later, it cost his government approximately $80,000,000. Unfortunately, these acts, so destructive to the national economy, had become part of the political culture.

The Tanks

Even more threatening was an uprising by junior officers on the morning of June 29, 1973. A tank regiment drove down the streets of Santiago, curiously stopping for red lights, as it headed for the defense ministry. Once at the ministry, the people on the tank fired numerous shots, killing 22 and wounding 32, in a violent uprising, which the press labeled as the *tancazo* or tank assault. They also attacked the government palace, but the commander of the army, General Prats, persuaded the rebels to lay down their arms. In the meantime, Allende broadcast a message to workers to defend their government. Many of them, encouraged by Socialist and MIR leaders who had organized *cordones industrials,* or industrial belts, took over more than 300 factories. That evening Allende's supporters organized a massive rally in front of the national palace to reassure everyone that the government was still in control.

Peace Negotiations

The *tancazo* warned both CODE and the Unidad Popular that if politicians did not compromise and uphold the democratic system, then the next time the military left the barracks, it would take over the government. This grim reality forced the two sides to negotiate. On July 30 Salvador Allende and Christian Democrat leader Patricio Aylwin discussed the points that might resolve the major differences between the two coalitions. When the press speculated whether Allende might offer the PDC positions in his cabinet, the majority of the PDC leadership publicly opposed such a move. Within the UP the Communists welcomed the prospect of some PDC cabinet members, hoping this would prevent a military coup, while the Socialists opposed it. Patricio Aylwin proposed the designation of military officers to important cabinet posts, the return of occupied private property, and the enforcement of the arms control law. With some reservations, Allende accepted most of these demands, but he rejected the return of occupied industries, knowing that Socialist and MIR leaders would veto such a move. Soon he felt additional pressure to negotiate a solution to the crisis, because the truck drivers, the merchants, and eventually most business owners and professionals joined in another national strike. In mid-August he and Aylwin again secretly met at the house of Cardinal Raúl Silva, but the discussion failed to produce an agreement.

Middle-Class Concerns

Rather than tensions subsiding, they increased. On August 22 CODE congress members passed a resolution accusing Allende of violating the constitution and taking private property without legal authority. Not only had CODE supporters lost their businesses, but also the Unidad Popular had dismissed them from the management and technical staff of many of these firms. Chilean professionals faced the reality that unless they belonged to the Unidad Popular they could not find work. As a result, engineers, chemists, accountants, and others sought jobs in other Latin American countries and the United States. Newspapers carried pages of advertisements titled *Por Viaje Vendo*, "For Sale, I'm Leaving," of professionals liquidating their home furnishings and apartments. Adding to employment anxieties were the threats of violence, which the *cordones industriales* made to Santiago residents if the military should try to overthrow the government. The military took these threats seriously and began raiding worker-controlled factories in search of arms caches. Periodically CODE newspapers ran photographs of guns and homemade weapons confiscated at a particular industry.

Moderate groups within the Unidad Popular were concerned with the "brain drain" and increased hostility of the middle class to their government. More radical groups, however, questioned whether the middle class should have any role in a socialist Chile. In an effort to respond to the oppositions' request for greater security, Allende decided to include General Carlos Prats and three other officers in his cabinet. Unfortunately, the MIR and radical Socialists undermined the military's trust in the government when they tried to infiltrate the armed forces and turn the recruits against their officers. Then on August 21, a bizarre confrontation occurred between General Prats and Alejandra Cox, while each was driving in separate cars on a Santiago expressway. Allegedly after she insulted him, he became furious, and pursued her car. The military officers' wives protested his behavior and demanded his resignation. Humiliated, Prats quit as Defense Minister and resigned from active duty. Allende then replaced him with Augusto Pinochet, believing that the latter would uphold the constitution.

Accomplishments and Problems

Although the intense conflict after October 1972 hurt many Unidad Popular programs, until then the government improved health, education, housing, and employment. The infant mortality rate dropped, and people ate better and lived longer. Schooling increased as Allende's government emphasized all levels of education. Kindergarten enrollment nearly doubled and the government built 122 new schools. Elementary and secondary school enrollments increased by 10 percent while university enrollments more than doubled from 70,000 to 145,000. In housing, the government began 110,000 new units but encountered a variety of problems and finished only 29,000.

From 1970 to 1973 employment grew, showing an increase of 235,000 employed, while in the same period unemployment dropped from 6.1 percent to 4.8 percent. The production of all goods increased during the first two years, but after the national strike in October 1972 a decline began. Strikes, a drop in investment, and the scarcity of raw materials caused GDP to drop by 3.6 percent in 1973. For two years, workers' incomes increased faster than inflation, but by late 1972 spiraling prices and scarcities caused them to fall behind. To expand employment and output, the government amassed large deficits, causing inflation to rise from 21 percent in 1971 to 381 percent by September 1973. In the farm sector, CORA and *campesino* land expropriations gave *campesinos* access to more land, but the change hurt production. In 1973, farm output was down 22 percent, with wheat output dropping by 40 percent. To compensate for this decrease, the government increased food imports from $135 million in 1970 to $511 million in 1973.

International trade and Chile's balance of payments experienced severe problems after Allende's first year in office. Partly due to strikes and partly due to new management, copper production and exports dropped. With imports rising, a trade imbalance grew and drained the country's financial reserves. Traditional economists warned the Unidad Popular that it needed to pay more attention to national finances and less to distribution and property ownership, but many UP leaders disregarded this advice as inapplicable to the socialist economy they were building. When the financial situation got out of control, unfortunately, the UP factions could not agree on a common policy.

Military Coup

Some members of Unidad Popular had urged workers to overthrow democratic institutions, which they claimed favored the enemies of a socialist state. Other members, who were committed to democracy, vented their anger at the opposition with derogatory epitaphs such as *momios,* or mummies, and fascists. The strategy of CODE supporters changed after the March elections to one in which they openly urged the military to overthrow the government. CODE supporters derogatorily referred to members of the Unidad Popular as "Upientos," or scum. The epitaphs and vehemence with which both sides condemned each other augured ill for the survival of democracy.

The national strike continued while rumors of an impending military coup circulated daily. Early in the day on September 11, 1973, the military left their barracks before dawn and occupied most of the radio stations. They began broadcasting marches and periodic bulletins that they were assuming control of the country. They offered Allende a plane to fly out of the country and declared a national curfew that would begin at 11:00 A.M. Informed of the military's demands, Allende first told all the workers to go into the streets and defend the government, but he later changed his mind and asked them to remain alert at their factories. Allende refused to surrender, so at noon the air force bombed the national palace. Allende died. According to one version, the army shot him, and according to another, he committed suicide. The military began arresting a number of prominent government leaders while others sought refuge in foreign embassies. Rumors of a possible civil war proved false. The sporadic armed resistance of some Unidad Popular followers proved futile when confronted by a professional army.

Immediately an international debate began over key issues raised by the tragedy of Chile. Concerned people asked who was responsible for the military coup, had the Unidad Popular adopted a rational strategy for transforming Chile, and was it possible for a revolution to be achieved through democratic means? Regarding the first question, many critics pointed their fingers at the Nixon administration, believing that it undermined Allende's government. A Congressional investigation headed by Senator Frank Church found that the CIA tried to block Allende's election and then provided financial support to opposition groups. But, it encountered no evidence that the CIA had participated in the overthrow of the Unidad Popular government.

Rival factions of Allende's government, once in exile, frequently blamed each other for the military coup. While the radical left condemned the Communist Party for slowing down the pace of revolution, the Communists condemned the left for its failure to support negotiations. In fact, all the political actors bore responsibility for the tragic end of democracy. The extreme divisiveness within the Unidad Popular, and within the country at large, undermined Allende's government. Class politics of the Unidad Popular split the nation and unleashed a violence that affected everyone. Looking for a mediator to end the violence, Allende invited the military into his cabinet. This worked temporarily, but when the left wing of his own party demanded their expulsion, once again violence stalked the country. The military overthrew the Unidad Popular on September 11, to end his popular revolution. From this experience, observers concluded that an elected government cannot undertake a revolution and preserve the consensus needed to govern a democracy.

9

Military Rule and Neoliberalism, 1973–90

No one in Chile anticipated how military rule would change their lives. For members of the Unidad Popular (Popular Unity), or UP, one day they were government leaders and the next they were fugitives. Although CODE supporters generally rejoiced with the overthrow of the Unidad Popular, most were naïve about their future political role. Christian Democratic leaders mistakenly believed that the military would soon restore civilian political institutions. They thought that their opposition to the Unidad Popular had earned them the right to help rebuild civic institutions. Conservative leaders were less eager for the restoration of democracy, for they feared a resurgence of left-wing parties. The Military Junta, which assumed power after the coup, worried that elections and public debate would create more unrest while blaming the nation's crisis on traditional politics. The Junta members had not decided how long they would be in office, whether they would eventually reinstate the 1925 Constitution, and how they would manage the economy.

Those voices within the CODE coalition, which wanted a quick reinstatement of the 1925 Constitution and civilian government, quickly lost out to those who wanted prolonged military rule. The Junta and some of its conservative civilian allies decided to drastically reshape national institutions. It ordered the termination of all civilian political activity, while behind the scenes two pro-military groups rivaled for leadership. A conservative Catholic group wanted the military to create a political movement similar to that of Spain's Francisco Franco, whereas a conservative economic group wanted the military to emphasize neoliberal fiscal change. Although both groups had influence in the government, within two years the economic group gained the upper hand.

The economists were foreign-educated, many with Ph.D.s from the University of Chicago, and therefore nicknamed the "Chicago Boys." They attempted to apply neoliberal principles to every aspect of Chilean life, not only privatizing businesses and farms expropriated by the Unidad Popular, but many traditional government services as well. The latter included health care, social security, and education. Conservative thinkers around the world watched this experiment in privatizing the state. As prosperity increased in the late 1970s, even Chilean skeptics began to believe in the new economic model. Some international observers recommended the model for the rest of Latin America. A drastic recession in the early 1980s, however, rapidly reversed these sentiments. As most financial institutions went bankrupt and the government failed to pay its international debts, even conservative supporters questioned the economic reforms.

Augusto Pinochet, president of Chile since late 1974, became a target for the regime's critics. They put together a broad spectrum of opponents who protested the lack of civil rights and demanded Pinochet's resignation. Although they failed to achieve their objective, in 1988 they defeated his bid for eight more years in the presidency. The following year they elected a president and a congress in preparation for the return of civilian rule. In 1990, with the inauguration of new leaders, seventeen years of military rule ended. Pinochet's shadow still lingered, but the new government inherited a flourishing economy to help it build a more equitable society.

MILITARY POLITICS

Like the members of many institutions in Chile, the leaders of the military came from diverse backgrounds and espoused a variety of beliefs. Most officers came from middle-class families with the exception of the navy, which drew more from the upper class. Before the military coup, a minority of senior officers, but many enlisted men, supported the Unidad Popular. A larger number of senior officers sympathized with the Christian Democrats. On the right, a minority of hard-liners, or *duros*, occupied a militant position. All officers shared deep feelings of patriotism, complemented by a loyalty to their branch of service and their commanders. They were also under pressure to advance their careers, because if they were passed over for promotion they were forced to resign. The hierarchical structure of the military assured that if a highly influential group could assume command they could count on most officers and servicemen to obey orders even if they disagreed with their politics.

During the last nine months of the UP government, Allende asked various military officers to serve in his cabinet in an attempt to restore confidence in his administration. Because intolerance had eroded civil society as people attacked each other with a vehemence seldom seen in Chile, the officers in Allende's cabinet experienced enormous frustration governing the country. Particularly galling to them was the daily political haggling within the Unidad Popular government, leading them to question who was in charge.

As the country seemed headed for chaos, a consensus began to develop within a core of military commanders that they had to take over the government. The hard-liners took the initiative in organizing the coup, so that when they overthrew the Unidad Popular they imposed their version of order on the country rather than restore civil society. The head of the Military Junta, Augusto Pinochet, assured Chileans that the armed forces acted out of patriotism. He did not mention that he had arrested some of his own officers for their loyalty to Allende; rather, he stressed the unity of the armed forces. He blamed the deterioration of the nation on politicians, who he said put their own interests above those of the nation. Based on this rationale, he suspended all political activity, which he called a prerequisite to rebuilding the nation.

The Military Junta reminded the nation that in September 1973 the country was on the verge of civil war. It showed arms caches on television and published a white book on "Plan Z." This document alleged that Unidad Popular leaders planned to assassinate leading military officers during the country's independence celebration on September 19. For some Chileans, this assertion was credible, considering that the Movimiento de Izquierda Revolucionario (Revolutionary Left Movement), or MIR, and radical Socialists had urged workers to arm themselves. For other Chileans, the military's claims were a trumped-up justification for overthrowing Allende's government. As with most controversies, people drew their conclusions according to their political beliefs, not evidence.

Pinochet offered the people a similar scapegoat to the one Colonel Carlos Ibañez had used decades before. Politicians corrupted the nation. In 1973, as people looked for someone responsible for insecurity and scarcities, Pinochet assured them that not just the UP politicians had damaged the nation, but all politicians had. He contrasted the "self-serving politicians" to the patriotic military in hopes of uniting all people behind his government. After so much conflict, most Chileans desperately looked for leadership to give them peace and prosperity. CODE supporters especially saw the military as an answer. They did not foresee the military's disregard of civil rights or the economic experiments it would initiate.

Whereas people affiliated with the CODE initially supported the military, those belonging to Allende's government feared for their lives. The military rounded up thousands of Unidad Popular leaders and detained them in centers throughout the nation, the largest being the National Stadium in Santiago. After their arrest, some celebrities like folk singer Victor Jara "disappeared" until his cadaver later turned up. Likewise, activist and freelance writer Charles Horman "disappeared" after being incarcerated in the National Stadium. The heroic efforts of his father to find his body became the subject of the book and film *Missing*. As many as 3,000 people disappeared and only a decade or more later did information emerge about the location of their bodies.

High-ranking UP officials took asylum in embassies. Those who were unable to do so the military arrested and sent to various detention camps in the Sur and Zona Austral regions. The military imposed a state of siege and a curfew. Carabineros patrolled the street corners with submachine guns. Periodically the military swept the *poblaciones,* or poor neighborhoods, arresting people, holding them a day or two, and then releasing them without charges. The purpose was intimidation. Those particularly active in opposing the military were arrested, tortured, and sometimes executed. While the Catholic Church and other human rights activists protested these abuses, a number of important Christian Democratic leaders anguished over whether to publicly criticize the military. In 1976 former president Eduardo Frei decided that he must challenge the government's human rights abuses. Although he originally sympathized with the military coup, now he called for the restoration of democracy. Pinochet immediately sought to discredit him with accusations of being unpatriotic and naïvely collaborating with the left wing. So intense was the government's harassment that when Frei died mysteriously in January 1982 during a routine operation, his family and friends conjectured that the military might have poisoned him. Coincidentally, a month later, labor leader Tucapel Jiménez died at the hands of an assassin. Like Frei, he originally supported the military regime but had turned against it.

Some Chileans living in exile vocally opposed the military government. Fearful of these voices, the *Dirección de Inteligencia Nacional* (National Intelligence Service), or DINA, designed overseas operations to silence them.

A year after the coup, a car bomb blew up the former commander in chief of the armed services, Carlos Prat, and his wife in Buenos Aires. The following year Christian Democratic leader Bernardo Leighton was shot, but not killed, in Rome. In 1976, a car bomb killed Allende's former ambassador to the United States, Orlando Letelier. Since the latter assassination occurred in Washington, D.C., the United States Justice Department investigated the traces left by the hit squad. It found conclusive evidence that DINA had carried out the bombing using both its own operatives and Cuban exiles. Although the United States' investigation discovered the identity of the bomber and extradited him, it had no success in extraditing the head of DINA, who authorized the killing. As international attention focused on DINA, Pinochet decided to dissolve it, but he created another intelligence service in its place.

At great personal risk, some people within Chile resisted military rule. Union members, supported by moderate Unidad Popular sympathizers and Christian Democrats, engaged in peaceful strikes and protests. Unfortunately, they often faced arrest, torture, and exile. In contrast to the peaceful demonstrations, the left-wing groups of the Unidad Popular, such as MIR, chose to engage in armed struggle. They organized urban guerrilla units, which engaged the carabineros in numerous shoot-outs. In 1983, they succeeded in assassinating the mayor of Santiago, causing the military to retaliate with the arrest and assassination of many guerrilla members. Fearing the worst, prominent MIR leader Pascual Allende sought asylum in Costa Rica. Amid the violence, the Vicaría de la Solidaridad, or Solidarity Vicariate of the Catholic Church, offered legal support to those arrested and helped relatives find the "disappeared." Civil courts continued to function during this period, but most judges were either sympathetic to the military or intimidated by it and therefore provided little human rights protection.

The military's anti-Marxist crusade made it blind to the universal repugnance its acts of vengeance caused abroad. For observers outside Chile, these arrests and assassinations confirmed previous accounts of the regime's brutality. Pinochet, however, believed that he was engaged in a holy war and increasingly ran the country without much accountability even to his fellow officers. He demanded that the other members of the Junta name him president. General Gustavo Leigh of the air force repeatedly opposed Pinochet's aggrandizement, but to no avail. In revenge, Pinochet forcibly removed Leigh in July 1978, prompting nine Air Force generals to resign in protest. To shore up support within the military, Pinochet promoted loyal followers, purchased new equipment, and increased salaries and benefits. To further assure that the armed forces had adequate resources, in 1976 he decreed an allocation to them of 10 percent of all the copper export revenue.

He also appointed a commission to rewrite the constitution, which enshrined the military's protective role over the state. According to this document, if the state was threatened, the military had a right to intervene on its behalf. The constitution created a National Security Council to help the military recognize if a threat existed. The new charter did provide for a congress, but the first election would not occur until 1989 at the earliest. The system for conducting elections guaranteed strong minority party representation, capable of blocking attempts to amend the constitution. In 1988, a referendum would determine if Pinochet would continue in the presidency until 1997, or whether other candidates could run for the office. To give this new charter the aura of public support, he held a tightly managed plebiscite in 1980. When Chileans overwhelmingly ratified the constitution, this gave more institutional legitimacy to military rule. It also established a system, however, to which even the military had to adhere. This limitation was not obvious to Pinochet in 1980. His regime exercised nearly unlimited power and was buoyed by the prosperous economy, but crises came later and his own constitution turned against him.

PRIVATIZING THE ECONOMY

While the military tried to pacify the country and legitimate its rule, it also struggled to fix the economy. In an attempt to restore markets and property rights, it loosened price controls and returned some businesses to the former owners. As inflationary pressures pushed up prices, store shelves filled up again, but only the affluent could afford the goods. Unemployment grew, adding another problem to the woes of the working class. With criticism rising both at home and abroad because of the lack of civil liberties, the generals hoped to quickly return the country to affluence and thus gain new support. They looked at the problem from an engineer's perspective, believing that development was a process of planning and building. Although few of them had studied economics, they considered it a science closely related to their own engineering background. They failed to recognize the social implications of economic theory.

When the University of Chicago–trained economists approached Augusto Pinochet with a plan for transforming the country, he immediately liked the idea. They offered to bring their mentor, Milton Friedman, to Chile to conduct a seminar for policymakers and business leaders. Friedman's credentials as Nobel laureate in economics and advisor to nations around the world also had the potential of raising the military's prestige in the international business community. In March 1975, Milton Friedman arrived in Chile with much fanfare. In a three-day seminar, he outlined how to create a market economy by privatizing most state activities, slashing government spending, and encouraging foreign trade and investment. Rather than implement such drastic changes over a long period, Friedman recommended doing so immediately. He called this "shock treatment." In the short run, he recognized the high social costs of the program. Tight money would reduce demand, raise unemployment, and produce hardships. Yet Friedman predicted an economic turnaround so dynamic that everyone would benefit. According to this vision, Chile's long-standing development problems would finally end. Believing that Friedman's plan would work, Pinochet authorized the "Chicago Boys" to put together a program which would shock the nation toward development.

INDUSTRY

Pinochet's economic minister, Fernando Léniz, began the process of returning industries expropriated during the Unidad Popular. His successor, Sergio de Castro, accelerated a process that privatized 25 banks and over 400 other companies. But privatization was only one piece of a plan developed by a group of economic professors at Universidad Católica with Ph.D.s from institutions like the University of Chicago. They intended to restructure the entire economy along neoliberal guidelines.

To undertake their task, they reversed the policies of most twentieth-century Chilean economists who had used a variety of government subsidies such as tariffs and credits to stimulate industrial development. The Católica economists, however, rejected these methods. According to them, protection and subsidy had encouraged inefficient and noncompetitive industries. To expose national industry to foreign competition, from 1973 to 1980, they dropped the average tariffs from 100 percent to only 10 percent. By removing tariff protection, they forced industry to become efficient and quality conscious. If the prices of Chilean goods were not competitive with those of Asia, Europe, and North America, then the industry would perish.

To accomplish this radical transformation the economic team recognized that Chilean industry had to reduce its production costs. To this end the team implemented labor reforms that weakened unions and allowed manufacturers to lower wages, fringe benefits, and employment taxes. Neoliberal economists, ironically, did not consider these labor-cutting measures to be subsidies to industry.

Plants and machinery had severely deteriorated during the Unidad

Popular government and entrepreneurs sorely needed outside capital. To give them access to credit with which to buy or modernize factories, the economic team encouraged new financial institutions and lifted restrictions on foreign borrowing. Taking advantage of these opportunities, a group of aggressive business leaders borrowed funds both at home and abroad to build large conglomerates.

Pinochet's economic team implemented this new model at a time when Chilean industry was least prepared for international competition. Following the military coup, the local market had shrunk in response to higher prices and unemployment. The shock treatment initially crippled manufacturing, which shrank by 25 percent in 1975 before beginning to grow at the healthy rate of 6 to 7 percent in the years 1976–80. For government economists, this four-year boom seemed to confirm the validity of neoliberal manufacturing policies.

Although Milton Friedman provided much of the theory behind these policies, his colleague from the University of Chicago, Arnold Harberger, played an even more important role as he commuted regularly to Chile. He encouraged the Chilean economic team to diversify exports and lessen its dependence on copper through favorable exchange rates. Two of his former students, Jorge Cauas and Sergio de Castro, led Pinochet's team. They gave priority to reducing government spending in an effort to lower inflation. From 1973 to 1981, inflation dropped from over 600 percent to less than 10 percent, an accomplishment that both Chileans and foreigners considered "miraculous." Confident they had whipped this perennial scourge, in 1979 they froze the exchange rate of the peso to the dollar. They overlooked how a fixed exchange rate can hurt exports and subsidize imports. As a result soon famous brands, which had rarely been available in Chile, filled the stores and displaced local produce. National firms struggled to survive, but many did not. Between 1977 and 1980, almost 1,300 failed.

Unfortunately, the crisis soon became worse. In an effort to fight its own problems of inflation, the United States Federal Reserve Board decided to raise interest rates. This tightened credit worldwide while driving up the value of the dollar. During the late 1970s with easy credit available, Chilean business owners had borrowed almost $11 billion abroad and were largely responsible for pushing the nation's foreign debt from $5.3 to $17.3 billion. With credit tight and the dollar more expensive, neither business owners nor the state could pay their foreign debts.

Large Chilean conglomerates pressured the government not to devalue the peso because the dollars they needed to repay their debts would become too expensive. Yet by 1982, the government had no choice. At first, the economic team lowered the peso by only 18 percent, but soon it devalued it further. As debtors needed more and more pesos to buy dollars, soon their debts exceeded their equity. Banks were some of the most severely effected. A study by economist Rulf Lüders showed startling evidence that most had a negative worth. With a total collapse of the nation's financial institutions imminent, the government took them over. Suddenly the military found itself controlling more firms than those expropriated by the Allende government. The fluctuations of the global market could be more devastating to private firms than socialism. Neoliberal economists had failed to adjust national monetary policy to the volatile world market. Like the Unidad Popular, they had pushed Chilean capitalism again toward extinction.

Economists from the earlier Alessandri and Frei administrations, who never agreed with the University of Chicago economic model, now proclaimed that it had failed. According to them Chile needed to return to the days of protectionism and subsidy. Desperately looking for a solution, Pinochet listened to this criticism and changed his economic team. The new leaders quickly implemented higher tariffs and fiscal controls to help local industry and financial institutions. Nevertheless, as these measures began to resurrect the economic system of the 1950s and 1960s, the business community feared abandoning neoliberal policy completely. So as soon as the economy showed signs of recuperation, business leaders persuaded Pinochet to appoint Hernán Büche as finance minister. With his degree from the Columbia University School of Business, he seemed to combine the theory and practice of running the nation's economy. He even expanded the policies of privatization by selling state firms such as the large utilities. He also allowed foreign investors a greater participation in Chilean business.

Although neoliberals debated privatizing the Gran Minería or large copper mines, Pinochet was adamant that the state retain ownership. He recognized that this industry was a major source of government revenue and foreign exchange. Even during the convulsions of the Unidad Popular, copper output grew by an average of 4 percent per year. Though this was less than projected, strikes and other disruptions kept production down. After the military took over, in four years it boosted output by 21 percent, reaching approximately 990,000 metric tons in 1977. A decade later production exceeded 1,400,000 tons and then 1,588,000 tons in 1990. Although these increases seem impressive, they were gradual rather than spectacular. In fact, by 1990 many areas of the economy exceeded copper's rate of growth. The shift in exports demonstrates this trend. Whereas copper represented 75 percent of exports in 1973, by 1990 it represented less than 50 percent. Chile's new exports of agricultural, forestry, and fishery products suddenly attracted worldwide attention.

AGRICULTURE, FORESTRY, AND FISHERIES

The restructuring of natural resource activities represented a formidable challenge to the military's economic team. The Frei and Allende administrations had expropriated over 5,000 properties representing 60 percent of Chile's arable land, yet neither government had settled the legal status of these lands. The Corporación de la Reforma Agraria, or CORA, had acquired many of these *fundos* legally, but others the workers had simply taken over by force. Workers operated the CORA-expropriated properties as communities, while the state held the legal titles. The Junta's economic advisors objected to these state-owned farms so they divided them up, issued property deeds, and converted the workers into owners. This represented about one-third of the total expropriated farmland. Another third of the lands that the CORA had not expropriated legally, the government returned to their former owners. The remaining third of the lands officials sold on the commercial market.

Not only did this distribution radically change land ownership patterns, it introduced a new concept of agricultural investment as well. As the government promoted exports, the farm sector began to emphasize overseas rather than domestic markets. Instead of raising the traditional grain and beef, the new farmers planted orchards and vineyards to export fresh fruit, largely to the United States. For example, in 1973, Chile had 66,000 acres of fruit trees and by 1989 this expanded to 173,000 acres. To compete in the overseas fresh produce markets nevertheless required substantial investments.

Many new owners borrowed heavily to modernize their technology and ran their farms like a business. They had no hereditary or emotional ties to the land, only economic ones. Furthermore, they had no family ties to the labor force. Contrary to the traditional *fundos*, which had a large number of workers living on the land, the new owners reduced the number of tenants and subcontracted workers through a labor broker. The former tenants therefore had to move to nearby towns and commute to work. They had no place to plant a garden or raise a sheep or cow. The new relationship between landowners and the workers was now temporary. Many seasonal workers who picked and packed the fruit were now migrants. The 1981 labor code made it extremely difficult for them to organize. Consequently, rural union membership declined from approximately 120,000 in 1973, to less than 30,000 in 1981, and workers lost the right to bargain over their wages and working conditions.

Large packing companies emerged that subcontracted with small growers to buy their fruit. The biggest Chilean company, owned by David del Curto, competed with the multinationals Dole, Chiquita, and Del Monte. The industry grew explosively from only $40 million in exports in 1974 to nearly $1 billion in 1991. Chile became the largest exporter of table grapes in the world. The fact that the Chilean summer corresponds to the Northern Hemisphere's winter was extremely helpful. Likewise, Chilean technology, infrastructure, and low wages gave the country an advantage over other Southern Hemisphere competitors such as Argentina, Australia, and South Africa. The new agribusiness model even transformed the production of traditional farm products. Wheat productivity per hectare nearly tripled from 1969–70 to 1990–91. Similar gains also occurred in corn and potato production.

Many of the new small farmers, unfortunately, did not have the knowledge or the capital to modernize their farms and participate in the export boom. In 1979, when the government allowed them to sell their land, many of them did so. With a small amount of capital, they moved to an urban area hoping to find work or set up a small business. An indirect consequence of the agrarian reform, therefore, was an accelerated migration of farm workers to the cities. During times of expanding jobs, this new source of labor furthered development, but during economic slumps they joined the mass of street venders trying to peddle enough to survive.

Two other activities that experienced enormous growth during the Pinochet regime were fishing and forestry. The migrating anchovy off Chile's northern seacoast served as the basis for a booming fishmeal industry. Whereas in 1973 the country exported $48 million, in 1987 this had risen to $934 million, with the country ranked fourth in the world in total catch. Although in 1990, the industry employed 60,000 workers, overfishing and changing ocean currents made employment and annual production unpredictable. It also became a highly concentrated industry with the Angelini family and a New Zealand partner controlling over 75 percent of production.

In addition to fishmeal, Chile developed many fish farming operations. Investors built pens in lakes and bays where they fed and harvested the fish. When Chile began exporting salmon all over the world, people viewed this new industry as a magnificent accomplishment. Fresh fish exports grew to $837 million in 1988. Then people began to observe how fish food and fecal matter fouled the waters and they lamented the environmental damage. Ecologists pushed for regulation of this industry in order to protect the nation's waters.

In the forestry industry, tree farming also became big business. Since its inception, foreign species rather than native species predominated. In its efforts to promote exports the Pinochet government subsidized the reforestation of almost 2 million acres with two species. The first, the fast-growing Monterrey pine, is especially suitable for pulp and paper, and the second, the slower-growing Douglas fir, makes excellent lumber. Trees planted in earlier decades created the opportunity for expanding the paper mills in the 1970s. Chile also began to sell prefabricated houses to various countries along with other wood products. Whereas in 1970 forestry exports were only $42 million, by 1989 they reached $784 million. These successes in agriculture, fishing, and forestry produced a dramatic shift in the nation's trade. The value of exports grew from $2.2 billion in 1974 to $8.1 in 1989 with new products predominating. Pinochet's economic team largely achieved its goal of diversifying trade and overcame the traditional dependence on copper.

WORKERS

Although the Military Junta publicly stated that it was apolitical and intended to govern for the benefit of all Chileans, it soon decreed labor measures that belied this impartiality. Some workers like the copper miners had protested against the Unidad Popular, so the Junta considered them as allies. By contrast, the majority of workers had collaborated with the Unidad Popular, so the Junta considered them as enemies. To combat them, the Junta tried to root out the Communist and Socialist influence in the labor movement by prohibiting political activity and dissolving activist unions. It did not intervene when management dismissed labor activists and laid off other workers regardless of previous contracts.

The neoliberal economic team that took over in 1975 claimed that it wanted to eliminate the "monopolies" in labor markets. The Junta and President Pinochet regulated labor through a series of decrees that bypassed many provisions of the 1931 labor code. In 1978, Labor Minister and neoliberal economist José Piñera issued a new code. Although this code recognized labor's right to organize and to engage in collective bargaining, it abolished closed shops, limited strikes to 60 days, and permitted employers to hire replacement workers. In addition, it eliminated labor courts, while allowing employers to fire workers without cause and pay overtime only to those working 12 or more consecutive hours. The new code also encouraged employers to subcontract workers in order to avoid direct responsibility for them.

Piñera talked about creating a free market labor system, but in practice the new system's intent was to curtail labor organization and collective bargaining. Measured by its own goals, the government succeeded in reducing union membership from a height of 650,000 in 1973 to less than 400,000 in 1981. Thereafter membership stabilized and began to increase slowly to 425,000 in 1988. Then, during the campaign to restore democracy, membership jumped up to 600,000. Although membership approached early 1970s levels, unions still faced many hurdles to gain the rights and protection that they enjoyed two decades earlier.

Workers' most difficult period occurred when the government implemented Friedman's shock treatment. Unemployment ballooned from 4.8 percent in 1973 to 14.5 percent in 1975, while the economy contracted 13 percent. To provide some relief, the government created public jobs called "minimum employment." It intended that these low-paying jobs be undesirable so that as other employment opportunities emerged, workers would quit. In 1976, however, jobs became so scarce that more than 150,000 people scrambled for minimum employment. In the following year, the figure reached over 185,000, but after 1977 as the economy picked up the number declined sharply.

THE MIDDLE CLASS

Whereas a majority of laborers had supported the Unidad Popular, with the middle class the reverse was the case. Many participated in the March of the Empty Pots, the national strikes, and other boycotts. Most were relieved, therefore, when the military took over. Older Chileans nostalgically envisioned the new government to be like the Carlos Ibáñez years, perhaps forgetting some of the economic hardships of his two presidencies. Originally, most of the middle class was grateful for the heavy hand with which the military imposed order. After the constant clashes of the previous few years, a loss of liberty seemed a reasonable price to pay for apparent tranquility. Most did not want to believe the atrocities, which the foreign press reported was occurring in the National Stadium. They believed foreign reporters were dupes of an international left-wing conspiracy. When international church bodies condemned the military for its violation of human rights, Chilean churches of the same denomination often argued that the military saved the country from communism.

Although the majority of the middle class supported CODE and the military coup, an important minority supported the Unidad Popular. Most UP leaders were middle class, with all but three of Allende's cabinet ministers and many of his agency directors holding college degrees. A sizeable number of professors and a majority of public school teachers belonged to the Unidad Popular. Artists, writers, and performers likewise belonged to Allende's coalition. Between 1973 and 1979, at least 28,000 Chileans left the country as refugees, the majority being middle class. Some calculate that approximately 200,000 fled during the military regime, with the middle class predominating. Sweden, Italy, Canada, Great Britain, the United States, Mexico, Venezuela, Australia and Eastern European counties received thousands of refugees. Some of the poor who supported Allende crossed the mountains into Argentina, but most remained in the country with their families, trying to survive under difficult conditions.

At first, the refugees' experiences outside of Chile were difficult, especially in Eastern Europe. They faced unemployment, language and cultural problems, and anxiety about their future. With time, some developed permanent attachments in their country of exile. Even after the end of the Pinochet regime, they visited, but never resided in Chile. Perhaps the greatest tragedy of both the Allende and Pinochet governments was how it divided families. Another tragedy was the loss of tolerance. Until the late 1960s, Chileans enjoyed discussing controversial issues with people of all political convictions. This openness unfortunately disappeared, as politics became messianic, then vengeful, and later, dangerous.

Somewhat naïvely the majority of the middle class believed that the military would quickly restore prosperity. In October of 1973, when the Junta removed price controls, causing food and rent prices to skyrocket, they were shocked. The black market of the UP years quickly disappeared, however, and store shelves filled. The illusion was that the consumer culture had returned even though people had little money. Likewise, when the Junta returned many agricultural and industrial properties to their former owners, people had the notion that private property was now safe. A year later, however, as prosperity declined and unemployment rose, people began to worry.

Then came the Católica economists' shock treatment. Middle-class supporters imagined that privatizations and budget cuts would only eliminate jobs created by the Unidad Popular. Such was not the case. In the public sector, opponents of the UP who had held onto their jobs during Allende's three years suddenly received severance notices. Patricia Goycolea, for example, who worked for the Corporación de la Vivienda, or the Public Housing Administration, lost her job and spent two years looking for another one. Juan Torres, an employee of Vialidad, or the Highway

Department, since the 1960s was encouraged to resign. He finally found a job building the Trans-Amazonian highway in Brazil. These workers and thousands of others the government persuaded to quit and receive generous severance packages, or remain and risk being fired.

After three years of hardship, in 1977, the promised economic takeoff began. Unemployment dropped and imports and credit became plentiful. A construction boom transformed Santiago, invading residential neighborhoods with high-rise apartments called *torres*. The capital's suburbs marched toward the Andes, filling in the open spaces in Barrio Alto, the premier middle-class neighborhood. With credit, people bought homes and cars for commuting to the suburbs. By 1984 more than 40 percent of Santiago's residents took advantage of consumer loans. The nation's automobiles doubled from 1975 to 1981. It certainly appeared that the military had delivered to the middle class a long awaited consumer revolution. The military and its economic team were never more popular.

The flood of imports that helped fuel this revolution, unfortunately, severely damaged local industry. When the bubble burst, Chileans belatedly recognized that international credit had funded much of the consumer revolution. The roller-coaster money market cost people their farms, their businesses, and their houses. This time the cause was global financial markets, not socialism. After a major reorganization and considerable hardship, in 1985 the economy recovered. It fueled another consumer boom larger than the first, but this time less based on foreign credit.

THE ELITE

This group almost universally supported the military coup. They believed that the Junta would restore both their property and their social dominance. Two different elite visions of Chile emerged during the first year of the Junta. One was a trade union movement called *gremialismo* headed by the conservative law professor Jaime Guzmán of the Universidad Católica. Guzmán advised President Pinochet to create a protected democracy based on trade unionism and controlled by the military. The other was market capitalism as interpreted by neoliberal economists. Both vied for Pinochet's support. Whereas the first urged the military to create a political movement with strong state control of the economy, the second urged the military to concentrate on restructuring the economy so as to reduce state control. When Pinochet opted for the latter, the *gremialistas* were shocked. The first consumer boom, however, converted many of them, including Jaime Guzmán, to neoliberalism. They became convinced that rising affluence would convert more people to the regime than a mass political movement. Most, however, feared the return of democracy, believing that the Christian Democrats might regain power. Although they had worked with them in the CODE coalition, they did not forgive them for supporting land reform and undermining property rights.

The elite erroneously believed that the military would return to them all of their expropriated properties. The government, however, did not return *fundos* or businesses expropriated legally. Many families with aristocratic roots, whose estates had reinforced their status for generations, found themselves landless. The government sold land and businesses, but many elite members lacked the capital to buy them. The new owners were often the leaders of financial institutions with access to credit. Entrepreneurs emerged who not only bought national firms, but acquired firms in Argentina, Brazil, Peru, and Bolivia as these nations also privatized their economies. This new elite was far more affluent and cosmopolitan than their predecessors but also more dependent on foreign credit. The elite also depended on the military's neoliberal policies. An important question was whether this group could survive and prosper when Pinochet's rule ended.

UNIVERSITY REFORM

The first objective of the military for the universities was to uproot Marxism. The second objective was to apply the neoliberal economic model to them. Uprooting Marxism was clearly ideological, yet the neoliberalism that replaced it was ideological as well, even though its leaders often denied this. At first, the implementation of these two objectives shrank university faculties and enrollments, but in the 1980s important expansions occurred in all aspects of higher education.

The first step for the Junta was to dismiss the existing rectors, or presidents, and to replace them with military officers. They fired professors, eliminated some departments, and moved others to new locales. For example, they transferred the University of Chile history faculty to an aging Santiago mansion, miles from the main campus and library, and later moved it to La Reina on the eastern outskirts of the city. They divided the excellent library collection, located on the main campus, among the various academic departments in the metropolitan region, losing many books in the process. Some conservatives also wanted to limit the influence of the Christian Democrats in the universities. The Junta agreed and dismissed Edgardo Boeninger, who had run the University of Chile during the conflictive times of the UP. Almost universally, the new rectors denied PDC professors positions as department chairs or deans.

Another element of university reform was the partition of the Universidad de Chile. Until 1973, this venerable institution supervised most of Chilean higher education. The university had an extensive regional campus system with the Santiago faculty actually administering final examinations on provincial campuses. In an effort to diminish the university's power, the military gave complete autonomy to the regional campuses. As a result, by 1981 the original eight universities became seventeen. In Temuco, for example, the branch campuses of the Universidad de Chile and the State Technical University fused to become the Universidad de la Frontera, or the Frontier University. As an independent institution, it added new programs, built a new campus, and developed research programs. Located in the Mapuche heartland, it also promoted Mapuche education through extension services. The combination of national and local funding made a more dynamic university than the two branch campuses. Here, as well as at other new institutions, the communities now felt greater ownership. The University of Chile faculty, nevertheless, worried that this autonomy might cause a decline in academic standards.

An even more explosive revolution occurred, however, when Pinochet's economic team applied its neoliberal policies to higher education. Their first step was to end the tradition of free university tuition. They raised tuition to between $1,000 and $2,000 per semester, according to the school and the major. For poorer students, they created scholarships, though in insufficient numbers. Then they encouraged the creation of private universities that received no state funding. Suddenly new universities sprouted up throughout the country, especially in Santiago, more than doubling the national total by 1980. Only a few like the conservative Catholic Opus Dei had a religious affiliation. Most were secular and for profit. These new institutions had few full-time professors, preferring when possible to hire well-known professors from established institutions on a part-time basis. With lower admissions requirements than established universities, some of these for-profit institutions threatened to become "diploma mills."

Although university enrollment declined from 146,000 in 1973 to 118,000 in 1982, the opening of new institutions caused it to rise to 153,000 by 1989. New types of post-secondary institutions, called professional institutes and technical training centers, enrolled an additional 76,000 students. The first were four-year institutions where students could study such subjects as bookkeeping, secretarial skills, and marketing. All these centers were for profit and ranged considerably in quality. The centers advertised widely, but, since the government did not accredit them, students found it hard to judge the quality of their programs. For students who could not afford a university education, these centers were attractive, enrolling about one of every three students engaged in post-secondary education. By the late 1980s, there were over 20 professional institutes and 150 centers for technical training.

While post-secondary enrollments grew, state support of universities and training centers as part of the general education budget declined. Whereas in 1974 the state spent 47 percent of all public education dollars on universities, by 1989 this had more than halved, to 22 percent. Following the North American model, student tuition covered declining state support. Even with some scholarships available, workers' children found a college education increasingly out of reach.

Chilean university students had a long tradition of political activism. To curtail this tradition, the Junta replaced academicians with military officers as the campus rectors or presidents. As long as these new leaders maintained a tight control and the economy was growing, they succeeded in minimizing open political activity. In 1982, however, when the economy crashed, students filled the streets, marching against the military. Protests also flared up within the university itself. Students held meetings, distributed flyers, and put up posters criticizing the military. Some like the philosophy students at the Universidad Católica were more daring and occupied the department's administrative offices until the carabineros stormed in to evict them.

In the 1980s, important intellectual activities occurred outside of the universities. European and North American governments, which wanted to support a transition to democracy, began funding independent research institutes. The members of these institutes often were university professors frustrated by the lack of academic freedom on their campuses. One institute, the Facultad Latinoamericana de Ciencias Sociales (Latin American Social Science Faculty), or FLASCO, ran opinion polls, conducted research, published, and held conferences emphasizing democratic institutions. Another, created by Cardinal Raúl Silva Henríquez and called the Academia de Humanismo Cristiano, or the Academy of Christian Humanism, published a journal called *Alternativas* that supported political change. Often the Academia sponsored seminars with international and Chilean scholars who discussed the road back to democracy. Scholars from these institutes, who had close ties to the Christian Democratic Party, provided intellectual leadership in the campaign against Pinochet and in the transition to democracy.

PUBLIC SCHOOL REFORM

Just as dramatic as the university reforms were the military's reforms of K–12 education. Not surprisingly, the administration began by eliminating Marxist influence from the classroom. It dismissed teachers who were known members of the Unidad Popular parties. Then it restructured the Pedagógico, the most important teacher-training school in the country. Originally this school belonged to the Universidad de Chile, but the administration converted it into a separate institution called the Instituto Pedagógico. At first its faculty and students were fearful of engaging in any political activity, but like at other universities, when the economic crisis disrupted national life in the 1980s, Pedagógico students began to march in the streets again.

Two years before this crisis, in 1979, the administration totally restructured the national school system by placing public schools under municipal control and financing. In an effort to undermine teacher tenure, a 1988 law allowed the municipal school districts to dismiss longtime teachers. The stated objective of these reforms was to give local authorities more control over education, but many communities lacked the resources to support schools. Therefore, the national government continued to subsidize local districts. The affluent municipalities, however, had greater resources and paid their teachers higher salaries. The national government also funded private schools that charged no tuition. In Santiago, for example, only 22 percent of students attended the latter in 1980 while six years later, 47 percent attended them. The objective was to show that students performed better in publicly funded but privately managed schools than in the traditional state-run schools. A national testing of fourth and eighth graders showed slightly higher scores in the former, but the most important score discrepancy was between students in wealthy and poor municipalities. Parents' income and school resources continued to be the best indicators of student performance. One category of schools unaffected by these reforms were the private, elite schools, often run by religious organizations and which charged high tuition.

The military also attempted to de-politicize the schoolteachers and, in 1974, abolished the National Teachers' Union. The government replaced it with the Colegio de Profesores, or Teachers' Association, then in 1981 substituted it with the Asociación Gemialista de Educadores Chilenos, or Chilean Educator's Association. Neither of these organizations helped draw up the dramatic educational changes of the 1970s and 1980s. Likewise, in their weakened condition they could not energetically push for improved salaries and working conditions. Teachers' salaries were discouragingly low and affected the profession's morale. Classrooms lacked repairs, instructional materials, and books, but the military failed to remedy the situation.

Enrollments decreased or were stationary in K–12 institutions in the years from 1973 to 1980, but the following decade some important growth occurred. Secondary education, which traditionally lagged far behind elementary education in enrollments, grew from 53 to 75 percent of the eligible population. Another area in which enrollments grew significantly was preschool education. In 1974, only 109,600 attended whereas in 1989 the figure reached 213,200. The growth in these two areas meant students were better prepared to enter first grade and stayed in school longer. In an urban, more technical Chilean society, these accomplishments enabled more young people to participate fully in the country's modernization.

SOCIAL SECURITY

The Chilean social security system was broken in 1973, with pensioners receiving hardly enough to buy food. Due to inflation, most retired workers either took another job or lived in abject poverty. Even so, social security absorbed an increasingly large proportion of the government budget. From 20 percent in 1973, it grew to 50 percent in 1980. Following the neoliberal model, the Minister of Labor, José Piñera, drew up a proposal to privatize the system. According to his plan, workers contributed monthly to private companies called Administradoras de Fondos de Pensiones (Pension Fund Administrators), or AFPs, that invested their money. Upon retirement, the AFPs would pay them a pension based on the value of their investment. Under this system, employers did not contribute any funds, whereas the workers had to contribute a minimum of 10 percent of their earnings. Workers could switch their account from one company to another, but they could not participate in the investment decisions of the companies. The companies charged an annual management fee, which according to critics was excessively high. The government offered incentives for all workers to switch to this private system. However, those workers vested in the old public social security system could remain.

The most remarkable aspect of this private social security system was not the benefits it offered workers, but the amount of capital the fund managers had available to invest. Never in Chile's history had so much capital entered the private market. These funds transformed the Chilean equity market and served to create large domestic conglomerates. Unfortunately, fund managers failed to invest conservatively. When the economic shock hit the country in 1982, the funds went bankrupt and the government had to take them over. Later the government sold them, requiring stricter management guidelines but opening participation to foreign investors. Soon foreign corporations controlled half of the AFPs. Concentration in the industry occurred so that by the 1990s two companies controlled over 60 percent of the nation's pension funds. Although the Chilean model of privatized social security has attracted considerable admiration worldwide, so far it has benefited the equity market more than it has benefited workers. Once, it collapsed during a major economic downturn and it has yet to prove that it can pay large numbers of retirees and remain solvent.

HEALTH CARE

Before the military government, Chile delivered universal health care through a two-tier system. One tier was the free public system while the other was a pay-for-service system administered through the employees' pension system. In the public system, an expectant mother, for example, had lengthy waits before she could see a nurse or physician. When she gave birth, a midwife would attend her unless complications occurred. Although the maternity ward only had eight or ten beds, the baby's delivery and hospital stay were free. In the private system, by contrast, the expectant mother visited her physician monthly. Her physician then attended her during birth. The mother shared a room with only one other patient. The pension system, however, paid only part of the total costs and the patient paid the difference.

Two major problems existed with this system: one was its inequality and the other was its cost. To resolve both problems the military's economic team implemented health care reform. So that the public system would respond to the needs of local communities, the team transferred the administration of local clinics to municipal governments funded by the national government. An attempt was made to give workers a choice of physician through the government-run Fondo Nacional de Salud (National Health Fund), or FONASA. Approximately one-fourth of all Chileans participated in this system. In accord with the neoliberal economic policy, the government also created a new private system called the Instituto de Salud y Prevención (Health and Prevention Institute), or ISAPRE. Employers paid a monthly quota to various private firms that shared the market. When employees received health care, the ISAPRE paid part of the fee and they paid the difference. Chilean-owned firms dominated this new health care industry, with two North American firms, Aetna and Cigna, gaining about a quarter of the market by the late 1990s.

These health care changes provided improved coverage for many people, but the public system used by the majority of Chileans still needed improvements. Prenatal, maternity, and infant care for all Chileans improved through a national program. It succeeded in lowering the mortality rate from 82 in 1000 in 1970 to 15 in 1000 in 1990, or five times lower.

Adult life expectancy also increased, but less dramatically, from an average of 65 years in 1970 to 71 years in 1990. In general, however, the middle class benefited the most through the FONASA and ISAPRE systems. For those who could afford them, they provided care equivalent to that of European and North American systems. The excellent training of physicians and nurses, along with the importation of medicine and technology, provided first-world health care to middle-class Chileans.

WOMEN IN POLITICS

Women played a major role in creating political change in Chile in the 1970s. However, national issues rather than feminist ones motivated them. Prominent women leaders from various parties had served in congressional or ministerial positions since the 1950s. First enfranchised in 1949, women voters increasingly decided the outcome of elections. By the presidential election of 1964, half of the voters were women. They leaned more toward centrist and rightist candidates, as the 1970 presidential election demonstrated. Whereas over half of Alessandri's and Tomic's votes were female, only 41 percent of Allende's votes were female. Three years later in the parliamentary elections, this trend was more pronounced, with the Unidad Popular receiving less than 40 percent of the female vote while the opposition received almost 60 percent.

The Frei administration sought the support of women, especially those of the working class, through its *promoción popular*. It developed Centros de Madres (Mothers' Clubs), or CEMA, to educate women and to help them market their homemade crafts. Neither the Christian Democrats nor any other party in the 1960s raised critical issues about society and gender. Rather they tried to respond to women's family roles. The Unidad Popular followed a similar philosophy, seeking to help working-class women through extension work, publications, and distribution of food. It did not challenge traditional roles either.

As in much of the developing world in the 1960s and 1970s social class rather than gender dominated the political debate in which women defined themselves. Middle-class and upper-class women were usually well educated and employed maids who handled the cooking, housework, and child care, enabling them to work in professions outside the home. Although they experienced some gender barriers in these professions, they were not ready to form a multi-class alliance to fight these barriers, especially when the political culture threatened the survival of their social class.

Middle- and upper-class women protested against the Unidad Popular, not only because it did not provide abundant consumer goods for their families, but because it threatened their jobs and their property. They also objected to Marxist conceptions of women from a conservative, usually Catholic perspective. Although numerous female leaders gained prominence through their opposition to the Allende regime, their vision was limited to achieving his overthrow. They did not envision developing personal political careers.

In recognition for their work in the protest movement, Pinochet named a few conservative women to his administration, but he never gave them key policy roles, which he assigned to male technocrats. The most important woman in his administration turned out to be his wife, Lucía Hiriart. She headed the Secretaría Nacional de la Mujer, or National Secretariat of Women, as well as 49 different charities. Most significantly, she led CEMA, which had over 10,000 centers around the nation with more than 200,000 members. Other military wives and middle-class volunteers assisted working-class women in domestic concerns, crafts, and the sale of products. They emphasized Christian, as opposed to Marxist, values. Although CEMA groups were supposedly apolitical, since their inception the parties had used them for political purposes, and the military was no different. Lucía Hiriart encouraged CEMA women to turn out for important public events staged by the military. When Pinochet presented himself for a plebiscite in 1988, she and her fellow volunteers persuaded CEMA members to campaign on his behalf. Their efforts succeeded, for women gave him a slight majority of their votes in contrast to men, who opposed him by a majority.

The working-class women who supported Pinochet did so because they feared the insecurity of the Allende years or else they benefited in some fashion from his regime. Nevertheless, many other working-class women's husbands, children, and relatives suffered from the arrests and torture by the regime. Furthermore, the economic shock treatment had left family members unemployed and family members hungry. The working members of the family also found that the new labor law effectively lowered salaries and undermined job security.

An entirely new group of female leaders emerged to support those oppressed by the military regime. The Agupación de los Familiares de Detenidos-Desaparecidos, or Families of the Arrested and Disappeared, formed in 1974 to help find arrested family members. They organized conspicuous protests such as when they chained themselves to the fence of the Supreme Court Building in 1979. Most of these women had never participated in political activities, but with their family's integrity threatened, they became activists. In 1978, women celebrated the Primer Conferencia Nacional de la Mujer, or the First National Women's Conference, with approximately 300 attending. This modest number was considered a large turnout for a women's group until the economic crisis of 1982.

Suddenly people from all social classes and political persuasions lost their jobs and their possessions. This frustration fueled a new protest movement, which included the Movimeinto Feminista, or Feminist Movement, that staged a dramatic protest in front of the National Library in August 1983. Women also founded Mujeres por la Vida, or Women for Life, in 1983, inspiring 10,000 women to pack Caupolicán stadium to protest the military's policies.

"NO" CAMPAIGN

The constitution ratified in 1980 specified that there would be no election until 1988 and then it would be a plebiscite to determine whether Pinochet would continue to govern eight more years. In 1980, few doubted that the government would alter this timetable given the booming economy and the repressed opposition. Then came the economic crisis of 1982 when even the regime's most ardent supporters questioned its competence to rule. Whereas the regime's civil rights record had raised the voices of the Christian Democrats and the left wing, now the country's financial woes added new voices from the right.

As long as the middle and upper classes feared a return of the left and new attacks on private property, they silently acquiesced to military rule. The economic crisis of 1982, however, caused as many people to lose property as had lost it under the Unidad Popular. Farmers who had defended their lands against campesino occupations during the UP now had their lands foreclosed on by the banks. Their grateful feeling toward the military now turned to one of betrayal. They blamed the Chicago Boys' credit policies, which made them more financially vulnerable than ever in the nation's history.

As support for the military waned, the opposition began holding protests, which quickly gained sympathy. Opposition leaders decided to hold rallies on the eleventh of every month to protest the day the military took power. The protest on June 11 was so massive that the press speculated that the following month's protest might force Pinochet's resignation. The July 11 protest was huge and convinced Pinochet to change his cabinet, but he was not intimidated by it. On August 11, he fought back, positioning armed troops in many cities with orders to fire on unruly marchers. In Santiago, the troops killed various protesters, sending a chilling message to future participants. To this confrontation, Pinochet added a rhetorical one aimed at frightening the middle class away from an alliance with the left wing. This two-track strategy had the short-term effect of deflating the protest movement and giving Pinochet time to fix the economy. He also tried to divide the opposition by appointing Sergio Onofre Jarpa, a former National Party senator, as minister of interior. Jarpa gave a civilian face to the regime, as well as reminded CODE supporters of the anti–Unidad Popular rallies he had led. At the same time, Lucía Hiriart and other generals' wives campaigned for support in the *poblaciones,* or working-class districts.

A less visible but more tenacious opposition developed to Pinochet in Washington during Ronald Reagan's second term. After criticizing Jimmy Carter's human rights policy and defending his own support of authoritarian regimes, Reagan reversed himself and decided that the best defense against communism was democracy, not dictatorships. He discovered how a human rights campaign and free, open elections could be useful against both Cuba and Nicaragua's Sandinista regime. Reagan also had second thoughts about supporting military regimes after the Argentine military invaded the Malvina/Falkland Islands. By 1985, only two military regimes remained in South America: Paraguay and Chile. For civic-minded Chileans, this stigma was humiliating. More importantly for the United States, in every South American country in which democracy was restored, the governments were either centrist or conservative. The specter of left-wing democracies of the 1960s and 1970s had vanished. Given this major change in political ideology, Pinochet's regime became a liability, rather than an asset, to United States' policy. The Reagan administration, therefore, began to shift support to pro-democracy groups.

In 1985, the economy recovered, but the belief that the military offered security for private property was lost. The opportunity emerged to convince a majority of Chileans that democracy is the best guarantee of their rights. In 1985, the Catholic Church committed its support and leadership to the democracy campaign. Cardinal Juan Francisco Fresno brought together all non-Marxist groups to sign a National Agreement for a Transition to Democracy. Pinochet, who earlier had complained about the Church's human rights activities, now told the Cardinal to keep out of politics. Violence almost derailed discussions about democracy when, in September of 1986, a left-wing terrorist group, the Manuel Rodríguez Patriotic Front, tried to assassinate Pinochet. Using machine guns and rockets, the group killed five of Pinochet's body guards, but Pinochet escaped in an armored car.

In April 1987, hope of peace returned when Pope John Paul II visited Chile. He referred to the country's government as a dictatorship and called for a restoration of social justice. Pinochet did not intend to give up power, but in accord with the 1980 Constitution, he prepared to hold the 1988 plebiscite. His officials established the procedures for voter registration and the recognition of political parties. He then tried to convince Chileans that by retaining him eight more years in the presidency they would guarantee their security and prosperity.

To prepare the Christian Democratic Party's campaign against eight more years of Pinochet, Gabriel Valdés, the party president, stepped aside in favor of Patricio Aylwin. In early 1988 Aylwin negotiated an alliance of center and left-wing parties called the Concertación de Partidos por el No, or the Coalition of Parties to Vote "No." The Socialist Party under the moderate leader Ricardo Lagos played a very dynamic role in the campaign. The "No's" innovative use of television spots and community organizations built up a momentum that caught Pinochet's supporters by surprise. Additionally the United States and European democratic organizations contributed generously to the "No" campaign. In October 1988, the people spoke with their ballots, giving the Concertación a victory with 54 percent of the vote to Pinochet's 43 percent.

In a different era, Pinochet might have falsified the results, or even refused to abide by them, but most governments in the Western Hemisphere were now democratic. Even Pinochet could not buck this trend. Furthermore, the U.S. policy was highly unfavorable to military regimes. Still, it was uncommon for a military leader to terminate his own regime, especially with a booming economy like Chile's in the late 1980s. Perhaps Pinochet was overconfident that Chileans, who opposed the Unidad Popular, would always show him their gratitude at the polls. If so, he was wrong; now he had to conduct the first open election since 1973.

Parties picked their candidates and began to campaign. The Concertación, composed of the Christian Democrats, Socialists, and minor left-wing parties, selected Patricio Aylwin as its candidate. A coalition of two right-wing parties, Renovación Nacional (National Revolution), or RN, and Unión Democrática Independiente (Independent Democratic Union), or UDI, picked Hernán Büchi, Pinochet's former finance minister. A second right-wing candidate, Francisco Javier Errázuriz, helped split the conservative vote and guaranteed Aylwin's victory even before the election took place. The Concertación also won large majorities in both branches of Congress with 72 of 120 Deputy seats and 22 out of 38 Senate seats.

The Concertación tried to persuade Pinochet even before the election to make constitutional revisions. He agreed to additional democratic procedures but refused to revise the congressional election system that favored party alliances. Pinochet also remained inflexible about retaining his commander in chief position in the armed forces until 1998. He thus denied the president control over the military. Finally, Pinochet refused to give any assurance that he would not decree additional laws before his term of office expired. Although this process of restoring democracy was imperfect, it did not prevent the inauguration of Patricio Aylwin on March 11, 1990. He became Chile's first elected president in seventeen years and faced the challenge of restoring democracy.

10

The Democratic Transition after 1990

When Patricio Aylwin was inaugurated March 11, 1990, as the first elected president in 17 years, he inherited a growing economy but a divided nation. Glass framed office towers, high-rise apartments, shopping malls, and sprawling suburbs had transformed Santiago and provincial capitals. Clogged highways, overflowing supermarkets, and well-stocked department stores were now commonplace. Vacations in Paris and Cancún or shopping excursions to Miami and New York were no longer unique. Nevertheless, 40 percent of Chileans lived below the poverty line. Many rural areas were without services such as potable water and electricity. Most anguishing, however, was the unknown fate of more than 3,000 Chileans. The courts refused to hear any cases covered by a blanket amnesty decree and there had been no official investigation of those who had disappeared or suffered human rights abuses.

Though the painful situation of many families had not been resolved, society was not clearly divided into the haves and the have-nots. Most Chileans had experienced some rise in their standard of living during the prosperous years of the late 1970s and late 1980s. Although the new government wanted to resolve social justice questions, it also wanted to maintain economic growth. These conflicting aims had made social and economic questions more complex. The Christian Democrats and the Socialists, who now controlled the government, did not intend to create a revolution but wanted to make the existing system more socially responsible.

MAKING DEMOCRACY WORK

Constitutional Issues

The Constitution of 1980 imposed the institutional framework within which the new democratically elected president and congress governed. Although Patricio Aylwin and successive presidents tried to amend it and remove key undemocratic articles, the authors of the constitution had made this virtually impossible without the approval of the conservative opposition. The latter did agree to amendments that streamlined government but balked at those that threatened their power. Amendments they opposed would eliminate nonelected senators, grant the president the power to name the head of the armed forces, and would revise the electoral system. Due to the conservative intransigence, these changes would take years to accomplish.

The Concertación did win ample majorities in both houses, but in addition to the elected senators, the Constitution authorized Pinochet and the armed forces to designate nine others. Not surprisingly the designated senators voted with the other conservatives to block many of Aylwin's proposals. They frustrated his efforts to revise the labor code, to prosecute the military leaders accused of civil rights abuses, and to reform the judicial system. The Concertación thus found itself captive to a process it did not create and seemed incapable of revising. For those who expected the new government to reject the Pinochet legacy, the Constitution and the neoliberal economic model made this extremely difficult.

Augusto Pinochet remained as commander in chief of the armed forces until 1998. During Aylwin's four-year presidency, Pinochet relied upon intimidation to veto any measure that might affect him or the military. When congress investigated his son for insider business deals with the army, Pinochet ordered Santiago troops to feign an uprising, in a maneuver Chileans later referred to as the *boinazo*, in reference to the soldiers' berets. To calm Pinochet's indignation, Aylwin agreed to table the investigation and other demands. When reporters or political figures publicly derided Pinochet, to assuage him the government arrested the alleged offenders on libel charges.

In March 1998 Pinochet's term as commander in chief expired so, according to the constitution, he then assumed a lifelong seat in the senate.

Due to health problems, however, he flew to England to receive treatment. In his role of senator, not only did he claim diplomatic immunity, but he believed that his close friendship with former prime minister Margaret Thatcher and British military officers assured him preferential treatment. He had solidified this relationship during the Falkland/Malvinas Island War when Chile quietly provided England with logistic support. Yet to his surprise and indignation, the Labor government that replaced Thatcher failed to recognize this relationship. When a Spanish court filed an extradition request to prosecute him for the death and torture of its citizens, the English judiciary placed him under house arrest while it reviewed the case.

Pinochet's detention inflamed Chilean political debate just as the country prepared for the 1999 presidential elections. Neither the conservative candidate, Joaquín Lavín, nor the Concertación candidate, Ricardo Lagos, made Pinochet's detention an issue, but the press made it a cause célèbre. Lagos won narrowly, and, just before his inauguration, the English courts found that due to Pinochet's failing health he was unfit for trial and allowed him to return home. Nevertheless, even in Chile he was not safe, for the national courts suspended his senatorial immunity. Bitter debates ensued as the tribunals dealt with the most explosive case in the country's history. A resolution finally occurred in June 2002 when the Chilean Supreme Court, following the English example, also declared Pinochet unfit for trial. In an act of apparent compromise, a few days later he renounced his senate seat. The general thus gave up his last forum for intimidating elected leaders and, with his health declining, grudgingly separated himself from national politics.

Lagos, in contrast to his two predecessors, seemed freed from Pinochet's threats. The new head of the armed forces, General Ricardo Ilzurieta Caffarena, installed in March 1998, fully cooperated with civilian authority. Ilzurieta spent four years trying to modernize the armed forces and to subordinate them to civilian control. After successfully accomplishing this transformation in March 2002, he stepped down and was replaced by Juan Emilio Cheyre.

In a startling statement three months later Cheyre condemned the leaders of the military coup of 1973 and recognized that the armed forces had violated human rights. Though this declaration did not make him popular with many former colleagues, it signaled a responsibility of the military in reconciling the nation's wrongs.

In June 2003, conservatives joined the Concertación in amending the Constitution. They agreed to eliminate the military's right to protect Chilean democracy and instead subordinated all institutions to the rule of law.

While the transition to democracy appeared nearly complete, a declining economy and a resurgent conservative political movement created new challenges for Lagos. Perhaps the biggest complication that he faced was that the Christian Democrats threatened to pull out of the Concertación if the Socialists failed to give them important concessions.

Evolving Politics

With the return of democracy in the 1990s, many former protest leaders became legislators and cabinet ministers. They soon left behind marches and strikes in an attempt to reform the system from within. Even young leaders often brought with them considerable experience. They often came from families of prominent 1960s politicians. For example, Eduardo Frei's daughter, Irene, became a senate leader while his son, Eduardo Frei Ruiz-Tagle, became president from 1994 to 2000. Patricio Aylwin's daughter, Mariana, headed the Ministry of Education during the Lagos administration, while Orlando Letelier's son, Felipe, won election to the House of Deputies. When Ricardo Lagos named Michelle Bachelet, the daughter of former air force general Alberto Bachelet, Defense Minister in 2002, she became the first woman to hold this post. Equally significant in 2003 was the election of Isabel Allende, the former president's daughter, as speaker of the House of Deputies. Although in Chile prominent political families have held office through various generations, for the first time daughters followed in their father's careers.

Electoral campaigns seemed surprisingly similar to those of an earlier era. Candidate placards with respective party acronyms blanketed walls and light posts. The television and radio stations blared jingles and songs. Marches and rallies concluded with charismatic speeches and chants from loyal supporters. Magazines and newspapers offered political commentary to inform voters of the issues and electoral strategies. At coffee, lunch, and dinner, citizens debated the candidates' strengths, weaknesses, and pedigrees. Politics made everyone part of the national debate as democracy emerged from a long hibernation.

During the 1990s the political spectrum shifted away from the conservative right, associated with the former military regime, to the moderate center represented by the Concertación. The Communists on the far left and the UDI on the far right appealed to voters with extremist views but failed to attract a large following. Voters consistently gave the Concertación more than 50 percent of their support during the 1990s, while the conservative coalition received less than 40 percent, and the Communists received approximately 5 percent.

In the year 1999, however, voting patterns began to change. In the first round of the presidential election, the Concertación's tally dropped below 50 percent. In a second round, it squeezed out slightly more than 51 percent, giving Ricardo Lagos the victory. Among female voters, Lagos lost by 3 percent. Male voters, therefore, gave him his victory, supporting him by a 9 percent margin. After a decade in office, voters' enthusiasm for the Concertación had eroded, in large part due to an Asian economic crisis that raised unemployment to nearly 10 percent.

In 2000, another economic crisis began in the United States and Europe and further eroded the Concertación's appeal. Partly as a result, a disturbing trend of voter polarization emerged in the 2001 congressional elections. Votes for the center shrank, while those for the right and left grew. Shocked Christian Democrats discovered that UDI had now displaced them as the largest party in the country. The polarization was partly attributable to economic factors. Nevertheless, Chile's unresolved past increasingly galvanized public discussion, compelling people to look backward rather than forward.

The continual revelations of the Pinochet regime's assassinations and torture separated Chileans into hostile camps. Likewise, Spain's attempt to extradite Pinochet from England sharply divided opinions. Those who wanted the general prosecuted, even if by a foreign country, widely supported Spain's action. Just as passionately, Pinochet's conservative supporters protested in front of the British and Spanish embassies in Santiago demanding his release. The right and the left both used this issue to rally their respective supporters, while the Christian Democrats, caught between the warring factions, wished the issue would go away.

Another disturbing voting trend is that Chileans showed some ambiguity about going to the polls once their initial enthusiasm for elections had passed. From the election of 1993 to that of 1996, participation dropped by nearly one million votes. The following year, it dropped another 600,000. The presidential election of 1999, however, caught the public's attention and turnout increased by 1,300,000 over that of 1997. The congressional elections of 2001, nevertheless, repeated the trend of declining participation, with voter turnout 850,000 less than in 1999. Within this pattern, it is important to note that presidential elections drew the most voters, followed by municipal, and finally, congressional elections.

With increased television and radio ownership, the media gained greater access to the public than ever before. Perhaps the media was part of the problem of declining voter turnout because parties invested more money in advertisements and less effort in creating a political community. The post-Pinochet political system also offered voters fewer direct benefits.

The patronage system, which so highly energized Chilean politics in the pre-1973 era, continued to create jobs for the educated middle class but few for the working class. Privatization had eliminated the public corporations, which politicians could use to reward workers. Also, with the new emphasis on economic management, government touted growth statistics and figures on job creation, but these numbers did not motivate many voters. As the country's consumer culture increasingly reflected that of Europe and the United States, voter apathy followed a similar pattern. No longer was it obvious what the politicians delivered; they had become system managers. During sharp economic downturns, like in 2001, party preferences began to change, but voter turnout failed to rebound. The disturbing trend of citizens becoming consumers instead of voters seemed to have spread to Chile.

Intellectual Trends

Public debate on national issues resurged in the 1980s, yet only in the 1990s did the government succeed in restoring freedom of the press and full ideological diversity in the universities. With this new freedom, each political and intellectual group sought to gain support for its cause through impassioned narratives of the nation's past. The left's vision increasingly attracted student support as it elected leftist leaders to head its federations. Such agendas as funding and access impassioned students and led to protests such as the one in April 2002 that provoked clashes with the police. In contrast to the 1960s, student activism did not aim to destroy the old system but to reform it.

Intellectual critics of the military concentrated on revealing the regime's hidden past and class inequalities. Jorge Edwards, ambassador to Cuba during the Unidad Popular, in his novel *Los convidados de piedra,* or *The Guests of Stone,* condemned the elite for its role in overthrowing Allende. Nobel Prize–winning poet Pablo Neruda, who died within days of the military coup, protested the Military Junta on his deathbed. Mourners turned his funeral into an antimilitary demonstration. Antonio Skármeta transformed Neruda from rebellious poet to romantic matchmaker in *Ardiente paciencia,* or *Burning Patience,* popularly known as *Il postino,* the award-winning film version. In *La casa de los espíritus,* or *The House of the Spirits,* Isabel Allende revealed how deeply rooted family tensions and social inequalities provoke violence. More recently, journalist Patricia Verdugo exposed the military's brutal assassinations in her work *Los zarpazos del puma,* published in English as *Chile, Pinochet, and the Caravan of Death.*

Sociologist Tomás Moulián pointed his attack at the injustices of neoliberal economics in *Chile actual, anatomía de un mito*, or *Today's Chile: The Anatomy of a Myth*.

Conservative supporters of the regime feared that these writings would strengthen the left and revive the confrontations of the pre-1973 era. In an attempt to justify the acts of the military regime, Pinochet and others published their versions of the past. In three volumes the general repeatedly emphasized how the armed forces had saved the country from Marxism. His minister of interior, Sergio Fernández, in *Mi lucha por la democracia*, or *My Struggle for Democracy*, justified his efforts to create a workable political system. Although some authors conceded that the military committed abuses, Rafael Valdivieso in *Crónica de un rescate, Chile 1973–1988*, or *The Story of a Rescue . . .* claimed that only through force did the military avoid civil war.

In journalism, traditional newspapers such as the *Mercurio* and *La Tercera* dominated national readership, but critical publications such as *La Epoca* presented a more liberal perspective. Headed by Christian Democratic journalists and supported by the Catholic Church, *La Epoca*'s well-documented articles on human rights abuses and economic inequalities complemented the Concertación's agenda of political reform.

Beginning in the late 1990s, the satiric magazine *The Clinic* used fictitious interviews and outrageous humor to highlight national faults and foibles, while the on-line magazine *El Mostrador* irreverently satirized public figures of various stripes.

Academic publications, though less sensational, helped build support for the transition to democracy. Government research support enabled scholars to produce works that strengthened the political center. Cristian Gazmuri's two-volume biography, *Eduardo Frei Montalva y su época*, or *Eduardo Frei Montalva and His Times*, critically assessed the record of the first Christian Democratic presidency. Pamela Constable and Arturo Valenzuela's thorough analysis of the divisiveness of the Pinochet regime appeared in *A Nation of Enemies: Chile Under Pinochet*, while Elizabeth Lira and Brian Loveman in *Las ardientes cenizas del olvido*, or *The Burning Embers of Forgetfulness*, emphasized Chile's tradition of amnesty in healing political confrontations.

Considering the wrenching economic experiments of both Allende and Pinochet, scholars sought to offer a balanced, historical perspective of Chile's economic development. Armando de Ramón and José Manuel Larraín in *Orígenes de la vida económica chilena, 1659–1808*, or *Origins of Chile's Economic Life . . .* undertook an innovative study of colonial economic trends. Eduardo Cavieres supplemented this perspective with an examination of foreign trade in *Comercio chileno y comerciantes ingleses 1820–1880,* or *Chilean Trade and English Merchants*. . . . A view of national development and the stock exchange appeared in *Historia de la Bolsa de Comercio de Santiago, 1893–1993,* or *History of the Santiago Stock Market* . . . , by Juan Ricardo Couyoumdjian, René Millar, and Josefina Tocornal. These works and others contributed to an informed, democratic discussion of economic policy.

Accomplishments

When the Concertación assumed control of government in 1990 it had a concrete legislative agenda, yet more important than specific programs was the need to win long-term support for democratic institutions. Many conservative Chileans believed that only authoritarian rule could prolong stability and progress. In the 1989 plebiscite they represented the 43 percent of voters who favored eight more years of Pinochet's rule. Could the Concertación convince them that democracy offered more benefits than authoritarian rule? Perhaps it might even win over some of these people and broaden the center of the political spectrum.

Another major challenge was how to incorporate a substantial percentage of Chile's poor into the consumer revolution. Liberalizing labor laws to strengthen collective bargaining would help raise wages. Not only would pro-labor measures improve workers' welfare, they would prevent labor from supporting the far left. The problem with making major revisions to labor laws was that the right wing had sufficient veto power in legislature to prevent their passage. So the Concertación would have to negotiate a consensus.

The Concertación's economic teams proved equally adept as their predecessors in fine-tuning the economy to achieve a maximum of economic growth while avoiding inflation. During most of the 1990s the economy grew at a rate equal to or above that of the best years under the military. The programs for the extremely poor had a major impact on all areas of Chile. In rural areas, the government funded potable water, electricity, roads, and telephones. Suddenly people who had been on the periphery of modernization had running water and color television.

But in doing so, concertación leaders could not play their traditional role of working-class mobilization. They had to gain the support of the working class through a raised standard of living and increased social services. Again, they were very successful, but as a consequence, people increasingly believed that their vote did not count.

For those workers who would not benefit from expanded labor organization, the Concertación sought to protect them through a partial re-suscitation of the welfare state. The government's economists recognized that they would have to allocate resources carefully to avoid slowing down the high performing neoliberal model. They stuck to the principal of balanced budgets, preferring to raise taxes for social welfare programs rather than use deficit spending. Finance ministers tenaciously refused to endorse a populist agenda of consumption paid for by inflation.

The Concertación made important gestures to the business community by continuing the military's policy of privatization. It sold utilities such as water, sewage, and electricity. It encouraged foreign capital investment. Spanish capital acquired large stakes in Chilean banks and utilities while North American and Japanese capital opened up new mining ventures. It was hard to determine what would be the long-term consequences of these investments, especially since they were reminiscent of the domination that foreign capital had in Chile until the 1960s. To what extent would these investments expand production and jobs as opposed to repatriating profits from existing operations? Books like *Mapa actual de la extrema riquesa en Chile,* or *A Current Map of the Extreme Wealth in Chile,* by Hugo Fazio Rigazzi alerted Chileans of the extent to which conglomerates were penetrating vast sectors of the national economy. It was less certain the extent to which these multinationals were reshaping the country's political landscape.

Chile's human development as measured by such indicators as life expectancy, infant mortality, literacy, and income placed it ahead of all other Latin American nations. Similarly, Chilean women improved their status in society more than other Latin American women. To further encourage them, Aylwin created the Servicio Nacional de la Mujer, or National Women's Agency, at a ministerial level. President Lagos named women to important government roles; in 2002, 5 of his 16 cabinet members were women. They pushed for economic opportunity and the legal equality of women. The Frei Ruiz-Tagle and Lagos governments urged their legislatures to pass a divorce law to overcome the existing limitations of legal separations, but the Catholic Church lobbied hard for Christian Democrats to vote against the proposal.

As in many countries, violence against women increased in Chile during the 1990s with the reported number of rapes rising from 9.61 to 10.63 per thousand. These numbers, however, are only one-third the level of the United States. Also, births out of wedlock continued to increase. Some other indicators of crime such as the murder rate and arrests decreased in the 1990s. Car and home thefts, however, continued to rise, prompting people to install more security devices in both their vehicles and residences. To protect their property, home owners joined together to hire a neighborhood guard or security agency. Many people, however, moved to high-rise apartments believing that they offered more security than private homes. Chileans were fortunate, however, that the extreme violence of paramilitaries and drug traffickers, which threatened civil society in many Latin American large cities, did not invade Santiago, Concepción, or Valparaíso. Neither did population growth exceed economic growth. In Chile, new jobs and welfare programs actually reduced the nation's poverty level.

Human Rights

The most difficult problem that the Concertación undertook in the transition to democracy was addressing human rights abuses which occurred during the 17 years of military rule. The dismal spectacle of other South American nations' trying to resolve human rights abuses under military rule suggested the difficulties ahead. When the armed forces in Argentina, Uruguay, and Brazil turned their governments over to civilians in the 1980s, they sought to limit their accountability. Only Argentina successfully prosecuted some members of the military junta, largely because of the armed forces' humiliating defeat in the Malvinas/Falkland Islands War.

The Chilean case was different. By 1990 the neoliberal economic model was so successful that countries throughout the hemisphere were also implementing it. Among many Chileans, the military retained strong ideological and economic support. Even among those who opposed military rule, there were Christian Democratic leaders who originally encouraged the military coup. These leaders had to act cautiously because the military might possess sensitive information. Civilian politicians, therefore, sought a balance between the pursuit of justice and not alienating the military's cooperation in the democratic transition.

In anticipation that someday civil authority might hold the military accountable for human rights violations, in 1978 Pinochet decreed a broad amnesty for anyone who had committed crimes between September 11, 1973, and March 10, 1978. The Supreme Court later upheld the constitutionality of this decree. The prosecution of human rights violations was additionally stymied because it was difficult to amend the constitution and restructure legal procedures. Furthermore, Pinochet threatened civilian politicians with dire consequences if they even "touched his men." To prevent another military intervention, therefore, civilian leaders proceeded cautiously within the limitations imposed on them.

Approximately 3,000 Chileans were executed or disappeared during the

Pinochet regime and in many cases their bodies were never found. Thousands of others had been tortured. The Supreme Court decided that the government had the right to investigate, but not prosecute, the crimes covered by the 1978 amnesty decree. To undertake the investigation, Congress created the National Truth and Reconciliation Commission and authorized it, for a limited period of nine months, to investigate human rights abuses. Named to head the eight-person commission was Raúl Rittig, a longtime leader of the Radical Party and an ambassador during the Allende era. His conscientious leadership soon prompted people to refer to the commission as the "Rittig Commission" rather than by its official name.

The commission asked that anyone with knowledge of persons killed, tortured, or having suffered other abuses testify before it. Thousands of citizens provided testimonies that became the basis of the 2,000-page report the commission presented in March 1991. The report's narrative of assassinations, torture, and disappearances prompted President Aylwin to publicly apologize to all the family members of the victims. He also called for the military to recognize the pain that they had inflicted on their victims and their families. Neither Pinochet nor other members of the armed forces offered apologies; rather, they claimed that they had acted in the line of duty

Although moderates desired a reconciliation, extremists did not. Two political assassinations in early 1991 showed that the spirit of revenge was very much alive. In March, a leftist group gunned down a military doctor who had allegedly participated in political torture. A month later the Manuel Rodríguez Patriotic Front shot the author of the 1980 Constitution, law professor Jaime Guzmán, near the Catholic University. Aylwin reacted quickly and created an Office of Public Security to assure Chileans that he would not tolerate vindictive violence. The closely linked Communist Party and the Rodríguez Front came under considerable pressure for this use of violence, leading one faction of the latter group to reject arms and declare itself in favor of the democratic process.

The government, to promote justice within its institutional constraints, followed up the work of the Rittig Commission by creating the National Corporation for Reparation and Reconciliation. The twofold task of this body was to discover who was responsible for human rights abuses and to provide the victims or their families some compensation. To encourage testimonies from military personnel, in 1994 President Eduardo Frei Ruíz-Tagle offered immunity to those who would testify. Some did come forward to reveal new evidence of torture and assassination. One of the most dramatic revelations was that of a former employee of DINA, the military intelligence, who not only confessed to murdering labor leader Tucapel Jiménez but named his commanding officers who he claimed ordered him to do so.

New disclosures prompted a few politicians and journalists to berate the military and the courts for impeding justice. In an effort to appease disgruntled military leaders, the government detained these critics and confiscated objectionable publications. In 1996, for example, a court incarcerated the communist leader Gladys Marín for two days for her derogatory statements about Pinochet. Two years later the government seized *El libro negro de la justicia chilena,* or *The Black Book of Chilean Justice,* by Alejandra Matus for its scathing indictment of both the armed forces and the courts.

In response to increasing public pressure, the government's efforts to guarantee the military immunity from prosecution eroded. In 1995 Manuel Contreras, former head of DINA, was sentenced to seven years in prison for his role in the assassination of Orlando Letelier and his colleague, Ronni Moffit. Three years later Contreras declared that Pinochet was directly responsible for DINA's activities. The courts then indicted Pinochet but later found him unfit for trial. Another controversy errupted in 2003 when President Lagos proposed to grant amnesty from prosecution to lower-ranking military personnel who divulged the human rights abuses of their commanders during Pinochet's regime.

Investigations of human rights violations spread outside the country and even former Nixon-administration officials became potentially accountable for allegedly supporting Chilean violence in the early 1970s. The most dramatic case was initiated by the descendents of General Rene Schneider. They filed a $3 million civil suit against Henry Kissinger, Richard Helms, and other Nixon officials for their role in Schneider's assassination in 1970. Joyce Horman, the widow of Charles Horman, filed a similar suit that charged Nixon officials with collaborating with South American military leaders to eliminate leftists through a program called Operation Condor. The question in these suits was a new principle in international law. Could key Western leaders be prosecuted for their roles in clandestine operations during the Cold War?

THE ECONOMY

Fine Tuning

When Patricio Aylwin took charge of the economy in 1990, Chile enjoyed a high growth rate but inflation was up. In the election campaign, his political coalition had emphasized that in spite of economic growth, almost 40 percent of Chileans lived below the poverty level. Now as president, his challenge was how to improve these people's lives without undermining the positive features of the economy. He decided to continue with the neoliberal model with its emphasis on privatization and exports, but to increase jobs, taxes, and public services in an effort to lower the poverty level. A key element of his plan was to encourage manufacturing by offering subsidies but without raising tariffs. Manufacturing promised more, higher-paying jobs as well as innovative technology.

In spite of the overall goals of the government, Finance Minister Alejandro Foxley believed that his first priority was to cut inflation if the country were to achieve long-term growth. With inflation over 27 percent in 1990, Foxley raised both interest rates and taxes, although in the short run this meant lower growth and employment. On the positive side, he predicted that a tight monetary policy would encourage high rates of savings and investment and attract foreign capital. By 1994 he'd achieved his goal, having cut inflation to less than 9 percent. Additionally, he reduced import duties from 15 to 11 percent and encouraged exports through a favorable exchange rate. Unfortunately, his tight money policy dropped growth from nearly 10 percent in 1989 to 4.2 percent in 1994 while the unemployment rate increased slightly.

When Eduardo Frei Ruíz-Tagle became president in 1994, the outlook for the Chilean economy was far more positive. Nevertheless, his economic team, led by Finance Minister Eduardo Aninat, continued to fight inflation, lowering it to 4.5 percent by 2000. Aninat followed his predecessor's example and lowered tariffs from 11 to 6 percent over a five-year period. He also continued earlier privatization initiatives, even leasing the port of Valparaíso to a private firm. During Frei's first two years, economic growth jumped to over 7 percent, but when the Asian economic crisis hit in 1998, it dropped off to 3.4 percent. The following year the economy declined even more to –1 percent, the first negative figure since 1983, while unemployment ballooned to nearly 10 percent. With exports representing an ever larger percentage of the Chilean economy and Asian exports approximately one-third of the total, the "Asian flu" of the late 1990s had a particularly harsh impact on Chile.

In 2000 the Lagos government came to power just as the Asian economies were recovering, but then the European and North American economies entered a recession. Inflation increased somewhat in 2000, but Lago's restrictive monetary policy lowered it in 2001. The economy began to grow again in 2001, but at the modest rate of 2.8 percent, less than half that of the previous decade. Utilities and production for internal consumption, not exports, led the recovery.

To stimulate trade, Lagos signed free trade agreements with the European Union, Mexico, and Canada. With the United States, 11 years of negotiations produced the agreement both countries signed and ratified in 2003. Effective January 1, 2004, it reduced many tariffs immediately, but agricultural tariffs will be phased in over an eight-year period. With this stimulus, bilateral trade is expected to grow from its 2002 level of $8.8 billion. Nevertheless, some worried Chilean *fundo* owners called for subsidies to insulate them from the projected onslaught of cheap U.S. farm goods.

As early as 1998, the troubled foreign markets showed the vulnerability of the Chilean export model. Yet as neighboring Argentina's economy collapsed in 2002 and other Latin American nations experienced crises, by comparison, the Chilean economy appeared healthy. Economists succeeded in cushioning both internal and external shocks with adjustments in monetary policy. Lagos refused to stimulate the economy through deficit spending, but in 2002, to restart the sluggish economy, he did agree to lower interest rates. Although initially he proposed a new labor law to strengthen the unions' collective bargaining power, when business leaders protested that any labor changes would discourage investment, he put the legislation on hold.

Since the return of democracy in 1990, economists have avoided the temptation of seeking short-range fixes at the expense of the nation's long-range prosperity. The wide margin of support voters gave to the Concertación allowed policy makers to adopt strict monetary policies to cool off inflation even though this lowered growth and raised unemployment. Economists used technical criteria, not the need to win votes, in making these policies. The strengthening of the conservative coalition in 1999 and 2001 may change the Concertación's priorities, however, with the short-term urgency to win elections influencing policy.

Mining

The great changes occurring in the Chilean economy are most graphically seen in the area of mining. Although copper continued to be the most important industry, it no longer monopolized exports. Also, the expansion of private mining overtook the large public mines. Whereas in 1973 all large mining companies belonged to the state-owned copper firm, CODELCO, in the 1980s and 1990s new private mines led to a renaissance of the Gran Minería. La Escondida opened in 1990 and soon overtook Chuquicamata to become the country's largest copper mine. Other new mines such as La Disputada and Collahuasi contributed additional private production. Multinational firms such as Utah International, Rio Tinto Zinc (both U.S. companies), Mitsubishi, Nippon Mining (both Japanese), Falconbridge (Canadian), and the Anglo-American (South African) formed joint ventures to develop these mines in what marked an important departure from the largely U.S.–owned firms of the 1960s. With these new mines, approximately two-thirds of all output was now private. Moreover, the lower production costs of the private mines over the costs of CODELCO led to an intense debate as to whether the latter should not also be privatized. Scandals about financial losses in CODELCO's international trading further undermined public confidence in the state-owned sector.

Manufacturing

With the Chilean economy wedded to an export model, many people wondered if Chile would become locked into producing only raw materials. In the 1970s manufacturing's contribution to the GNP declined then stabilized. It continued to be sluggish in the 1980s, but during most of the 1990s industry and manufacturing grew at 6 percent per year, a figure better than in all but two of the other Latin American nations. Much of the industrial growth occurred in metal, pulp, and paper export products. Some industries, such as food and beverages, produced largely for local consumption. They tailored prepared meals and drinks to local tastes. In spite of low tariffs, these industries managed to keep 90 percent of the products in supermarkets of national origin.

Some economists claimed that if Chile aggressively supported manufacturing the nation could become another Korea. More than half of Chilean raw material exports, however, were completely unprocessed. In 1990 only 13 percent of total exports were manufactured goods; in 1996 this figure increased to almost 22 percent. Manufacturing potentially offered more jobs, wages, and technology, but could Chilean goods compete in the world market? Chilean leaders' decision to lower tariffs unilaterally in the 1990s and sign numerous free trade agreements meant the nation would not follow the Asian strategy of protecting local manufacturing. The Concertación economists preferred the Canadian or the Scandinavian model of exporting natural resources but processing them as much as possible. They looked to PROCHILE to promote exports and raise the quality of Chile's infrastructure, technology, worker training, and marketing in the belief that these efficiencies would stimulate manufacturing. Interestingly enough, small and medium-sized firms emphasized manufactured exports more than large ones, finding their best markets in the MERCOSUR nations of South America. Economists had yet to find how to stimulate large firms to export Chilean goods to Europe and the United States.

Information Technology

By the year 2000 one of every ten Chileans owned a computer. The same year the country spent $1.1 billion on computer product imports as the government invested heavily in information technology for schools and universities. To help less affluent Chileans, President Lagos supported the growth of a National Network of Infocenters which gave people free access to the Internet. When he met with Microsoft chair Bill Gates in November 2000, they signed a number of software agreements. With Chile already a leading Latin American software exporter, these agreements sought to build on this position.

Digital economy revenues grew at a yearly rate of above 25 percent, reaching $5.7 billion in 2001 and $7.7 billion in 2002. E-commerce was the fastest growing sector, representing $1.5 billion in 2001. In an attempt to accelerate e-commerce development, in 2002 the Lagos administration sponsored a six-step promotion process. Most importantly, it created the legal framework to guarantee private contracts negotiated over the Internet. It also encouraged on-line business between private companies and the government. To encourage small and medium-sized Chilean firms to sell directly to European markets via the Internet, it targeted this sector in the trade agreement it signed with the European Union in 2002.

Forestry

Exports of logs, lumber, and pulp grew rapidly from $870 million in 1990 to $2.3 billion in 2000. Even though falling world prices decreased earnings by 10 percent in 2001, this activity still produced about 13 percent of the nation's exports. If less raw materials and more finished wood and paper products were exported, this would raise both income and employment, but without government support it is unlikely to occur.

Creating future forests is a high priority as Chileans planted more than 200,000 acres of trees in the year 2000. Although none of these were genetically altered species, a biotechnology firm, Genfor, intends to change this. Genfor headed a joint venture of U.S., Canadian, and Chilean firms that used both gene splicing and cloning technology to develop a pest-resistant Radiata pine tree. In addition, this firm worked with Cellfor, a Canadian company, to introduce a Radiata pine tree with a 20 percent higher cellulose content. Once planted in Chile, Genfor expects both of these new species to increase forest productivity. In the long run, however, they encourage the monoculture of Radiata pine, which already represents 80 percent of Chile's tree plantations.

With these new species, Chilean commercial forestry continues the questionable practice of overlooking native species. Neither the industry nor the government plants native trees, but the forestry department has improved its management of national parks and restricted the farmers' use of fire to clear natural forests. Still, during the chronic drought of 1998, fires burned over 200,000 acres. Ecologists are becoming increasingly concerned about the country's forests and rallied to oppose a massive wood chipping project in the austral region by Trillion, a U.S. forest products company. In a number of well-publicized protests the Chilean Green Peace chapter has tried to halt this project.

Agriculture

The bright spot of Chilean agriculture was that fruit production continued to grow. By 1998 fruit represented 12 percent of the value of Chilean exports. Table grape exports led the way as they rose from 178,000 tons in 1984 to 513,000 tons in 1996. Planting paused in the mid-1990s as world prices dropped 15 percent due to overproduction. The decline in prices for other fruits such as peaches and kiwis sometimes exceeded 40 percent. California grape growers and Oregon pear and raspberry growers complained that Chilean imports were lowering prices below profitability. As prices stabilized, farmers began planting again in 1998. To assist in this expansion, in 2003 the government undertook new irrigation works in the fertile Colchagua Valley. Simultaneously, farmers raised the productivity of their vineyards to a level approaching the United States'. The European Union trade agreement opened more markets to Chilean fruit exporters and established a system to handle trade disputes. Trade agreements with Mexico, Canada, and the United States should also favor Chilean fruit exporters.

In addition to fresh fruit, Chile gained recognition as a major wine exporter. Brands such as Concha y Toro, Santa Carolina, and San Pedro became commonplace in supermarkets throughout the world. Another sign of the maturing wine industry is that some Chilean companies purchased vineyards in Argentina, while companies from both the United States and Spain formed joint ventures with Chilean vineyards.

Whereas lower tariffs and trade promotion helped fruit growers, it severely hurt producers of traditional crops such as grain. The MERCOSUR trade agreement dropped tariffs on Argentine grain, which is produced more cheaply than in Chile. In the late 1990s farmers in the Sur protested the impact of this agreement and demanded government support for their industry. Congress temporarily responded with a tariff increase. So pessimistic have some southern farmers become, however, that they are planting trees rather than traditional crops on their farmland. If the government is unwilling to offer grain price supports as do other nations, southern farmers will have to experiment with vineyards, orchards, or other innovative crops to remain on their lands.

Another negative note to Chilean agriculture was the decline in the number of peasant farmers. The World Bank actually encouraged this process by emphasizing the advantages of large farms in global market competition. According to its calculations, the cost of planting table grapes and producing export-quality fruit is about $14,000 per acre. The rationale is that since small farms cannot get credit to finance this level of investment, large farms are preferable. Small farmers are failing to compete and selling their land and moving to the cities. Agricultural workers left the countryside as well and rural employment fell from 902,000 in 1992 to 816,000 in 1997. Workers who remain on farms have had difficulty organizing due to restrictive legislation, so, not surprisingly, rural poverty remains high.

Fishing

During the 1990s Chile continued to expand its fish and seafood exports, which approached $1.5 billion and represented more than 11 percent of total exports. The catch included native species as well as the fish-farmed foreign ones. Most were destined for human consumption rather than for animal feed. In 1999 fresh and frozen fish represented over 60 percent of fish exports, canned and prepared fish and shellfish nearly 24 percent, and fish meal only 16 percent. Salmon exports alone reached $625 million. Especially important were Asian markets, where Chile captured a major part of the Japanese salmon and fresh trout sales. In spite of all this growth, a shadow hung over the fishing industry. U.S. health officials worried about possible toxic residues in Chilean salmon raised in fish farms. Could ocean fisheries sustain ever larger catches and was fish farming affecting the water quality of lakes and bays? Environmentalists and the tourism industry understandably demanded increasing accountability from this industry.

Telecommunications

This industry has thrived in Chile largely due to deregulation. The General Law of Telecommunications of 1982, modified in 1987, 1994, and 1997, created the basis for open access to this industry. Nevertheless, the Compañía de Teléfonos de Chile (Chilean Telephone Company), or CTC, has done its best to discourage competition through its pricing policies for connecting to its system. In 1996 the three largest companies accounted for a total of over $2 billion in revenue. The system is 100 percent digital and has competing cable television and mobile telephone networks. Preparations are underway to bring broadband Internet access to Chilean businesses and homes. Cell phones are ubiquitous, with rival companies enticing Chileans in shopping malls and through the media. To provide public telephone service to rural areas as well as Internet service to public schools and universities, the government set up a special fund. The government wants no one left behind in this communications revolution.

SOCIAL CLASSES

Workers

From the late 1980s through most of the 1990s Chilean laborers saw growing opportunities for employment. Whereas approximately 3.6 million Chileans were employed in 1985, this figure rose to 5.4 million by 1998. During the same period, the unemployment rate dropped from nearly 12 percent to 5.3 percent. The growth of labor unions was rapid in the latter 1980s but slowed down in the 1990s. While employment grew by 900,000 during the decade, labor union membership grew by less than 60,000. Restrictions on affiliations and collective bargaining imposed by the Pinochet government continued to dampen union growth. The three democratic administrations have attempted but failed to revise these restrictions.

Frustrated in their efforts to revise the constitution, Concertación leaders have emphasized the management of a growing economy to increase worker income rather than encourage the use of collective bargaining. The workers' reward for tacitly accepting this model is that national growth raised real wages more than 25 percent over a decade.

This income growth plus an increase in social expenditures since 1990 have cut the poverty rate from about 40 to 20 percent of the population. From 1989 to 1995, social expenditure expanded by 50 percent. Public housing construction, electricity, and potable water have all improved the lives of the poor.

As in most developed nations, the largest number of Chileans found employment in services. During the 1990s employment in this area rose from 55 percent to 59 percent, industrial employment remained constant at 24 percent, and agricultural employment declined from 19 percent to only 12 percent. Throughout most of the 1990s the construction boom offered many new jobs, but with the economic contraction that began in 1998, this area suffered the most. Projected new malls and industrial parks along with the government's intention to spend $15 billion by 2004 on airports, highways, jails, and schools should add new construction jobs.

The Middle Class

The affluence of the 1980s and 1990s created a consumer revolution that especially benefited the middle class. People in the middle class bought homes, cars, and prepared foods; they shopped in malls and banked through ATMs. A second home at the beach or in the southern lake region was common. If they had a cabin in the Sur, no longer did they use it only in the summer; now with multiple flights available daily, they could escape there on long weekends. In 1999, however, when the economy began to turn sour, credit card debts and other easy loans left people vulnerable to collection agencies and foreclosures.

Even during the recession, cable companies frantically installed lines in middle-class neighborhoods in expectation of future broadband use. Already cable television, Internet dialups, and video games brought electronics into homes. Fortunately young people unplugged to play *futbol* or, in the evening, dance at the local disco. For education, students had more choices. In addition to new professional schools and universities, many college graduates sought advanced degrees in Europe or the United States. In business and economics, for example, diplomas from Harvard University, the University Chicago, or the University of Wisconsin became increasingly common.

Professionals spent an important part of their workday in front of a computer. They e-mailed colleagues, locally and overseas, and accessed international data banks. In the academic world as well as other fields, research played an ever-increasing role. Library collections, government services, and company records became available on-line. Attending and presenting papers at American or European conferences was an expected professional role. Chilean middle-class culture rapidly homogenized with that of Europe and North America. Language and cultural barriers made this less the case with the Far East, although a third of all national trade is with that region.

As with advanced countries, the accelerated pace of life raised the stress in Chileans' lives. The tradition of lunch at home with the family was now more difficult. Working late, arriving home at eight or nine o'clock, and eating dinner in front of the television was now common. Many business leaders commuted regularly from Santiago to provincial capitals and to other South American countries, Europe, or the United States.

Although affluence has transformed the Chilean middle class, it has conserved some of its unique character. In an upscale supermarket, not just frozen pizzas and hamburgers are available in the prepared food section; the traditional *pastel de choclo,* or corn casarole, *arroz a la marinera,* or seafood rice, and *empanadas de mariscos,* or shellfish pies, are there as well. At the juice bars, such local fruits as *lucuma* and *chirimoya* compete with orange, grape, and vegetable juices. Many middle-class Chileans avoid malls, preferring to shop in their neighborhood. People still flock to the open markets to buy fresh produce. On Sundays families still gather for the noon meal as relatives drop by and the elderly narrate family genealogies and traditions to those who listen. In spite of rapid change, the extended family remains the center of national life.

Middle-class households always depended heavily on maids who, in addition to cleaning and cooking, often served as surrogate parents. As more attractive employment opportunities opened up for women, maids became increasingly difficult to find. Fewer girls from southern Chile were available and so more undocumented migrants from Peru and Bolivia filled this role. While most of these migrants pour into Santiago, the city, with its traffic and pollution, is losing its attractiveness for some college-educated youth. The availability of the Internet, cell-phone service, and efficient air travel enables young people to try life in the provinces and still stay connected. Provincial cities have become more cosmopolitan while offering a clean environment, less crime, and easy commutes.

The Elite

Important changes have occurred in the composition of the elite. The neoliberal model allowed brash entrepreneurs to form conglomerates surpassing the fortunes of any previous era. Whereas some traditional families like the Edwards remained prominent, new figures became the nation's economic power brokers. Many of these corporate leaders invested heavily in neighboring nations. According to one estimate, one-fourth of new foreign investment in Peru is Chilean with Chilean capital entering Argentina as well.

The elite continues to enjoy a level of consumption far surpassing other groups, but with the consumer revolution they no longer have a monopoly on such amenities as two cars, a second house, and foreign travel. The elite no longer dominates cultural and government institutions. For the first time in history, therefore, the elite has had to accept that Chile has definitely become a middle-class society.

CHANGING LANDSCAPES

Economic development in the 1980s and 1990s had a profound impact on both the urban and rural landscapes throughout Chile. In Santiago, perhaps most notable was the movement of the affluent business and commercial districts eastward into the Providencia and Vitacura districts. High-rise glass and steel office buildings converted a middle-class residential area into a banking, insurance, and real estate center. Department and jewelry stores, an occasional supermarket, and upscale restaurants added diversity to the area. *Torres,* or multistoried apartments, sprang up along sycamore-lined streets like Los Leones or América Vespucio, replacing single-family dwellings. Neighborhood associations trying to preserve their privacy occasionally succeeded in preventing the intrusion of these high-rise apartments

To handle the rise in traffic from the suburbs, which sprawled in all directions, the government invested heavily in urban commuter highways. When traffic was light on weekends, these arteries enabled people to move around the urban environment with ease, but during weekday rush hours congestion was like that of big cities everywhere. When the government proposed the widening of Bella Vista, a picturesque road on the north side of the Mapocho River, a major battle occurred. Neighbors opposed sacrificing their serenity to commuters who chose to live in distant suburbs.

Luxurious stucco homes with brick trim and ceramic tile roofs took over the grazing lands on the rolling hills east of Santiago. Developers built luxurious subdivisions such as Los Trapences with palm-lined avenues and Spanish revival homes right up to the base of the Andes. In the opposite direction, toward the national airport, as well as south toward San Bernardo, stretched miles of working-class apartments. They were less drab than low-cost public housing built in the 1960s and early 1970s but still far from comfortable. Few green spaces surrounded them. For the many rural migrants who occupied this monotonous landscape, urban living seemed particularly hostile.

Most urban areas in Chile expanded both up and out. In Viña del Mar rows of apartments blocked the ocean view. In Temuco, a modest-sized city of 300,000, where only a handful of five-story buildings existed before the 1980s, a *torre*-building frenzy hit, and soon dozens dotted the skyline.

Even in small, lakeside tourist towns like Villarrica and Pucón, high-rise apartments and hotels added a cosmopolitan air.

The rural landscape went through a transformation. On the road from Santiago to Valparaiso, truck farms and pastures ceded to miles of newly planted vineyards all with a standardized look. Similarly regimented orchards lined the Pan-American highway heading south. Quickly disappearing was the nostalgic, rustic, and timeless look of the pastoral landscape. In the Andean lake region, farm areas were increasingly filling up with summer homes surrounded by a small acreage. In the stretch between Villarrica and Pucón, which as late as the 1960s was made up of dairies and farms, summer homes predominated by the late 1990s.

In spite of periodic droughts, Chile was becoming greener. Throughout rural areas, especially in the coastal mountains and the Andes, a change in vegetation occurred. In some areas of the Andes stricter regulation of slash-and-burn agriculture was bringing back the native forests. East of Santiago, for the first time in hundreds of years, the lower steps of the Andes were covered with evergreens. Heading south, huge areas that were once marginal grazing ranges were now covered with tree farms. Symmetrical rows of Radiata pine now stretched over the horizon.

The Environment

Without full regard to the environmental consequences, for decades the Chilean economy emphasized the harvesting of natural resources. Although the return of democracy in 1990 opened up a debate over environmental issues, the government gave priority to continuing the economic growth rate achieved in the later Pinochet years. The Aylwin government did create the National Environmental Commission, or CONAMA, but did not give it strong enforcement power.

Various protests by a fledgling environmental movement demanded the reconsideration of some major projects. The Mapuche opposed the Ralco hydroelectric dam on the Bio-Bio River, which would flood part of their native lands. Their repeated attacks on the construction firm led the Biobío governor, Esteban Krause, to apply the antiterrorism law against those responsible. The Mapuche also torched numerous tree plantations, demanding the return of native lands that the government annexed in the 1880s. To ameliorate these demands, President Lagos appropriated $130 million to help 650 Mapuche communities. One goal was to purchase privately held lands and return them to the Mapuche.

In the Austral region a Canadian aluminum company, Noranda, proposed building three hydroelectric dams to power a large aluminum smelter. The company intended to invest $2.75 billion in the project, which would produce 440,000 tons of aluminum annually. Because the project would raise wages and employ hundreds of workers, labor unions and local economic interests favored it. Environmentalists, by contrast, protested that it would despoil an unpolluted area. In what appeared as a victory for environmentalists, Noranda announced that it postponed the project indefinitely. Although such debates make decisions more complicated and projects more costly, free expression gives all parties a chance to find a balance between growth and the environment.

THE FUTURE

As Chile looks forward, it also looks backward. In September 1990, for example, thousands of Salvador Allende's supporters attended a public funeral denied to his family 17 years earlier by the Military Junta. In 1998, on the twenty-fifth anniversary of Pablo Neruda's death, the University of Chile commemorated his work with a widely publicized exhibit of his writing. In 2000, the same year Chile inaugurated as president Ricardo Lagos, a former member of the Unidad Popular, dignitaries gathered to dedicate a statue of Salvador Allende in Santiago's Plaza de la Constitución. On nearby kiosks, Chileans read newspaper headlines of torture and clandestine burials. When new members joined the Supreme Court, this body reversed an earlier decision and now allowed military officers to be prosecuted for human rights abuses. Looking backward, Chile tried to reconcile itself with its past, so that in the future it could look forward.

Among moderate Chileans, cooperation occurred, if not reconciliation. Christian Democrats and Socialists worked together during the "No" campaign and three presidential administrations. Even the conservative Renovación Nacional showed a willingness to compromise so that the democratic transition might succeed.

As September 11, 2003, the thirtieth anniversary of the military coup, approached, President Lagos dedicated a room in the presidential palace to Salvador Allende. In memory of the dead, human rights advocates marched to Santiago's General Cemetery. In an effort to diminish Pinochet's stature in the armed forces, current Commander in Chief Juan Emilio Cherye canceled all military commemorations for the day. Nevertheless some of Augusto Pinochet's supporters held a rally in front of the Diego Portales Center and booed Cheyre for his alleged disloyalty to his former leader. Although antagonisms remain between the left and the right 30 years later, civil expression and elections have largely replaced violence.

Among Communists on the left and UDI supporters on the right less reconciliation has occurred. For both practical and ideological reasons, the Communists raised their voices against alleged abuses by those in power. Not only were their ideological positions predictable, they carried the burden of their own connections to terrorism and a name that tied them to the collapsed system of the Soviet Union. Their indignation against the government, therefore, failed to attract much support. In reaction to a sluggish economy, in August 2003 some Socialist leaders rebelled against Lagos's leadership and supported a nationwide workers strike.

Divisive politics on the right have found considerable success. The UDI, under the leadership of Pablo Longueira, has used Pinochet's legal problems and the economic recession of 1998–2002 to rally supporters. In the human rights campaign, UDI supporters see an agenda of discrediting the military and, indirectly, the party.

Although Joaquín Lavín, the 1999 conservative coalition candidate, publicly rejected polarizing politics, other members of the UDI find that this strategy wins elections. Longueira believes that after the 2001 congressional showing, in 2006 his party now has the momentum to end the Concertación's sixteen-year monopoly on the presidency.

Despite problems and clouds on the horizon, the democratic transition has worked. The election of Ricardo Lagos and the moderating influence that he exercised over his fellow Socialists show how far the transition has come. But to say that the politics of confrontation is buried and will not return is naïve. Especially when international recessions slow down the economy, political differences become exaggerated. A chronic economic downturn, therefore, could prove explosive. To their credit, however, Chilean economists and politicians have demonstrated both resolution and skill in adjusting policy to changing international conditions.

Much of Chile is new. Not only have urban and rural landscapes changed, but people's thinking has changed as well. Long conversations over tea or dinner are more rare as a practical, ambitious people rapidly build a first-world, material culture. They are proud that the rest of Latin America looks to them as a model for the future, yet only a few recognize that progress in its current form threatens their land. To protect it they must change their priorities. They still painfully relive their past, but they also recognize that many traditions unite them, especially their democratic heritage. As they look backward and come to terms with the past, their heritage gives them many positive reasons to be optimistic about their future.

Notable People in the History of Chile

Aguirre Cerda, Pedro (1879–1941). President from 1938 to 1941. His electoral victory was based on a coalition of parties from the center-left, including the Radical, Socialist, and Communist parties, which enabled him to narrowly defeat the rightwing candidate, Gustavo Ross. While in office he dealt with the Chillán earthquake by creating the Corporación de Fomento (Development Corporation), or CORFO, which became the leading agency for promoting industrial development.

Alessandri Palma, Arturo (1868–1950). Nicknamed the "León de Tarapacá" (Lion of Tarapacá) for his combative senatorial campaign in 1915 in Chile's northern-most province. He served two non-consecutive terms as president from 1920 to 1925 and from 1932 to 1938. His first term was interrupted twice by the military. Although he proposed a variety of legislative reforms during his first term, the conservative-dominated senate blocked them. To overcome legislative intransigence, he supported a new constitution in 1925 which strengthened the power of the presidency. In his second term he confronted a country devastated by the Depression. His Finance Minister, Gustavo Ross, succeeded in restarting the economy, but his conservative policies as well as his deployment of force against both workers and Nazi youth alienated many Chileans. Among conservatives, however, he remained immensely popular and twice they elected him senator after his presidential term ended.

Alessandri Rodríguez, Jorge (1896–1986). President from 1958 to 1964. Presidential candidate again in 1970, but narrowly defeated by Salvador Allende. His administration passed the first agrarian reform law, cooperated with Alliance for Progress programs, and rebuilt the Valdivia region after the 1960 earthquake. His father was president Arturo Alessandri.

Allende, Isabel (1946–). Chile's best-known, living novelist. Her novel *House of the Spirits* is widely acclaimed, as are her subsequent novels. Like many Latin American writers, she employs magic realism as a means to heighten the psychological reality of her characters. Her father was a cousin of former president Salvador Allende.

Allende Gossens, Salvador (1908–73). President from 1970 to 1973. On three previous occasions he had been defeated as candidate for president, but in 1970 he won a narrow victory with slightly more than 36 percent of the total votes. A coalition of left-wing parties called the Unidad Popular participated in his government. During his administration he tried to socialize the economy by nationalizing the Gran Minería, most banks, hundreds of industries, and the food distribution system. His supporters accelerated the expropriation of large landholding. Employment rose and student registration increased. In the third year of his administration, with inflation rampant, private property in jeopardy, and consumer goods chronically scarce, strikes and confrontations disrupted all activities. Likewise, congress accused him of violating the constitution. On September 11, 1973, the military overthrew him. The cause of his death remains a controversy.

Almagro, Diego (1480–1538). From 1535 to 1536 he experienced great hardships as he crossed the desert and the Andes to explore Chile. He failed to find the riches he had sought, but provided valuable information for the Valdivia expedition, which followed four years later. Upon returning to Peru, he opposed the Pizarro brothers in a civil war, was captured, and executed. Only seven years earlier, in 1530, he had helped Francisco Pizarro conquer the Inca Empire.

Aylwin Azócar, Patricio (1918–). President from 1990 to 1994. Elected by the Concertación, which included the Christian Democrats, the Socialists, and the Party for Democracy. As the first elected president after the Pinochet regime, he dexterously steered a transition toward democracy. Previously, he held many important positions in the Christian Democratic Party and was his party's chief negotiator with Allende in 1973, when the latter sought to resolve the nation's political crisis.

Blamaceda, José Manuel (1840–91). President from 1886 to 1891. He governed during a period of growing nitrate wealth, which he funneled into public works such as railroads, ports, and public buildings. He clashed with congress, however, over ministerial appointments and the budgetary process. Congress challenged his authoritarian style and, with the support of the navy, defeated his forces. Balmaceda sought asylum, but, rather than leave the country, he chose suicide instead.

Barros Arana, Diego (1830–1906). Best known for his sixteen-volume masterpiece, *Historia general de Chile.* An additional two volumes, *Un decenio de la historia de Chile, 1841–1851 (A Decade of Chilean History),* enabled Barros Arana to cover history from prehistoric times to the middle of the nineteenth century. He also served as Chile's representative in negotiations with Argentina over the two nations' common border. Nationalists, however, blame him for allocating too much of the Patagonia to Argentina in the 1881 treaty.

Bello, Andrés (1781–1865). Although Venezuelan by birth, he helped found the University of Chile and served as its rector for more than twenty years. He acted as consultant for the 1833 Constitution, codified Chile's civil law, wrote extensively on grammar, and served in congress. He and Domingo F. Sarmiento, later president of Argentina, engaged in a famous debate over usage of the Spanish language.

Bulnes Prieto, Manuel (1799–1866). President for two consecutive terms: 1841 to 1851. Great economic progress occurred during his decade in office including the initiation of steamship service and the first railroad. Also founded during his administration were the University of Chile and the town of Punta Arenas in the far south. Previous to being elected president, he commanded Chile's troops in the war with the Peru-Bolivian Confederation.

Carrera, José Miguel (1785–1821). Independence leader who grew impatient with a divided congress and imposed his own authoritarian rule. He both accelerated and divided the independence movement. Unfortunately, in 1814, a feud between he and Bernardo O'Higgins aided the Spanish in their effort to reconquer Chile. He fled to Argentina where he and his brothers began reorganizing their forces. Their efforts clashed with those of O'Higgins and San Martín and led to his brothers' execution in 1818, followed by his own execution in 1821. Even today Chileans are divided into "Carrerista" and "O'Higginista" camps, based on their loyalty to each of these early independence leaders.

Caupolicán (?–1558). Mapuche leader who assisted Lautaro in his victories over the Spaniards in the 1550s. Governor García Hurtado de Mendoza, aided by a Mapuche informer, defeated and killed Caupolicán near Concepción in 1558. Alonso de Ercilla extolled Caupolicán's extraordinary strength in *La araucana.*

Cochrane, Thomas Alexander (1775–1860). Vice admiral of the Chilean navy from 1818 to 1822. He successfully eliminated all Spanish shipping on the coasts of Chile and Peru and captured the port of Valdivia from Spanish forces. In 1820 he supported the liberation of the Peruvian Vice-royalty by transporting the army, commanded by José de San Martín, from Valparaíso to southern Peru. In 1822, however, he resigned his position and accepted the command of the Brazilian navy.

Ercilla Y Zúñiga, Alonso de (1533–94). Although he spent less than three years in Chile, his epic poem, *La araucana,* is the most important literary work of the colonial period. The poet transforms the Spanish and Map-uche combatants into heroic Greek archetypes, thus ennobling New World figures for European culture. The work became an important source of Chilean identity and nationalism.

Frei Montalva, Eduardo (1911–82). President from 1964 to 1970. During his administration he expanded educational enrollments, accelerated the agrarian reform, began copper mine nationalization, and built thousands of low-income houses. Unfortunately, two left-wing groups split from his party and his economic plans faltered. After his presidency, he led the senate's opposition to Allende's accelerated socialization. When Allende was overthrown, Frei Montalva originally supported the military, but later became a sharp critic of its human rights abuses. In 1982, he died during a routine operation, leading his relatives to raise the question of a con-spiracy. (Note: Frei's second last name is only used when an ambiguity exists with his son.)

Frei Ruíz-Tagle, Eduardo (1942–). President from 1994 to 2000. During the first four years of his administration, the country's economy had a stellar performance. With the onset of the Asian financial crisis in 1998, Chile lost markets. Growth faltered during his final two years as president. Frei was reticent to push too aggressively on human rights cases. In 1998 when Augusto Pinochet's term expired as commander in chief of the armed forces, he replaced him with General Ricardo Izurieta Caffarena. Eduardo Frei Ruíz-Tagle is the son of Eduardo Frei Montalva.

Freire, Ramón (1787–1851). Leader of Chile from 1823 to 1827. Succeeded in driving the Spanish out of the island of Chiloé. He supported liberal ideas including federalism, but he aggravated, rather than solved, the nation's financial problems. He relied upon a monopoly, the *estanco,* to pay the installments on a British loan. When it defaulted, this ruined the country's international credit. During the civil war of 1830, Freire's troops were defeated at the battle of Lircay and he fled into exile. In 1836, with Peruvian support, he tried but failed to overthrow Chile's conservative government.

Gay, Claudio (1800–73). French naturalist contracted by the Chilean gov-ernment in 1830 to undertake a study of the nation's flora, fauna, and geography. Gay spent more than a decade gathering his materials which he eventually published in a twenty-four-volume work, along with two illustrated atlases. He also wrote a multi-volume history of Chile which inspired Chileans to cultivate historical research.

González Videla, Gabriel (1898–1980). President from 1946 to 1952. Originally the center-left parties including the Radicals, Socialists, and Communists supported him, but in 1948 he persuaded congress to outlaw the Community Party with a measure titled the *Ley de Defensa de la Democracia* (Democratic Defense Law). While antagonizing this group of voters, he attracted another group by signing a bill granting women the right to vote. He is best remembered in La Serena where generous federal subsidies remodeled the city in an attractive neocolonial style.

Grove Vallejo, Marmaduke (1879–1954). As minister of defense during the Socialist Republic in 1931, he was the power behind the throne. This short-lived government attempted many reforms, but was soon overthrown. In the presidential election of 1932, Grove came in second to Arturo Alessandri. Later he served in congress, was general secretary of the Socialist Party, and helped engineer the victory of Pedro Aguirre Cerda and the Frente Popular in the 1938 presidential election.

Ibáñez del Campo, Carlos (1877–1960). Twice president: from 1927 to 1931 and from 1952 to 1958. He rose to power in the 1920s when he assumed a tutorial role toward civilian presidents Arturo Alessandri and Emiliano Figueroa. After the latter resigned, Ibáñez received overwhelming support in a special election. He began with administrative reforms and impressive public works which, unfortunately, were accompanied by severe repression of both labor and the press. He also created the Carabineros, or national police. On the international front, he returned the province of Tacna—which Chile had occupied since the War of the Pacific—to Peru. The 1930 Depression devastated Chile's economy, leading to widespread protests and Ibáñez's resignation in 1931. During his second presidency, Ibáñez spent most of his time battling labor and negotiating with an uncooperative congress.

Lagos, Ricardo (1938–). Inaugurated president in 2000 to a six-year term. Lagos belongs to the Socialist Party but was elected with the support of the Concertación. Although wanting to promote labor and other reforms, the world economic recession of 2000–2002 obligated him to postpone these proposals and struggle to reactivate the economy. Lagos was a member of Salvador Allende's administration and lived briefly in exile during the Pinochet government. In 1988 he assumed a dynamic leadership position in the "No" campaign to deny Pinochet eight more years as president. During the Aylwin and Frei R. administrations, he held various ministerial positions. In 1999 Lagos defeated the Christian Democratic candidate, Andrés Zaldivar, in a primary election held by the Concertación, thus winning the support of the coalition in his bid for the presidency.

Lastarria Santander, José Victorino (1817–88). Professor of law and Liberal congressional leader. In a famous University of Chile seminar, Lastarria condemned the nation's conservative Spanish heritage and urged leaders to look to more liberal nations for direction. He published widely on themes of literature and the law. He served as a minister in several administrations and on one occasion represented Chile in diplomatic negotiations.

Lautaro (1534–57). Mapuche military leader who defeated the Spanish in important battles. In 1553, his troops killed Pedro de Valdivia at Tucapel. Other victories followed, including the capture of the city of Concepción in 1556. He intended to attack Santiago, but in 1557 Pedro de Villagra surprised him in his camp and killed him. Alonso de Ercilla immortalized Lautaro's bravery in his epic poem, *La araucana*.

Mistral, Gabriela (1889–1957). Awarded the Nobel Prize in Literature in 1946. She was the first Latin American to receive this award. Her love for children, nature, and her Native American roots are important themes in her poetry. She also served as a diplomatic representative of Chile in various countries. For a partial list of her works, see the bibliography. Gabriela Mistral is a pseudonym; her given name was Lucia Godoy Alcayaga.

Montt Alvarez, Jorge (1845–1922). President from 1891 to 1896. When congress rebelled against the authoritarian measures of president José Manuel Balmaceda, Montt supported congress from his position as navy captain. He played an important role in defeating Balmaceda's forces and was elected president the same year. During his regime, congress dominated, as it would until a new constitution was ratified in 1925. Montt did reform the electoral system, which diminished presidential manipulation of elections. He also auctioned numerous nitrate fields, often to foreign companies.

Montt Torres, Manuel (1809–80). President for two consecutive terms: 1851 to 1861. Governed during a period of great progress in telegraph, railroad, and public works construction. Montt encouraged public education, agricultural credit, and efficient administration. Nevertheless, he clashed with both the Church and mining entrepreneurs. In 1859 a civil war broke out in the north and then spread south to Concepción. After an early loss, government troops defeated the rebels. Although Montt claimed victory, his successor recognized the need to heal the nation's divisions with a general amnesty.

Neruda, Pablo (1904–73). One of the greatest poets of the twentieth century. Awarded the Nobel Prize in Literature in 1971. The dominant themes of his work include erotic love, Native American heritage, workers' rights, and communion with nature. He served in various diplomatic missions to foreign countries. He was also a member of the Communist Party, receiving its nomination for president in 1970. He died just after the military coup. His home on the coast at Isla Negra has been converted into a private museum by his many loyal followers. For a partial list of his works, see the bibliography. Neruda is a pseudonym; he was born Neftalí Reyes Basoalto.

North, John Thomas (1842–96). Ambitious English entrepreneur who bought up nitrate certificates during the War of the Pacific. He also gained monopoly railroad rights, enabling him to overcharge competitors. His skill at creating corporations and selling their stock made him one of the richest men of his era.

O'Higgins, Ambrosio (circa 1720–1801). Governor of Chile from 1788 to 1796 and viceroy of Peru from 1796–1801. As governor he established new towns, encouraged major public works in Santiago, and built the first road from the capital to Valparaíso. He also eliminated the encomienda and encouraged commerce. He was Irish, emigrating first to Spain and then to Chile in 1761. He began as a merchant but he soon entered the military to build fortifications and pacify the Mapuche. His exceptional military record earned him the trust of the king, who named him governor. His son, Bernardo, was born from a relationship which he had with Isabel Riquelme. Although Bernardo was never legitimized, his father paid for his education in England and willed him his estate when he died in 1801.

O'Higgins, Bernardo (1778–1842). Supreme Director of Chile from 1817 to 1823 and considered "the father of his country." With José de San Martín, he defeated the Spanish forces at the Battle of Chacabuco on February 12, 1817. He then organized the government and planned the liberation of Peru. He liberalized many of Chile's laws, especially in commerce, but encountered opposition by entrenched elite families. In 1823, these family leaders pressured him to resign. He did so rather than provoke a civil war. He voluntarily went into exile in Peru, expecting to be called back to govern Chile, but this never happened. He died in exile. His father was Ambrosio O'Higgins.

Pérez Mascayano, José Joaquín (1801–89). President for two consecutive terms: 1861 to 1871. Pérez began his presidency with a general amnesty for those guilty of political crimes, which helped to unify the country after the civil wars of 1851 and 1859. He also abandoned the conservative policies of his three predecessors and allied himself with the liberals. Important liberal reforms included two bills: one guaranteeing freedom of religion and one prohibiting consecutive presidential terms. In 1866 his government declared war on Spain for the latter's attack on Peru. In revenge for this action, the Spanish fleet shelled Valparaíso, severely damaging its commercial warehouses.

Parra, Violeta (1917–67). Musicologist and folksinger who gave new life to Chile's rich musical heritage. She also composed numerous songs, the most famous being *Gracias a la vida*. Her children, Angel and Isabel, have carried on their mother's tradition both as composers and singers in their Santiago nightclub.

Pinochet Ugarte, Augusto (1915–). President of Chile from 1974 to 1990. He was commander in chief of the armed forces during the overthrow of Salvador Allende's government in 1973. As head of the military junta, he disbanded the congress and left-wing political parties. There is still debate about his personal responsibility for human rights violations. In 1975 he authorized the economists from the Catholic University to implement neoliberal reforms, which radically transformed the national economy. He also supervised the ratification of the 1980 Constitution which replaced the one of 1925. After stepping down as president in 1990, he continued as head of the armed forces until 1998. Attempts to try him for human rights violations have failed. Both English and Chilean courts have found that due to his failing health he is unfit for trial.

Pinto Garmendia, Aníbal (1825–84). President from 1876 to 1881. He confronted a severe world recession which hurt all aspects of the Chilean economy. To prevent bank failures and a crisis in international payments, he supported legislation which liberalized exchange rules, raised tariffs, and taxed inheritances. He is best known for his leadership in the War of the Pacific. He declared war on Bolivia and Peru in 1879. Though Chile's military was generally unprepared for the conflict, by January 1881 it successfully occupied Lima. In the process, the Chilean armed forces annexed the valuable nitrate fields of Bolivia and Peru.

Portales Palazuelos, Diego (1793–1837). Political leader largely responsible for the initiation of the conservative regime in 1830. He held numerous cabinet positions, but, more importantly, he exercised great influence over president Prieto. As a merchant, he encouraged trade but had little tolerance for liberal political innovations. He sought the preeminence of Valparaíso as the leading port of the Pacific. To promote this end, he encouraged war with the Peru-Bolivian Confederation. In 1837, he was assassinated by opponents in an uprising near Valparaíso.

Prats González, Carlos (1915–74). Commander and chief of the military from 1969 to 1973. He supported constitutional government and strongly opposed those who wanted the military to overthrow Salvador Allende. A humiliating confrontation with Alejandra Cox led the wives of his colleagues to demand his resignation. When he did resign in August 1973, his replacement was Augusto Pinochet, who supported plans for a coup d'état. Prats went into exile in Buenos Aires where he maintained an active correspondence with opponents of the military regime. In revenge, DINA operatives assassinated him and his wife a year later with a car bomb.

Prieto Vial, Joaquín (1786–1854). President for two consecutive terms: 1831 to 1841. He was Diego Portales's protégé, lending his military leadership to the conservative regime established after the Battle of Lircay. The Constitution of 1833 took effect during his first term as did the important fiscal reforms initiated by finance minister Manuel Rengifo. New silver and copper mines contributed to growing prosperity. During his second term, Chile defeated the Peruvian-Bolivian Confederation. However, his close collaborator, Diego Portales, was killed in a Valparaíso uprising.

Rengifo Cárdenas, Manuel (1793–1845). Minister of finance from 1830 to 1835 and from 1841 to 1844. To balance the national budget during the administration of Joaquín Prieto, Rengifo lowered taxes and rationalized the customs legislation to reduce tax evasion and smuggling. He also restored the nation's internal credit by establishing a debt amortization plan. In spite of his success, Prieto dismissed him when Rengifo considered running against him in the 1836 presidential election. Five years later, president Bulnes named him again to head the ministry of finance. His great accomplishment was to renegotiate Chile's loan with London bond holders, thus reestablishing the nation's foreign credit. Like United States treasurer Alexander Hamilton, Rengifo established the financial basis for successful government and national progress.

Santa María González, Domingo (1825–89). President from 1881 to 1886. He achieved a settlement in 1884 ending the war with Peru. He also encouraged a conflict with the Mapuche, forcing them to forfeit ancestral lands to the government. The biggest political conflict of his administration was a proposal for the state to control cemeteries, marriages, and birth registrations. Although this legislation passed, it profoundly aggravated relations with the church and the Conservative Party.

Silva Henríquez, Cardinal Raúl (1907–99). Archbishop of Santiago from 1961 to 1983; raised to cardinal in 1963. This liberal leader of the church approved of most of Frei M.'s reforms. During the Allende government he abstained from criticizing the Unidad Popular's programs until a national education reform, la Escuela Nacional Unificada, threatened to impose a fixed curriculum on Catholic schools. He offered his services to Salvador Allende and Patricio Aylwin in 1973 when they tried to resolve the nation's political turmoil. After the military overthrow, much to president Pinochet's displeasure, Cardinal Silva advocated human rights through the creation of the Vicaría de la Solidaridad.

Tomic Romero, Radomiro (1914–). Christian Democratic candidate for president in 1970, who placed third behind Salvador Allende and Jorge

Alessandri. Earlier, he helped found the Falange Nacional as well as its successor, the Christian Democratic Party. During the first half of Eduardo Frei M.'s administration, he served as Chile's ambassador to the United States. After losing the 1970 election, he congratulated Salvador Allende. Some conservative Christian Democrats blamed him for the party's defeat because he failed to campaign on Frei's record and chose to propose more radical reforms. After the military coup, he went into exile where he strongly criticized the Pinochet regime.

Valdivia, Luis de, S.J. (1561–1642). Jesuit priest who gained royal approval for a peaceful relationship between the Spanish and the Mapuche, called the "Defensive War." This policy, which became effective in 1612, granted the Jesuit Order unique missionary responsibilities in the Mapuche heartland, while restricting the access of other Spaniards. To implement this policy, Valdivia conferred with many Mapuche leaders. Unfortunately, one angry chief ordered the massacre of three Jesuit priests at Elicura that same year. Civil authorities, who disagreed with the policy, now openly rejected it, although the crown did not officially revoke it until 1626. Luis de Valdivia had no blood relationship with Pedro de Valdivia.

Valdivia, Pedro de (1502–53). Explorer, conqueror, and governor of Chile. In 1540 he traveled overland from Peru to the Valle Central of Chile. There he founded the capital, Santiago de la Nueva Extremadura, on February 12, 1541. The town's council elected him governor, a position later confirmed by the king. After distributing lands and the service of Indians to his comrades, in 1550 he marched south into the dense forests of the Mapuche heartland. There he audaciously attacked the Indians, establishing forts, small towns, and encomiendas. He underestimated the Mapuche and their military prowess. Under Lautaro's leadership, the Mapuche rebelled and killed him at the Battle of Tucapel in 1553.

Glossary of Selected Terms

Aduana: Customs agency which assesses tariff duties and checks the credentials of international travelers.

Afuerino: An agricultural worker who does not live on the property where he works.

Aguardiente: Grape brandy, although the word literally means "firewater."

Alacalufes: Indians who lived by fishing in the north of the Magallanes province.

Alcalde: The chief administrative officer of the town council.

Araucanians: Term used by the Spanish to refer to the Indians who lived south of the Biobío River. Current usage is to call them Mapuche.

Arroz a la Marinera: Casserole of rice with shellfish.

Audiencia: Colonial judicial and administrative body which handled civil and criminal cases as well as checked the authority of the chief executive.

Boleadora: An Indian weapon, adopted by some mestizos and used for hunting and war. Consists of two or three round stones attached to a leather thong. Thrown at game or at enemies on the battlefield.

Bomberos: Firemen; usually volunteers.

Cabildo abierto: The *cabildo* was the colonial town council. During the independence, this institution was open, or *abierto*, to include all community leaders.

Campesino: Yeoman farmer, but often used as a generic term for rural people who are not large landowners.

Carabineros: National police force; also considered the fourth branch of the armed services.

Casa de la Moneda: Originally the colonial mint, but today it is the president's mansion.

Chamber of Deputies: Lower house of the Chilean congress.

Chicha: The Indians made this fermented beverage of corn or pine nuts, but today the Chileans use grapes or apples. In the Sur it is hard cider.

Chilote: A person from the island of Chiloé.

Chonos: Native Americans who lived in the Aisén region, largely on the archipelago of the same name. Subsisted largely by fishing.

Chupilca del Diablo: The *chupilca* is an alcoholic drink, usually wine, mixed with ground, toasted wheat. According to mythology, it became *diabolic* when Chilean soldiers added gunpowder during War of the Pacific.

Concertación: Coalition of the Christian Democrats, the Party for Democracy, the Socialists, and the Social Radicals that has functioned since 1988.

Consejales: Elected members of the town council. Formerly called *regidores*.

Consulado: In the colonial period this was the merchant guild. Today this term refers to the consulate of a diplomatic mission.

Cordones industriales: Industrial belts especially in Santiago. The Unidad Popular mobilized the workers in these industries to lock out the owners and participate in political rallies.

Criollo: In the colonial period, a person of Spanish ancestry born in Chile. Today it refers to something authentically Chilean; for example, a *caballo criollo* is a national breed.

Cuña: An influential contact or connection who can resolve a bureaucratic impasse.

Curanto: A shellfish dish traditionally cooked in a pit.

Cuyo: Today the western Argentine provinces of Mendoza, San Juan, and San Luis. Before 1776, however, this area fell under the administrative jurisdiction of Chile.

Dieciocho: Reference to Independence Day, celebrated on the eighteenth of September.

Diezmo: Tithe or agricultural tax which the crown collected and distributed to the church.

Empanada: Baked or deep-fried turnover filled with ground beef, chopped eggs, olives, and onions. Traditional for celebrations such as Independence Day.

Encomendero: An individual awarded Indian tribute for service to the crown. Often exploited Indian labor in violation of edicts prohibiting this practice.

Encomienda: Group of Indians who owe tribute to an *encomendero.* After 1542 the crown ordered this tribute paid in goods, not labor, but rarely was this order enforced.

Escudo: Monetary unit introduced in 1959 to replace the peso and eliminated in 1975 when the peso was restored. The more general meaning is shield or coat-of-arms.

Estanco: In the independence period, a monopoly franchise granted by the government to a private firm in return for an annual fee. Products included in the monopoly were tobacco, imported spirits, and playing cards.

Fiducia: Magazine published by the conservative Catholic organization La Sociedad Chilena de Defensa Tradición, Familia y la Propiedad (The Chilean Society for the Defense of Tradition, Family, and Property), or TFP. Opposed to the Frei and Allende regimes, as well as the liberal members of the church hierarchy.

Filopolitas: Liberals within president Prieto's administration who supported the candidacy of Manuel Rengifo as Prieto's successor.

Fogón: Rustic wooden structure with an earthen floor and a hearth; used by Mapuches and rural Chileans for cooking and socializing.

Fundo: Term that means large estate and replaces *hacienda* in the nineteenth-century Chilean lexicon.

Gran Minería: Large-scale, industrial mines.

Gremialismo: Conservative political movement of employer and professional associations intended to counterbalance the power of labor unions.

Gremio: Employer or professional association, such as a truck owners or engineers association.

Habilitadores de minas: Merchants who advanced goods to miners as credit in return for an exclusive right to market their ores.

Huaso: An elegantly dressed *fundo* owner mounted on his best horse; or, a country bumpkin unfamiliar with modern urban life.

Huilliches: Mapuche clans who lived between the Maule River and the Valdivia region.

Inquilino: Tenant laborer on a hacienda or *fundo.*

Intendente: In the late colonial period, a regional administrator created by the Bourbon kings. After independence, the top provincial administrator; appointed by the president, not elected.

Junta: Small ruling committee; often a transitional government.

Maloca: Mapuche raiding party.

Mapuche: Native Americans who lived in the Central Valley and Southern Chile. Also referred to as the Araucanians. Divided into various subgroups.

Mestizo: A person with both European and Native American ancestry.

Navío de Registro: Merchant vessel authorized by Spain to trade with Spanish America.

Norte Chico: Mining region which encompasses the provinces of Atacama and Coquimbo.

Norte Grande: Desert mining region which encompasses the two northernmost provinces of Chile, Antofagasta and Tarapacá.

Onas: Native Americans who hunted various animals in the Tierra del Fuego region.

Opus Dei: Conservative Catholic religious order; influential in the Pinochet government.

Padrino: Godfather. *Slang:* a contact who dispenses favors.

Palita: An influential contact or connection who can circumvent a bureaucratic impasse.

Papelera: Pulp and paper company named the Compañía Manufacturera de Papeles y Cartones and partly owned by Jorge Alessandri. The Unidad Popular threatened to take it over.

Pastel de choclo: Casserole or pie made of corn, ground beef, and other select ingredients.

Patria y Libertad: An ultra-conservative political organization, which conspired to overthrow Allende and replace him with a fascist-style regime.

Pedagógico: The school of education of the University of Chile known for its militant politics.

Pehuenches: Mapuche who lived in the Andes mountains. The *Pehuén* is the Araucanian pine tree; *che* means people.

Pelucones: A slang term for nineteenth-century conservatives. Literally, *peluca* means wig; *pelucón* means bigwig.

Peña: Folk music venue, often a nightclub.

Peninsulars: Spaniards born in the Iberian Peninsula, as distinguished from Spaniards born in America.

Picunches: Northern clans of the Mapuche who lived in the Maule River region.

Pipiolos: A slang term for nineteenth-century liberals.

Pisco sour: Traditional aperitif especially offered to foreign guests, consisting of *pisco* (a grape brandy), lemon juice, powdered sugar, and other select ingredients.

Poblaciones: Working-class neighborhoods that were highly politicized during the Frei and the Allende regimes; subject to search and seizure operations under the military.

Promoción popular: Frei's effort to encourage worker organizations to solve their community problems and participate in the political process.

Puelches: Mapuche clans who lived on the eastern side of the Andes.

Pulpería: Hacienda or company store that sells largely dry goods.

Roce de fuego: Slash-and-burn agriculture, especially prevalent south of the Maule River.

Roto chileno: Poor urban worker with great spunk for overcoming adversity.

Situado: Annual subsidy which the Viceroyalty of Peru paid Chile to defray some of the cost of the wars with the Mapuche.

Tacnazo: A rebellion by the Tacna army regiment on October 21, 1969, led by General Roberto Viaux, which demanded increased military salary and equipment.

Tancazo: June 29, 1973, tank assault on central Santiago that left 22 dead. Prelude to military coup three months later.

Tierra del Fuego: Island south of the Strait of Magellan jointly owned by Chile and Argentina. Name derived from fires lit by natives and observed by European mariners.

Torres: High-rise apartments.

Trapiche: Grinding mill used to break up ore. In Caribbean, used to grind sugarcane.

Tribunal de Minería: In the late colonial period, a court and a guild which handled mining litigation and resolved mine owners' problems.

Vicaría de la Solidaridad: Support group run by the Catholic Church to help those being persecuted by the military.

Vino tinto: Red wine.

Viva Chile mierda: Irreverent but triumphal cheer of patriotism.

Volcán: Volcanically formed mountain; can be active or inactive.

Yaganes: Indians in the south of the Magallanes province; dedicated to fishing.

Suggestions for
Further Reading

The suggestions that follow include general works on Chile, Internet sources, and works that refer to the themes treated in each chapter. I have included works in both English and Spanish, but very few journal articles and no dissertations. This does not mean that the latter two sources are not important; rather, within the limited scope of this essay, it was not possible to include them. Please note that many works encompass periods far broader than that of a specific chapter, but for economy's sake I have chosen to list them only once. It is also important to emphasize that scholars writing in English have explored the colonial period and the years from 1830 to 1960 far less than they have late twentieth century. I also want to emphasize that history is created by a community of scholars, and without the studies listed below this present work would not have been possible.

General Works

Two excellent surveys of Chilean history are available in English. Simon Collier and William F. Sater, *A History of Chile, 1808–1994* (Cambridge: Cambridge University Press, 1996) provides unique insight into the country's social and political evolution. Brian Loveman, *Chile: The Legacy of*

Hispanic Capitalism, 3rd ed. (New York: Oxford University Press, 2001) unravels the complex political history while providing a wealth of tables and bibliographical suggestions. Paul W. Drake et al., *Chile: A Country Study* (Washington, D.C.: Library of Congress, 1994) contains essays on the history, society, economy, politics, and security of Chile by experts in these respective areas. A concise general study is Jay Kinsbruner, *Chile: A Historical Interpretation* (New York: Harper and Row, 1973). *The Cambridge History of Latin America* (Cambridge: Cambridge Univ. Press, 1984–) has chapters on Chile by Simon Collier, Harold Blakemore, Paul Drake, and Alan Angell, who have all published extensively on Chile. Julio Heise González, *150 años de evolución institucional* (Santiago: Editorial Andrés Bello, 1960) is a valuable summary of Chile's political history. An older, but fascinating, survey is Luis Galdames, *A History of Chile* (Chapel Hill, University of North Carolina Press, 1941).

The most admired history of Chile, which covers the colonial and early independence periods, is Diego Barros Arana, *History general de Chile,* 16 vols. (Santiago: Rafael Jover, 1884–1902). Immensely popular among Chileans, but of less rigorous scholarship, is Francisco Encina, *Historia de Chile desde la prehistoria hasta 1891,* 20 vols. (Santiago: Editorial Nacimento, 1948–55). Alberto Edwards Vives, *La Fronda Aristocrática* (Santiago: Editorial Del Pacífico, 1928) proposes a provocative interpretation of the elite in Chile's history. A useful general text is Sergio Villalobos R., Osvaldo Silva G., Fernando Silva V., and Patricio Estellé, *Historia de Chile,* 4 vols. (Santiago: Editorial Universitaria, 1974). Villalobos has published volumes of a multivolume social history, *Historia del pueblo chileno* (Santiago: Empresa Editora Zig-Zag, 1980–). A contemporary textbook, edited by Nicolás Cruz and Pablo Whipple, written by specialists from the Catholic University, is *Nueva historia de Chile desde los orígenes hasta nuestro días* (Santiago: Zig-Zag, 1996). For an overview of Chilean literary trends and selected readings see Hugo Montes and Julio Orlandi, *Historia y antología de la literature chilena,* 8th ed. (Santiago: Editoria Zig-Zag, 1969).

More specialized studies cover a substantial part of the nation's past. Looking at economic policies and challenges is Markos Mamalakis, *The Growth and Structure of the Chilean Economy: From Independence to Allende* (New Haven: Yale University Press, 1976). Valuable for anyone engaged in demographic and economic research is his *Historical Statistics,* 6 vols. (Westport: Greenwood Press, 1979–89). For an economic history that is considerably more broad than the title suggests, see Juan Ricardo Couyoumdjian, René Millar Carvacho, and Josefina Tocornal, *Historia de la Bolsa de Comercio de Santiago, 1893–1993: un siglo del mercado de valores en Chile* (Santiago: Bolsa de Comercio de Santiago, 1993). Examining Chile's attempt to build its own shipping industry is Claudio Véliz, *Historia de la marina mercante de Chile* (Santiago: Universidad de Chile, 1961). For those interested in how the armed forces became involved in politics see Fredrick M. Nunn, *The Military in Chilean History* (Albuquerque: University of New Mexico, 1976).

Numerous analyses of Chile's political evolution are available. To understand how government institutions evolved, Federico Gil, *The Political System of Chile* (Boston: Houghton Mifflin, 1966), is excellent. Looking at the dynamics of parties and elections is Germán Urzúa Valenzuela, *Historia política de Chile y su evolución electoral desde 1810 a 1992* (Santiago: Editorial Jurídica de Chile, 1992). Presenting a historical analysis of the complicated multiparty system is Timothy R. Scully, *Rethinking the Center: Party Politics in Nineteenth and Twentieth Century Chile* (Stanford University Press, 1992). Critical of the political system's ability to address major social and economic problems is James F. Petras, *Politics and Social Forces in Chilean Development* (Berkeley: University of California Press, 1969). Offering Chileans insight into the ways past amnesties have restored the nation's political health is Brian Loveman and Elizabeth Lira, *Las suaves cenizas del olvido: la vía chilena de reconciliación política 1814–1994*, 2 vols. (Santiago: LOM Ediciones, 1999).

Fredrick B. Pike, *Chile and the United States, 1880–1962* (University of Notre Dame Press, 1962), compares Chile's social policies with those of the United States. Robert N. Burr, *By Reason or Force: Chile and the Balancing of Power in South America, 1830–1905* (Berkeley: University of California, 1965) provides the most complete analysis of Chilean diplomacy. Heraldo Muñoz and Carlos Portales, *Elusive Friendship: A Survey of U.S.-Chilean Relations* (Boulder: Reiner, 1991) is often critical of the United States' influence in Chile.

Internet Sources

Chilean government and private institutions widely use the Internet to communicate with the public. National, regional, and local government institutions maintain Web sites to advise citizens about programs. Sites also provide a wealth of information for researchers. Chilean universities' Web sites are similar to those of European and U.S. institutions, with program descriptions and online library catalogs. Major businesses, whether copper companies, vineyards, or publishing houses, maintain Web sites. Professional organizations like the Colegio de Ingenieros (Engineer's Association) as well as employer organizations such as the SOFOFA (Manufacturers' Association) are accessible on the Internet.

For information about the national government, www.estado.cl has a menu that links to the various ministries and administrative subdivisions. For excellent statistical information visit the Internet sites of the Instituto Nacional de Estadisticas, www.ine.cl/chile, and the Banco Central, www.bcentral.cl. Information on Chilean elections can be found at www.Georgetown.edu/pdba/Elecdata/Chile. The Latin American Studies program at the University of Texas Internet site, www.lanic.utexas.edu/la/chile/, provides portals to hundreds of Chilean institutions, including most universities and many NGOs.

Information on Chilean trade opportunities is available from ProChile at www.chileinfo.com and the U.S. Commercial Service at www.usatrade.gov/website/ccg.nsf/ccGurl/CCG-CHILE. Also, the United States embassy, www.usembassy.cl, has useful information and links.

Most Chilean newspapers and magazines are partly or wholly available online. *El Mercurio*, www.mercurio.cl, founded in Valparaiso in 1827 and in Santiago in 1900, publishes news on this site as well as through its on-line service at www.emol.com/noticias. Chile's first online news broadcast is the satirical, *El Mostrador*, www.elmostrador.cl. The most widely circulating paper is *La Tercera*, www.latercera.cl. Regional newspapers such as *La Estrella de Iquique* or *El Dario Austral* of Temuco can also be easily accessed online. Magazines offering valuable political commentary are *Ercilla*, www.ercilla.cl, *Qué Pasa*, www.quepasa.cl, and *Punto Final*, www.puntofinal.cl. *Vea*, www.vea.cl, and *Paula*, www.paula.cl are the most widely circulating women's magazines.

Some Chilean radio stations broadcast online and others publish online news. For example, visit the sites of Radio Cooperativa, www.cooperativa.cl, Radio Agricultura, www.radioagricultura.cl, and Radio Concierto, www.concierto.cl. Some television stations such as Television Nacional de Chile—Canal 7, www.tvn.cl, and Televisión de la Pontificia Universidad Católica de Chile—Canal 13, www.canal13.cl, present news summaries and programming on the Web.

Chapter 1: A Crazy Geography

The title for this chapter comes from Benjamín Subercaseaux, *Chile, o una loca geografía* (Santiago: Ediciones Ercilla, 1940), which was published three years later in English with the more serious title, *Chile: A Geographic Extravaganza*. Harold Blakemore provides a valuable vision of Chile in chapter 10 of a work that he and Clifford T. Smith edited, *Latin America: Geographical Perspectives* (London: Methuen and Co, 1971). Pedro Cunill,

Visión de Chile (Santiago: Editorial Universitario, 1972) provides an expanded view of the country, whereas George Pendle, *The Land and the People of Chile* (New York: Macmillan, 1960) compliments geographic material with a general history. For recent information, the chapter "Chile" in *South America, Central America, and the Caribbean* (London: Europa Publications: 2001) is quite helpful as is "The World Factbook—Chile," www.odci.gov/cia/publications/factbook/.

Chapter 2: Origins of the Chilean People, 500–1750

A summary of early human occupation in Chile appears in *South American*, vol. 3 of Stuart Schwartz and Frank Solomon, eds., *Cambridge History of the Native Peoples of the Americas* (Cambridge: Cambridge University Press, 1996–2000). Karen Olsen Bruhns, *Ancient South America* (Cambridge: Cambridge University Press, 1994) also discusses the earliest inhabitants. Description of an interesting but controversial archeological site in southern Chile appears in Tom D. Dillehay, *Monte Verde: A Late Pleistocene Settlement in Chile*, 2 vols. (Washington, D.C.: Smithsonian Institution Press, 1989–97). For archeological work done largely in the 1930s see Julian Steward, ed., *The Handbook of South American Indians*, 6 vols. (Washington, D.C.: Smithsonian Institution, 1946–50). A summary of pre-Columbian Chile appears in Grete Mostny, *Prehistoria de Chile*, 14th ed. (Santiago: Editorial Universitaria, 1999). Anthropological studies of twentieth century Mapuche appear in L. C. Faron, *Mapuche Social Structure* (Urbana: University of Illinois Press, 1961) and L. C. Faron, *Hawks of the Sun* (Pittsburgh: University of Pittsburgh Press, 1964).

A number of Spaniards who participated in the wars with the Mapuche wrote chronicles. A captured officer who wrote a sympathetic account of the Mapuche was Francisco Núñez de Pineda y Bascuñán, *Cautiverio feliz* (Santiago: Editorial Universitaria, 1973). Alonzo de Ercilla wrote the famous epic poem, *La araucana* (Buenos Aires: Espasa-Calpe, 1947). The exiled Jesuit, Juan Ignacio Molina, described both Mapuche and Spanish colonial society in *The Geographical, Natural, and Civil History of Chile* (New York: AMS Press, 1973). Alvaro Jara, *Guerra y sociedad en Chile* (Santiago: Editorial Universitaria, 1971) discusses Spanish land and labor policies that prolonged hostilities with the Mapuche. A study emphasizing social and commercial relations with the Mapuche is Carlos Aldunate et al., *Relaciones fronterizas en la araucanía* (Santiago: Ediciones Universidad Católica de Chile, 1982), whereas discussion of the Jesuits' missions with the Mapuche appears in Eugene H. Korth, Society of Jesus (S.J.), *Spanish Policy in Colonial Chile: The Struggle for Social Justice, 1535–1700* (Stanford University Press, 1968).

Some excellent works examine the development of Spanish colonial society in Chile. Mario Góngora, *Origen de los inquilinos en Chile central* (Santiago: Editorial Universitaria, 1960) looks at the development of hacienda labor institutions. Eugene H. Korth and Della M. Flusche, *Forgotten Females: Women of African and Indian Descent in Colonial Chile, 1553–1800* (Detroit: B. Ethridge Books, 1983) outlines the condition of subjugated women in the colonial era. Marcelo Carmagnani, *El salario minero en Chile colonial* (Santiago: Universidad de Chile, 1963) describes how salaried labor replaced conscripted labor in mining. Benjamín Vicuña Mackenna, *La edad de oro en Chile*, 2nd ed. (Buenos Aires: Editorial Francisco de Aguirre, 1968) along with his other works on copper and silver, romanticizes Chile's mining traditions. A major study of prices and trade by Armando de Ramón and José Manuel Larraín, *Orígenes de la vida económica chilena, 1659–1808* (Santiago: Centro de Estudios Públicos, 1982) outlines the economic trends in colonial history.

Chapter 3: Independence, 1750–1830

A number of important studies have examined the economic origins of Chilean independence. Jacques A. Barbier, *Reform and Politics in Bourbon Chile, 1755–1796* (Ottawa: University of Ottawa Press, 1980) underscores fiscal problems, whereas Sergio Villalobos, *El comercio y la crisis colonial* (Santiago: Universidad de Chile, 1968) shows the frustrating attempts of Spanish merchants to monopolize trade. Eduardo Cavieres Figueroa, *El comercio chileno en la economía mundo colonial* (Valparaíso: Edicioners Universitarias de Valparaíso, 1996) discusses late-colonial trade patterns that transcend independence. Eugenio Pereira Salas, *Buques norteamericanos en Chile a fines de la era colonial, 1788–1810* (Santiago: Universidad de Chile, 1936) documents the magnitude of United States trade in Chile before independence. Luz María Méndez Beltrán, *Instituciones y problemas de la minería en Chile, 1787–1826* (Santiago: Universidad de Chile, 1979) illustrates the often frustrated efforts of the Chilean mine owners' guild to deal with economic and political issues.

There are some excellent first-hand accounts by foreign visitors in Chile during the independence period. After encountering many obstacles that prevented him from building a copper industry, a somewhat embittered entrepreneur, John Miers, *Travels in Chile and La Plata*, 2 vols. (London: Baldwin, Cradock, and Joy, 1826), offers advice on Chilean society and mining conditions. John Mayo and Simon Collier, eds., *Mining in Chile's*

Norte Chico: Journal of Charles Lambert, 1825–1830 (Boulder: Westview Books, 1998) published the personal observations of Chile's most successful immigrant mine owner.

An excellent study of independence issues and leaders is Simon Collier, *Ideas and Politics of Chilean Independence* (New York: Cambridge University Press, 1967). Julio Heise González, *Años de formación y aprendizaje politicos, 1810–1833* (Santiago: Editorial Universitaria, 1978) emphasizes the important institutional experiments of the independence era. Two biographies of Chile's independence leader are Stephen Clissold, *Bernardo O'Higgins and the Independence of Chile* (New York: Praeger, 1969) and Jay Kinsbruner, *Bernardo O'Higgins* (New York: Twayne, 1968). Kinsbruner also looks at the dominant political boss of the era in *Diego Portales: Interpretative Essays on the Man and Times* (The Hague: Martinus Nijhoff, 1967). Alfredo Jocelyn-Holt Letelier, *El peso de la noche: Nuestra frágil fortaleza histórica*, 2nd ed. (Santiago: Planet, 1998) asserts that an elite civic culture created the Chilean state. Donald Emmet Worcester explores Lord Cochrane's role in the Chilean fleet in *Seapower and Chilean Independence* (Gainesville: University of Florida Press, 1962).

An examination of the politics of prominent families is by Mary Lowenthal Felstiner, "Kinship Politics in the Chilean Independence Movement," *Hispanic American Historical Review* 56, no. 1 (February 1976): 58–80. Maria Graham presents a fascinating first-hand account of her conversations with important leaders in her *Journal of a Residence in Chile, During the Year 1822* (London: Longman, Hurst, Rees, Orme, Brown, and Green, 1824). Eduardo Pöppig, *Un testigo de la aborada de Chile, 1826–1829*, trans. Carlos Keller (Santiago: Zig-Zag, 1960) offers a very optimistic view of the future progress of Chile, while Alexander Caldcleugh, *Travels in South America During the Years 1819–20–21*, 2 vols. (London: John Murray, 1825) is more realistic.

Chapter 4: Miners, Merchants, and Hacendados, 1830–61

Arnold Bauer, *Chilean Rural Society from the Spanish Conquest to 1930* (New York: Cambridge University Press, 1975) provides far more than a history of Chilean agriculture; his work offers an inclusive vision of the nation's economic development. Claudio Gay, *Historia física y política de Chile: Agricultura*, 2nd ed., 2 vols. (Santiago: ICIRA, 1973), although overly optimistic about the future of Chilean agriculture, presents an encyclopedia of material for the mid-nineteenth century.

A study that illustrates a wide variety of commercial, agricultural, and industrial activities of early merchants is that of Juan Eduardo Vargas Cariola, *José Tomás Ramos Font: una fortuna chilena del siglo XIX* (Santiago: Ediciones Universidad Católica de Chile, 1988). Ricardo Nazer Ahumada, *José Tomás Urmeneta: un empresario del siglo XIX* (Santiago: Dirección de Bibliotecas, Archivos y Museos, 1993) likewise reveals the diversity of activities of leading mine owners. For an opportunity to read both the diary and correspondence of a leading mining entrepreneur see Simon Collier and John Mayo, eds., *Mining in Chile's Norte Chico: Journal of Charles Lambert, 1825–1830* (Boulder: Westview Press, 1998). Steven S. Volk, "Mine Owners, Moneylenders, and the State in Mid-Nineteenth-Century Chile: Transitions and Conflicts," *Hispanic American Historical Review* 73, no. 1 (February 1993): 67–98 presents the best analysis available of the vital role of mining credit. Pierre Vayssière, *Un siècle de capitalisme minier au Chili, 1830–1930* (Paris: Editions du C.N.R.S., 1980) studies technical and economic changes of the mining sector. Leland R. Pederson, *The Mining Industry of the Norte Chico, Chile* (Evanston: Northwestern University, 1966) studies the region that dominated Chilean mining before the annexation of the Norte Grande during the War of the Pacific. Eduardo Cavieres Figueroa, *Comercio chileno y comerciates ingleses 1820–1880: Un ciclo de historia económica* (Valparaíso: Universidad Católica de Valparaíso, 1988) clearly documents Chile's global commercial relations in the nineteenth century. A complementary study that illustrates the interactions of commercial firms with other sectors of the Chilean economy is John Mayo, *British Merchants and Chilean Development, 1851–1886* (Boulder: Westview Press, 1987).

For the most in-depth political history of the Portalian Era, see Simon Collier, *Chile: The Making of a Republic, 1830–1865* (Cambridge: Cambridge Univ. Press, 2003). Maurice Zeitlin, *The Civil Wars in Chile, or, The Bourgeois Revolutions That Never Were* (Princeton University Press, 1984) suggests that the political frustration of the new economic elite led to revolution. Another perspective on radicalism and its diversity is Cristián Gazmuri, *El "48" Chileno: Igualitarios, reformistas, radicales, masones y bomberos* (Santiago: Editorial Universitaria, 1992). Two revealing personal accounts of the mid-nineteenth century are James Melville Gillis, *Chile; Its Geography, Climate, Government* (Washington, D.C.: A.O.P. Nicholson, 1855) and Vicente Pérez Rosales, *Recuerdos del Pasado, 1814–1860* (Santiago: Editora Nacional Gabriela Mistral, 1973). Among his many activities, Pérez Rosales organized the German colonization of southern Chile. A century later, Ricardo Donoso contributed incisive analyses of the nation's political development in *Desarrollo político y social de Chile desde la Constitución de 1833* (Santiago: Imprenta Universitaria, 1941) and *Las ideas políticas en Chile* (Mexico: Fondo de Cultura Económica, 1946).

Chapter 5: The Triumph of Congress, 1861–91

Julio Heise González, *Historia de Chile: El Período Parlamentario, 1861–1925*, 2 vols. (Santiago: Editorial Andrés Bello, 1974 and Editorial Universitario, 1982) presents the best overview of the variety of changes that transformed Chile during this period. Francisco A. Encina, *Nuestra inferioridad económica* (Santiago: Imprenta Universitaria, 1912), by contrast, presents an early critique of the nation's economic priorities. Harold Blakemore, *British Nitrates and Chilean Politics, 1886–1896* (London: Athlone Press, 1974) explains how British nitrate entrepreneurs promoted their own interests, but these did not include civil war. Oscar Bermúndez Miral, *Historia del salitre desde sus orígenes hasta la Guerra del Pacífico* (Santiago: Universidad de Chile, 1963) includes fascinating biographical information on nitrate entrepreneurs, whereas Thomas F. O'Brien, *The Nitrate Industry and Chile's Crucial Transition, 1870–1901* (New York: New York University Press, 1982) observes how the nitrate industry stifled development. Julio Pinto Vallejos, *Trabajos y rebeldías en la pampa salitrera* (Santiago: Universidad de Santiago, 1998) looks at labor organization and conflict in the nitrate industry. Baldomero Lillo, *Sub terra, cuadros mineros*, 2nd ed. (Santiago: Nascimento, 1931) narrates a stark story of the life of a coal miner while Eduardo Barrios, *Gran señor y rajadiablos* (Santiago: Nascimento, 1967) depicts that of an aristocratic hacendado.

Michael Monteón, *Chile in the Nitrate Era* (Madison: University of Wisconsin Press, 1982) presents an overview of Chile in the late nineteenth century. In an innovative work, Henry W. Kirsch, *Industrial Development in a Traditional Society: The Conflict of Entrepreneurship and Modernization in Chile* (Gainesville: University Press of Florida, 1977) shows the early structure of Chilean manufacturing. By contrast, Arnold J. Bauer, "Industry and the Missing Bourgeoisie: Consumption and Development in Chile, 1850–1950," *Hispanic American Historical Review* 70, no. 2 (May 1990): 227–54 asks why Chile failed to develop a strong middle class.

Robert McCaa, *Marriage and Fertility in Chile: Demographic Turning Points in the Petorca Valley, 1840–1976* (Boulder: Westview Press, 1983) examines the evolution of families in a rural valley north of Santiago. A complementary interpretation appears in Ann Hagerman Johnson, "The Impact of Market Agriculture on Family and Household Structure in Nineteenth-Century Chile," *Hispanic American Historical Review* 58, no. 4 (November 1978): 625–48. George Young, *The Germans in Chile: Immigration and Colonization, 1849–1919* (New York: Center for Migration Studies, 1974) narrates the history of this influential group in southern Chile. William F. Sater, *Heroic Image in Chile: Arturo Prat, Secular Saint* (Berkeley: University of California Press, 1973) tries to understand Chilean society through an analysis of its most popular hero, while his *Chile and the War of the Pacific* (Lincoln: University of Nebraska, 1986) takes a more realistic look at Chile's conflict with its northern neighbors. An important examination of the evolution of the University of Chile is Sol Serrano, *Universidad y nación, Chile en el siglo XIX* (Santiago: Editorial Universitaria, 1994).

Chapter 6: New Classes and Conflicts, 1891–1925

Gonzalo Vial Correa, *Historia de Chile*, 4 vols. (Santiago: Editorial Santillana del Pacífico, 1981–) presents a detailed overview of the post-1891 period. René Millar, *La elección presidencial de 1920* (Santiago: Editorial Universitaria, 1981) highlights the changes in Chilean society that contributed to Arturo Alessandri's election. Robert Alexander, *Arturo Alessandri: A Political Biography*, 2 vols. (Ann Arbor: University of Michigan, 1977) provides a useful analysis of this important national leader, whereas Ricardo Donoso, *Alessandri, agitador y domoledor: Cincuenta años de historia política de Chile*, 2 vols. (Mexico and Buenos Aires: Fondo de Cultura Económica, 1952–1954) makes a strong critique of his political role. A very valuable study of the early history of organized labor is Peter de Shazo, *Urban Workers and Labor Unions in Chile, 1902–1927* (Madison: University of Wisconsin Press, 1983). Carl Solberg, *Immigration and Nationalism: Argentina and Chile, 1890–1914* (Austin: University of Texas, 1970) explains why Chile failed to attract the number of immigrants that Argentina did.

Chapter 7: Experiments in Democracy, 1925–58

An exceptional generation of writers began publishing in this era. Gabriela Mistral, *Desolación* (New York: Instituto de las Españas en los Estados Unidos, 1922) began her poetic career while Pablo Neruda, *Twenty Love Poems and a Song of Despair*, trans. W. S. Merwin (New York: Penguin Books, 1993), *Crepusculario*, 3rd ed. (Santiago: Nacimento, 1937), *Canto general*, trans. Jack Schmitt (Berkeley: Univ. of California, 1991), and *Odas elementales* (Buenos Aires: Losada, 1954) became the foremost poet in the Spanish language. An earlier, experimental poet was Vicente Huidobro, *Altazor, or a Voyage in a Parachute* (Saint Paul, Minn.: Graywolf Press, 1988). Two creative experimental novelists were Augusto d'Halmar, *Pasión y muerte del cura Deusto* (Berlin: Editora Internacional, 1924) and Pedro Prado, *Alcino*, 2nd ed. (Santiago: Nascimento, 1928). Marxist interpretations of the history of Chile gained prominence through the works of Julio César Jobet, *Ensayo crítico del desarrollo económico-social de Chile* (Santiago:

Editorial Universitario, 1955), and Hernán Ramírez Necochea, *Historia del imperialismo en Chile* (Santiago: Editorial Austral, 1960).

Dealing with the complex and conflicting role of the military during this period is Fredrick M. Nunn, *Chilean Politics, 1920–1931: The Honorable Mission of the Armed Forces* (Albuquerque: University of New Mexico, 1970). By contrast, Paul W. Drake, *Socialism and Populism in Chile, 1932–1952* (Urbana: University of Illinois Press, 1978) analyzes the political alliances of the Popular Front administrations. Ernst Halperin, *Nationalism and Communism in Chile* (Cambridge: MIT Press, 1965) and Julio Faúndez, *Marxism and Democracy in Chile: From 1932 to the Fall of Allende* (New Haven: Yale University Press, 1988) examine the rise of the Communist and Socialist parties. Tomás Moulián, *El gobierno de Ibáñez, 1952–1958* (Santiago: Programa FLASCO, 1985) criticizes Ibáñez's conservative second regime. A unique contribution to the study of government is Germán Urzúa Valenzuela and Anamaría García Barzelatto, *Diagnóstico de la burocracia chilena, 1818–1969* (Santiago: Editorial Jurídica de Chile, 1971), which observes the long-term development of public administration.

The United States ambassador during the Popular Front, Claude G. Bowers, *Chile through Embassy Windows, 1939–1953* (New York: Simon and Schuster, 1958) left a valuable memoir as Franklin D. Roosevelt's representative in Chile. Another perspective of Bowers, especially his Chilean role, appears in the latter chapters of Peter J. Sehlinger and Holman Hamilton, *Spokesman for Democracy: Claude G. Bowers, 1878–1958* (Indianapolis: Indiana Historical Society, 2000). Michael J. Francis, *The Limits of Hegemony: United States Relations with Argentina and Chile during World War II* (Notre Dame, Indiana: Univ. of Notre Dame Press, 1977) describes the negotiations that finally led Chile to break with the Axis, whereas William F. Sater, *Chile and the United States: Empires in Conflict* (Athens: University of Georgia Press, 1990) presents an excellent overview of the relations of the two nations.

A path-breaking work on the development of women's organizations and their political activities is Felícitas Klimpel, *La mujer chilena: el aporte feminine al progreso de Chile, 1910–1960* (Santiago: Editorial Andrés Bello, 1962). Two more recent contributions are Elizabeth Quay Hutchison, "From 'La Mujer Esclava' to 'La Mujer Limón': Anarchism and the Politics of Sexuality in Early-Twentieth-Century Chile," and Karin Alejandra Rosemblatt, "Charity Rights and Entitlement: Gender, Labor, and Welfare in Early-Twentieth Century Chile," *Hispanic American Historical Review* 81, no. 3/4 (2001): 519–54; 555–86.

The lack of agricultural modernization during the period first attracted the attention of George M. McBride, *Chile: Land and Society* (Baltimore:

American Geographic Society, 1936). Later scholars like Brian Loveman, *Struggle in the Countryside: Politics and Rural Labor 1919–1973* (Blooming-ton: Indiana University Press, 1976), who looked at agricultural labor, and Thomas C. Wright, *Landowners and Reform in Chile: The Sociedad Nacional de Agricultura 1919–1940* (Urbana: University of Illinois, 1982), who looked at agricultural employers, studied the origins of rural conflict. For a more global analysis of the impact of the Depression and the war on Chile see P. T. Ellsworth, *Chile: An Economy in Transition* (New York: Macmillian, 1945).

Chapter 8: Reform Turns to Revolution, 1958–73

Whereas no adequate study of Jorge Alessandri's administration has yet appeared, works abound on the Frei and Allende administrations. Background works include Weston H. Agor, *The Chilean Senate* (Austin: University of Texas, 1971), which describes the functioning of this pow-erful political body before the crisis in the early 1970s. An extremely useful historical analysis of the interaction of labor and political parties is Alan Angell, *Politics and the Labor Movement in Chile* (London: Oxford University Press, 1972). James O. Morris, *Elites, Intellectuals, and Consensus: A Study of the Social Question and the Industrial Relations System in Chile* (Ithaca: Cornell University, 1966) describes social dynamics of labor relations in Chile. George Grayson, *El Partido Demócrata Cristiano chileno* (Buenos Ai-res: Editorial Francisco de Aguirre, 1968) outlines the rise of the Christian Democratic Party while Michael Fleet, *The Rise and Fall of Chilean Christian Democracy* (Princeton University Press, 1985) explains the errors that caused the party to lose power in 1970. Cristián Gazmuri, *Eduardo Frei Montalva y su época*, 2 vols. (Santiago: Aguilar, 2000) is an extremely in-formative biography of the first Christian Democratic president.

Some excellent economic studies exist for this period. Markos Mama-lakis and Clark Reynolds, *Essays on the Chilean Economy* (Homewood, Ill.: R.D. Irwin, 1965) question the politics of favoring some economic sectors while punishing others. Ricardo French-Davis, *Políticas económicas en Chile, 1952–1970* (Santiago: Universidad Católica, 1973) defends the economic performance of the Frei administration while Jere R. Behrman, *Macroeco-nomic Policy in a Developing Country: The Chilean Experience* (New York: Elsevier/North–Holland, 1977) offers a more impartial assessment. Theo-dore H. Moran, *Multinational Corporations and the Politics of Dependence: Copper in Chile* (Princeton: Princeton University Press, 1974) presents an overview of the conflictive copper politics while Barbara Stallings, *Class Conflict and Economic Development in Chile 1958–1973* (Stanford: Stanford

University Press, 1978) shows how class issues exhausted traditional institutions.

No subject has attracted more interest in Chile than Salvador Allende and the Unidad Popular. He made his ideas available in *Allende: Su pensamiento politico* (Santiago: Editorial Quimantú, 1972). Paul Sigmund, *The Overthrow of Allende and the Politics of Chile* (University of Pittsburgh, 1977) provides a useful contrast of the Frei and Allende regimes. Nathaniel Davis, *The Last Two Years of Salvador Allende* (Ithaca: Cornell University Press, 1985) criticizes Allende's policies while exonerating him from responsibility for his overthrow. Both Ricardo Z. Israel, *Politics and Ideology in Allende's Chile* (Tempe: Arizona State University, 1989) and Edy Kaufman, *Crises in Allende's Chile: New Perspectives* (Westport: Praeger, 1988) argue that many of Allende's troubles resulted from his own policies. For a literary perspective see novelist Jorge Edward, *Los convidados de piedra* (Barcelona: Seix Barral, 1978) and *Persona Non Grata: A Memoir of Disenchantment with the Cuban Revolution,* tr. Andrew Hurley (New York: Paragon House, 1993). Isabel Allende, *House of the Spirits* (New York: A.A. Knopf, 1985) with her tragic story of family politics became Chile's most famous novelist. Antonio Skármeta, *Burning Patience,* trans. Katherine Silver (New York: Pantheon, 1987) transforms Pablo Neruda into cupid.

Other studies that examine the crises of the Unidad Popular are Stefan De Vylder, *Allende's Chile: The Political Economy of the Rise and Fall of the Unidad Popular* (Cambridge: Cambridge University Press, 1978), Ian Roxborough, Philip O'Brien, and Jackie Roddick, *Chile: the State and Revolution* (New York: Holmes and Meier, 1977), and Arturo Valenzuela, *The Breakdown of Democratic Regimes: Chile* (Baltimore: Johns Hopkins University Press, 1978). Brian H. Smith, *The Church and Politics in Chile* (Princeton: Princeton University Press, 1982) observes rising church involvement in the political process while Peter Winn, *Weavers of Revolution: The Yarur Workers and Chile's Road to Socialism* (New York: Oxford University Press, 1986) chronicles textile workers' expropriation of a major factory. Cristóbal Kay and Patricio Silva, eds., *Development and Social Change in the Chilean Countryside: From the Pre-Land Reform Period to the Democratic Transition* (Amsterdam: Center for Latin American Research and Documentation, 1992) presents varied viewpoints on the crises of Chile agriculture. Heidi Tinsman, "Good Wives and Unfaithful Men: Gender Negotiations and Sexual Conflicts in the Chilean Agrarian Reform, 1964–1973," *Hispanic American Historical Review* 81, nos. 3–4 (2001): 587–619 looks at land reform from a female perspective.

Two evaluations of Unidad Popular's failures are Robert Moss, *Chile's Marxist Experiment* (Newton Abbot, England: David and Charles, 1973)

and Mark Falcoff, *Modern Chile, 1970–1989: A Critical History* (New Bruns-
wick: Transaction Publishers, 1991). Joaquín Fernandoes, *Chile y el mundo
1970–1973: la política exterior del gobierno de la Unidad Popular* (Santiago:
Ediciones Universidad Católica de Chile, 1985) clarifies the issue of international credit during the Unidad Popular. Other important works documenting changes during this period are Kathleen Fischer, *Political Ideology
and Educational Reform in Chile, 1964–1976* (Los Angeles: University of California at Los Angeles, 1979), Hannah W. Stewart-Gambino, *The Church
and Politics in the Chilean Countryside* (Boulder: Westview Press, 1992), Dale
L. Johnson, ed., *The Chilean Road to Socialism* (Garden City: Doubleday and
Co., 1973), Edward Boorstein, *Allende's Chile: An Inside View* (New York:
International Publishers, 1977) and Sergio Bitar, *Chile: Experiment in Democracy* (Philadelphia: Institute for the Study of Human Issues, 1986).

Chapter 9: Military Rule and Neoliberalism, 1973–90

The three dominant subjects covered by works on the Pinochet years
are human rights abuse, institutional reform, and the return of democracy.
Pamela Constable and Arturo Valenzuela, *A Nation of Enemies: Chile under
Pinochet* (New York: W.W. Norton, 1991), Lois Hecht Oppenheim, *Politics
in Chile: Democracy, Authoritarianism, and the Search for Development*, 2nd
ed. (Boulder: Wesview Press, 1999), and Genaro Arriagada, *Pinochet: The
Politics of Power* (London: Unwin Hyman, 1988) offer critical perspectives
on the entire period of military rule. By contrast, James R. Whelan, *Out of
the Ashes: Life, Death and Transfiguration of Democracy in Chile 1833–1988*
(Washington, D.C., Regnery Gateway, 1989), Rafael Valdivieso Aristía,
Crónica de un rescate (Santiago: Andrés Bello, 1988) and Sergio Fernández,
Mi lucha por la democracia (Santiago: Editorial Los Andes, 1994) credit the
military with rebuilding civil society. Helen Mary Spooner, *Soldiers in a
Narrow Land: The Pinochet Regime in Chile* (Berkeley: University of Califor-
nia, 1994) details both corruption and human rights violations under
military rule. Cathy Lisa Schneider, *Shantytown Protest in Pinochet's Chile*
(Philadelphia: Temple University Press, 1995) and Pamela Lowden, *Moral
Opposition to Authoritarian Rule in Chile, 1973–1990* (New York: St. Martin's
Press, 1996) chronicle the protests that led to the restoration of civil society.
Another form of protest was through music, as discussed by Nancy E.
Morris, "Canto Porque Es Necesario Cantar: The New Song Movement in
Chile, 1973–1983," *Latin American Research Review* 21, no. 2 (1986): 117–36.
Larissa Lomnitz and Ana Melnick, *Chile's Middle Class: A Struggle for Sur-
vival in the Face of Neoliberalism* (Boulder: Reinner, 1991) shows that the
neoliberal reforms could have unintended effects on the middle class. An

interesting autobiography by a leading Socialist and opponent of the military regime is Clodomiro Almeyra Medina, *Reencuentro con mi vida* (Santiago: Ediciones Ornitorrinco, 1987).

For overviews of the neoliberal transformation of the Chilean economy see Sebastián and Alejandra Edwards, *Monetarism and Liberalization: The Chilean Experiment* (University of Chicago, 1991) and Javier Martínez and Alvaro Díaz, *Chile: The Great Transformation* (Washington, D.C.: UNRISD, 1996). Joseph Collins and John Lear, *Chile's Free Market Miracle: A Second Look* (Oakland: Institute for Food and Development Policy, 1995) presents a critical view of these reforms on such areas as health care, housing, and social security. Equally critical of neoliberal changes in agriculture is Lovell S. Jarvis, *Chilean Agriculture under Military Rule: From Reform to Reaction, 1973–1980* (Berkeley: University of California Press, 1985). A thoroughly documented analysis of the health care reforms is Joseph L. Scarpaci, *Primary Medical Care in Chile: Accessibility under Military Rule* (Pittsburgh: University of Pittsburgh, 1988).

Works that map the road from military rule to democracy are J. M. Puryear, *Thinking Politics: Intellectuals and Democracy in Chile, 1973–1988* (Baltimore: Johns Hopkins University Press, 1996) and César N. Caviedes, *Elections in Chile: The Road toward Redemocratization* (Boulder: Rienner, 1991). Other essays that discuss the opportunity for political change are in Paul Drake and Iván Jaksić, eds., *The Struggle for Democracy in Chile, 1982–1990* (Lincoln: University of Nebraska, 1991).

Chapter 10: The Democratic Transition after 1990

Various authors analyze the modifications that democratic regimes have made to neoliberalism. A somewhat critical view is that of David E. Hojman, "Poverty and Inequality in Chile: Are Democratic Politics and Neoliberal Economics Good For You?" *Journal of Interamerican Studies and World Affairs* 38, no. 2/3 (1996): 73–97. This contrasts with Hojman's earlier, more positive, evaluation, *Chile: The Political Economy of Development and Democracy in the 1990s* (Pittsburgh: University of Pittsburgh, 1993). Kurt Weyland, "Economic Policy in Chile's New Democracy," *Journal of Interamerican Studies and World Affairs* 41, no. 3 (Fall 1999): 67–97 questions whether the democratic regimes' use of the neoliberal model really addresses salient social problems. A revealing study of globalization and the role of foreign corporations in Chile's new economy is Hugo Fazio, *La transnacionalización de la economía chilena: Mapa de la extrema riqueza al año 2000* (Santiago: LOM Ediciones, 2000). A critique of export agriculture under neoliberalism is Marcus J. Kurtz, "Free Markets and Democratic

Consolidation in Chile: The National Politics of Rural Transformation," *Politics and Society* 27, no. 2 (June 1999): 275–302. Optimistic views of the Chilean telecommunications and software industries are offered by Jorge Rosenblut, "Telecommunications in Chile: Success and Post-Deregulatory Challenges in a Rapidly Emerging Economy," *Journal of International Affairs* 51, no. 2 (Spring 1998): 565–82 and R. A. Baeza-Yates et al., "Computing in Chile: The Jaguar of the Pacific Rim?" *Communications of the ACM* 38, no. 9 (September 1995): 23–28.

A source that lists major events and issues in human rights is www. derechoschile.com/cronologia. The most graphic depiction of military persecution is Patricia Verdugo, *Chile, Pinochet, and the Caravan of Death* (Coral Gables: North-South Center Press, 2001) while Alejandra Matus, *El libro negro de la justicia chilena* (Santiago: Planeta, 1999) condemns the quiescence of the courts. A comparative study on the southern cone nations' attempts to deal with human rights is Luis Roniger, "Human Rights Violations and the Reshaping of Collective Identities in Argentina, Chile and Uruguay," *Social Identities* 3, no. 2 (June 1997): 221–47. Tomás Moulián, *Chile actual: anatomía de un mito* (Santiago: LOM, 1997) questions whether democracy is possible under the Constitution of 1980. Ana Cecilia Vergara and Jorge Vergara Estévez, "Justice, Impunity and the Transition to Democracy: A Challenge for Human Rights Education," *Journal of Moral Education* 23, no. 3 (1994): 273–85 fear that without the public school curriculum addressing human rights, civil society will not heal.

David Carruthers, "Environmental Politics in Chile: Legacies of Dictatorship and Democracy," *Third World Quarterly* 22, no. 3 (2001): 343–58 calls for a more concerted political effort to resolve decades of environmental degradation. Philip D. Oxhorn, *Organizing Civil Society: The Popular Sectors and the Struggle for Democracy in Chile* (University Park: Pennsylvania State University, 1995) sees new organizations rising to address local issues. On the international level, David R. Mares and Francisco Rojas Aravena, *The United States and Chile: Coming in from the Cold* (New York: Routledge, 2001) believe democracy presents an opportunity for improved United States–Chilean relations.

Index

Abalone, 6
Abascal, José Fernando, 65
Abbot Laboratories, 124
Academia de Humanismo
    Cristiano, 202
Acción Nacional de Mujeres de
    Chile, 118
Aconcagua, exploration of, 31–32;
    river, 86; valley, 11, 13
Administradoras de Fondos de
    Pensiones (AFPs), 204
Aduana, 60. *See also*
    Customshouse
Aetna corporation, 205
African slave trade, 44
Afuerinos, 47, 58
Agrarian reform. *See* land reform
Agriculture: church, 42; colonial,
    33, 57–58; commercial farms,
    12, 194–95; expansion, 95, 121,
    194; exports, 105; decline in
production, 141; imports, 141;
land sales, 194; loans, 122;
machinery, 84, 106, 121, 150;
pre-Columbian, 28; price
freeze, 141; production, 181;
tax cuts, 89; taxes, 61;
transformation, 194; World
Bank policy, 230
Agrupación de los Familiares de
    Detenidos-Desaparecidos, 207
Aguirre Cerda, Pedro, 140, 151
Aguirre, Francisco de, 34
Air Force, 148, 189
Air transportation, 15–16, 18, 166,
    232–33
Alacalufes, 29
Alcalde, 22. *See also* mayor
Alcino, 137
Alessandri Besa, Arturo, 21
Alessandri Palma, Arturo, 114,
    117, 120–21, 131; labor

relations, 145; policies, 150; resignation, 148; second term, 150

Alessandri Rodríguez, Jorge, 155, 159–61; candidate 1970, 170–71

Allende, Isabel (congresswoman), 216

Allende Lloren, Isabel (author), 8, 218

Allende, Pascual, 189

Allende, Salvador: attempt at compromise, 176; death, 182; economic change, 15; educational programs, 8; election 1958, 155; election 1964, 162; funeral, 136; government, 22, 172–83; inflation, 18; negotiations with CODE, 179; nomination, 136; overthrow, 7; reforms, 23; statue, 126; victory, 170–72

Alliance, 120, 130–31

Alliance for Progress, 160

Almagro, Diego de, 30–32, 48n

Altamirano, Carlos, 176

Altamirano, Luis, 131

Alternativas, 202

Altiplano, 4, 6

American Federation of Labor, 146

American Revolution, 59

Americo Vespucio, 234

Amnesty, 78, 213, 222, 224

Amunátegui, Miguel Luis, 96

Anaconda Copper Company, 127, 141; chilenización, 164

Anarcho-Syndicalists, 119; apolitical stance, 119, 145

Anchovies, 5, 11, 195

Ancud, 14

Andes Mountains, 3–4, 6, 27, 64–66; exploration, 30–31

Andina copper mine, 12

Anganamon and spouse, 39

Angelini family, 195

Anglican Church, 24

Anglo-American Corporation, 227

Angol, 49n

Aninat, Edwardo, 225

Antarctica, 3, 5

Antique shops, 23

Antofagasta, 6; exports, 11; population, 125; in War of the Pacific, 100–102

Antofagasta Nitrate and Railroad Company, 99, 102

Anwandter, Carlos, 123

Arab immigrants, 10

Arabian Orthodox Church, 24

Araucana, La, 35

Araucanian pine, 29

Araucanos. *See* Mapuches

Arauco, 49n, 105

Archbishopric of Santiago, 23

Archeologists, 28

Architecture, 15, 24, 60

Arcos, Santiago, 92

Arequipa, Peru, 30

Argentina, 3, 7; border agreement, 102; Chilean investment, 233; contraband, 143; economic crisis, 226; embassy, 110; exploration, 30–31; Ibáñez exile, 149; military prosecution, 222; negotiations, 100; railroad, 83, 130; refuges to, 198; secession movements, 74; tango, 135; tourism, 13; trade, 17, 66; unions, 119; vineyard purchases, 229

Arica, 3, 6; Battle of, 101; railroad, 17; transfer to Chile, 102, 149

Aristocrats. *See* elite

Arms caches, 180, 187

Army, 68; support of Balmaceda, 110

Arqueros silver mine, 11

Art, 18, 24; artists, 135, 198;
   commune, 137; religious, 41
Artisans, 24, 47, 60, 72, 92; mutual
   societies, 119
Asia, 17, 30, 75; recession, 225
Asociación de Damas Protectoras
   del Obrero, 119
Asociación Gremialista de
   Educadores Chilenos, 203
Asylum, 188–89
Atacama Desert, 3, 27;
   exploration, 31
Audiencia, 36, 46, 52, 60, 62
Augustinians, 41
Austral region: highway, 15;
   aluminum and dam project,
   236–37
Australia, 195, 198
Authoritarian rule, 70–71, 73, 91;
   under Alessandri, 132; in Latin
   America, 133, 150; under
   military, 150, 185–90
Automobiles, 199; traffic, 234
Axis, 151–52
Ayacucho, Battle of, 68
Aylwin, Mariana, 216
Aylwin, Patricio, 19, 22; apology
   for human rights abuses, 223;
   economy, 224–25; formation
   of Concertación, 210;
   inauguration, 211–13;
   negotiations with Allende, 179

Bachelet, Michelle, 216
Baides, Marquis de, 39
Balmaceda, Manuel, 103, 109, 111,
   128, 130
Baltra, Alberto, 170
Banco Nacional de Chile, 79, 85
Banks: ATMs, 232; foreclosures,
   208; influence of nitrates, 103;
   investments, 82; loans to UP,
   177; nationalization, 167;
   negative worth, 193;

nineteenth century, 79;
   privatization, 191; role of
   church, 41; Spanish
   acquisitions, 221
Baptist Church, 24
Baquedano, Manuel, 102
Barnard, Juan Diego, 82
Barrio Alto, 199
Barrios, Eduardo, 106, 137
Barros Arana, Diego, 8, 96, 100
Barros Luco, Ramón, 130
Basque-Castilian aristocracy. *See*
   Elite
Basques, 55
Bauer, Arnold, 84
Bécquer, Gustavo, 135
Bella Vista, 234
Bello, Andrés, 74
Bernstein, Julio, 107
Bilbao, Francisco, 92
Biobío region, 10
Biobío river, 37; proposed dam,
   235
Biotechnology, 228
Bishops, 46, 52
Black market, 158, 198
Bland, Theodoric, 67
Boeninger, Eduardo, 169, 200
Boinanazo, 214
Boleadoras, 29, 48n
Bolívar, Simón, 68
Bolivia: exploration, 31;
   immigration, 10, 233; mining,
   95, 97; oil nationalization, 141;
   railroad, 11, 130; treaty, 99;
   wars with Chile, 3, 7, 90, 95
Bonaparte, Joseph, 62
Bonded warehouses, 68, 89
Bookstores, 134
Bossay, Luis, 155
Bourbons reforms, 52–53, 60
Boxer, Charles, 27
Braden, William, 126
Brain drain, 180

Bratz, Berni, 166
Brazil: Dutch occupation, 37; exploration, 30; independence, 68; jobs, 199; monarchy, 62; secession movements, 74; trade, 17
Bremen, 75
Breweries, 14, 81, 123
British American Tobacco Company, 125
British Columbia, 28
British: invasion of Buenos Aires, 63; investors, 76, 83, 102–3; loan, 69, 82; mediation, 65; merchants, 80; trade, 45
Buccaneers: Dutch, 37; English, 37
Büche, Hernán, 193, 210
Buenos Aires, 3; British invasion, 63; contraband, 45, 56; Lambert's arrival, 76; residence of Waddington, 86; slave trade, 44
Bulnes, Manuel, 88, 90–92
Bunker, Tristan, 62
Bureaucracy: colonial, 60; negotiations with, 157
Burning Patience, 218
Butte, Montana, 127
Byron, Lord, 135

Cabildo, 53, 55, 60, 62–63, 69
Cádiz, 44, 75
Caldera, 78
California: environment, 28; Gold Rush, 80–81; grape growers, 229; trade, 75
Camanchaca, 6
Cámera de Comercio, 118
Campesinos, 57, 142, 144; fundo takeovers, 167–68, 176; working conditions, 159
Camping, 25
Canada, 177, 198; forestry company, 228; industrial model, 227; Noranda Aluminum Corporation, 235–36; trade agreements, 226, 229
Canasta popular, 174
Canto general, 136
Capital: flight, 156; foreign, 64, 166, 193; return to Chile, 159
Carabineros, 22, 142, 148, 164; at fundo San Miguel, 167; street patrols, 188
Caracoles silver mine, 97
Carrera, José Miguel, 65; arms purchases, 66; brothers executed, 66
Casa de la Moneda, 60
Casanova, Archbishop Mariano, 109
Castillo Velasco, Fernando, 168
Castro, Fidel, 175
Castro, Sergio de, 191–92
Catalans, 52
Catholic Action, 144
Catholic Church: affiliation, 23; agriculture, 42; bells, 41; Chilean bishops, 46; clergy, 41; colonial reform, 53; conflicts with government, 93, 108; construction, 41; defense of Indians, 38–39; education, 42; finance, 41, 53; government conflicts, 93, 108; historical criticism, 96; humanism, 161; land, 41; missionary work, 38; opposition to divorce law, 221; progressive ideas, 161; property expropriated, 69–70; sacraments, 41; support of democracy, 209; under O'Higgins, 68; views on women, 207
Catholic University of Chile. See Universidad Católica de Chile
Cattle, 5 12, 33, 85; export, 57, 80;

in the Sur, 142–43; trade with Mapuche, 40, 42
Cauas, Jorge, 192
Caupolicán, 8, 35
Cavieres, Eduardo, 219–20
Cea, José Manuel, 82
Cell phones, 231
Cellfor Inc., 228
CEMA, *See* Centro de Madres
Cement industry, 124, 140
Censo, 53
Central America, 10
Central Bank, 148
Central Intelligence Agency. *See* CIA
Central Unica de Trabajadores, 146
Centro de Madres (CEMA), 165, 206–7
CEPAL, 162
Cerro Grande, 78
Cerro Santa Lucía, 32
Chacabuco, Battle of, 66
Chamber of Commerce, 118
Chamber of Deputies, 19
Chañarcillo, 77–78
Charles III, 54–55
Charles V, 31–32
Charquicán, 42
Chemical industry, 12, 14, 17, 123
Cheyre, Juan Emilio, 215, 236
"Chicago Boys," 186, 191, 208
Chicha, 29, 43, 99, 143
Chiclayo, Peru, 205
Chile actual, anatomía de un mito, 219
Chile, Pinochet, and the Caravan of Death, 218
Chilean-Argentine Treaty, 3
Chilean Electric Company, 164
Chilean Mining Association, 76
Chilean Society for Tradition, Family, and Property, 23
Chilean Telephone Company, 231

Chilenization of copper, 16, 164
Chillán, 5, 140
Chiloé, 6, 14; exploration, 35; freed from Spain, 38
Chilotes, 14–15
China: credit, 177
Chinese workers, 81
Chinook, 48n
Chiquita Brands International, 195
Choncha y Toro SA, 229
Chonchol, Jacques: conflict with Frei, 166; head of CORA, 174
Chonos, 29
Chonos Archipelago, 15
Chorrillos, Battle of, 102
Christian Democratic Party (Partido Demócrata Cristiano), 20, 144; divisions, 163; election results, 162, 170; elite concerns, 200; government 155, 162–72; no campaign, 210–11; reaction to Pinochet's policies, 200; role under military, 185; student activism, 168–69; vote for Allende, 172; women's roles, 206
Chupilca del Diablo, 8, 101
Chuquicamata copper mine 11, 126; chilenización, 164
Churchill, Sir Winston, 134
CIA, 165, 171–72, 176; role in military coup, 182. *See also* Track II
Cider. *See* chicha
City council, 22, 53. *See also* cabildo
Civic institutions, 19, 133, 150, 185
Civil liberties, 70, 87–88
Civil rights, 87, 91; abuse of, 186, 208
Civil war, 95, 113
Classical music, 23
Clergy, 42, 51–52, 54

Clinic, The, 219
Club de Bomberos, 118
Club de la Unión, 130
Club de París, 177
Club de Señoras, 118
Coal, 79, 83; mine working conditions, 99
Coalition, 130
Cochrane, Lord, 67
CODE, 176–83; middle class backing, 198; resolution against Allende, 180; supports military, 188; urges overthrow of Allende, 182
CODELCO, 227; privatization rejected, 193
Coihaique, 15
Colchagua valley, 229
Cold War, 164
Colegio de Profesores, 203
Collective bargaining, 158, 166, 197, 220, 231
Colonia do Sacramento, 45
Colonization: Santiago, 32; of Sur, 4, 122, 142–43
Columbia University, 193
Columbus, Christopher, 30
Commerce, 65, 68–68; Bourbon reforms, 54
Communist Party, 144–46; abolished, 140; blame for coup, 182; established, 120; links to terrorism, 223; marginalized, 216; middle class membership, 148; nomination of Neruda, 136; Popular Front, 145; rejects violence, 172; rural unions, 159; strategy in 1970, 170
Compañía Cervecerías Unidas (CCU), 123
Compañía de Acero del Pacífico (CAP), 151
Compton Family, 143

Comptroller-General, 19, 148, 172
Computers, 228. *See also* Internet
Coñaripe, 5
Concepción: coal mines, 79; earthquake, 5; elite, 63; founded, 49n; industries, 13, 123; Mapuche rebellion, 35; military, 70; opposition to Montt, 92; population, 9, 13; port, 13; rainfall, 12; whaling, 75
Concertación, 20–21, 216–17; government of, 220–27
Concertación de los Partidos por el No, 210–11
Concón refinery, 12
Conde de la Conquista, 63. *See also* Mateo de Toro Zambrano
Condorito, 8
Confederación de Tabajadores de Chile, 145, 159
Confederación Democrática. *See* CODE
Conglomerates, 192, 204, 233
Congress, 19–21, 84; affluence of members, 94; censors cabinet, 95; conflict with president, 95; election of Allende, 171–72; elections 1965, 163; prestige, 130; proposed unicameral legislature, 172; resolution opposing Allende, 180
CONICYT, 165
Conquest, 32–35, 47
Consejales, 22
Conservatives, 70–71, 85, 87–89, 109; appeal to upper middle class, 148; in Coalition, 130; reticence to restore democracy, 185; under Pinochet government, 186
Constable, Pamela, 219
Constitution: of 1823, 69; of 1828, 70; of 1833, 78, 89; of 1925,

113, 132, 185; of 1980, 20, 190, 214; amendments, 214–15; commissions, 132, 190; experiments, 74; proposal of "tres areas," 176; revisions, 210

Construction industry: Alessandri stimulus, 150; boom, 199, 232; colonial, 60; contraction, 232; Lagos' proposals, 232; roads, 165; schools, 165; under Frei, 166

Consulado. *See* Tribunal del Consulado

Consumer society, 147, 154, 158, 198–99, 213, 218; revolution in, 232–33

Contraband: Argentine, 143; British, 45, 49n, 62; French, 59; United States, 60

Contraloría General. *See* Comptroller-General

Contreras, Manuel, 224

Cooperatives, 165; on expropriated fundos, 167; Peace Corps program, 165

Copiapó, 3, 31, 77

Copper: colonial mining, 34, 59; copperware, 24; deposits, 4, 11; exports, 17; growth, 125–27, 140–41, 193; investment, 126; nationalization, 16, 172; prices, 152, 166; production, 78–79, 126–27, 166; sulfide ores, 77; technology, 126

Coquimbo, 75; government, 77; licensed port, 64

Córdoba, Argentina, 83

Cordones industrials, 179–80

CORFO. *See* Corporación de Fomento

Corn, 28–29, 32, 43, 58; productivity, 195

Corning Glass Company, 125

Corporación de Fomento (CORFO), 140, 151

Corporación de la Reforma Agraria (CORA), 161, 167, 174; area expropriated, 194

Corporación de la Vivienda (CORVI), 198

Corporación del Cobre (CODELCO), 163

Corsairs, 65

"Cosmic race," 27–28

Costa Rica, 189

Council of Indies, 3, 7, 46

Courcelle-Seneuil, Jean Gustave, 91, 108

Cousiño, Matías, 79–80, 83

Couyoumdjian, Ricardo, 220

Cox, Alejandra, 180

CRAC. *See* Republican Confederation for Civic Action

Crafts: CEMA, 206; colonial, 47, 60; contemporary, 24; Mapuche, 14

Creationism, 135

Credit: agricultural, 16, 106, 122; colonial, 45, 56; lack of, 128; national, 90; Nixon boycott, 177; under Allende, 177; under Frei, 70

Crepusculario, 136

Criollo, 46, 52, 61; colonial advisors, 57, 62; merchants, 58

Cristalerías de Chile, 123, 125

Cruz, José María de la, 88, 92

CTCH. *See* Conferación de Trabajadores de Chile

Cuba: exiles, 189; Revolution, 161, 170; unions, 119; US human rights campaign, 209

Cueca, 14, 107

Cunco, 143

Curanto, 14

Customs house, 52, 60, 110

CUT. *See* Central Unica de Trabajadores
Cuyo, 3

Dairy industry, 14, 121, 142, 165
Dams, 13
Dance, 29; disco, 232; at Tirana festival, 107. *Also see* Cueca
Darwin, Charles, 5, 74
David del Curto SA, 195
Dávila, Carlos, 149
Dawson, John, 103
Daza, Hilarión, 90, 100
De las Casas, Fr. Bartolomé, 38
Decentralization, 22
Decree of Free Commerce, 65
Deer, 29
Defensive War, 38–40
Del Monte Food Company, 195
Democratic guarantees, 171
Democratic Party (Partido Democrática), 119
Democratic rule, 150, 155, 237; conservative shift, 209; elite concerns, 200; tensions, 182
Depression, 16, 139; impact on nitrates, 141
Deputies, 73, 78–79, 87
Desolación, 136
Detention camps, 188
Devaluation, 108, 192
D'Halmar, Augusto, 136
Diaguitas, 28
Dieciocho, 8
Diego Portales center, 236
Diezmo. *See* Tithe
DINA (Dirección de Inteligencia Nacional), 188–89, 224
Disappeared, 213, 223
Disease: impact on Mapuche, 30, 43–44; in mining camps, 98
Dobson, Charles, 76
Dole, 195

Domestic service, 10, 14, 58, 119, 122, 144, 147, 206, 233
Domeyko, Ignacio, 91
Dominican Monastery, 24, 41
Donoso, Ricardo, 8, 137
Dresden, 131
Dungan, Jimmy, 165
Durán, Julio, 162
Duros, 186–87
Dutch West Indies Company, 37–38

Earthquakes, 5; in Chillán, 140; in Valdivia, 160; in Valparaiso, 127
Easter Island, 3, 4, 149
Eastern Europe, 198
Echaurren Larraín, Dolores, 86
Ecologists, 229
E-commerce, 288
Economics: CEPAL model, 162; contraction, 197; crisis, 181; decline, 215; development, 3, 7; distribution, 16; fine tuning, 220; freedom, 75; growth, 15–16, 160, 213; impact on landscapes, 234; planning, 164, 190; policy, 70, 108; publications, 18; state-led, 155; subsidies, 191; theory, 160; transition, 190
Ecuador, 5; colonial trade, 44, 59; settlement patterns, 28
Edner, Andrés, 123
Education: Allende accomplishments, 8; church, 53; colonial, 42, 51, 52; enrollments, 8; expansion, 16, 115; government support, 76, 115; hacendado children, 106; Jesuits, 42; Mapuche, 144; privatization, 16, 22; Protestant, 24; reform, 91; rural schools, 107; under

O'Higgins, 68; under Popular
  Front, 151
Edwards Bello, Joaquín, 136
Edwards Eastman, Agustin, 171,
  233
Edwards, Jorge, 8, 52, 218
Edwards Ossandon, Agustín, 86,
  122
Edwards Ross, Agustín, 122, 126
Edwards Vives, Alberto, 137
Egaña, Mariano, 89
E.I. du Pont Nemours and
  Company, 124
Elections: campaigning, 216;
  congressional, 19, 20, 153;
  fraud, 129; manipulation of,
  89, 95; municipal, 167;
  parliamentary, 1973, 178;
  reform, 109, 129; role of
  women, 206
Electoral college, 130
Elicura massacre, 39
Elite: Basque-Castilian, 137; in
  church, 41; coalitions, 113;
  colonial, 48, 59, 61;
  divisiveness, 70; industrial
  ownership, 124; land
  investments, 84; opposition to
  Allende, 133; role in
  independence, 62; tourism, 13;
  under Prieto, 70
Employment, 17; public, 147;
  redistribution, 149; rural
  decine, 230
Empresa Nacional de Electricidad
  (ENDESA), 117, 151
Empresa Nacional de Petroleo
  (ENAP), 152
Encina, Francisco, 8, 137
Encomenderos, 38, 44, 46–47
Encomienda, 12, 32–33, 35; in
  mining region, 55
England, 215; immigration to
  Chile, 52; trade, 56

Ensayo crítico del desarrollo
  económico-social de Chile,
  138
Entailed estates, 12, 52, 57, 62, 70,
  84; abolished, 93
Environment, 195–96; water use,
  230
Epoca, La, 219
Equity market, 204–5
Ercilla, 176
Ercilla, Alonso de, 8, 35
Errázuriz, Cardinal Francisco
  Javier, 23
Errázuriz, Francisco Javier
  (presidential candidate), 210
Errázuriz, Maximiano, 79
Escondida copper mine, La, 11
Escuela Nacional Unificada
  (ENU), 17
Esmeralda, 101
Estanco, 46, 60, 66; under Freire,
  69, 82
Europe: films, 134; intellectual
  and social trends, 184; study,
  91; trade, 75
European Union, 17, 210; credit,
  177; trade agreement, 226,
  228–29
Exchange rate, 156, 192; frozen,
  192
Exiles, 188, 198
Existentialism, 138
Exploration, 30–32, 35, 80
Export-Import Bank, 140, 153
Exports: agriculture, 58, 81;
  colonial, 44–45; copper, 56;
  diversification, 17; forestry
  products, 228–29; fruit, 229–30;
  gold, 56; grain, 12, 58; growth,
  17; hides, 59; nitrates, 97; port
  volume, 13; seafood, 230;
  silver, 56, 89, 97; wool,
  229–30
Eyzaguirre, Jaime, 137

FACH. *See* Air Force
Factory seizures, 179
Falange, 161
Falconbridge, 227
Falkland Islands/Malvinas
    Islands, 209, 215, 222
Family: life, 232; networks, 158
Farellones ski resort, 13
Fascism, 161, 182
Fazio Rigazzi, Hugo, 221
Federación de Estudiantes
    Chilenos (FECH), 115
Federación de Obreros de Chile,
    120, 144
Federación Nacional de
    Trabajadores Agrícolas, 144
Federalism, 21, 70; eliminated, 89
Felstiner, Mary Lowenthal, 84
Ferdinand VII, 62
Fiducia, 169
Figueroa, Emilio, 148
Films, 134
Filopolitas, 90
Finances, 181; crisis in 1815, 66;
    reform, 89; under Freire, 69
Financial institutions, 186, 192;
    AFP funds, 204; government
    takeover, 193
Fine Arts Museum (Palacio de
    Bellas Artes), 23
Firefly, 77
Fish: abundance, 5, 11, 14;
    consumption, 99; exports, 195,
    230; farming, 195; industry
    growth, 194–95; meal, 17, 195,
    230
FLASCO, 202
Flourmills, 79–81, 106, 123
FOCH, 144–45; supports
    campesinos, 167
Fogón, 29, 142
Folk music, 14, 22–23
Fondo Nacional de Salud
    (FONASA), 205–6

Food: colonial, 42–43;
    distribution, 16; imports, 181;
    prices, 121; processing, 12, 233;
    traditional, 233
Foreign: corporations, 124; debt,
    16, 90; investment, 52, 64; loan
    default, 150; nitrate
    ownership, 102, 141; policy,
    153–54; press, 197; technology,
    76
Forests: biotech, 228–29; fires, 229;
    growth, 194; industries, 14; in
    the Sur, 13, 123, 142; native
    species neglect, 229; planting,
    186; pre-Columbian, 12, 33;
    recreation, 25
Foxley, Alejandro, 225
Franchises, 99, 108
Franco, Francisco, 186
FRAP, 153
Free trade, 91, 96, 108; agreements
    with Canada, European
    Union, Mexico, and United
    States, 226
Frei, Irene, 216
Frei Montalva, Eduardo:
    accomplishments, 166;
    challenges military, 188; death,
    188; education program, 21;
    election 1958, 155, 162; election
    1964, 162; government, 162–70;
    Tacnazo, 169
Frei Ruíz Tagle, Eduardo, 21, 216;
    immunity offer, 233
Freire, Ramón, 69–70, 88, 90
French: case of Toumens, 105;
    education, 91; immigration, 10,
    52, 105; investors, 102;
    merchants, 59, 80; Revolution,
    61; trade, 45, 64
Frente de Acción Popular (FRAP),
    153
Fresno, Cardinal Juan Francisco,
    209

Friedman, Milton, 190–91, 197
Friendly Indians, 29, 36
Fronda aristocrática, La, 137
Fruit: exports, 229; price decline, 229
Frutillar, 14
Fuerza Aérea de Chile, 148, 189
Fundo San Miguel, 167
Fundos: changing labor system, 194; defense of, 174; expropriations, 12, 156, 167, 174; labor costs, 156; owners, 144

Gallo, Miguel, 77–78
Gallo, Pedro León, 73, 78
Gandarillas, Manuel José, 89
García Carrasco, Francisco Antonio, 49n, 62, 84; arrest of criollos, 63; resignation, 63
García Huidobro, Francisco, 55
García Oñez de Loyola, Martín, 37
Gas lighting, 79, 82
Gates, Bill, 228
Gaucho, 48n, 143
Gay, Claudio, 74, 96
Gazmuri, Cristián, 219
GDP (gross domestic product), 16
General Song, 175
General Teachers' Association, 116
Genfor Technologies Inc., 228
German: farmers, 143; immigrants, 10, 14, 24, 105, 143; merchants, 80; metallurgist, 56; synthetic nitrates, 126
German-Chileans, 151
Gill y Gonzaga, Antonio de, 54
Godoy, Juan, 77
Gold: amalgamation, 55; discovery, 48–49n; mines, 30–32; panning, 33, 54; standard, 148–49

Góngora, Mario, 138
González, Fr. Gil, 38
González Videla, Gabriel, 146, 152
Government: colonial, 46, 52; expenditures, 192; growth, 115; instability, 130; revenue, 75; subsidies, 83, 87
Goycolea, Patricia, 198
Goyenechea, Candelaria, 78, 83
Gracias a la vida, 22
Graham, Maria, 85
Grain, 11–12, 32–33, 40; exports prohibited, 65; merchants, 79–80; tariff reduction, 229
Gran Minería, 127
Gran señor y raja diablos, 106, 137
Grapes export growth, 195. See also Vineyards
Great Britain, 198; capital, 83; mail subsidy, 83; mediation offer, 101
Green Peace, 229
Gremialista movement, 199
Gremios, 177
Gross Domestic Product. See GDP
Grove, Marmaduke, 149
Guaico, El, 86
Guayacán, 79
Guayaquil, 44, 57, 83
Guerrillas, 189
Guests of Stone, The, 218
Guggenheim brothers, 125
Guill y Gonzaga, Antonio de, 54
Gunpowder, 56
Guzmán, Jaime, 168, 199, 223

Habilitadores, 56
Hacendados, 46, 58, 80; migration to city, 106
Hacienda, 12; church owned, 41–42; meat and wine production, 106; mine owners, 57; owned by Ramos, 82

Hambriento, El, 82
Hamilton, Alexander, 90
Happy Captivity, 40
Harberger, Arnold, 192
Hardliners, 186–87. *See also* Duros
Harvey, Robert, 103
Hawkins, Richard, 37
Health, 221; care, 205; effect of
    fish toxins, 230; free care, 16;
    miners, 98; Popular Front
    program, 151; privatization,
    205
Heise González, Julio, 8, 130, 138
Helms, Richard, 171
Hemenway, August, 81
Highway Department
    construction, 15, 18
Hiking, 25
Hillyar, Captain James, 65
Hiriart, Lucía, 207–9
Historia de Chile, 137
Historia del imperialismo en
    Chile, 138
Historians, 7, 8, 96, 135
Hitler, Adolf, 134
Homesteaders in the Sur, 15, 122,
    142–43
Hoover, Herbert, 149
Horman, Charles and Joyce, 188,
    224
Horses, 33, 42
Housing. *See* public housing
Huanchaca, Bolivia, 97
Huáscar, 101
Huasos, 12, 42, 48n, 80
Huasos Quincheros, 23
Hudson River Valley, 37
Huidobro, Vicente, 135
Huilliches, 29, 48n
Human Rights, 162; activists, 188;
    prosecution for violations
    allowed, 236; violations, 188,
    213, 215, 222–24
Humanist Party, 20

Humbolt, Alexander, 5
Humitas, 43
Hunting, 29
Hurtado de Mendoza, García,
    34–36
Hydroelectric power, 13, 140, 151

Ibáñez, Colonel Carlos: anti-
    politics, 148; election of 1942,
    151; government, 118, 132,
    137; labor relations, 144–45,
    148; middle class support, 148;
    nostalgia for, 197; platform of
    1952, 152; resignation, 149
Ideas políticas en Chile, 138
Illiad, 35
Ilzurieta Caffarena, Ricardo,
    215–16
IMF, 177
Immigration, 10; colonial, 51; to
    Mapuche territory, 105; role in
    industry, 123
Immunity, 223
Imperial, 49n, 105
Imports: agricultural, 141;
    colonial, 44, 59; growth of,
    160; machinery, 108, 127; port
    volume, 13; subsidized, 192
Incas: Almagro's expedition, 31;
    defeat by the Mapuche, 29, 33;
    expansion, 27; trade, 30
Income: distribution, 17; family,
    17; government, 66, 75, 110,
    129, 179; personal, 17
INDAP, 161, 165
Independence Day, 8
Independencia, 101
Independent Democratic Union
    Party (UDI), 216–17
Indians: labor, 31–32. *See also*
    Diaguitas; Incas; Mapuches
Indigenismo, 135
Industrial belts. *See* Cordones
    industriales

Industrial Workers of the World (IWW), 145–46
Industrialization, 91, 107–8, 123–25; Aylwin policy, 225; contraction, 192; expansion, 192; foreign participation, 124; forest products, 228; government role, 140; growth of, 160, 166; model, 154; neoliberal program, 191; policy debate, 227; state ownership, 156; worker seizures, 179
Industries: brewing, 14, 81, 123; food, 123; lumber, 5, 11, 13, 58, 123, 195; textiles, 12, 40, 80. *See also* Chemicals; Fishing; Mining; Oil; Steel
Infant mortality, 147; decline of, 181, 205, 221
Inflation, 18, 104, 108, 120, 122, 134; during War of Pacific, 128; fear of, 220; rampant, 158; rates, 139; reduction of, 159, 192; supporters of, 129; under Alessandri, 150, 160; under Aylwin, 225; under González Videla, 152
Inquilinos, 47, 57, 121; expulsion of, 194
Inquisition, 41, 96
Institute of Chilean Engineers, 117
Instituto de Desarrollo Agropecuario (INDAP), 161; union organization, 167
Instituto de Salud y Prevención (ISAPRE), 205–6
Instituto Forestal, 166
Instituto Nacional, 68, 78, 85, 91–92, 107; law school, 96
Instituto Pedagógico, 168–69, 203
Insurance companies, 79, 82
Intendente, 7, 22, 53, 60, 96
International Telephone and Telegraph Company (ITT), 164, 171–72
Internet, 4, 15, 18, 228, 231–32; business use, 191
Inti Illimani, 23
Investment: foreign, 166; private, 131, 156, 166; public, 131, 156, 166
Iquique, Battle of, 101; population, 125; port, 11; water, 102–3
Irish immigration, 52
Iroquois, 29
Irrigation, 85–87; Colchagua valley, 229; colonial, 42, 57; Limache, 86; Norte Chico, 11; Valle Central, 6
Isla Negra, 13
Islam, 24
Italian immigration, 10, 105
Italy, 54; merchants, 80; receives refugees, 198
Itata River, 13, 31
IWW, 145–46

JAP (Juntas de Abstecimiento y Precios), 174
Japan: capital, 221; mining investment, 227; seafood imports, 230; trade, 17
Jara, Victor, 22, 188
Jarpa, Sergio Onofre, 209
Jefferson, Thomas, 54
Jesuits: agriculture, 42; church, 41; expulsion of, 53–54; missionaries, 38–40
Jewish community, 24
Jiménez, Tucapel, 188, 224
Jobet, Julio César, 138
Jobs: creation of, 158, 218; unskilled, 10, 14
John Paul II, 209
Juan Fernández Island, 3; incarceration, 66–67; World War I, 131

Junta: independence, 63–65; of 1924, 131; of 1932, 149
Juntas de Abastecimiento y Precios, 131

Kemmerer, Edwin, 148
Kennecott Copper Company, 126, 141
Kennedy Administration, 155
Kerensky Chileno, El, 169
Kindergarden, 181
Kiosk, 18
Kissenger, Henry, 171–72, 177, 224
Klein-Saks Mission, 153, 160
Korea: economic model, 227; war, 146
Körner, Emil, 110
Krause, Esteban, 235
Krebs, Ricardo, 114

La Caja de Colonización Agrícola, 142
La Plata, Viceroyalty of, 45, 59
La Serena: attacked, 37, 70; mineralogy education, 91; opposition to Montt, 92; population, 9
Labor: colonial reforms, 35; Indian, 35, 38–39; laws, 220; Pinochet policies, 196; reforms, 191
Labor Code: of 1931, 144–45, 150; of 1978, 196; of 1981, 194
Lagos, Ricardo, 19, 21, 210, 215; commemorates Allende, 236; offers land to Mapuches, 236; president, 217, 224; relationship to Socialists, 237
Laissez faire, 131
Lake Caburgua, 143
Lake District, 3, 25
Lambert, Carlos Segundo, 77
Lambert, Charles, 76–77
Land: church estates, 41;

ownership, 57, 122, 194; purchases, 84; values, 57
Land reform, 12, 16, 151, 156; Frei's bill, 167; PDC goals, 162; under Alessandri, 155, 161; under UP, 174
Landlords rent control, 156
Language, 22
Larraín family, 84
Larraín, José Manuel, 219
Larraín, José Toribio, 62, 84–85
Larraín Moxó, Rafael, 85
Lastarria, José Victorino, 91
Latin America, 16–17; instability, 74
Lautaro, 33–34
Lavín, Joaquín, 21, 215
Law for the Permanent Defense of Democracy, 146
Lazcano Echaurren, Fernando, 86
Lazcano Mujica, Fernando, 85
Leigh, Gustavo, 189
Leighton, Bernardo, 189
Léniz, Fernando, 191
Letelier, Felipe, 216
Letelier, Miguel, 117
Letelier, Orlando, 189, 224
Levies, 66; by O'Higgins, 67
Ley de Seguridad Interior del Estado, 150
Liberal Party, 108–9, 113; middle class support, 148
Liberals, 69–71, 73, 87–89; exile of, 89; favor Rengifo, 90; ideas, 91; revolt, 93
Life span, 147, 181, 206, 221
Lillo, Baldomero, 99
Lima: battle for, 102; merchants, 58, 65, 81; San Martín invasion, 67; slave trade, 44
Limache, 86
Lira, Elizabeth, 219
Lircay, Battle of, 70, 89
Literacy rate, 8, 107, 115, 147

Literature, 8, 22
Liverpool, 75, 78
Liverpool Nitrate Company, 103
Livestock, 43, 57
Llaima (mountain), 6
Llama, 29, 43
Llanquihue, 14
Loa river, 11
Loans: British, 69; church, 41;
   foreign, 110; government, 56,
   66; US, 148, 153
Locke, John, 54
London market, 76, 164
Longueira, Pablo, 237
Los Loros, Battle of, 78
Loveman, Brian and Sharon, 165,
   219
Lüders, Rulf, 193
Luengo, Segundo and Zoila, 143
Lumber, 5, 11, 13, 58, 123, 195
Lutheran Church, 24
Lynch, Patricio, 103

Mackenna, Juan, 52
Magellan, Ferdinand, 30
Maipo River, 13, 85
Maipú, Battle of, 66
Malleco, 105
Malocas, 29
Manuel Rodríguez Patriotic Front,
   22, 209
Mapocho: exploration, 31–32, 110;
   market, 12, 233; river, 234
MAPU, 159, 168
Mapuche: alliances, 29; cattle, 43,
   104–5; cavalry, 36–37;
   conquest, 3, 33–38; defense, 29;
   enslavement, 36, 39; history,
   96; horsemanship, 33; land
   expropriation, 142, 235;
   language, 22, 48n; lost
   autonomy, 104; military
   strategy, 37; missionaries, 24;
   population, 9, 14, 28; protest

of dam, 235; rebellion, 33–34,
   61; territory, 28–31; textiles, 43;
   trade, 30, 40, 43, 104;
   university education, 201
March of the Empty Pots, 174,
   197
Marco del Pont, Francisco, 66
Mardones, Francisco, 117–18
Marga Marga gold mines, 32
Marín, Gladys, 21
Maritain, Jacques, 161
Marriage, 42
Martínez de Rozas, Juan, 62
Marxist: class warfare, 161;
   education, 178, 203; faculty,
   200, 203; fear of takeover, 169;
   idealists, 146; military crusade
   against, 189; socialism, 149;
   views on women, 207
Masons, 108–9, 115, 118
Matta, Guillermo and Manuel
   Antonio, 73
Matte, Eugenio, 149
Matus, Alejandra, 224
Maule River, 13, 29–30, 33
Mayorazgos. *See* Entailed estates
McBride, George, 142
Medina, José Toribio, 96
Meiggs, Henry, 108
Mendiburu, José de, 58
Mendoza, Argentina, 35; railroad,
   130; trade, 45; trail, 60
Mercantilism, 46; reformed, 54,
   63–64
Mercedarians, 41
Merchants: criollo, 58, 68, 80;
   foreign, 64, 68, 90; guild, 45;
   Lima, 58, 65, 81; Spanish,
   46–47, 58, 66–67; trade with
   Mapuche, 40
MERCOSUR, 227, 229
Mercurio, El, 18
Mercury, 44–45, 54–56;
   amalgamation process, 55

Mestizos, 44, 46; in mining, 55; women, 48

Methodist Church, 24

Mexico: ballads, 135; commerce, 30; instability, 74; militia, 38; oil nationalization, 141; per capita income, 74; population, 10, 44, 139; reception of refugees, 198; trade agreement, 226, 229

Microsoft, 228

Middle class: affluence, 233; diversity, 114; employment, 147; health, 206; leaders, 111, 147; political affiliation, 157; in politics, 93, 113, 116, 133; salaries, 147; travel, 13, 233; voting, 129

Migration, 10, 11–14; Chilotes, 14; farm workers, 195; inquilinos, 142; nitrate workers, 125; to cities, 138

Military: arrests, 182, 187; army benefits, 189; conservative support, 169; coup, 182; detention camps, 188; Junta, 185–87; patriotism, 186–88; political preferences, 186; president's cabinet, 178, 187; promotion, 186–87; prosecution of officers, 236; role of officers' wives, 180; salaries, 189; social origins, 186; *tacnazo*, 169; *tancazo*, 179; university administration, 200–202

Militia, 38, 52, 60–61

Millar, René, 220

Minimum employment, 197

Mining: business model, 98; colonial production, 42, 54; expansion, 95–96; expropriation, 172; franchises, 99; guild, 56–57; history, 76–80,

96; internationalization, 227; investment, 86; methods, 125; owners, 46; private companies, 226; taxes, 61; technology, 54, 56, 76, 79, 97; wages, 55; workers, 55, 96, 98

Mint, 52, 55–56, 60, 82; reform, 89

MIR, 168, 174, 179; armed resistance, 189; infiltration of armed forces, 180; Plan Z, 187

Miraflores, Battle of, 102

Missing, 188

Mistral, Gabriela (Lucila Godoy Alcayaga), 8, 135–36, 175

Mitsubishi, 227

Modernization, 95–96, 121, 166

Moffit, Ronni, 224

Molina, 166

Momios, 182

Moneda, La, 182; celebration by PDC, 169

Monopoly of liquor and tobacco. *See* Estanco

Monte Verde, 28

Montero, Juan Esteban, 149

Monterrey Pine. *See* Radiata pine

Montt, Jorge, 110, 130, 132

Montt, Manuel, 78, 85, 88, 92–93

Montt, Pedro, 86

Mormon church, 24

Morro, 101

Mortgage Loan Bank, 93, 122

Mostrador, El, 219

Mothers' Clubs. *See* Centro de Madres

Moulián, Tomás, 218

Mountain climbing, 25

Movimiento de Acción Popular Unitaria. *See* MAPU

Movimiento de Izquierda Revolucionario. *See* MIR

Movimiento Feminista, 208

Moxó, Dolores, 85

Mujeres por la Vida, 208

Mulattos, 44
Municipal government, 19, 46; health care management, 205
Municipal Theater of Santiago (*Teatro Municipal de Santiago*), 23
Muñoz de Guzmán, Luis, 62
Museum of Santiago (*Museo de Santiago*), 23
Music: ballads, 135; classical, 135; Mapuche, 29; tangos, 135
Mussolini, Benito, 134
My Struggle for Democracy, 219

Nahuel, Hilario, 143
Nahuel, Segundo, 143, 166
Ñandú, 29
Napoleon Bonaparte, 51, 61; war, 59
National Agreement for a Transition to Democracy, 209
National Agricultural Society, 85, 118
National Archive, 13, 23
National Cathedral, 23, 41
National Congress, 64–65, 67
National Corporation for Reparation and Reconciliation, 223
National Energy Commission, 19
National Environmental Commission (CONAMA), 235
National Falange, 144
National Guard, 89
National Historical Museum, 23
National identity, 7, 96
National Library, 23, 68, 137, 208
National Network of Infocenters, 228
National Railway Company, 117
National Renovation Party. *See* Renovación Nacional
National Security Council, 19, 190
National Stadium, 188, 197

National Strike, 180–82
National Teachers' Union, 203
National Truth and Reconciliation Commission, 223
Nationalism, 7
Nationalist Party, 170; joins CODE, 176; supports Alessandri, 170
Nationalization, 157
Navíos de registro, 59
Navy, 67, 100–101
Nazar Ahumada, Ricardo, 79
Nazi youth, 150–51
Neoliberal economic model: Aylwin support, 225; health care, 205–6; Latin American interest, 237; performance, 221–22; social security, 204–5
Neoliberals, 16, 186, 191; labor policy, 191, 196; monetary policy, 192
Neruda, Pablo (Nefatlí Reyes Basoalto), 8, 13, 22, 27, 135–36, 175, 218; commemoration, 236
New Song movement, 22
New Toledo, 31
New Zealand, 195; dairy specialists, 165
Newspapers, 18, 134
Nicaragua regime, 99; human rights record, 209
Nitrates: Bolivia, 95; cartel, 104; certificates, 99, 102; investments, 125–26; markets, 120; mining, 3, 95, 125; ownership, 126; production, 97, 104; synthetic, 126; taxes on, 99; wealth, 11
Nixon Administration, 176–77, 182, 224
No Campaign, 208–11
Nobel Prize in Literature, 136, 175
Noble titles, 52, 57; abolished, 68
Noranda Corporation, 235–36

Normilla, Flora, 77
Norte Chico, 4, 11, 76, 96
Norte Grande, 4, 11, 96–97, 114
North, John Thomas, 102–3, 108, 125
Nuestra inferioridad económica, 137
Núñez de Pineda y Bascuñan, Francisco, 40
Nurses, 206

Odas elementales, 136
Office of Public Safety, 223
Oficina de Planificación Nacional (ODEPLAN), 163
O'Higgins, Ambrosio, 52, 56
O'Higgins, Bernardo, 52; abdication, 69; Freire's challenge, 88; government, 65–69; historical interpretations, 96, 137
Oil: exploration, 140, 151; industry, 16, 153–54; refineries, 12, 14; sabotage, 175
Onas, 29
Opera, 23
Operation Condor, 224
Opus Dei, 23, 201
Orchards, 12, 57, 85; expansion, 194, 235; in Sur, 143
Oregon, 6, 28, 108; pear and raspberry growers complain, 229
Oruro, Bolivia, 97
Osores de Ulloa, Pedro, 39
Osorio, Mariano, 65–66
Osorno, 14; founded, 35

Pacific Northwest, 13, 28, 48n
Pacific Ocean, 3, 4, 30, 60; currents, 5, 27
Pacific Steam Navigation Company, 83
Painting, 23, 41

Palace of Fine Arts (Palacio Nacional de Bellas Artes), 13
Paleolithic era, 28
Palma, Gabriel, 108
Pan de rescoldo, 49n
Panama: canal, 127; colonial trade, 30, 44
Pan-American Highway, 4
Pando, Juan Antonio, 80
Pangipulli, 14
Papelera, La, 176–77
Paper industry, 12, 14, 17, 123, 196, 227
Paraguay: Jesuits missions, 39; trade, 45
Paraguayan tea, 44–45. *See also* Yerba mate
Paris, 91, 135
Parks, 25
Parliamentary era, 94, 110
Parque Cousiño, 80
Parque O'Higgins, 24, 80
Parra, Angel and Isabel, 22
Parra, Violeta, 22
Partido Obrero Socialista, 120
Partido por la Democracia (Party for Democracy) (PPD), 20
Partido Radical Social Demócrata, 20
Patagonia, 3, 4, 5, 7; Chilote migration, 14; coal mines, 143; Indians, 29; settlement of, 93; sheep ranches, 121; treaty, 100
Patria y Libertad, 175, 178
Patriotism, 186–87
Patronage, 157, 217
Payador, 22
Peace Corps Volunteers, 165–66
Peace Treaty: with Mapuche, 40; with Peru, 102
Pehuenches, 29, 48n
Pelucones, 87–88, 92–93
Peña, 22
Peninsulares, 61, 64

Pentacostal church, 24
Pequeña minería, 127
Pereira Salas, Eugenio, 138
Pérez, José Joaquín, 78, 93–94
Pérez Rosales, Vicente, 91
Pérez Zujovic, Edmundo, 175
Peru: blockade, 67; Chilean
    investments, 233; colonial
    trade, 44, 58; guerrilla warfare,
    102; loan, 69; migrants, 233;
    nationalized nitrates, 99;
    nitrate certificates, 99;
    settlement patterns, 28; trade
    restrictions, 65; trade rivalry,
    90; war, 3, 7, 90. *See also* War
    of the Pacific
Peru, Viceroyalty of, 3, 34, 36;
    expedition to Chile, 65; fear of,
    63; invasion of, 67–68; militia,
    38; population, 44; subsidy for
    Chile, 38; trade, 44, 59
Peruvian-Bolivian Confederation,
    87; war with, 90
Peruvian early cultures, 28
Pezuela, Joaquín de la, 67
Philadelphia, 75
Phillip V, 59
Physicians, 206
Picunches, 29, 48n
Pilcomayo, 101
Piñera, José, 196–97, 204
Pinochet, Augusto: Allende
    names head of armed forces,
    180; arrest in England, 215,
    217; Contreras' revelations,
    224; federalism, 21–22;
    government, 185–211; human
    rights revelations, 217;
    intimidation tactics, 214;
    named president, 189;
    neoliberal reforms, 15;
    plebescite, 19; senator, 214, 215;
    threats, 222; unfit for trail, 215
Pinto, Aníbal, 102

Pinto, Francisco Antonio, 70, 91
Pipiolos, 87–88
Pirihueco, 14
Pisagua, 101
Pisco sour, 11
Pizarro, Francisco, 30–31
Plan Z, 187
Plebescite, 190, 207, 208–11
Poblaciones, 188, 209
Pocahontas, 40
Poetry, 135–36. *See also* Vicente
    Huidobro; Gabriel Mistral;
    Pablo Neruda
Police, 19, 60. *See also* Carabineros
Political culture, 84, 87–88;
    campaigning, 178, 216;
    changed by military, 185–86;
    discussions, 7; independence,
    64–65; Junta blames
    politicians, 187; patronage,
    157; political parties, 20–21;
    reform, 155–56; role of
    women, 206; strikes during
    UP, 179; supporters, 133;
    theory of change, 183; under J.
    Pérez, 94; with FRAP, 153
Polynesian workers, 81
Popular Front, 7, 114, 145, 151
Population: colonial, 43–44, 48n;
    economically active, 158;
    growth, 10, 114; native, 9, 28;
    Norte Grande, 125; rural, 122
Portales, Cea and Company,
    69–70, 82
Portales, Diego, 82–83, 88–90
Portales, Santiago, 82
Portillo, 13
Portrerillos copper mine, 11, 127
Portugal, 62
Portuguese immigration, 52, 81
Poverty, 15, 17, 220, 231
PPD. *See* Partido por la
    Democracia
Prado, Pedro, 137

Prat, Captain Arturo, 101
Prats, Carlos, 178–179; assassinated, 189; resignation, 180
Pre-Columbian Art Museum, 23
Pre-natal care, 205
President, 19, 73; competition for, 157
Prices: cereals, 106; consumer, 134; beef and grain, 106; freeze, 140, 173; minerals, 76
Prieto Vial, Joaquín, 82, 88–91
Prieto, Victoria, 83
Primary School Teachers' Society, 116
Primer Conferencia Nacional de la Mujer, 208
Private enterprise, 75, 140, 190
Private property, 16, 46, 117, 155, 176, 198, 208
Private schools, 203
Privatization, 191, 198; businesses, 16, 186; health care, 16, 22; land, 186, 194; social security, 205; social services, 186; utilities, 193, 221
ProChile, 227
Professional institutes, 201
Professionals: commuting, 233; impact of Internet, 232; job loss, 180; new roles, 232; opposition to UP, 180; organizations, 118; party loyalty, 109; political roles, 133, 139; sale of property, 180; strikes, 177, 180; women, 206
Property rights, 157, 190
Protectionism, 193
Protestant churches, 24, 68, 92
Protests: against Allende, 177–78, 180; against Ibáñez, 149; against Pinochet, 208–9; students, 202–3; supporting

Pinochet, 217; use of music, 22; women, 208
Public education, 8, 96
Public employees, 147; bonuses, 4; colonial period, 61
Public housing, 16, 151, 161; distribution, 157; PDC goals, 162; under Concertación, 231, 234; under UP, 181
Public services, 131
Public works, 54, 60, 69, 75–76, 110, 128; railroads, 130; under Alessandri, 150; under Frei, 162; under Ibáñez, 148
Publishing industry, 68, 134; acquisition by UP, 170
Pucón, 14, 165; growth, 235
Puelches, 29, 48n
Puerto Montt, 6; commercial center, 14, 15; death of squatters, 175; railroads, 130; rainfall, 13
Puerto Yunguay, 15
Pulpería, 98
Punta Arenas, 3, 5; population, 15
Purén, 49n

Quadragesimo Anno, 161
Quilapaiyún, 23
Quillín conference, 39–40
Quiroga, Rodrigo de, 36

Radiata pine, 228–29, 235
Radical Party, 109, 115; in Alliance, 130; election of 1964, 163; growth of representation, 116, 117; image, 152; middle class support, 147; platforms, 117, 152; in Popular Front, 151; strategy in 1970, 170
Radical Social Democratic Party. *See* Partido Radical Social Demócrata
Radio, 134; campaigns, 217;

military broadcasts, 182; political advertisements, 178; receivers, 18, 23

Railroad, 4, 11, 16; construction, 107, 110, 128, 130; Copiapó-Caldera, 78, 83; industry, 107; international, 130; loss of passenger service, 17; in Mapuche heartland, 105; modernization, 166; role of Wheelwright, 83; Santiago-Talca, 85, 93; Santiago-Valparaiso, 87, 93

Ramírez Necochea, Hernán, 138

Ramón, Armando de, 219

Ramos Font, José Tomás, 80

Ranco, 14

Ranquil, 142, 150; labor union, 159

Rapel river, 13

Reagan, Ronald, 209

Real estate, 86

Rebellions, 73, 177

Recabarren, Luis Emilio, 120

Recession, 16, 186, 237; Asia, 225; Europe and North America, 225

Recreation, 25

Reducciones, 14. *See also* Reservations

Reforestation, 12–13, 165, 196

Refugees, 198

Rengifo, Manuel, 75, 88–91

Renovación Nacional, 20, 210; cooperation with Concertación, 236

Rent control, 156–57

Republican Confederation for Civic Action, 144

Rerum Novarum, 161

Reservations Mapuche, 14

Retail merchants, 177, 180

Revolutionary theory, 183

Ribera, Alonso de, 37

Riñihue, 14

Río Negro Valley, 143

Rio Tinto Zinc, 226

Ríos, Juan Antonio, 151–52

Rittig Commission, 223

RN. *See* Renovación Nacional

Road construction, 60, 76, 166

Rodeo, 14, 42, 106

Rodríguez Grez, Pablo, 175, 180

Rolando Matus, 174

Roman Catholicism. *See also* Catholic church

Roosevelt, Franklin D., 134

Rosario, Argentina, 83

Rosas, Juan Manuel de, 74

Rose del fuego. *See* Slash and burn

Ross, Gustavo, 150–51

Ross, Juana, 122

Roto chileno, 8, 101

Rousseau, Jean Jacques, 54

Royalists, 63, 67

Ruíz de Gamboa, Martín, 35

Rural landscapes, 235–37

Russell, William H., 125

Russian Orthodox Church, 24

Russian Revolution, 120

Saavedra, Colonel Cornelio, 104

Sabotage, 175

SAG, 165. *See also* Servicio Agrícola y Ganadera

Saint Augustine Convent, 87

Sales tax, 89, 93

Salmon, 230

Salvador Copper Mine, El: chilenización, 164; strike, 164

Salvation Army, 119

San Antonio, 12

San Borja Hospital, 60

San Francisco, California, 5, 80–81

San Francisco Church, 23, 41

San Isidro, 86

San Juan, Argentina, 35

San Martín, José de, 66–68

San Miguel, Fr. Antonio de, 38
San Pedro, 229
Sanfuentes, Enrique Salvador, 130
Santa Carolina, 229
Santa Cruz, Andrés, 90
Santa María, Domingo, 109
Santiago: aristocracy, 68–70;
    church schools, 24; commercial
    changes, 234; founded by
    Pedro de Valdivia, 32;
    industry, 107, 128; mayor
    assassinated, 189; migration,
    233; planning, 32; pollution,
    233; population, 9–10, 139;
    region, 7; trade with Buenos
    Aires, 45; traffic congestion,
    10–11; transportation, 213;
    urban sprawl, 234; weather, 4
Santillán, Hernando de, 35
Sarmiento, Domingo F., 74
Savings, 166
Schneider, René, 172, 224
Scientific management, 117
Scorpion, 49n, 62, 84
Sculpture, 23
Secret Ballot, 153
Secretaría Nacional de la Mujer,
    221
Secularization, 87, 92, 96, 108
Senate, 19; representation, 73,
    78–79, 85; under O'Higgins, 67
Servicio Agrícola y Ganadera
    (SAG), 165
Servicio Nacional de la Mujer, 221
Servicio Nacional de Salud, 147
Seville, 44
SFF (Sociedad de Fomento
    Fabril), 118, 124
Sharp, Bartholomew, 37
Sheep industry, 14, 42, 80, 121,
    165
Shellfish, 5, 14
Shock treatment (economic),
    191–92

Siemens-Schuchart, 124
Silva Henríquez, Cardinal Raúl,
    24
Silver, 54–56, 75, 77–78; exports,
    97; production, 97
Situado (Royal), 38
Siúticos, 138
Ski resorts, 5, 13, 24
Slash and burn, 13; in Sur and
    Zona Austral, 15, 142
Slavery, 57; abolished, 69; African,
    44; Mapuche, 36, 39
Slavs, 24
Smith, Captain John, 40
Smuggling. See contraband
Sobremonte, Viscount Rafael, 63
Soccer, 25. See also World Cup
Social Conservative Party, 161
Social Democrats, 146
Social justice, 156, 162, 210, 213
Social mobility, 52
Social security, 204–5
Social services, 22, 156; by church,
    41
Socialist Party, 20; blame from
    coup, 182; in FRAP, 153;
    infiltration of armed services,
    180; internal divisions, 176;
    middle class membership, 148;
    new strategy, 167–68; Plan Z,
    187; reaction of Lagos'
    policies, 237; role in no
    campaign, 210; rural unions,
    159; union relations, 145–46;
    withdrawal from Popular
    Front, 151
Socialist Republic, 140, 149
Socialist Workers' Party, 120, 146
Sociedad Chilena de Historia y
    Geografía, 137
Sociedad Chilena de la Tradición,
    Familia y Propiedad, 169
Sociedad de Fomento Fabril, 118,
    124

Sociedad del Apostulado Popular, 119
Society for Equality, 92
Software, 228
Solar, Bernardo del, 77
Solidarity Vicariate. *See* Vicaría de la Solidaridad
Soloman, Patricia, 165
Sopaipillas, 42
South Africa, 195
South America military rule, 169
South American Power Company, 164
South Sea Company, 59
Soviet Union, 145–46
Spaniards: Almagro expedition, 31; banks, 221; casualties, 38–39; Civil War, 136; colonization, 31, 47; conflicts with Mapuche, 29; conquest, 27, 33–38; deserters, 39; flight to Peru, 66; merchants, 58–59, 64; military officers, 53; Pinochet extradition petition, 215; population in Chile, 44; southern towns abandoned, 37; union influence, 119
Spanish Empire, 27, 59
Spich, Robert, 165
Sporting clubs, 25
State of siege, 73, 89–90, 150; of 1973, 188; under Ibáñez, 153
State Technical University, 201
Steamships, 75, 79, 82
Steel, 13, 16, 107–8, 140, 151, 153; role of state in industry, 153–54
Strait of Magellan, 3, 5, 30, 35, 44, 93
Street venders, 195
Strikes: against military government, 189; campesinos, 144; coal miners, 120, 146; copper miners, 120, 153, 164, 178; frequency and length, 158–59; general, 177, 182; in Iquique, 120; nitrate miners, 99, 120; railroad workers, 145, 150; stevedores, 120; students, 168–69, 202; truckers, 177
Suárez, Inés, 32
Subercaseaux, Benjamín, 1
Subway, 18, 162, 166
Sugar: imports, 107; industry, 140, 153–54; national company, 152; refinery, 107; scarcity, 173; trade, 44, 81; tariff war, 90
Supreme Court, 19, 93, 236
Sur, 4–5, 13–15; agricultural production, 142; climate, 6; farm protests, 230; defense of fundos, 174; population growth, 114, 142; reforestation, 230
Swansea, South Wales, 77
Sweden, 198
Swiss immigrants, 10, 105
Swiss Match, 125
Symphony orchestra, 25

Tacna, 101–2, 149
Tacna Regiment, 169
Tacnazo, 169
Talca, 85, 93
Talcahuano, 5, 10; licensed port, 64
Tallow, 42, 58
Tamaya copper mine, 11, 79
Tancazo, 179
Tarapacá, 102
Tariffs: of 1833, 89; increases, 150, 193; for industry, 124, 154; reductions, 80, 89, 191, 225; tariff war with Peru, 90
Taxes: collection, 44, 46, 60; colonial, 54, 57, 60; copper, 139, 141; farm, 53, 60, 139; increases, 160, 221; lack of representation, 61; liquor, 106;

mining, 74; nitrates, 104, 139;
percent of GDP, 147; rate, 60;
reduction, 75, 104, 150; reform,
89; revenue, 16, 70; sales, 147
Teachers, 198; dismissal, 22;
salaries, 203; training, 8
Technical training centers, 201
Telecommunications, 231
Telegraph, 83; in Mapuche
territory, 105
Telephone, 231
Television, 4, 18, 210, 217; cable,
231–32
Temblor, 5
Temuco, 14; education, 24;
growth, 234
Teniente copper mine, 12, 126;
government acquisition of,
164; strike, 178
Tennis, 25
Tercera, La, 219
Textiles, 12, 40, 80, 123; Mapuche-
woven, 104
Theater, 23, 107
Thieme, Roberto, 175
Tiahuanaco civilization, 28
Tierra del Fuego, 5, 30
Tithe (diezmo) 53, 61; eliminated,
89, 93
Tobacco, 46, 60, 66, 69, 82, 121. See
also Estanco
Tocornal, Josefina, 220
Toiber, Rigo and Gabriela, 165
Tolerance, 27, 198
Tomic, Radomiro, 171
Tongoy, 79
Toro Zambrano, Mateo de (Conde
de la Conquista), 63
Torres (high rise apartments), 199,
234
Torres, Juan, 198
Torture, 188–89
Totoralillo, 79
Toumens, Orélie-Antoine de, 104

Tourism, 5, 6; artisan products,
24; in foreign countries, 213;
Norte Grande, 11; Sur, 14, 235;
Valle Central coast, 13
Track II, 172
Trade: British, 128; colonial,
44–45, 58; contraction, 69;
deficit, 160, 181; growth, 9;
guild, 45; international, 64;
monopoly, 45; O'Higgins'
policy, 68; reforms, 63–64, 89;
in slaves, 44; with US, 128
Trade unions. See Gremios
Trans-Amazonian Highway, 199
Transportation, 95, 128
Trapences, Los, 234
Trapiche, 55
Treaty of Ancón, 102
Tres Areas, 176
Tres Puntos silver mine, 77
Tribunal de Minería, 56–57
Tribunal del Consulado, 44, 60,
64
Trillion, 229
Trotskyists, 146, 147
Trovolhué, 165
Truckers' strike, 177, 180
Tsunami, 160
Tucapel, 33, 49n
Twenty Love Poems, 175

UDI. See Unión Democrática
Independiente
UECH. See Unión de Empleados
de Chile
Under the Earth, 99
Unemployment, 19, 98–99; after
coup, 190, 197; decline, 173,
199; nitrates, 141; in public
sector, 149
Unidad Popular:
accomplishments, 181; divisive
actions, 182–83; formation of,
170; government, 172–83;

leaders arrested, 182, 185, 188;
middle class leaders, 198;
platform, 170; reforms, 155;
women's voting patterns, 206
Unión de Empleados de Chile,
116
Unión Democrática
Independiente, 20–21, 210;
voter appeal, 216–17
Unions, 144–47; campesino, 120,
167; decline, 194; growth, 158;
membership, 114, 119, 144–45;
mining, 99; in the 1990s, 231;
politics, 139; rural, 159, 162;
weakened, 191
United States: acceptance of
refugees, 198; arbitration, 149;
arms sales, 66; Articles of
Confederation, 74;
Constitution, 74; Declaration
of Independence, 64;
diplomacy, 152–53, 209;
Federal Reserve policy, 192;
fishing, 59; fruit imports, 194;
early instability, 74; Justice
Department, 189; loans, 153;
mediation offer, 101;
merchants, 80; Nixon credit
reduction, 177; support of
independence, 61; support of
"no" compaign, 210; trade, 17,
56, 59–60, 64
United States Steel, 125
Univeridad Católica de Chile,
115, 137, 161, 168–69, 191, 199,
201, 223
Universidad Católica de
Valparaíso, 168
Universidad de Chile, 74, 91, 93,
138, 168–69; history
department, 200; exhibit of
Neruda's works, 236;
Pedagógico, 203
Universidad de la Frontera, 201

Universidad de San Felipe, 51, 53,
62, 84
Universities: autonomy of
regional campuses, 201;
declining government
funding, 201; dismissed
faculty, 200; enrollment, 115,
157, 161, 165, 201; entrance
exams, 164–65; military
governance, 200;
neoliberalism, 200; new
institutions, 201; protest
against military, 201; tuition
costs, 201
University of Chicago, 186, 190,
192–93, 232
University of Wisconsin, 232
Upientos, 182
Urban growth: landscapes, 236–37
Urbanization, 9–10, 114, 136; in
Norte Grande, 125
Urmeneta, José Tomás de, 79–80,
87, 97–98, 126
Utah International, 226

Vaccinations, 166
Valdés, Gabriel, 210
Valdivia (city), 5; commercial
center, 14; founded, 49n;
industry, 123; licensed port,
64; 1960 earthquake, 5, 160;
paleolithic site, 28; weather,
13
Valdivia, Fr. Luis de, 38–40
Valdivia, Pedro de: assists
Pizarro, 31; criticized, 38;
encomienda policy, 47;
estimates native population,
48n; execution, 34;
explorations, 32–33, 49n
Valdivieso, Archbishop Rafael
Valentín, 92–93
Valdivieso, Rafael, 219
Valenzuela, Arturo, 219

Valle Central, 1, 4; population, 9, 11–12, 30; weather, 6

Valle Nevado ski resort, 13

Valparaíso: attacked, 37, 87; colonial port, 44; congress building, 19; customs house transfer, 68; 1906 earthquake, 5, 127; history, 96; impact of Panama Canal, 127; industry, 84, 107, 123; licensed port, 64; lost business, 127; population, 9–10; progress, 75; Wheelwright's business ventures, 83

Varas, Antonio, 93

Vargas, Juan Eduardo, 81

Vatican, 69, 168

Vega, Alfonso, 166

Vegetables: beans, 28–29, 43; peppers, 28–29, 43; potatoes, 14, 28, 29, 43, 58, 195

Veinte poemas de amor, 136

Venezuela, 68, 74, 198

Verdugo, Patricia, 218

Vialidad (highway department), 198

Viaux, Robert, 169

Vicaría de la Solidaridad, 24, 189

Viceroy. *See* La Plata; Peru viceroyalties

Vicuña Mackenna, Benjamín, 8, 73, 96

Vidaure, Colonel José Antonio, 90

Video games, 232

Vietnam War impact on copper prices, 164

Villagra, Francisco de, 34, 36

Villarrica, 14, 49n, 105; growth, 235; vaccination campaign, 166

Viluco, 85

Viña del Mar: expansion, 235; population, 9; tourism, 13, 107

Vineyards, 11–12, 43, 57, 85, 99; expansion, 106, 194; joint

ventures, 229; production costs, 229–30; standardization, 235

Virginia, 40

Volcán Villarrica, 5, 6

Volcanoes, 1, 5

Voting: apathy, 218; decline, 217; limits on, 73, 88; patterns in 1960s, 163; patterns in 1990s, 216–17; purchase of, 109, 129–30

Vuskovic, Pedro, 173

Waddington, Josué, 86–87

Wages, 17; agricultural, 107, 122, 141; colonial, 47; contraction of, 152; farm worker, 195; freeze, 139–40; frustrated union bargaining, 146; growth in 1990s, 231; increase during UP, 173; stagnation, 157–58; under Frei, 166; urban, 122

War of the Pacific, 3, 8, 78, 100–104, 128

Washington State, 6, 28, 108

Weather, 4–6

Weber, Bruce, 165

Websites, 15, 18

Welfare: improvements, 231; programs, 221–22

Whaling, 5, 75

Wheat: exports, 57; planting, 32, 58; productivity, 43; San Isidro, 86; tariff war, 90

Wheelwright, William, 82–83

Whitman, Walt, 135

Wine: colonial, 43; exports, 12, 229; mine worker consumption, 99; trade, 40; use in war, 8

Women: captives, 37; colonial status, 47–48; education, 118; family roles, 206; illegitimacy, 221; in Lagos' cabinet, 221;

marriage, 47; military wives, 180; opposition to Allende, 174; opposition to Pinochet, 207–8; rights, 118; suffrage, 119, 152, 206; violence against, 221; workers, 17, 119

Workers: copper strike, 178; health, 147; Indian, 30; living conditions, 98; Mapuche, 48; mines, 79, 98, 127; Pinochet policies, 190; population, 139; rebellion, 12; rural, 194, 230; seizure of factories, 176; soldiers, 8, 101; specialization, 98; student support, 115; votes, 121, 129; women, 207

Working class, 113
World Bank, 230
World Cup, 25
World War I, 131
World War II, 141, 146; diplomacy, 151–52
Writers, 135

Yaganes, 29
Yerba mate, 14, 44, 45
Yugoslav immigration, 10
Yungay, Battle of, 90

Zig-Zag Publishers, 176
Zona Austral, 4; climate, 6, 15, 140

About the Author

JOHN L. RECTOR is Professor of History at Western Oregon University.

Other Titles in The Greenwood Histories of the Modern Nations
Frank W. Thackeray and John E. Findling, Series Editors

The History of Argentina
Daniel K. Lewis

The History of Australia
Frank G. Clarke

The History of Brazil
Robert M. Levine

The History of the Baltic States
Kevin O'Connor

The History of Canada
Scott W. See

The History of China
David C. Wright

The History of Congo
Didier Gondola

The History of Cuba
Clifford L. Staten

The History of France
W. Scott Haine

The History of Germany
Eleanor L. Turk

The History of Holland
Mark T. Hooker

The History of India
John McLeod

The History of Iran
Elton L. Daniel

The History of Ireland
Daniel Webster Hollis III

The History of Israel
Arnold Blumberg

The History of Italy
Charles L. Killinger

The History of Japan
Louis G. Perez

The History of Mexico
Burton Kirkwood

The History of Nigeria
Toyin Falola

The History of Poland
M. B. Biskupski

The History of Portugal
James M. Anderson

The History of Russia
Charles E. Ziegler

The History of Serbia
John K. Cox

The History of South Africa
Roger B. Beck

The History of Spain
Peter Pierson

The History of Sweden
Byron J. Nordstrom

The History of Turkey
Douglas A. Howard